THE NEW COOKBOOK

MIRIAM POLUNIN
Photographs by Roger Phillips

Macdonald

Author's acknowledgements

I don't believe that there is such a thing as a new original recipe. If there is, I doubt whether it will taste very good. Every combination of foods worth eating must have been tried somewhere in the thousands of millions of meals cooked every day.

My recipes don't claim to be original: they are variations. I am glad to thank those who've most helped me with their ideas about cooking – though some of us have never met. I thank too the people who've particularly contributed to this book: Florence Greenberg; Gayelord Hauser; Lelord Kordel; Peter and Joan Martin; Nathan Pritikin; Howell Roberts, on yeast baking; Nathalie Hambro, on food style; Rose Elliot; Mary Dodwell, for help with recipe testing; my neighbour Nicholas Vester, for reminding me regularly that healthy food has to win hearts by its taste; Rita Greer, for allowing me to use her recipe for gluten-free brown bread; my mother and father, who fed me well and biased me towards natural foods; Lorna Polunin, for lots of ideas; and Jill Metcalfe, of the British Diabetic Association, for help with the diabetic section.

I am indebted to Roger Phillips whose photographs make my recipes look mouth-watering and to the cooks Jane Suthering and Caroline Ellwood who prepared the food for photography.

A *Macdonald* Book

First published in Great Britain in 1984
by Macdonald & Co (Publishers) Ltd London & Sydney
A member of BPCC plc

The New Cookbook was conceived, edited and designed by
Frances Lincoln Limited, Apollo Works, 5 Charlton King's Road, London NW5 2SB

British Library Cataloguing in Publication Data
Polunin, Miriam
    The new cookbook.
    1. Cookery
    I. Title
    641.5   TX717
    ISBN 0-356-10550-4

Filmset by Tradespools Ltd, Frome, Somerset
Printed and bound in Spain by Artes Graficas Toledo S.A.

Macdonald & Co (Publishers) Ltd
Maxwell House 74 Worship Street London EC2A 2EN
D. L. TO: 1205 -1984

THE NEW COOKBOOK

CONTENTS

INTRODUCTION

Would you like to eat delicious meals – and know that they also happen to be good for you? This book is about making favourite dishes healthier while keeping them tasting good, and how to combine dishes into meals with balanced food value.

Most people now accept that what we eat affects how well we feel. After years of confusion – 'eggs are good for you, eggs are bad for you' – a clear picture of the eating pattern that can help health has emerged. It's accepted by governments and expert opinion, and it isn't going to change.

This book is based on these agreed guidelines, not on any revolutionary diet idea. The recipes put these principles into action in the kitchen. But they don't mean changing your style of eating beyond recognition. Making food healthier can be done unobtrusively. The main steps are to choose dishes that happen to be healthy anyway or can be adapted to healthy eating; to use the most nutritious form of ingredients; and to cook in a way that keeps the food value in the food. Then you need to combine dishes to make up balanced meals.

It's common sense – made easier by collecting the information together into a new look at how we choose and cook meals.

How you eat is largely a habit, shaped by how you were fed as a child, affected by where you live, your daily schedule, your family's habits, and more. The result may be eating habits that help your health, or that harm it. Why not choose the ones that help? After the first effort of changing, the new style of eating becomes a habit as easy and as satisfactory as the old.

It's also as easy or easier for the cook. As a working woman myself, I've deliberately picked recipes that do not need elaborate preparation or skill. The methods that maximize the health value of food are mainly simple ones.

Healthy food doesn't have to look primitive, though. As the photographs throughout this book show, your table can look sophisticated and mouth-watering.

HEALTH POINTS

Five simple rules – *less sugar, less fat, more fibre, more fruit and vegetables and less salt* – sum up the style of eating now accepted as positively helpful to your short-term and long-term health. They enable you to judge any food you come across in shop or restaurant, and pick the healthiest of what's available.

Far from losing your enjoyment of food, you'll find yourself freed from anxiety about weight control, and released from any sense of guilt at over-indulgence in food you know isn't good for you or your family. Having an occasional splurge of eating foods that aren't good for you doesn't do any damage. It's daily meal habits that make the difference.

Calories
Calorie counts given in this book are based on the metric measurements in the recipes and are therefore only approximate for the imperial conversions. In fact, the calories contained in natural foods vary and the calorie amounts can therefore be taken only as a guideline. Further information is given on page 309. Do consult the measurement information given on the same page before you start cooking.

Once you've used these rules for a while, they'll become second nature, without your having to think about it. Don't worry that you'll get so concerned about unhealthy food that you'll be too depressed to enjoy what you eat – or turn into a fanatic who'll bore your friends. It's true that many people are eating in a depressingly unhealthy way – but you needn't despair, because the situation is generally improving: more and more people are becoming aware of the pitfalls they are digging for themselves with knife and fork.

The key to the new style of eating is *food value per calorie*. Over the last 150 years, increases both in income and in the range of foods available have dramatically changed our eating habits. We've turned what used to be special occasion foods into foods for every day, because we can now afford to eat them regularly, and they're offered to us ready-prepared so we don't have to make an effort to get them.

These foods can be summed up by the word 'rich'. It sounds nice, but it really means that they are high in fat: buttery, creamy, slathered in mayonnaise, chocolate-coated or crunchy-fried. We've also increased our fat intake by shifting from staples like bread, beans or potatoes to meat, cheese and eggs as main cooking ingredients. Even lean meat is much higher in fat than the cereals or beans which used to provide more of our protein. We've developed the habit of eating much more sugar, which up to the nineteenth century was a luxury food.

The net effect of these changes has been that roughly three out of every five calories we eat comes from either sugar or fat – roughly one from sugar, two from fat. Unfortunately, the 20 per cent of our calories that we devote to sugar is 20 per cent that brings us none of the forty-plus vitamins and minerals we need for good health. The 40 per cent devoted to fat is about twice as much as we need for health. So around four in every ten calories are given to substances that provide no useful nutrients.

In the past, that would have mattered less because people – that is, those people who could afford to – ate more. They needed to, because they used up more energy. A world without vacuum cleaners, fork-lift trucks, cars or lifts meant that everyone used more muscle. Just keeping warm, before the invention of central heating, could use up a tidy number of calories each day.

The more food you eat, the more vitamins and minerals tend to come with it (especially when less sugar is eaten). So the less it matters if you eat some things which have little food value. Today we need – and eat – fewer calories. But we still need as many vitamins and minerals. So it's more important that everything we eat provides something useful: good value per calorie. That idea becomes even more essential if you are for any reason eating less, whether to lose weight, after an illness, or because you've lost your appetite through stress or a new set of false teeth! (If you eat better, you have a better chance of avoiding all these problems, by the way.)

LESS SUGAR

The commonsense idea that if you devote 20 per cent of your calories to a food without vitamins, minerals or fibre – like sugar – you end up with 20 per cent less chance of getting all the nutrients you need from food, is the main argument against eating sugar.

It applies equally to white crystal sugar, golden syrup, and the more refined brown sugars. Although less refined brown sugars have some trace elements, they still carry much less vitamin and mineral value than most foods.

When you eat sugar, you are using up the appetite and calories that could be spent on other foods – and any other food would provide more food value.

Another reason for avoiding sugar is that it is so easy to eat a lot of – and to absorb. Sugar packs almost 100 calories into each 25g (110 per oz), in such a small volume that it's easy for the average person to swallow around 100g (3½oz) or more every day – lots of it in drinks.

Sugar is established as the crucial influence in dental decay. Although cleaning teeth can help prevent gum disease – from which adults lose more teeth than they do from tooth decay itself – it's very doubtful whether cleaning can in itself stop sugar, in partnership with the natural bacteria present after eating anything, from rotting your teeth.

Although people who eat and enjoy a lot of sweet foods find it hard to imagine, the taste for sweetness isn't fixed. After a month or two of eating less sugary food, the sweet foods that have been longed for and missed may seem sickly and no longer attractive when eaten again. Given the large proportion of our food eaten in the form of sugar, this is a major step towards a healthier style of eating – and though any change requires effort at first, soon you won't even want anything sweeter than is provided by fruit, fresh and dried.

Although eating sugar does increase very quickly the level of sugar in our blood – and thus the resources of energy available to us – it doesn't automatically make us feel energetic! We have to be active already to benefit from the new reserve of energy.

In children, eating too much sugar has been associated with nervousness, restlessness and lack of concentration.

Why eat less sugar?
• It uses up calories you need to spend on foods which give you the vitamins, minerals and fibre you need.
• It is the principal factor in tooth decay – and brushing will make only a marginal difference.
• It's easy to eat a lot of because of its small volume for its calories, and so it encourages overweight.
• Some people over-react to the sudden arrival of a lot of sugar in the bloodstream, in such a way that the level falls very fast, resulting in a 'low' of energy – and the urge to eat another sweet thing, which can set off a vicious circle.
• High sugar intake seems to provoke some children to over-activity and lack of concentration.

That's almost 400 calories-worth. To eat the same amount of calories in the form of other foods, you'd have to tuck away 500g (1lb 2oz) peeled bananas, or 1.2kg (2½lb) apples, or 185g (6½oz) wholemeal bread, or 450g (1lb) potatoes.

Because the 400 calories-worth of sugar takes up such little space inside us, we may not feel much fuller for eating it – so may well eat other foods as well. The result is: we gain weight.

Not every calorie of food we swallow gets absorbed into our system, to be used as energy or stored as fat. And the evidence is that calories eaten in the form of high-fibre foods are less likely to be used fully. If you eat the same calorie-value of peanuts, peanut butter and peanut oil, for instance, you are likely to absorb almost all of the calories from the peanut oil, slightly fewer of the ones from the butter, and least from the peanuts. Calories from sugar, however, unless they are all used up in activity, are swiftly absorbed, again encouraging weight gain.

Although nine out of ten people you asked might agree that 'you need sugar for energy', your body certainly does not need crystal sugar – which is only a few centuries old in the aeons of human history. What it does need is a steady raised level of blood sugar, and any food will provide your system with the material for making blood sugar. Unlike sugar or glucose powder, the other ways of keeping your blood sugar at a level where energy is available to your body bring you useful vitamins and minerals at the same time.

They may also keep your blood sugar level up for longer. Some people's bodies react to eating sugar, and to the sudden rise in blood sugar it produces, by making every effort to reduce the surge. The result is that the level of sugar in the blood falls remarkably quickly and, a few hours after eating sugar, it can be lower than before they started.

This reaction is known as 'low blood sugar', or *hypoglycaemia*. It's become fashionable to have this condition, or diagnose people as having it. As most people have never been thoroughly tested, it's hard to know how many people do react this way.

But anyone who notices that around two hours after eating a sugary snack or meal, especially if they drank coffee or alcohol at the same time, they feel as lacking in energy and as 'low' as if they hadn't eaten for days, may find that avoiding sugar and coffee is the answer to the problem. The urge to 'perk yourself up' with a coffee and a bun or some chocolate should be resisted, as it can just set off the same cycle again – and low blood sugar means low mood, not only low physical energy. Sand-wiches, fruit and other non-sugared snacks, which will not provoke the 'let's clear some of that sugar out of the bloodstream' reaction from your body, will provide a way out of the vicious circle.

The sugar in fruit does not usually present any problems, because it is so diluted with water and fibre that you'd feel full before you ate a significant amount. Nor is it just supplying empty calories, as fruit provides minerals, vitamins A and C and fibre at the same time.

Honey has a substantial proportion of the same type of sugar as is found in fruit. This 'fruit sugar', 'fructose' or 'laevulose', does not provoke the low blood sugar reaction, but provides a supply of energy that is released more slowly. The other main sugar in honey – glucose or dextrose – is quickly absorbed. So honey has a partial advantage over sugar in how it is absorbed. It is also lower in calories and, thanks to its fructose content, somewhat sweeter, spoonful for spoonful, than sugar – so less should be needed.

However, although honey contains a wide spectrum of vitamins and minerals, it does so in such small amounts that they are only a minute

Artificial sweeteners aren't used, because they do nothing to 'de-programme' the sweet tooth we develop as we grow up.

contribution. Honey should not be used to replace the same weight of sugar, but in very small amounts when sweetness is wanted. The same is true of fructose or fruit sugar bought in packets, or maple syrup.

Putting it into practice
Good cooking doesn't demand sugar. None of the recipes in this book includes crystal sugar, because even desserts and cakes can be sweetened with much smaller amounts of honey or puréed dried fruit. Fruit sugar is used occasionally in small amounts.

Thanks to the advent of the freezer, foods can be preserved more effectively than when they had to be jammed or bottled – and without depending on sugar's preserving properties.

Dispensing with sugar has the benefit of encouraging you to use more fruit, with its vitamin, mineral and fibre content.

LESS FAT

Unlike sugar, fat isn't all empty calories. You definitely need some fat – the family name for a large group of substances including fatty acids, waxes, phospholipids and sterols.

Between them, they are necessary for dozens of normal body reactions, which is why no one should ever aim for a fat-free diet. However, the 40-plus per cent of all calories which the average Westerner eats as fat – much of it without realizing it's being eaten – is over twice as much as is needed for good health.

While controversy goes on about the effects on health of eating cholesterol, a sterol in animal foods that we also make in our bodies, expert opinion and government reports agree that Mr and Mrs Average would benefit by eating less fat in total.

As with sugar, this is partly because too much fat takes up the calories we should be spending on other nutrients we need: we spend about 20 per cent of all our calories on fats that are surplus to our need for fat. As with sugar, that means we are 20 per cent worse off for other nutrients that don't come with fat.

100g (3½oz) of fat at 9 calories per gram gives 900 calories, 40 per cent of 2250, a little over an average woman's intake. Most men probably get through around 2800 calories a day, and 125g (4½oz) of fat.

It's even easier to eat too much fat than too much sugar. It's the most calorie-packed of all our foods, with 'visible fats' such as butter, margarine, lard, oil and dripping carrying between 730 and 900 calories per 100g (3½oz). Ah, but I don't eat much fat, you may think. In fact, 100g (3½oz) per day is a typical fat intake for a man or woman eating some 2250 calories per day: just 40 per cent of their calories.

What does the surplus fat do to us? First, it will tend to fatten us up: high-fat meals are almost always high in total calories. Unless we are particularly energetic, or living in an icy climate where we use up extra calories keeping warm, we won't use up all the calories, and careful Nature will store them around our person.

Secondly, countries with a high fat consumption definitely have much higher rates of heart disease. Is this caused by the surplus fat in particular? Or by the body's inability to deal with all the extra calories that high-fat meals load it with? We're not sure.

What *is* known is that people with a high level of fat in their bloodstream are more likely to get heart disease.

The fats on which most attention focuses in heart disease are the fatty acids. These fall into three main groups:
1 Saturated fats, mainly but not solely found in animal foods, tend to be solid at room temperature. They get their name from their chemical

Although no one knows the perfect amount of fat to eat for good health, most official reports have settled on 25 to 30 per cent of energy as being the maximum that should come from fat. This figure is a good deal higher than the minimum requirement because it's hard to devise a Western-style diet with a lower level of fat. While the Japanese, when eating traditionally, may thrive on a diet that provides as little as 10 to 15 per cent of calories as fat, even reducing fat consumption from 38 per cent to 33 per cent of calories in the UK during the Second World War produced a lot of dissatisfaction. (On the other hand, there was a sharp drop in some of the diseases associated with high fat intake.)

Why doesn't expert opinion say that more fats should come from PUFAs? Other fats have uses, too, particularly as carriers of the fat-soluble vitamins A and D. In any case, most of the fats we eat contain a mixture of saturated fats, unsaturated fats and PUFAs. Safflower oil, for example, highest of all common oils in PUFAs, also contains about 11 per cent saturated fats. While a fat that we think of as hard animal fat, lard, has about 9 per cent PUFAs and 44 per cent unsaturated fats, as well as 44 per cent saturated.

In any case, just because a certain amount of PUFAs is good does not mean more is better: the evidence is that our bodies are not designed to deal with large amounts of any type of fat. In addition, PUFAs are vulnerable to rancidity unless accompanied by vitamin E – which they usually are in nature. In refining, some of the vitamin E is lost. Eating too many refined liquid oils may not be healthy unless they have vitamin E added.

A major reason for our high intake of hard fats is that, with affluence, we have moved from getting most of our protein from cereals and pulses to getting it from meat and dairy foods. The first two are very low in fat; the others, high. Even lean meat has a much higher fat content than bread, potatoes or rice.

structure, in which hydrogen atoms play a part. They are called 'saturated' because every point on the chemical structure to which a hydrogen atom can be attached has one: it's full, or saturated.
2 Unsaturated fats have some gaps on the structure. They are usually liquid but thick at room temperature.
3 Polyunsaturated fats have lots of gaps for hydrogen atoms unfilled. They are the softest fats.

The World Health Organization recommends that around 10 per cent of all our calories should come from polyunsaturated fats (often abbreviated to PUFAS). These are the only sources of the essential fatty acids which perform an assortment of important functions in the body. Lack of essential fatty acids, for instance in a fat-free diet, has produced loss of growth, eczema-like skin conditions and changes in cells in test animals. In humans, one particular essential fatty acid, linoleic acid, is associated with production of prostaglandins, substances with many vital roles.

For most people, the WHO figure means eating 25 to 30g (around 1oz) of PUFAS a day. What does this mean for you and me? That the same 2250-calorie-a-day person should eat no more than 75g (2½oz) fat, instead of 100g (3½oz). And the 2800-a-day man should go down from 125g (4½oz) to 93g (3¼oz). Both should aim to get about a third of all their fats from PUFAS.

It isn't a daunting reduction. If you measure out 25 or 30g (around 1oz) butter, for instance, you'll see that you don't have to lose very much – about two flat tablespoonfuls – from your plate. But you'll save over 200 calories. In theory, done daily that would produce a weight loss over a year of some 9kg, or 20lb!

And expert opinion considers that you'll also be safer from heart disease.

Because most of the fats in a Western diet come from the harder, saturated fats, it's these that need cutting back more sharply if they are to be reduced to two-thirds of total fat intake (in practice they will probably still come to more than that, since our PUFAS will also carry some saturated fats with them).

Reducing the amount of hard fat eaten means returning to the use of more of the low-fat proteins. But this needn't mean sacrifice: many favourite dishes work on this basis, including pasta, pizza, and chili with beans, to name just a few.

Contrary to people's fears, such foods are no more fattening than meat, as their calorie counts work out about the same. And eating low-fat rather than high-fat proteins inevitably increases the fibre eaten, making food more filling and, for many people, a lower total calorie count.

Putting it into practice
The fats that are easiest to reduce are the visible ones, such as cooking fats and oils, fat on meat and butter or margarine spread on bread. But invisible fats can't be forgotten. Some of these are in processed foods, for instance in bought biscuits, pies, salami, cakes, fried foods, chocolate and other sweets such as fudge, coffee creams and more. And these are usually processed fats.

That leaves the fats that exist in natural foods. Because the food may be high in food value, and you can't eat it without eating the fat, these foods should come last in your fat-cutting programme. Eggs, for instance, have about 11 per cent fat when raw, boiled or poached. But they also have a good level of protein and vitamins, so they're reasonable food value per fat gram. Other foods that fall into this

It's worth noting that the kind of fat in animals varies with what they eat. Inactive farm animals fed on carefully designed fattening rations have a harder kind of fat (and more of it) than game. This is one reason why game is used freely in the meat section of this book – and pork isn't in at all.

Why eat less fat?
• Half of the fat we eat is surplus to the fat we need. So we are using about 20 per cent of our calories on a high-calorie food whose nutrients are extra to requirements, when we could spend those calories on foods providing nutrients we do need.
• Because fat packs over 200 calories into 25g (under 1oz), a style of eating high in fat is almost always very high in calories, so it encourages unwanted weight gain.
• A high intake of fat in any country apart from one with an Arctic climate is linked both to a low-fibre intake (because people build up high fat intake by getting their protein from meat and dairy foods, instead of from low-fat cereals and pulses) and to a high rate of circulatory disease, particularly heart disease.

A link has been claimed between a low intake of fibre and the West's high rates of cancer of the colon and rectum, and of heart disease. It's hard to separate the contributions made by low fibre and by high fat, which almost always goes with it, since eating less fibrous food tends to go with getting more protein from fattier sources, such as meat and dairy foods. It's very difficult to prove that lack of fibre actually causes these problems, but the evidence gained by comparing communities and by treating diverticular disease and haemorrhoids with fibrous food is convincing.

Can fibre help you slim? If you stop eating when you feel full, eating fibre can help you feel full sooner, because it is bulky and swells up as it absorbs fluid in your tummy. It may also make you feel full for longer, by delaying the progress of food from stomach to digestive tract. And there's some evidence that on a high-fibre diet you'll absorb slightly fewer of the calories you eat. Although you may only 'lose' some 4 calories out of every 100 you eat, a person eating 2200 calories per day could 'lose' about 4kg (9lb) a year this way (454g or 1lb of fat represents approximately 3500 surplus calories).

Of course, many slimmers know that they don't stop eating when they feel full. They eat for emotional reasons, even to the point of discomfort. For them, a different approach is needed (see page 297).

category include nuts, seeds, cheese, oily fish, wheat germ and oatmeal. The first three have so high a level of fat that they should be eaten with caution, while most people would not eat the others often enough or in large enough amounts to overload their fat intake. With meat, it's simply a question of choosing the leanest, and eating less meat.

Throughout this book, fat has been minimized except where it goes with a particularly nourishing ingredient, such as sunflower seeds or wheat germ. In general, the soft fats are preferred, but in the context of a generally low-fat style of eating, some butter isn't likely to be a problem. For a diet that is very low in fat, see pages 276–8.

The low-fat style of cooking in this book has three elements:
1 A choice of recipes naturally low in fat. You can't have puff pastry, for instance, without a lot of fat (I've included a compromise with shortcrust), while strudel dough is low in fat – and uses oil.
2 Choosing the lowest fat ingredients that are compatible with a successful result. Using low-fat milk, for instance, rarely hurts the result of a recipe; using the lowest-fat meat positively improves results.
3 Trimming unnecessary fat while cooking. Ways of doing this range from using a brush to oil a pan, rather than pouring in a generous pool of oil or adding a slab of butter, to cooking Scotch broth in two stages, chilling it between times so you can lift off a generous layer of fat.

By giving a full repertoire using this approach, this book makes it simple for you to apply these ideas to any recipe.

MORE FIBRE

The cell walls of the plants that we eat contain a variety of carbohydrate structures that are not fully digested by our systems. For many years, these parts of foods were considered superfluous, and because they tend to give foods a chewier texture, they were often refined away – the prime example being the branny outer skin of the wheat grain which is removed to make white flour.

Although some pioneers were arguing that these substances – christened roughage or fibre – were important for health as long ago as the 1930s (and the ancient Romans knew that bran prevented constipation), fibre has been 'rediscovered' only in the last twenty years.

At first, research concentrated on wheat bran. Comparisons between communities which eat unrefined foods high in fibre and our own, where sugar has been separated from the fibre in sugar cane and bran removed from wheat, showed that the low-fibre eaters had a wealth of intestinal ailments from which the high-fibre eaters were almost entirely free. These included diverticular disease (pouches in the wall of the intestine which can trap waste food and become infected), varicose veins and haemorrhoids, gallstones, appendicitis and diabetes.

Over the years, it's become clear that different types of fibre in different foods have varied effects in the body. The definition of fibre widened when it was realized that some carbohydrates with no 'chewy' characteristics, such as pectin in fruit, also belong to the class of partially digested carbohydrates. All are now grouped together as 'dietary fibre'. The dietary fibre in a food can be several times more than the 'crude' fibre measurement.

Cereal fibre, such as that from wheat, appears to be the one which has most use in intestinal problems, absorbing fluid, bulking and softening the stools, and speeding the transit time of food and waste products through the body. This last effect is the one associated with avoiding

High-fibre foods don't have to taste tough and branny. In fact, you need never know the fibre's there. Raspberries, for instance, have a particularly high level of fibre; so does sweetcorn.

Why eat more fibre?
1 It's important for the smooth working of the digestive system. This in turn may reduce your risk of a range of intestinal ailments.
2 From population comparison evidence, though it's hard to prove in an individual, a high-fibre intake may provide protection against high levels of fat in the blood, a main risk signal for heart disease; against diabetes, especially the kind that takes hold in middle age; and against obesity. Some researchers claim that it will also protect against cancer of the colon and rectum, and breast cancer. In all these cases, a higher fibre intake should be coupled with eating less fat. If you eat unrefined foods, this will happen naturally.
3 A high-fibre diet tends to be lower in calories, both because it's more filling so less is eaten, and because it is usually lower in high-calorie fats.

There almost certainly isn't an ideal vitamin C intake which is the same for everyone. Government-recommended levels of vitamin C are based on the amount that will prevent obvious disease, not the amount that will maximize this vitamin's anti-infection, health-maintaining powers.

People's usage of the vitamin will vary with their lifestyle. Stress and smoking, for instance, are both known to use up vitamin C. As the body barely stores this vitamin, daily supplies are wise; and bearing in mind the way the vitamin may be reduced in food by the time you eat it, it's sensible to eat lots of fruit and vegetables every day, to allow for losses or special circumstances where you may use up more.

Some people, of course, may prefer to swallow a vitamin C supplement and forget about what they eat, but this is not the best answer. Other substances in vitamin C-rich foods, most notably the bioflavanoids which coexist with vitamin C in many natural foods, may be useful to the body.

cancer of the colon, claimed to be encouraged by the long contact in a constipated person between harmful substances in food wastes and the delicate wall of the bowel.

Recently, other kinds of fibre have been investigated, particularly in relation to the level of fat in the blood, and thus to heart disease. It's clear that fibre and fat are interconnected in the digestive process: a high-fibre style of eating means that more of the fat eaten is passed unused through the body. A high level of fibre may also discourage the body from producing excess cholesterol, or from laying down fat deposits along arteries. 'Gummy' fibres such as oats and beans appear to have most effect in changing blood fat levels. Slowing down the passage of food from stomach to digestive tract is associated with most kinds of fibre, particularly with gums. This effect may favourably influence blood sugar levels, and conditions such as diabetes.

Expert opinion is united in recommending that people restore more fibre to their food. At least 30g (just over 1oz) a day of dietary fibre is recommended – which can be 50 to 100 per cent more than the amount provided by a refined-food style of eating.

Putting it into practice
The simplest way to eat more fibre is to eat more unrefined foods – remembering that only plant foods have fibre. Recipes throughout this book use mainly unrefined ingredients, with fibre from all types, cereal, bean, nut, fruit and vegetable. For details of the fibre content of common foods, see page 275.

By cooking with unrefined foods, rather than adding bran to refined ones, you end up with less 'branny', more tasty results. You also gain the vitamins and minerals of the natural product, many of which would be reduced by refining.

It's important to go slowly when increasing the amount of fibre you eat, or you are likely to feel bloated by the extra bulk.

MORE FRUIT & VEGETABLES

For food value per calorie, fruit and vegetables are hard to beat. They're prime sources of vitamin C, vitamin A (in carotene form), folic acid, vitamin E, vitamin K and a whole range of minerals.

The calcium value of leafy green vegetables is particularly important to those who don't eat dairy food. Leafy greens are also the richest sources of almost all the nutrients listed above.

The exception is vitamin A, in carotene form, richest in carrots, apricots, yellow melon and other yellow or orange vegetables or fruit. However, the level in leafy greens is still considerable.

Vegetables are much more useful for nutrients than most fruits, although some varieties of fruit are particularly rich in vitamin C. Most people think first of oranges and blackcurrants, but don't forget strawberries, lemon juice, gooseberries and grapefruit. Fruit also comes into its own as a way of satisfying the sweet tooth healthily.

The quantity of fruit and vegetables eaten varies widely from individual to individual. It's greatly influenced by family habits, and by where you live. How far the poor supply is a result of poor demand, and how far a cause of poor demand, is an interesting subject. While it isn't necessary to have a variety of vegetables or fruit to eat well – cabbage and carrots would do the job – the wide range now available does encourage using more.

The golden rules for keeping food value in vegetable and fruit produce are as follows:
• Look for the freshest – or grow your own. Organically grown produce is safer, keeps better and may taste better too.
• Keep produce the minimum of time before use.
• Protect it from light and heat by keeping in a refrigerator.
• Chop fruit and vegetables – thus exposing more surface area to light and heat – just before you cook them. Don't keep prepared vegetables soaking in water, as vitamins and minerals can dissolve away.
• Use cooking methods that keep produce away from contact with water, which can leach out nutrients.
• Don't keep food hot or reheat it.

Why eat more fruit and vegetables?
• They are almost the only sources of vitamin C, necessary for maintaining or recovering general health. Much of the vitamin C can be lost between harvest and plate, so it's sensible to eat plenty.
• Vegetables, particularly the leafy greens, are also prime sources of folic acid (a B vitamin necessary for the formation of red blood cells), vitamin E and vitamin K. Greens are an important source of calcium and also of other minerals, including iron.
• Orange vegetables and fruits, notably carrots, apricots, yellow melon, pumpkin, sweetcorn, sweet potatoes and tomatoes, are the richest sources of carotene, from which the body makes vitamin A. Leafy greens are also very rich in carotene.
• Virtually all this high food value is provided in a low-calorie form that is fairly filling because of its fibre content.
• Fruit and vegetables contribute a wealth of flavours, colours and textures to cooking, helping to make food more attractive.

Common table salt consists almost entirely of sodium chloride. Sodium teams with potassium in the body in the fluid-regulating system. While most natural foods contain either roughly equal amounts of each, or more potassium, a Western diet that includes a large amount of made-up foods is far higher in sodium.

A link between high blood pressure and excess salt was established as long ago as 1928. The average Westerner may eat around 12g (almost ½oz) of salt a day. This is at least ten times the level the body needs. However, reducing salt intake to 6g (⅕oz) a day is enough to produce a fall in blood pressure in most people; strict low-salt diets may aim for as little as 3g (⅒oz) of sodium a day.

Two other important influences on your vegetable and fruit intake are where you usually eat, and the state of your teeth. People who regularly take a high proportion or all of their meals in staff catering facilities, whether in army, hospital, industrial or educational establishments, are likely to have a far lower intake. So will anyone whose poor teeth put them off chewing.

All these influences on how much fresh vegetable and fruit produce you eat will also affect how many vitamins and minerals you get out of what ends up on your plate. Storage time, cooking times and methods, and the length of time cooked produce is kept hot, are also influenced by family habits, by how easy it is to shop frequently, by mass cooking practices, and even by whether you want your vegetables mushy to make them easier to chew.

The vitamin C level in vegetables can drop by 80 per cent with poor treatment, while other vitamins and minerals are affected to a lesser extent. Length of exposure to air – whether during storage in a shop or in your kitchen or, worst of all, when chopped up ready to be cooked – is a major influence on vitamin loss.

Remember that fruit and vegetables are virtually your only sources of vitamin C. Although fresh milk contains a significant amount, pasteurization and exposure to light will reduce it.

Putting it into practice
It's a good principle to include something from the fruit and vegetable world in every meal. Use the types rich in vitamins A and C most, especially the leafy greens, which are definitely the most nutritious type of produce. This book shows how to make more of vegetables and fruit, though with fruit, really, recipes are hardly needed: it's the ideal convenience food, for snacks or any meal.

Get used to avoiding vitamin-destructive but common habits of handling fruit and vegetables. Throughout this book, you'll find vegetables and fruit used plentifully, cooked for the minimum time and with the least contact with water.

Keep any water that has been in contact with vegetables during cooking (apart from brassica water) for the stock jug, and use it within a day or two for another recipe. By doing this routinely, you will repossess much of the food value inevitably lost even in careful cooking.

LESS SALT

Salt is added to almost every food in the making, whether it's bread made at a bakery, cheese at a dairy, or a pie made at home.

In theory, the surplus salt should be excreted via the kidneys. In practice, some people's bodies seem to stand up to the daily glut of salt better than others.

Too much salt not only creates extra work for the kidneys, but may result in excess fluid being retained.

Roughly one in four of us is likely to suffer from raised blood pressure later in life. Blood pressure is a measure of how hard the heart is having to work to push the blood round the body. High blood pressure is a prime sign that the heart is having to work too hard, and that there is a higher risk of either a heart attack or a stroke, or kidney disease.

Although it's clear that some people don't suffer at all from a high salt intake, are you willing to bet that you're one of them? Even if you are, extra sodium puts an unnecessary workload on your kidneys.

Why eat less salt?

• Too much salt makes extra work for the kidneys, one effect being that fluid can be retained in the body. This waterlogging can reduce circulation, resulting in less oxygen being fed to cells.
• In those vulnerable to high blood pressure, eating too much sodium in salt encourages this symptom of higher heart attack or stroke risk.

People who take diuretic drugs lose potassium. To counteract this, such drugs often include potassium, whose chemical symbol, 'K', will probably figure in the drug brand name. Or separate potassium tablets may be prescribed. Potassium in these concentrated forms can irritate the stomach and encourage ulceration. Taking extra potassium in the form of unsweetened fruit or vegetable juice (about 600ml or 1 pint total per day is preferable.) Bananas, leafy greens and citrus fruits are particularly rich in potassium.

Putting it into practice

Reducing the amount of salt eaten is difficult – for most people more difficult than reducing sugar or fat. While a salt-free diet is virtually impossible (since there is sodium in most natural foods) and unnecessary, eating much less salt – around half your present amount or less – is sensible, and tastebuds gradually adapt. This means cooking foods with little or no salt, and restraining its use at table. Recipes throughout this book keep the salt level down by using less added salt; by using unrefined foods which haven't had salt added to them and have more of their natural flavour intact; and by flavouring foods with lower-sodium tastes such as lemon juice, yogurt, mustard, herbs and spices. For details of salt substitutes, see page 278. For lists of foods high and low in sodium, see pages 279.

The other side of the balance is potassium. Processed foods may lose potassium in the refining, and people who eat only small amounts of fruit and vegetables – particularly rich sources, although potassium occurs in many foods – may not get good supplies. Eating natural, unrefined foods, with plenty of fruit and vegetables, gives a much better supply of potassium, so it can keep its delicate balance with sodium.

HEALTHY MENUS

Menu-making for health doesn't mean sacrificing the pleasure of good meals. It just means choosing some delicious dishes – which happen to be healthier – in preference to others, and getting into the routine of cooking in health-building ways.

A good way to start is with a party game. Each person in a household sits down and makes a list of the forty foods or dishes he or she likes best. Some people will be surprised to find they don't have forty favourites to list: they tend to eat the same meals often.

You can then put the lists in order of healthiness. Foods such as baked potatoes or bananas come top. Low in fat, free from concentrated sugar, complete with natural fibre, low in salt and with vitamins and minerals intact because they haven't been refined, they naturally match the five guidelines. With a little luck, there's a healthy filling for baked potatoes you like too: say, sweetcorn and cottage cheese, baked beans or mashed sardines.

Next come dishes which can easily be made healthy. If you like shepherd's pie, for instance, or baked apples, you can use leaner meat and less butter for the first, and dried fruit instead of sugar for stuffing the second, and come up with two perfectly healthy dishes that you'd not even notice had changed.

Then come dishes which can be made healthy by cooking them differently. If you list apple tart as a favourite, try making it with yeasted wholemeal pastry instead of white shortcrust pastry. It will then match the low-fat and high-fibre guidelines, but still taste good, if different (you may easily like it better). You can use eating apples instead of cooking apples and sprinkle them with currants or raisins and cinnamon for extra sweetness, to avoid having to add sugar, so your tart is low in sugar. Use plenty of apples, and you're meeting all the guidelines.

Even people who think they only love rich food will find that their list of favourites includes many dishes which are either healthy or can be made healthy. The first step towards healthier eating is just to eat these dishes more often than the ones it's difficult to make in a healthier way – such as cream-based ice creams.

SPANISH MENU

Gazpacho with chopped
vegetables **75 cals**
Wholemeal bread **90 cals**

— • —

Hazelnut trout in an overcoat
400 cals
Radish and new potato salad
170 cals

— • —

Orange slices in liqueur **70 cals**

Total calories per person **805**

Throughout this book, you'll find a selection of favourite recipes that have been made healthier. As well as enjoying them, you can adapt the ideas used to other recipes you like. Explore some of the recipes for dishes you've not made before, too. All the recipes have been planned to fit the five guidelines as closely as possible while still keeping the dish both tasting and looking good.

But it would still be possible to pick dishes from this book, and make a meal that wasn't balanced. If, for example, you picked individual cheese soufflés, followed by fish kebabs, followed by cheesecake, you'd end up with a lot of protein – much of it surplus to your needs – but almost no fibre. If you served plenty of fresh vegetables with your fish, you'd be getting one sort of fibre (and providing the 'more vegetables' element), but the meal would be more balanced if it also contained some cereal or pulse fibre, and another course which included fruit or vegetables.

To make healthy menus as well as healthy dishes, judge your plans against the essentials detailed in this chapter: protein, fibre, freshness, and colour and texture.

With this menu (see opposite) freshness and colour are provided by the vegetables in the gazpacho, the radish and potato salad and the fruit in the orange dessert. These also provide fibre, together with cereal fibre from the bread served with the gazpacho and from the low-fat yeast pastry around the hazelnut trout. The protein in the trout is topped up by the hazelnuts in the trout stuffing and by the pastry overcoat, and there's protein in the bread and potatoes as well.

PROTEIN

Westerners still tend to think of meat as essential for an adequate supply of protein – or, at least, they feel that if meat is not eaten then it should be replaced by fish, eggs and dairy foods. These are certainly main sources of protein for us now, but this is not a necessary, or even traditional, state of affairs, more an effect of affluence. In the past, the main sources of protein were cereals and pulses. This is still the case today in most countries.

A feast of fresh foods in this menu provides colour and crunch from vegetable strips, served with taramasalata, chunks of vegetables with the kebabs and from the orange and watercress salad, and from the fruit with the dessert. The protein comes from all three courses with fibre provided by the vegetables, brown rice and the honey cake made with wholemeal flour.

Most of us eat considerably more protein than we need. Excess isn't stored as protein by the body, but converted into energy and either used up by activity, or stored as fat, just like any other calories.

It's not established that excess protein is harmful, but it's unlikely to do us good. Animal experiments have shown that animals live longest on a diet that is relatively low in calories, which usually means fairly low in protein; and that rats fed a fairly low-protein diet can stand up to stresses such as exercise, injury, infection and restricted amounts of food as efficiently as rats given a surplus of protein.

This is not to deny the vital importance of protein, especially during the years of growth but also, in smaller amounts, throughout life, for the continuous repair and replacement of tissues.

The lower-fat animal proteins – fish, low-fat cheese, low-fat milk and meats such as rabbit and turkey – are also being chosen by more and more people in preference to red meat.

This trend does not threaten health or vitality – on the contrary. First, any slight drop in protein intake is unlikely to matter, because of the

How much protein do you need?

A rough and ready guide for adults is 1g of protein per kg (2.2lb) of body weight. For children, much more protein in relation to their weight is recommended.

For most people, the level will be between 50 and 75g (2 to 3oz) of pure protein a day. As no food is pure protein, and few more than a quarter protein, working out how much you are eating takes a little effort. And although it can be interesting to do, for most of us it's not necessary. Almost any meal plan we come up with that provides a filling number of calories, and is low in sugar and fat, will provide enough protein – whether or not it contains meat or fish.

One point is worth stressing here. In natural foods, the richest sources of B vitamins are all the protein foods. Get your protein, and you'll automatically get the B vitamins too. Unless, that is, you choose to get your protein from white bread, white rice or pearl barley. They've still got most of their protein after refining, but they've lost most of their B vitamins. So if you want to turn to the low-fat cereal protein as part of reducing the amount of fat you eat, it's important to safeguard your B vitamin supply by choosing unrefined bread, rice and flour.

considerable surplus in the average diet. Secondly, cereals and pulses provide almost exactly the proportion of protein recommended for good health: about 10 per cent of their calories come as protein. Thirdly, they have the benefit of saving fat: lentils and bread, for example, contain 1 per cent and under 3 per cent respectively, compared with over 7 per cent for even lean rump steak or 5 per cent for roast chicken (without its skin, which is fattier). Only fish and the lowest-fat cheese rival this leanness. Fourthly, pulses and wholemeal cereals provide fibre, which is not supplied by meat.

But what about first-class protein? you may worry. This term refers to those foods which contain all of the nine protein substances called 'essential amino-acids', because the body cannot make them itself from other ingredients in food, but must eat them as they are. Animal proteins have all nine essential amino-acids; most vegetable proteins don't. However, this is only important for people who rely very heavily on a single vegetable food, such as millet, for their protein; or for those, like vegans, who use no animal foods at all. For other people, a mixture of plant sources of protein, each containing a different balance of amino-acids, plus the 'complete protein' of milk, cheese, yogurt or eggs, will supply all nine acids even if they never touch meat or fish.

The combination of plant proteins that provides all the essential amino-acids can be summed up by the phrase 'beans with everything'. The type of protein found in beans complements that in grains or in nuts. A bean and rice salad, lentil soup with pizza, beans on toast or chili beans with tortillas are all examples of such happy partnerships.

For those who do use dairy foods, such careful matching is unnecessary.

Nor does it have to be a main course that provides protein. A first course such as butterbean soup, or a dessert such as cheesecake, will do just as well. And throughout the day little bits of protein add up, from the milk in your drinks, from the sunflower seeds on top of a salad, from the nuts in biscuits, from the flour in a cake, from eggs, from potatoes.

FIBRE

Aim to build more than one kind of fibre into your meals.

For most people, breakfast is the main cereal fibre source, because almost everyone who has breakfast at all will include cereal, toast or another grain-based food. If this comes in wholemeal form, it is likely to provide about a fifth of the day's fibre needs. Fruit eaten at breakfast will add another kind of fibre. Soft fruit, especially berries such as blackcurrants, raspberries and blackberries, are outstandingly rich.

Apart from breakfast, you'll need three or four other helpings of fibre per day. So when you choose food, keep this in mind. Don't eat a fibre-free main course, such as meat, fish, cheese or eggs, more often than once a day. Within a meal, when you have such a main course, pick an accompaniment such as brown rice or a bean salad. If you're in a restaurant, a wholemeal roll may be the only high-fibre option. A first course can provide the fibre – for instance, lentil soup or won ton Chinese dumplings (when made with wholemeal flour). So can a dessert, for instance a wholemeal fruit tart with dried apricots. Aim to have a 'gummy' fibre such as oat (porridge, oatcakes) or pulse (lentil soups, salad, casseroles, side vegetable) at least once a day, and a wheat, rice or other grain fibre at least once apart from breakfast. Generous use of fruit and vegetables will supply the remaining fibre.

DINNER MENU

Taramasalata with crudités
115 cals

—•—

Lamb kebabs **260 cals**
Brown rice **160 cals**
Watercress and orange salad
90 cals

—•—

Honey cake **260 cals**

Total calories per person **885**

Use parsley by the handful, not the sprig, adding it only at the end of cooking, as this is one of the most versatile flavours. Watercress is an excellent regular for your shopping list: it can be used in salad, in soup or, lightly cooked, mixed with another vegetable. Mustard and cress and beansprouts have the advantage that they are growing – and maintaining their food value – right up to the moment you eat them.

FRESHNESS

Make a habit of having some kind of raw fruit or vegetable at almost every meal. Start at breakfast with fresh fruit; include a salad in your meals each day; favour fruit desserts; use carrot sticks, celery, tomatoes and other vegetables or fruits as snacks.

When you are planning a meal, if you won't be having a salad with your main course, make sure one of the other courses is based on a fruit or vegetable, preferably uncooked.

Remember that you don't need a solid slice of protein at every meal. Light meals, based on salads but far more lively than the lettuce-and-tomato formula (see pages 148–61), give your digestion a rest, and your vitamin C and minerals a boost.

You can also plan meals based just on lightly cooked vegetables, combining three or four that contrast and complement each other.

Fruit provides useful nutrients, but vegetables, especially the leafy greens, are indispensable in a healthy diet. Get into the routine of having some kind of green leafy vegetable every day, and buying enough to make this easy.

COLOUR & TEXTURE

No one should sit down to a meal thinking 'This is going to be good for me.' It should look so delicious that all you want to do is tuck in.

Choosing foods which both contrast and complement each other in colour is an essential part of that appeal. It doesn't matter how delicious a plateful of chicken, brown rice and browned mushrooms might be: it all looks the same monotonous light brown. Aim for colour contrasts on the plate, and between different courses.

Fruit and vegetables supply most of the brightest natural food colours – another reason for using plenty of them. Serving them uncooked or lightly cooked isn't just good for their food value, it also keeps their brightness and, the other side of a good meal, their texture.

How often have you heard complaints about an unsatisfactory meal that centre on poor texture? Flabby fish, limp salads, hard pastry, stale bread, soggy pasta.... The shortest possible cooking time is your best safeguard against spoiling the natural textures of food.

But equally important is choosing foods that provide a contrast of sensations. Don't include more than one 'wet' course such as soup, or more than one 'soft' course such as taramasalata in a meal unless you are cooking for the toothless. Chinese people admire the texture of 'crispiness' in food, and have excellent methods of achieving it without the obvious route of frying. Very lightly cooked vegetables or salads chilled to crunchiness are ideal ways to introduce this texture.

Crisp foods are a world away from 'chewy' foods. They still call for chewing, but it doesn't seem like hard work. Food that needs some chewing is particularly good at the beginning of a meal: part of hunger is wanting to get your teeth into something. Chewing stimulates the stomach to start producing digestive juices. Salads and dips which are eaten with crisp sticks of raw vegetable or wholemeal toast both make good first courses.

Providing variation between hot and cold courses is another part of the art of menu-making. Although we tend to look to hot food in cold weather, it doesn't really warm us up except psychologically. Only a few extra calories are contributed by the heat of the food. Your body

---

JAPANESE MENU

Miso soup **50 cals**
Japanese chicken wings
265 cals
Aubergine with sesame **65 cals**
Spring onions **10 cals**
Cucumber **10 cals**
Brown rice **160 cals**
Fresh fruit platter **50 cals**

Total calories per person **610**

wouldn't care if you never ate hot food again. Because salads are such good vitamin and mineral carriers, don't give them up in cold weather. Warm them up psychologically by having hot soup first, or a hot jacket potato or wholemeal pitta bread with them.

MEAL PLANNING

In more and more families, fewer meals are eaten by everyone together: members of the family who may be working different hours, or spending evenings at sports or courses, want to eat at different times. And where the family does eat together, the cook is likely to be under greater time pressure, from a job or caring for children. There are three kinds of meal which are convenient in these circumstances: instant convenience or take-away meals, casseroles and soups which can simmer gently until wanted, and quickly made meals.

While convenience and take-away meals aren't always unhealthy, a high proportion of the foods on offer are particularly high in fat, sugar and salt, with little fibre or fresh food.

In this Japanese-style menu, strips of cucumber and spring onion, as well as the fruit dessert, provide the main fresh elements with protein from the soya bean curd and paste in the miso soup, from the sesame seeds with the aubergines, from the brown rice and from the chicken wings. The rice, sesame seeds and fresh foods provide a good mix of fibre.

Meals which include at least one crisp and crunchy course may also help you avoid overeating. They take longer to eat, and fast eating is a trait consistently found in overweight people – it's common sense to think that finishing first is an encouragement to having a second helping.

Quick-to-make meals include these options:
Fish dishes of all kinds; although some may benefit from being marinated beforehand, cooking rarely takes longer than ten to fifteen minutes. Thin frozen pieces can be cooked without thawing.

Liver and kidneys, which take under ten minutes, and toughen if overcooked.

Pancakes, using wholemeal batter; you can serve filled pancakes, stuffed with vegetables or fish in sauce, in around twenty minutes.

Pasta dishes; wholemeal pasta cooks in under twelve minutes, which is long enough to make a sauce.

Pizza, using scone dough base, is ready in about twenty minutes.

Risottos made with quick-cooking bulgur wheat.

Salads, especially if you make a habit of cooking double batches of beans and rice, so you often have a bowl of cooked rice or pulses in the refrigerator. Adding these to salad produces a kind of substantial salad many people find more acceptable as a main meal, as well as adding protein and fibre.

Substantial soups: fish chowder, chawanmushi, lentil soup, Vichyssoise, for instance.

Tofu burgers.

Quick desserts include the following;
Baked apples, which will cook in time for dessert if they're put in the oven before the meal is prepared, or take only about three to five minutes, depending on size, to cook in a pressure cooker.

Dried fruit compôte, made in a vacuum flask while the meal is being eaten, or pre-prepared and chilled in the refrigerator.

Fresh fruit.

Fresh fruit salad (use fruit juice instead of sugared syrup).

Pancakes, with stewed fruit filling.

Quick cheescake sundaes.

Ready-made ices and sorbets.

Wholemeal cake, in slices, served with yogurt or custard and stewed fruit, will make an impromptu trifle.

Yogurt with chopped fresh fruit or cooked dried fruit added just before serving.

Casseroles and soups are a good choice provided they aren't the only source of vegetables in the meal. Slow simmering will reduce the vitamin value, although minerals will just float from the vegetables into the stock, and still get eaten. In this situation, each person eating from the casserole or soup pot should cook a small batch of vegetables separately to eat with it, or even better, eat them uncooked in a salad or just cut in chunks.

The fibre for such a meal needs to be provided separately too, unless the casserole contains rice, barley or dumplings. Wholemeal bread is the easiest option, but keep in mind the quick-cooking grains – millet, buckwheat, wholewheat pasta or bulgur wheat, which can be ready in around fifteen minutes once they come to the boil. Or, instead fibre can be provided by a dessert that includes grain – for instance, a fruit crumble, a fruit tart, or one of the low-fat, low-sugar wholemeal cakes. All these stand up to 'shift' meals. Use fresh fruit regularly as pudding. If members of a family don't enjoy eating fruit it doesn't matter, provided they eat some vegetables. However, resistance to vegetables calls for more concern. Persuasion rarely works, and can put someone off even more, so the main tactic is to find a way of presenting vegetables differently. The main three methods are making vegetable soups; puréeing vegetables or soups, as many who dislike chewing vegetables will eat them once they are puréed; making juice. Most of the fibre is lost by this last method, but at least most of the vitamins and minerals are kept. Juices of assorted vegetables can be added to tomato juice or, surprisingly, to apple juice, for flavour. Purées and juices are particularly useful for old people, who may absorb food less efficiently and often have teeth problems that deter them from eating vegetables.

Children will often eat and enjoy pieces of raw vegetable which they wouldn't eat when cooked. Carrot sticks, pieces of cauliflower, celery, fingers of cucumber, raw mushrooms and slices of young turnip may all be happily munched, perhaps when a child is hungrily waiting for a meal. Many children particularly resist the dark leafy greens that are so rich in food value – but a soup including them, or a mixture of minced greens with potato, may meet with more approval.

For parties, plan a meal using the same five principles as for every day. You may feel more pressure to serve meat, or to make desserts sweeter. However, don't underestimate your guests' flexibility: for many people, one of the attractions of a party is encountering something new. For the same reason, 'theme' meals, picking all the courses to make a Russian-style, Japanese-style or Indian-style meal, are fun – and no more difficult to arrange. Suggested menus are featured throughout the book.

From the host's point of view, there's a considerable advantage in arranging a buffet-service meal, even for a dinner party for six people. It can include hot dishes, using a Chinese restaurant-style heater, and still avoid last-minute preparation and much handing of dishes round the table. Guests can help themselves and return to the dinner table, which remains uncluttered, easy to clear for dessert, and more devoted to conversation than to doling out food. The host can enjoy the meal far more if he or she isn't constantly springing up to fetch new courses. The buffet method particularly suits meals where there are many dishes, for instance an Indian curry meal or an assortment of salads.

RECIPES

NEW BASICS

A good sauce makes a meal, the saying goes. Yes, and the sauce is all too often what makes a meal bland, indigestible and fattening too.

Conventional sauce-making relies heavily on butter and cream, two flavours that certainly make a sauce taste 'rich' but which can also blot out the taste of what they are supposed to enhance. Their high fat content means that your digestive system can be struggling hours after your meal should be no more than a happy memory. The most lasting souvenir from a super-rich meal is likely to be a marginal increase in your waistline.

Take one of the classic summer meals. You start with avocado – and double the calories with a rich dressing. You go on to salmon – with a hefty dollop of hollandaise (mainly butter) or mayonnaise (mainly oil). Your new potatoes have a generous pat of butter melting over them. Even your peas are likely to be buttered. Finish with strawberries – and there will be more butter fat in the cream. Oh, and that roll and butter . . . .

This chapter shows how to escape from the heaviness of high-fat side dishes, which often contain more calories than the whole of the meal they accompany. And that doesn't mean doing without sauces. Here are some of the standards and some more original sauces, to suit every kind of meal, deliciously. An extra benefit is that most of these sauces are very simple to make, provided that you have an electric blender.

You will find that yogurt and low-fat soft cheese are staple ingredients of many of the new sauces, and indeed of many recipes throughout this book. Yogurt provides food value similar to that of milk, in a form that many people find more digestible. It is almost always easy to find in low-fat form, too. The low-fat soft cheeses contribute creamy textures and dairy flavour with only a fraction of the fat of cream or butter. Many different varieties of yogurt and soft cheese are now available (see Glossary, pages 310–12), but it is simple, and economical, to make them at home. I hope you will be tempted to try the recipes which I give for these versatile ingredients.

Another advantage of using soft cheese instead of butter or cream is that it provides much more protein, together with B vitamins. Most of us don't need extra protein (although extra B vitamins, which tend to occur with protein in food, can be very useful). What higher-protein sauces enable you to do is confidently to use more meatless and fishless main meals, particularly salad and vegetable meals. The dressing can provide protein you might otherwise be concerned about missing, particularly if you are cooking for people with high protein needs, such as teenagers and those recovering from surgical operations.

When you come to my baking recipes, you will, I hope, be delighted to find that cakes, made with the right ingredients, can

Tomato sauce, carrot purée vegetable sauce and pesto, a sauce made with basil

count as good food value just as much as other dishes. This chapter shows how cake fillings and toppings, many of which can double as sweet spreads for toast, scones and waffles, need not make you feel that you have to eat some other food as well to make up for 'empty calories', nor, on the other hand, that you have eaten so many calories you ought not to eat again for the rest of the day!

YOGURT

Yogurt is readily available from shops, but home-made yogurt is fairly easy to make at home. You don't need elaborate equipment, although you can buy special yogurt-makers of various kinds. From the user's point of view, the chief difference between electric and non-electric yogurt-makers is that with non-electric ones the milk must first be heated to the correct temperature. A wide-mouthed vacuum or insulation flask will work like a non-electric yogurt-maker. You can also use a warmed glass jar with a lid; during the period when the yogurt is incubating, keep the jar in a warm, draught-free place, such as an airing cupboard.

Bacteria love milk, so to ensure that only the ones you want thrive, all equipment must be thoroughly cleaned before use.

You can make yogurt from any kind of milk, and some of the many possibilities are listed below. I generally use skimmed UHT (long-life) milk. Thicker yogurt is much more useful in cooking than thin yogurt, and UHT milk seems to produce thicker yogurt than ordinary pasteurized milk. In particular, yogurt made with skimmed UHT milk is much thicker than yogurt made with skimmed pasteurized milk. There is the added convenience that UHT milk, because of its heat treatment, need not be scalded and then cooled – you can just warm it, or, if you are using an electric machine, simply pour it straight from the carton.

The recipe given here includes skimmed milk powder, to thicken the yogurt further. If you want very thick yogurt, add more milk powder.

You can buy special yogurt cultures to start your home-made yogurt, but, in general, using just under half a small shop-bought plain yogurt works just as well. The attraction of the dried cultures is that they may provide a culture not used commercially; in particular, there is one called *acidophilus*, which is credited with being beneficial for intestinal flora. The dried cultures are also useful for people with an allergy to cow's milk, who, of course, cannot use ordinary cow's milk yogurt as a starter. When you buy a shop yogurt as a starter, make sure it has not been pasteurized – usually stated in small letters somewhere on the tub; and that it is likely to be fresh, coming from a shop with a brisk turnover. If you like a particular shop yogurt, choose that one to start yours, as different brands use different cultures and yours is likely to turn out with at least some of the characteristics of the starter yogurt.

Does yogurt have the power to prolong your life? If it helps you eat a generally lower-fat diet, perhaps – especially if you also adopt some of the other aspects of the lifestyle of those communities famed for long-life-with-yogurt: daily exercise and eating no more calories than you need, staying active when old, living at high altitude (or practising deep breathing).

HOME-MADE YOGURT

Makes 600ml (1 pint)

600ml (1 pint) UHT or pasteurized skimmed milk

15ml (1 heaped tbsp) skimmed milk powder

30ml (2 tbsp) fresh unpasteurized natural yogurt

1 If you are using a non-electric yogurt-maker, warm UHT milk to 43°C (110°F). More roughly, the milk should be warm but far from uncomfortably hot to the finger – cooler than a bath. Scald pasteurized milk and leave it to cool to 43°C (110°F). Then mix the liquid milk with the milk powder and the yogurt starter and put the mixture into the yogurt-maker.

2 If you are using an electric machine, mix the UHT milk or the scalded and cooled pasteurized milk with the other ingredients and place the mixture in the jar, or jars, according to the machine's instructions.

3 In 3 to 4 hours the yogurt should have set. Transfer it to a refrigerator, where it will thicken further on cooling.

4 Remove several tablespoons of the yogurt to a very clean covered container to keep in the refrigerator for up to 1 week, to start the next batch.

5 If you intend to cook with yogurt, you will need to stabilize it to prevent it from curdling when it is heated. You can do this by blending in – for up to 1 litre (2 pints) of yogurt – either 1 egg white or 15ml (1 tbsp) cornflour mixed to a smooth paste with a few drops of water. If you use cornflour, any sauce in which yogurt is incorporated will need to be simmered for at least 1 minute or it will taste of the cornflour.

VARIATIONS

Goat's milk produces runnier yogurt. To thicken the yogurt, add *25g (1oz) milk powder* per 600ml (1 pint) of liquid milk: if you are using goat's milk because of an allergy to cow's milk, be sure to use *goat's milk powder*. Goat's milk is seldom available skimmed.

Soya milk can also be used, although the results taste different – slightly sweet and more granular. The milk is usually boiled for half a minute, instead of just being scalded.

Greek and Yugoslav yogurt acquires its attractive texture and skin by being made with milk boiled for 30 minutes or more to evaporate off some of the water. This reduces its food value, however, so it is preferable to thicken yogurt with skimmed milk powder.

Sterilized milk produces thick yogurt, but has a slightly burnt, cara-melized taste and has lost more vitamins because it has been cooked for a considerable period.

Yogurt can be made entirely from *skimmed milk powder*, but most people prefer the taste and texture of yogurt that has been made with liquid skimmed milk.

SOFT CHEESE

Lower-fat soft cheeses – their taste and texture varying with the milk, culture and recipe used – are becoming some of the most versatile kitchen ingredients, as people move towards a lighter style of cooking, with less butter, cream and high-fat cheese.

Soft cheese can be used in both sweet and savoury dishes. Making

Calories About 310 for 600ml (1 pint); add another 15 if stabilizing with egg white, 55 for cornflour.

• Suitable for diabetics
• No fibre
• Gluten-free

Thanks to the addition of skimmed milk powder, this yogurt has more protein than milk, and 300ml (½ pint) a day (used on cereal, in cooking or eaten straight from the jar) will provide about 14g (½oz) of protein, or about a quarter of an adult's average protein need. Yogurt also has a higher protein level of calcium than milk, together with substantial amounts of several B vitamins. Natural yogurt that is 'live', that is, has not been pasteurized after making, seems to relieve some stomach upsets, especially those that may follow taking antibiotics.

Useful recipe for making soya cheese from soya yogurt, for milk-free diets.

Boiling cheese cloths
Boil cloths used to make your own soft cheese every time you use them, to make sure you free them from any stale bacteria which could spoil your next batch. A 5- or 10-minute boil is enough, following a scrub in soapy water to get rid of any visible bits of cheese left on the cloth.

Calories About 325 for 600ml (1 pint).

Yogurt cheese – one of the most versatile ingredients to keep in the refrigerator

your own saves substantial sums of money if you use it regularly. 600 ml (1 pint) of milk will make 125 to 175g (5 to 6oz) of soft cheese, at about a third of shop prices. You also avoid the preservative used in some brands.

Here are two ways of making smooth-textured low-fat soft cheese, which can be used in recipes throughout this book.

YOGURT CHEESE
Makes 125 to 175g (5 to 6oz)

1 Make thick skimmed milk yogurt, adding 25g (1oz) of skimmed milk powder to each 600ml (1 pint) of milk (page 00). Tip the cooled yogurt into a sieve or colander lined with muslin or fairly coarsely woven cotton cloth.
2 Leave the yogurt to drain for several hours, until the texture suits your needs.
3 Transfer the cheese to a container with a lid. It will keep in a refrigerator for up to a week.
4 Use the whey that has drained off in baking or sauces. It has considerable food value, and scones and soda bread made with whey are lighter than those made with milk.

Calories About 285 for 600ml (1 pint) using curd cheese and skimmed milk; about 260 using buttermilk and skimmed milk.

RENNET CHEESE

Makes 125 to 175g (5 to 6oz)

600ml (1 pint) UHT or pasteurized skimmed milk

15ml (1 tbsp) skimmed milk powder

25g (1oz) smooth medium-fat curd cheese or 30ml (2 tbsp) buttermilk

5 or 6 drops of vegetable rennet

1 Warm a wide-mouthed vacuum or insulation flask.
2 If you are using pasteurized milk, scald it and leave it to cool. If you are using UHT milk, warm it. Whichever type of milk you are using, it needs to be at approximately 21°C to 27°C (70°F to 80°F).
3 Off the heat, stir in the skimmed milk powder, the curd cheese or buttermilk and, finally, the rennet.
4 Pour the mixture into the flask, seal it and let it sit for about 6 to 8 hours, or until there is a firm 'clot'.
5 Tip the cheese into a sieve lined with coarsely woven cotton cloth.
6 Leave it to drain over a bowl for a few hours, until it is firm. It is then ready to use.
7 Use the whey in baking or sauces.

SAUCES

When using these recipes for the first time, try to judge them on their own merits of taste and texture; don't compare them to richer versions (which they aren't aiming to duplicate). Here, the goal is a sauce that's good to eat – not one that fits in with a 'classic cuisine' image.

WHOLEMEAL WHITE SAUCE

Calories About 300 for 300ml (½ pint).

• Suitable for diabetics
• Low fibre
• Milk-free (using soya milk)

This basic sauce uses only half as much fat as the standard recipe of equal amounts of fat and flour, but produces a good result. The amount of fat is further reduced by using skimmed milk.

Wholemeal flour gives a creamy and very slightly speckled result, but this is not unattractive and is anyway usually hidden because the sauce is mixed with another food. For a thick sauce – for example, to bind rissoles – halve the amount of milk. *Makes 300ml (½ pint).*

15ml (1 tbsp) soft margarine, butter or oil

25g (1oz) plain wholemeal flour

300ml (½ pint) skimmed milk

½ small onion

1 bay leaf

pinch each of white pepper and sea salt

1 Melt the fat in a thick-based saucepan set over a low heat.
2 Stir in the flour thoroughly. Remove the pan from the heat.
3 Add the milk little by little, stirring all the time.
4 Add the onion and the bay leaf. Increase the heat to medium, return the pan to the heat, and stir the sauce constantly until it comes to the boil.
5 Reduce the heat again and allow the sauce to simmer. I use this sauce after it has simmered for 4 to 5 minutes, but purists would say it should simmer for at least 15 minutes. If you simmer the sauce for as long as this, stir it from time to time to make sure it doesn't stick to the pan.
6 Remove the bay leaf and onion and season the sauce.

LOW-FAT WHITE SAUCE

Makes 300ml (½ pint)

15ml (1 tbsp) plain wholemeal flour*

300ml (½ pint) skimmed milk, liquid or reconstituted

15ml (1 tbsp) skimmed milk powder

1 bay leaf

½ small onion

pinch each of white pepper and sea salt

*15ml (1 tbsp) cornflour plus 5ml (1 tsp) wholemeal flour can be used instead, but the sauce will have less flavour, although it will be whiter.

1 Place all the flour in a large cup.
2 Mix to a smooth paste with a little of the milk.
3 Put the remaining milk, with the milk powder, bay leaf, onion and seasoning, into a saucepan. Stirring steadily (skimmed milk burns easily), bring the milk to the boil.
4 Still stirring, pour the boiling milk on to the flour paste.
5 Return the mixture to the pan, stir until it comes to the boil, then simmer for at least 4 to 5 minutes. Remove the bay leaf and onion.

VARIATIONS FOR BOTH WHITE SAUCES

Cheese sauce At the end of cooking, add 25g (1oz) grated Parmesan or mature Cheddar cheese and a good pinch of mustard powder. Stir in the cheese until it melts, but do not boil the sauce again or the cheese may become stringy.
Herb sauce At the end of cooking, add about 30ml (2 tbsp) finely chopped fresh herbs (such as basil, chives, fennel, marjoram or a mixture).
Milk-free sauce Using the basic wholemeal white sauce recipe including fat, you can substitute 300ml (½ pint) of any well-flavoured stock for the milk, to make a savoury (but not white!) sauce.
Onion sauce Boil a large (100g [4oz] approximately) onion in 300ml (½ pint) water in a covered pan for 20 minutes before making the sauce. Use the cooking water instead of milk if you are following the recipe including fat. If you are using the low-fat recipe, add 40g (1½oz) skimmed milk powder to the cooking water, then use it instead of the milk, milk powder and onion in the recipe. For both sauces, add the chopped cooked onion after the sauce has thickened smoothly.
Parsley sauce At the end of cooking, add a good handful of finely chopped fresh parsley.

VEGETABLE SAUCE

Purées of lightly cooked and seasoned vegetables make delicate hot or cold sauces to complement any firm-textured main course, such as terrines, soufflés, fish kebabs or grain-based savouries. *Makes a side dish for 4 to 5.*

450g (1lb) vegetables, trimmed and roughly chopped

75g (3oz) quark or other low-fat soft cheese

freshly ground pepper

herbs or spices, to taste

Electric blenders have made it possible to purée vegetables easily and without the necessity to cook them to a pulp – losing vitamins and flavour on the way – so that they will go through a sieve.

1 Bring about 150ml (¼ pint) of water to the boil in a thick-based pan.
2 Add the vegetables.
3 Bring back to the boil, cover and simmer for about 4 minutes for courgettes or leafy greens, up to 20 minutes for beetroot or carrots.
4 Drain the vegetables, retaining the cooking liquid. Place the vegetables in the goblet of a blender, adding just enough cooking liquid to cover the blades. Blend until smooth.
5 Remove the purée from the blender and stir in the soft cheese, seasoning and any other flavourings. Don't be tempted to add the cheese to the blender, as the texture of the cheese may be broken down in the process.

VARIATIONS

Beetroot purée Make with yogurt instead of soft cheese, blend with 1 egg white or 10ml (2 tsp) cornflour before mixing and flavour with lemon juice to taste. Complements game, bean burgers and loaves, and savoury pies.
Carrot purée Spice with chervil, caraway or coriander. Complements white fish, lamb kebabs or liver.
Celery or celeriac purée Flavour with caraway seeds, parsley or a very little rosemary. Complements cheese dishes, fish dishes and any grain dish, such as risotto.
Parsnip purée Try serving as a substitute for potatoes or rice. Complements light dishes such as watercress soufflé or baked onions.
Spinach purée Flavour with nutmeg, if liked, and lemon juice. Complements almost any kind of savoury dish, but especially fish, pasta and grain dishes.
Other vegetables Strong-tasting vegetables like Brussels sprouts, or watery ones like courgettes, can be cooked and puréed if 100g (4oz) of potato is incorporated with 350g (12oz) of the main vegetable.

TOMATO SAUCE

Calories 2 servings at about 50 each, 4 servings at about 25 each.

• Suitable for diabetics
• Medium fibre
• Very low fat
• Very low salt (omitting salt)
• Milk-free
• Gluten-free

As well as tasting fresher than longer-cooked versions of tomato sauce, this sauce also retains more of the tomatoes' vitamins.

The key to this recipe lies in cooking the tomatoes for only 5 minutes. Longer cooking just seems to reduce their sweetness and flavour. The dab of honey brings out the flavour of the onions. The texture of the sauce is rough-cut, but you could blend it to smoothness if you prefer.
Makes enough for 2 people's spaghetti or 4 servings of side sauce.

1 medium shallot, very finely chopped
5ml (1 tsp) olive oil, preferably cold-pressed
1ml (¼ tsp) clear honey
4 ripe tomatoes, chopped
5ml (1 tsp) tomato purée
15ml (1 tbsp) fresh basil leaves, chopped, or 5ml (1 tsp) each dried basil and oregano
pinch each of black pepper and sea salt

1 Cook the chopped shallot gently in the oil for 7 minutes, adding the dab of honey 2 minutes before the end.
2 Add the chopped tomatoes.
3 Mash the ingredients roughly, and simmer, uncovered, for just 5 minutes. Turn off the heat.
4 Add the tomato purée, herbs and seasoning.

MUSHROOM SAUCE

An extremely tasty savoury sauce with many uses – to enhance vegetables, plain fish or a vegetable terrine, for instance. *Makes 300ml (½ pint).*

100g (4oz) mushrooms
5ml (1 tsp) oil
15ml (1 tbsp) plain wholemeal flour
15ml (1 tbsp) soya flour
scant 5ml (1 tsp) vegetable concentrate
10ml (2 tsp) soft margarine
200ml (7fl oz) stock

1 Slice the mushrooms and sweat them in the oil in a thick-based pan set over a low heat.
2 Mix the wholemeal flour and soya flour in a small saucepan, then add just enough water to make a smooth paste. Stir in the vegetable concentrate, margarine and stock.
3 Bring the stock mixture to the boil, simmer for 2 minutes, then add the mushrooms. Rinse the mushroom pan with 15 ml (1 tbsp) water and add to the rest of the sauce.
4 Transfer three-quarters of the mixture to the goblet of a blender, blend it to a smooth consistency, then return it to the rest of the mixture in the pan. Reheat the sauce.

VARIATIONS

This sauce can be made with other vegetables, such as *celery*, *leeks*, *onions* or *fennel*. Go easy with the vegetable concentrate: its strong flavour can be overpowering.

BEAN SAUCE

This mildly hot sauce can be used to top pasta, rice or potatoes, or teamed with minced chicken or lamb to make a chili con carne. With or without meat, you can use it to fill tortillas (page 93) or savoury pancakes (page 102). The flavour improves with overnight keeping. *Makes 3 main course servings.*

175g (6oz) dried beans, haricot or any larger type except soya
1 large onion, chopped
5ml (1 tsp) oil
1 small chili, with seeds removed, chopped
2 cloves of garlic (optional), crushed
225g (8oz) tomatoes
225ml (8fl oz) stock
2ml (½ tsp) dried oregano or dill
75ml (3fl oz) tomato purée
freshly ground pepper
pinch of caraway seeds (optional), crushed with the back of a spoon

1 Soak the beans overnight or cover them with water, bring them to the boil, simmer for 2 minutes, then soak for 2 hours.

Calories About 230 for 300ml (½ pint).

- Suitable for diabetics
- Medium fibre
- Very low fat (omitting margarine)
- Very low salt (substituting low-salt stock cube for vegetable concentrate)
- Milk-free
- Gluten-free (substituting buckwheat flour for wheat flour)

Soya flour is extremely high in protein – around 40 per cent – so adding it to any savoury sauce markedly increases the protein content. This flour does not need boiling, as it is sold pre-cooked.

Calories Celery sauce, about 226 for 300ml (½ pint); fennel sauce, leek sauce, onion sauce, about 240.

Calories About 210 a serving.

- Suitable for diabetics
- High fibre
- Very low fat
- Milk-free
- Gluten-free

Adding bean protein to any other vegetable protein, such as the grain in pasta or tortillas, improves the value of the total protein, and a portion of this combination will provide a protein-rich main course.

Bean fibre seems to be particularly effective in lowering blood fat levels.

2 Drain the soaking water off. Add fresh water just to cover and simmer for 40 minutes to 1½ hours, according to the beans chosen, until they are just tender. Do not add salt, as it would harden the bean skins, making them tough.
3 Cook the onion in the oil with 15ml (1 tbsp) water over a low heat for 8 minutes. Add the chili, and garlic if using, and cook for a further 2 minutes.
4 Add the tomatoes, stock, oregano, tomato purée, pepper, drained beans and caraway seeds if using. Simmer for about 15 minutes or until the sauce is well blended.

EGG AND LEMON SAUCE

A delicately flavoured, light-textured sauce to use in the same way as hollandaise. *Makes 300ml (½ pint).*

300ml (½ pint) stock, preferably a light stock such as chicken
15ml (1 tbsp) plain wholemeal flour
2 eggs
juice of ½ lemon
pinch each of pepper and sea salt

1 Place all the ingredients in the goblet of a blender and blend until smooth.
2 Transfer to a double boiler or a pan sitting over a larger pan of simmering water.
3 Whisk often until the sauce thickens, after several minutes. Do not allow it to boil. Check the seasoning.

VARIATIONS

Rémoulade sauce When you blend the ingredients, add 10ml (2 tsp) each of: mild mustard, chopped fresh parsley, chopped gherkins, chopped capers; add a few drops of anchovy essence if liked. Complements cold fish, poultry, shellfish and egg dishes.
Tarragon sauce When you blend the ingredients, add 5 to 10ml (1 to 2 tsp) dried tarragon, powdering it between your fingers. Complements fish and chicken.

TARATOR HAZELNUT SAUCE

Used thick, this Turkish sauce makes a dip or a topping for avocado pears, baked potatoes or bread. Thin with a little yogurt, milk or water to stir into pasta or serve beside plainly cooked fish, chicken or game. *Makes enough for 2 people's pasta or serves 4 as a side sauce, dip or topping.*

50g (2oz) hazelnuts
50g (2oz) soft breadcrumbs
2 cloves of garlic
15ml (1 tbsp) water
15ml (1 tbsp) wine or tarragon vinegar
juice of 1½ lemons
pinch each of white pepper and sea salt

Calories About 210 for 300ml (½ pint).

- Suitable for diabetics
- Low fibre
- Milk-free

This traditional Greek sauce is a low-fat alternative to the much richer hollandaise sauce.

Calories Rémoulade sauce, 280 for 300ml (½ pint); tarragon sauce, 210.

Calories 2 servings at about 190 each, 4 at about 95 each.

- Suitable for diabetics
- High fibre
- Very low salt (using low-sodium bread and omitting salt)
- Milk-free
- Gluten-free (using gluten-free breadcrumbs)

The advantage of hazelnuts, apart from their delicate flavour, is that they contain about 50 per cent less fat than other nuts. The lemon juice in this sauce, like several in this section, contributes a good amount of vitamin C.

1 To bring out the flavour of the nuts, toast them in an ungreased thick-based pan over a low heat for 2 to 3 minutes. Grind them in a coffee mill, food processor or nut grater.
2 Place the ground nuts in a blender or processor with all the other ingredients, and blend until smooth. The consistency will be very thick. Adjust the seasoning if you like by adding a little extra vinegar or lemon juice.

VARIATION

Tarator can also be made with *walnuts*.

CREAMY HERB SAUCE

One of the most versatile and interesting sauces, as much at home with a baked potato as with cold salmon or a bowl of salad. If you like a slightly sharp taste, choose yogurt or smetana; for a thicker, milder result, use fromage blanc or quark. *Makes 300 ml (½ pint).*

1 egg white*
225ml (8fl oz) thick plain low-fat yogurt or quark or fromage blanc or smetana or a mixture of any of these
30ml (2 tbsp) fresh dill, fennel, basil, chervil or marjoram, finely chopped
5ml (1 tsp) onion, grated
15 to 20ml (3 to 4 tsp) fresh lemon juice
5ml (1 tsp) honey
large pinch of white pepper

*If the sauce is to be used cold, the egg white is unnecessary. But if you plan to heat it, whisking an egg white thoroughly into the dairy product chosen will stop it curdling or separating. 15ml (1 tbsp) of cornflour can be used instead, but the cornflour can be tasted, and the sauce will have to be simmered for at least 2 minutes.

1 If you are intending to use the sauce hot, whisk the egg white thoroughly into the dairy produce.
2 Stir in all other ingredients. This is best done by hand, as a blender or food processor may break down the texture of yogurt or cheese.
3 Adjust the seasoning. Heat if you wish, but avoid hard boiling. Serve to add body to vegetable dishes, or to moisten terrines, soufflés or plain fish and poultry.

VARIATION

For a richer-tasting sauce, include a spoonful or two of *soured cream*.

PESTO

Basil has one of the most wonderful smells I know – one sniff can convince you that life is worth living. Unfortunately, it loses even more than other herbs in drying, and, as it is an annual, it is a herb you have to wait for summer to enjoy. Not difficult to grow in a pot, basil thrives best indoors where it is warm. Grow lots to relish in recipes like this.

Pesto is traditionally stirred into pasta, but can enhance rice, potato and tomato dishes just as effectively. *Makes enough for 2 people's pasta or 4 servings of side sauce.*

Calories About 150 for 300ml (½ pint); add 15 if you use egg white to stabilize the dairy product, 55 for cornflour, and another 25 to 50 if you include a little soured cream.

- Suitable for diabetics
- No fibre
- Very low fat
- Gluten-free

Yogurt, smetana and the low-fat soft cheeses all provide a useful amount of protein, with very little fat indeed.

Soured cream has a much higher (average 18 per cent) fat content, but gives more body.

Calories 2 servings at about 135 each, 4 at about 65 each.

- Suitable for diabetics
- Low fibre
- Gluten-free

Using low-fat cheese instead of the considerable amount of oil in traditional pesto recipes saves you about 500 calories.
Once mixed with the curd cheese or quark the pesto won't keep for more than a few days.

1 clove of garlic
25g (1oz) Parmesan or mature Cheddar cheese
25g (1oz) pine nuts or walnuts, toasted
40g (1½oz) fresh basil
approximately 50g (2oz) curd cheese or quark

1 If you have a food processor, you can blend all the ingredients. Chop the basil in the processor first, then add everything else. Otherwise, proceed as follows.
2 Crush the garlic.
3 Grate the cheese finely.
4 Grind the nuts finely.
5 Mince the basil finely in a herb mill or pound it in a mortar.
6 Mix these items thoroughly, before working in curd cheese or quark until the mixture is creamy in texture but still fairly solid.

SPREADS

There is no point in giving up butter if you switch to eating the same amount of margarine. Margarines contain the same quantity of fat as butter, and the same number of calories. Although margarines which are made entirely from vegetable fats will contain hardly any cholesterol, most nutritionists are more concerned about reducing the total fat eaten than just cutting down on cholesterol, since the latter is also produced by the body.

So the main message is to eat less fat of all kinds.

Both butter and margarine contribute vitamins A and D, and butter also provides significant amounts of vitamin E.

If your general eating pattern is low in fat, there is no reason why you should not go on including some butter for your toast. If you eat less butter, you will be reducing the total fats *and* cholesterol eaten. On pages 34 and 35 you will find two ways of continuing to enjoy the taste of butter in a diluted form.

Don't bother with block margarine. It may be made with animal oils, and so contain roughly similar amounts of cholesterol to butter. In any case, it is not rich in polyunsaturated, or essential, fatty acids because when oils are artificially hardened, or hydrogenated, to make them into a solid product, their 'unsaturated' or 'polyunsaturated' chemical structure is 'saturated' with extra hydrogen atoms, and they become like animal fats in character.

Soft margarine that is labelled 'all-vegetable' and 'high in polyunsaturates' has the advantages that it is virtually free from cholesterol (even if the role of cholesterol in heart disease is still uncertain); and it provides more of the essential fatty acids, or polyunsaturates (PUFAS) that the body finds useful, because fewer of the oils have been hardened. However, it is still just as high in calories as butter, and just as fattening. Because it spreads easily, it may be easier to eat less of it.

Low-fat spreads are often thought of as margarine, but contain far more water and can't legally call themselves margarine. Two types are available: one is fairly similar to soft margarine but whipped up with water. It contains less fat and therefore fewer polyunsaturates, but still provides a reasonable level of this type of fat. The other is based on a mixture of buttermilk and vegetable oils. As a result, it does not have as many polyunsaturates, but tastes more buttery. Its cholesterol content is not high. Both types of spread are vitamin-fortified in the same way as all margarines in the UK, contain half the fat of butter or margarine and provide only half the calories, at about 105 calories per 25g (1oz). To my mind they are no more unnatural than margarine, although their extra water restricts their cooking uses. You can't fry with low-fat spreads, nor make shortcrust pastry that isn't rock-hard. However, you can use them for some recipes.

There is a wide range of sweet spreads, one of the most popular being jam. In the UK ordinary jam is two-thirds sugar, by law. Reduced-sugar jams are now appearing in shops, but these often have more preservatives and other additives.

No-added-sugar jam with no additives is sold in almost all health food stores. It is sweetened by including concentrated apple juice and more fruit. So it does contain natural fruit sugar, but only about half as much total sugar as ordinary jam. It also contains, weight for weight, only about half as many calories.

Honey is often dismissed by nutritionists as no better than sugar. It is certainly still a high-calorie food, although at about 85 calories per 25g (1oz), less so than sugar at 110 calories per 25g (1oz). Honey is preferable to brown sugar, whose only advantage over white is tiny amounts of trace elements. Honey does provide **1** more sweetness per ounce, so less is needed; **2** a form of sugar less liable to lead to rapid changes in blood sugar, and not normally requiring insulin for absorption; **3** assorted trace elements and other somewhat mysterious ingredients; **4** many delicious flavours, not just sweetness. Honey is used in small amounts in recipes throughout this book, and can also be enjoyed in small amounts on toast or other foods. In the section on Preserves, you will find recipes for spreads sweetened with honey (pages 263 and 264).

Thick fruit purées and flavoured soft cheeses make ideal breakfast spreads, providing delicious flavours without 'empty calories', since the fruits also contribute fibre, vitamins and minerals; and the cheeses B vitamins and protein and minerals.

Yeast extract would be an ideal, vitamin-rich spread if it were not for its very high salt content. It should, therefore, be spread very thinly. A low-salt yeast extract is available from good health food shops.

SUNSHINE SPREAD

Makes 700g (1½lb)

450g (1lb) butter, unsalted or slightly salted

200ml (7fl oz) sunflower or safflower seed oil

1 Leave the butter at room temperature to soften.
2 Using a food processor or a hand-held electric beater, slowly blend in the oil.
3 Chill to produce a soft spread.

DAIRY SPREAD

Makes 350g (12oz)

225g (8oz) butter, unsalted, or soft margarine

100g (4oz) smooth curd or quark cheese

1 Soften the butter or margarine at room temperature.

Calories About 200 for 25g (1oz).

- Suitable for diabetics (in small amounts)
- No fibre
- Very low salt (using unsalted butter)
- Gluten free

This spread has about the same number of calories as butter, but is much more spreadable, so it should be easier to use smaller amounts.

Calories About 150 for 25g (1oz).

- Suitable for diabetics (in small amounts)
- No fibre
- Very low salt (using unsalted ingredients)
- Gluten-free

A spread with far fewer calories than butter, because the proportion of fat is less.

2 Blend in the cheese gradually, using a food processor or a hand-held electric beater.
3 Chill to produce a firm spread. Use within a week, so only make up fairly small quantities at a time.

VARIATIONS FOR BOTH SPREADS

Garlic spread Add 2 crushed cloves of garlic per batch.
Herb spread Add 15 to 30ml (1 to 2 tbsp) freshly chopped herbs, such as parsley, basil, marjoram, fennel or chives – the more finely they are chopped, the more flavour will pass into the spread.
Peppery spread Add 10ml (2 tsp) very coarsely ground black pepper.
Savoury spread Add 5ml (1 tsp) crushed fennel, caraway or celery seeds for an aromatic savoury spread.

FILLINGS & TOPPINGS

These recipes provide a wide variety of flavours, good texture and a way of making cake a well-balanced food.

As well as making delicious toppings and fillings for cakes, the cheesecake-style and fruit mixtures can be used to fill sweet pancakes or top muffins or scones, replacing buttery, sugary alternatives. The confectioner's custard makes a delicious filling for pastries.

CHEESECAKE-STYLE FILLING OR TOPPING

Sufficient for an 18cm (7in) diameter cake, needing 1 layer of filling or topping

225g (8oz) firm curd cheese

One or more of the following:
50g (2oz) almonds, slivered and toasted, or walnuts, chopped

25g (1oz) coconut, unsweetened desiccated or grated fresh

15ml (1 tbsp) carob flour, sieved

5ml (1 tsp) decaffeinated instant coffee granules, powdered with the back of a spoon in a cup

45ml (3 tbsp) very thick prune purée (from 50g [2oz] prunes, stewed, stoned and blended)

45ml (3 tbsp) very thick dried apricot or peach purée (from 50g [2oz] dried-weight fruit, stewed and blended)

45ml (3 tbsp) no-added-sugar jam or marmalade

few drops of vanilla essence

15ml (1 tbsp) walnuts, finely chopped, mixed with 30ml (2 tbsp) purée or no-added-sugar jam

15ml (1 tbsp) preserved ginger, chopped

5ml (1 tsp) grated orange zest plus 10ml (2 tsp) orange juice

1 banana mashed with 10 to 15ml (2 to 3 tsp) fresh lemon juice

10ml (2 tsp) of your favourite liqueur

set honey, to taste

Calories About 355 for this quantity of filling, with 10ml (2 tsp) honey. Add about 280 for almonds; 260 for walnuts; 88 for coconut; 60 for carob flour; 5 for coffee; 80 for prune purée; 90 for apricot or peach purée; 60 for jam or marmalade; 120 for walnuts with purée or jam; 40 for ginger; 5 for orange zest and juice; 80 for banana and lemon juice; about 30 for most liqueurs, but this will vary depending on the liqueur.

• Suitable for diabetics (omitting honey or reducing quantity to 5 to 10ml (2 to 3 tsp)
• High fibre (using nuts or fruit)
• Very low fat (using low-fat cheese)
• Very low salt (using low-salt soft cheese)
• Gluten-free

1 Add the flavouring of your choice to the curd cheese. If the cheese is very dry and your flavouring is not one of the moist ones, add a *very* little milk to moisten.

2 Add honey, little by little, until the filling is sweet enough. Some people will find that 10ml (2 tsp) honey is enough, others may want much more. Choose a honey with a flavour you like.
3 After filling or topping, keep the cake refrigerated and use within 4 days.

FRUIT FILLING OR TOPPING

Sufficient for an 18cm (7in) diameter cake, needing 1 layer of filling or a topping

350g (12oz) red plums or eating apples or ripe gooseberries or 450g (1lb) rhubarb

2 sprigs of sweet cicely, if available

25g (1oz) arrowroot

honey to taste – about 15ml (1 tbsp)

1 Trim the fruit, chopping apples and rhubarb, into a saucepan. Add the sweet cicely, if you have it.
2 Add about 150ml (¼ pint) water, or less, to give a 1cm (½in) layer in the pan.
3 Bring to the boil, cover and simmer for about 4 to 5 minutes, until the fruit is just tender.
4 Transfer the fruit, but not the cooking water, to a blender, removing plum stones and sweet cicely if used.
5 Add just enough water to enable the machine to work (none if using a food processor) and blend the fruit to a very thick purée.
6 Mix the arrowroot to a smooth paste with a few drops of water. Add the paste to the fruit purée and return it to the pan.
7 Bring the purée to the boil and simmer it for 3 minutes. Cool, and sweeten to taste with the honey.
8 Use the thickened purée alone or mixed with low-fat soft cheese as a filling or topping for a cake.

CHEESECAKE-STYLE FRUIT FILLING OR TOPPING

This filling will not stay in good condition for more than a few hours.
Sufficient for an 18cm (7in) diameter cake, with 1 layer of topping or filling.

125g (5oz) soft fruit, such as ripe peaches, kiwi fruit or strawberries, sliced, or raspberries, mashed

100g (4oz) smooth low-fat soft cheese

5ml (1 tsp) honey

few drops of vanilla or almond essence

1 Mix the cheese with the honey and the vanilla or almond essence, and spread the cheese mixture over the cake.
2 Spread the fruit over the mixture.

VARIATION

Soft cheese can be mixed with a thick purée of any kind of fresh or dried fruit.

Calories About 260 for this quantity if using plums, apples or gooseberries, 160 if using rhubarb.

• Suitable for diabetics (reducing honey to 5 to 10ml (1 to 2 tsp))
• High fibre (using berry fruit); otherwise medium
• Very low fat
• Very low salt
• Milk-free
• Gluten-free

Calories About 150 for this quantity depending on type of fruit used.

CONFECTIONER'S CUSTARD

Calories About 400 for 300ml (½ pint).

• Suitable for diabetics
• Very low fat
• Very low salt
• Gluten-free

The eggs and milk make the confectioner's custard a protein-rich sauce. Because this version uses skimmed milk, it has less fat than conventional recipes.

Use instead of, or mixed with, cream to fill pastries. The egg yolks give it a good flavour. It is delicious used cold to fill éclairs, or spread on a tart base under a layer of fruit. *Makes 300ml (½ pint).*

300ml (½ pint) skimmed milk
15ml (1 tbsp) cornflour
15ml (1 tbsp) skimmed milk powder
5ml (1 tsp) honey
7ml (½ tbsp) soft margarine or butter
2 egg yolks, lightly beaten
few drops of vanilla essence

1 Use a little of the milk to mix the cornflour and skimmed milk powder to a smooth paste.
2 Heat the remaining milk, stirring to prevent it from burning. Pour it on to the cornflour mixture, stirring to avoid lumps.
3 Return the mixture to the saucepan and add the honey and margarine or butter. Simmer for about 3 minutes.
4 Remove from the heat and add the beaten egg yolks and the vanilla essence.
5 Reheat the custard in a double boiler or in a pan set over a larger pan of simmering water, stirring for a few minutes until the mixture thickens. Check the flavouring.

BREAKFASTS

Breakfast should be more than a refuelling stop: rather, a little ceremony of enjoyment that gets the day off to a good start. Having breakfast is a sign that life is under control, so you aren't in a frantic rush. It's a sign that you didn't eat so much, and so late, the previous night that you're still trying to digest the remnants. In many households it's one of the few times that a family sits down together – even if people have the day's plans on their minds and don't feel like chatting. It's a breathing space.

From your body's point of view, breakfast should be welcome after some ten to twelve hours without food. For children, that may well be thirteen or fourteen hours.

So why are many people less enthusiastic about breakfast than they are about other meals? Some people just can't face food in the morning. If this is how you feel, there is certainly no point in forcing yourself to eat at breakfast time. Especially as you may well feel ravenous by mid-morning, so you do get a sort of late breakfast then. However, if your idea of a mid-morning snack is a plateful of pastries bought in a sandwich bar, you may be throwing away a good deal of your day's calorie intake on foods that provide virtually none of the vitamins, minerals and fibre you need – although they will be rich in refined starch and sugar and fat, all of which are more than likely to make you fat in the long if not in the short run.

There are other people who can't face breakfast at home, yet enjoy it very much when they are staying away from home. They may usually be in too much of a rush to stop for breakfast, or still feeling the effects of a heavy dinner.

If you belong to one of these groups, is it worth becoming a breakfast person? If you're a bruncher, it's definitely worth changing your mid-morning food to something that does more for you. Take it with you, find a snack bar that provides good food, or, if you are at home, just eat the healthy breakfast a bit later. For the 'can't wake up, too much rush' brigade, the first thing to do is to revise your evening habits: eat earlier, eat lighter and reduce the number of late nights. Then it will be no hardship to get up earlier, and enjoy the calm, sitting down to the delicious ritual that breakfast can become.

Perhaps you skip breakfast to help keep your weight steady? The good news is that the more of your food you eat early in the day, the easier you will find it to control your weight, provided that your total food intake doesn't change. A test group lost weight consistently when they ate the same amount of calories as usual, but all at breakfast time. You won't want to go that far, but keep the principle in mind.

A freshly peeled orange or an appetizing bowl of apple muesli can do wonders for your health as well as your morale. Breakfast lifts your blood sugar (even if you eat no sugar), topping up the

Nutmeg waffles, served with cottage cheese and strawberries, make a quick but delicious complete breakfast

supply of energy to your system. For most people, it's the main fibre meal. It's a time when more people feel like eating fruit. After a good breakfast, you are less likely to feel that mid-morning fade-away of energy – or urge for a chocolate bar – so your total food intake is likely to improve in quality. Children's needs for many main nutrients are higher in proportion to their weight than are those of adults; and a good breakfast can turn a child's mood from sulky to sunny, as well as making him more independent of midday meals that may be poorly balanced.

So what is a 'good breakfast'? Working on the five principles, it could be anything from the Japanese choice of beancurd soup, rice and egg or fish, to the Californian's orange juice and wholewheat muffins. But if you want to stick to familiar patterns, just look for two things: some kind of cereal food that is unrefined, and some fresh fruit. Cereal supplies a surprising amount of protein, B vitamins, vitamin E and minerals as well as fibre. Fruit provides another type of fibre that works in different ways, more useful minerals, vitamin C and often vitamin A.

Eat your cereal and fruit, avoid refined sugar and too much fat, and you will be getting maximum food value. Cooked breakfasts can fit into this pattern too, if you use the low-fat ideas I give. There are plenty of choices – you won't feel deprived.

If you aren't very hungry at breakfast, just have fruit. Try one of this chapter's fruit ideas, and ring the changes so you enjoy the seasons with your breakfast, as well as getting a variety of vitamins and minerals. If you don't want to eat breakfast – drink it!

If you're hungrier, add one of the unrefined cereal dishes – from waffles to frumenty. Only if you've tried these and you're *still* hungry, add a cooked breakfast.

Top off your breakfast with a thirst-quencher that's up to the same standards of taste and food value – see pages 268–9.

JUICES

Freshly squeezed fruit juice captures the flavour and food value of fruit in a concentrated form. It's a wonderful waker-up and a way of enjoying nourishment when, for whatever reason, you aren't hungry.

Flavour and food value are both better in freshly squeezed juices than in bought juices, which have to be heat-treated to preserve them, and inevitably lose some vitamin value in storage. Even frozen juice is gradually losing its vitamin value.

Drink home-pressed juices when they are very fresh or they too will start to lose their flavour, colour and vitamin value.

Orange and grapefruit juices are the easiest to extract at home, using either a hand citrus press or an electric version of the same shape. These juices are not only among the richest in vitamin C, they are also particularly high in potassium, an element that processed foods often lose. (Choose small grapefruit, which are easier to squeeze.)

Using a juicer, you can extract juice from almost any fruit or vegetable. See page 307 for how to choose a juicer. Even allowing for preparing the produce, making a glass of juice takes no longer than making a cup of tea. You don't need to make large quantities: juice is concentrated, and you may often want to add a little water to dilute it, especially for children. You can also mix home-pressed and bought juices.

Orange juice is not only an excellent source of vitamin C. Along with other fruit juices, and vegetable juices, it is particularly rich in potassium, in a form which may be more effective and is certainly safer than most potassium supplements contained in, or taken in conjunction with, diuretic drugs. Two glasses of juice a day can often do the job just as well. Vegetable juices are only useful if made fresh, since the packaged varieties usually have added salt (sodium) that works against the potassium's effect.

Delicious mixtures
Apple and carrot: half and half □ Apple, carrot and celery: equal quantities □ Apple and grapefruit: half and half □ Carrot, celery and parsley: a few spoonfuls of parsley juice to a half and half blend of celery and carrot □ Carrot, celery and tomato: equal quantities □ Orange and cranberry: 3 parts orange to 1 part cranberry □ Pineapple and orange: 2 parts pineapple to 1 part orange.
Not all juices that are high in food value taste delicious on their own. Try adding beetroot, watercress, parsley and cabbage juices in small amounts to other juices – carrot and apple cocktails, for example.

WHOLE-FRUIT BREAKFASTS

Whole fruit provides more fibre than fruit juice, and is more filling while contributing no more calories. While all but freshly squeezed juices have lost some vitamin value, the whole fruit contains locked-in food value and flavour. To retain both, don't prepare fruit too far in advance. Here are some simple ways of preparing fruit for breakfast that take no longer than making toast. Dried fruit can be prepared in advance, as it does not contribute significant amounts of the fragile vitamin C □Half a grapefruit – try grilling with 5ml (1 tsp) of honey on top for maximum juiciness. Pink grapefruit are naturally sweeter □ A slice of melon or pineapple, sliced kiwi fruit, or any fresh fruit in season □ Liquidize half a banana in a cup of skimmed milk, buttermilk or plain low-fat yogurt. Add some orange juice, if you like □ Mix some dried fruit compôte (page 42) with chopped orange □ Chop a banana or apple on top of cereal □ Stir raspberries, blackberries or strawberries into some smooth low-fat soft cheese, such as quark. Mash slightly □ Make fruit salad from 3 easy-to-prepare fruits, such as, in winter, a mandarin orange, grapes (no need to peel, just halve and pip), and an apple (no need to peel, just scrub and slice); in summer, a peach, ripe gooseberries and a banana □ Chop any fresh fruit into plain low-fat yogurt, with 5ml (1 tsp) honey if wanted □ Mince fresh fruit in a food processor or, with a little orange juice, in a blender, add some wheat germ and eat on toast, pancakes or waffles.

GAYELORD HAUSER'S CURVACEOUS COCKTAIL

One of the pioneers of 'eating your way to health', Gayelord Hauser in his late eighties is a first-class advertisement for his own philosophy. The advice given in my favourite of his books, *Look Younger, Live Longer*, is still sound – and includes this recipe. He emphasizes that these drinks are best sipped, or drunk slowly through a straw. *1 serving.*

1 large chopped orange or 225ml (8fl oz) orange juice
1 egg yolk
15ml (1 tbsp) wheat germ
5ml (1 tsp) honey

1 Place all the ingredients in the goblet of an electric blender and blend until smooth.

Calories About 160 a serving.
- Very low fat
- Very low salt
- Milk-free

Dried fruit compôte

Calories Using buttermilk, about 105 a serving with apricots or raspberries, 125 with bananas. If you use low-fat yogurt instead of buttermilk, add another 35 a serving.

- Suitable for diabetics (in small amounts)
- Medium fibre (using berry fruits); otherwise low
- Very low fat
- Gluten-free

This breakfast provides some protein (from the yogurt or buttermilk), some vitamins (B group from yogurt or buttermilk, C and A from fruit) and some fibre.

Calories About 75 a serving, depending on the mixture of dried fruit chosen.

- Suitable for diabetics (in small amounts)
- High fibre
- Very low fat
- Milk-free
- Gluten-free

YOGURT FRUIT SHAKE

Yogurt brings out the taste of many kinds of fruit, but don't try this recipe with fresh pineapple or papaya, which won't blend well. The fruits suggested in the recipe are the ones I think go particularly well with yogurt. If you want a sweeter shake, include some banana or add some sultanas or dates. They'll darken the mixture but give sweetness. *1 serving*.

225ml (8fl oz) plain low-fat yogurt or buttermilk
100g (4oz) fresh fruit, such as apricots, raspberries or banana

Place the ingredients in a blender and blend until smooth.

DRIED FRUIT COMPÔTE

A delicious breakfast, hot or cold, and also a good dessert. Add chopped fresh fruit for a special fruit salad. *Serves 3*.

100g (4oz) mixed dried fruit
good grating of nutmeg
5ml (1 tsp) ground cinnamon (optional)
2 thin slices of fresh lemon

Add a little wheat germ and/or natural yogurt for a balanced breakfast. The liquid is sweet enough to make sugar unwanted if you add some compôte to your breakfast cereal, or to plain yogurt.

Calories About 315 a serving with rolled oats, 310 with muesli base.

• Suitable for diabetics (halving quantity of dried fruit)
• High fibre
• Very low fat (omitting nuts)
• Very low salt (using fruit juice and reducing dried fruit)
• Milk-free (by soaking in juice instead of yogurt)
• Gluten-free (substituting millet, buckwheat or rice for oats)

The original recipe uses 15ml (1 tbsp) cereal per person: muesli was designed as a fruit meal, not a cereal-rich one. Made with plenty of fruit, muesli provides a complete meal, with protein from oats and yogurt, both cereal and fruit fibre, a variety of B vitamins from fruit, cereal and yogurt and vitamin C from the fruit and citrus juice. If you sometimes use yellow fruit such as apricots, peaches or melon they will supply vitamin A as well.

Cereal breakfasts are now firmly established as healthier for current energy needs than cooked ones. Cereals, especially when you use lower-fat milk and avoid sugar, make ideal lean-line breakfasts to keep you going until lunch – with protein, fibre, B vitamins and minerals.

1 Soak the fruit overnight.
2 Bring the soaked fruit to the boil in the soaking water in an uncovered saucepan. At this point the water should just cover the fruit. Add the spices and lemon slices, put the lid on the pan and simmer the fruit for 20 to 30 minutes, until it is tender, checking it does not dry out.

VARIATION

Vacuum-flask method Wash the fruit in a sieve under a tap. Bring it to the boil in sufficient water to cover. Warm a wide-mouthed vacuum flask by pouring in some of the mixture. Return the mixture to the pan and bring it back to the boil, then tip it into the flask with the spices and lemon slices. Seal the flask. The fruit will be ready after 45 minutes.

ORIGINAL MUESLI

Soaking muesli overnight is part of the original recipe with which Dr Bircher-Benner achieved remarkable health recovery in his clinic in Zurich at the turn of the century. Having absorbed the soaking liquid, the cereal is easier to digest – and a small amount goes much further. I also find that muesli which has been soaked overnight is much more enjoyable to eat. I don't think flaked cereals which have only just met milk taste of much, but the soaked oats have a lovely flavour. Use muesli at any meal, not just breakfast – it's a far healthier late-night snack than a toasted cheese sandwich. *1 serving*.

| 25g (1oz) rolled oats or muesli base |
| 30ml (2 tbsp) raisins or sultanas |
| 45ml (3 tbsp) plain low-fat yogurt |
| 1 medium apple |
| a little lemon or orange juice |
| 5 hazelnuts |

1 Soak the oats and raisins or sultanas overnight in the yogurt plus enough water to cover.
2 In the morning, grate the apple, add a good squeeze of lemon or orange juice to stop it discolouring, and stir it into the muesli mixture.
3 Grate or chop the nuts and sprinkle them on top.

VARIATIONS

Any amount of *fresh fruit* goes well with muesli.
Add *wheat germ* for extra sweetness, vitamins and protein or *5 to 10ml (1 to 2 tsp) bran* for more fibre. *Hazelnuts* are the least oily nuts, but you can mix in *any dried fruit and nuts* that appeal to you. For more sweetness, soak oats in some of the juice obtained from cooking dried fruit compôte.

CEREALS

The move away from cooked breakfasts to cereal only doesn't have to be mourned. Firstly, you can still have cooked breakfasts when you feel like making and eating them. Secondly, those traditional breakfasts which arouse nostalgia usually included cereal too, and there are many long-established and delicious ones to choose from. Widen your repertoire, and you need no longer face a row of boring packets.

Calories Rolled-oat porridge, about 120 a serving; oatmeal, 150; barley flakes, 110; high-fibre, add another 20; sweet, add about 60 if using raisins, 55 if using dates; frumenty, about 155 calories, with about an extra 20 if raisins or sultanas are added.

- Suitable for diabetics
- High fibre
- Very low fat
- Gluten-free (substituting rice, millet or buckwheat flakes for oats)

Oat fibre has over the last ten years been shown to have particular benefits for diabetics and others whose blood sugar and energy levels are erratic; for those suffering from high blood pressure; and for heart patients, since oat fibre seems to help control blood fat levels. Porridge and muesli are the easiest way to enjoy oat fibre, which you can now buy as a separate product. Because a small quantity of oats will make a good amount of porridge, this is an excellent food for slimmers. It is genuinely filling. If sweetness is built into porridge with dried fruit, there will be no need to add sugar. The fruit also provides additional fibre.

Frumenty – similar to porridge, but made with whole wheat grains instead of oats

EASY PORRIDGE

Porridge has become neglected, perhaps because people have visions of long stirring and slimy, messy saucepans. Rediscover it – it doesn't have to take long to make or wash up after. It's also one of the most warming and one of the cheapest foods there is. *1 serving.*

30g (1 generous oz) rolled oats
75ml (3fl oz) each water and skimmed milk
pinch of sea salt

1 Combine the oats with the liquid in a thick-based saucepan and add the salt. Bring to the boil, stirring steadily.
2 Simmer the mixture, uncovered, stirring occasionally, for 4 to 5 minutes, until the desired consistency is reached.
3 Serve with extra milk, plus: a very little salt or salt substitute; molasses, black treacle or honey; no-added-sugar jam; home-made fruit purée.

VARIATIONS

Vacuum-flask method Warm a wide-mouthed vacuum flask (not an insulation flask, which loses heat too quickly) with very hot or boiling water. Bring the porridge to the boil in a saucepan, then transfer it to the warmed flask. Stir the porridge and seal the flask. The porridge will be ready in 1 hour. Left overnight, it will be fine in the morning, but may need reheating slightly. Advantages: no sticking or stirring, plus fuel saving.
Oatmeal If you enjoy rolled-oat porridge, you will probably like oatmeal even better, as oatmeal has not been subjected to the heat-

rolling process which impairs the flavour of rolled oats. For each person allow 25g (1oz) fine or medium oatmeal and 300ml (½ pint) half skimmed milk, half water. Simmer the porridge for about 30 minutes; or leave it overnight in a well-sealed casserole in the second (warm) oven of a solid-fuel cooker. You can also use the vacuum-flask method, but cook the porridge for 5 minutes before transferring it to the flask.

Barley flakes These, or indeed any other kind of rolled, flaked cereal, can be cooked as porridge in the same way as oats. Most take a little longer than rolled oats to cook, unless the cereal is first left to soak in the liquid in a warm oven overnight.

High-fibre Add to any kind of porridge 10ml (2 tsp) per person coarse wheat bran; and/or use 15ml (1 tbsp) oat bran instead of half the rolled oats. Wheat bran gives a chewier consistency. Oat bran makes a very gelatinous mix. The two kinds of fibre are complementary, working differently (see page 312).

Sweet porridge For those who prefer porridge with plenty of sweetness, 25g (1oz) raisins or chopped dried dates per person can be cooked with rolled oats, oatmeal or other cereals. If you liquidize the dried fruit in the milk and water for the porridge first, more sweetness will be released.

Frumenty A recipe that the Anglo-Saxons would have felt familiar with. Wash 25g (1oz) whole wheat grains per person in a sieve held under a cold tap, picking out any black or other foreign objects. Soak in cold water, using about 125ml (4fl oz) for each 25g (1oz) grain, for 12 to 24 hours. Bring to the boil, cover and simmer very slowly for about an hour, until the wheat grains burst. If the mixture is too dry, add some skimmed milk.

Eat as a savoury cereal with a little yeast extract and milk; or for a sweet cereal, cook some raisins or sultanas, plus a little mixed spice, with the wheat. Very filling, and can be eaten hot or cold.

BREADS

You'll find most of the bread recipes in the baking section, page 235, but here are some ideas that belong to breakfast time, either because you can make them so quickly, or because croissants, to me, still seem to sum up a civilized and scrumptious breakfast.

12-MINUTE ROLLS

A recipe everyone needs at some time – but good to make even when you haven't run out of bread. Sieving the bran out and using it as a coating produces much lighter rolls. Any bran left over can be added to breakfast cereal. *Makes 12*.

225g (8oz) plain wholemeal flour, any type
20ml (4 tsp) baking powder
large pinch of sea salt
25g (1oz) soft margarine or butter
scant 150ml (¼ pint) skimmed milk to mix

1 Heat the oven to its highest temperature. Grease a baking sheet.
2 Sieve the flour, baking powder and salt into a mixing bowl, reserving the bran in the sieve.

If you steer clear of making delicious home-made waffles and muffins because you're nervous you'll wolf the lot, remember that these versions are filling, and needn't be accompanied by oodles of butter or jam.

Calories About 80 a roll.

As with soda bread, you lose some vitamin B_1 by using baking powder – but only about 10 per cent. The skimmed milk used in this recipe provides some extra B vitamins to balance out the loss.

- Suitable for diabetics
- High fibre
- Very low fat
- Very low salt (using low-sodium baking powder and unsalted fat, and omitting salt)

3 Rub in the fat.

4 Add milk gradually until you have a very sticky, wet dough.

5 Using a tablespoon, shape the dough into balls. Drop the dough balls into the reserved bran and roll them in it to coat them thoroughly.

6 Place the rolls on the baking sheet and bake them for 10 minutes in the hottest part of the oven.

VARIATIONS

For more flavour, add *2ml (¹/₂ tsp) crushed caraway*, *celery* or *toasted sesame seeds* to the dough.

GRANARY CROISSANTS

I prefer to use granary flour for making croissants. Why less-than-wholemeal flour? You can certainly make this recipe using strong wholemeal flour, but, if your experience is the same as mine, you won't be able to get your croissants to keep their distinctive layers – so you may end up with delicious rolls rather than croissants; but you may be a better baker than I am. *Makes 12 large.*

30ml (2 tbsp) fresh yeast or 15ml (1 tbsp) dried yeast
5ml (1 tsp) honey
1 25mg vitamin C tablet
45ml (3 tbsp) cold water
30ml (2 tbsp) boiling water
450g (1lb) granary or malted wheatmeal flour
2ml (½ tsp) sea salt
2 eggs
150ml (¼ pint) lukewarm water
225g (8oz) unsalted butter, chilled

1 If you are using fresh yeast or large-particle dried yeast, put the yeast, honey and vitamin C tablet in a cup. Pour in the cold water, then stir in the boiling water. If using fresh yeast, move on to step 2. If using large-particle dried yeast, leave the yeast mixture in a warm place for 10 minutes, until it becomes frothy. If using micronized yeast, omit step 1 and add the yeast to the flour in step 2 and the honey and vitamin C with the water in step 3.

2 Put the flour and half of the salt in a warmed mixing bowl.

3 Beat 1 egg and add it to the flour, together with the yeast mixture and enough of the remaining water to make a softish but workable dough.

4 Knead the dough on a floured surface for 8 to 10 minutes.

5 Roll it into an oblong, about 15 × 55cm (6 × 21in). Cut a third of the butter into small cubes and dot them evenly over two-thirds of the dough. Fold the unbuttered end over, then the other end on top.

6 Turn the dough sideways and repeat the rolling and folding process twice, using the rest of the butter. For the best results, chill the dough for 20 minutes between rollings.

7 Chill the dough, covered with polythene, on a floured plate for 30 minutes.

8 Roll and fold the dough 3 more times, but without adding butter. Chill for another 30 minutes.

9 Roll the dough into a large circle about 45cm (17in) across. Don't stretch the dough – it must be moving without sticking to the surface

Calories About 275 a croissant.

- Suitable for diabetics (occasionally)
- Medium fibre
- Very low salt (using only 1 egg and unsalted butter, and omitting salt)

Croissants can never be low in fat, but at least the ones in this recipe have more food value from the flour. You must use butter, because it is important to have a fat with a fairly high melting temperature; professional bakers use either butter or super-hardened animal fats.

Croissants take time and trouble, so make lots at once. They freeze well for up to 3 months. Crisp them, without thawing, for up to 15 minutes in a medium oven.

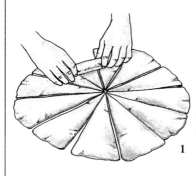

1

2

Rolling up croissants
1 With the dough divided into 12 wedges, roll each wedge from the outside to the centre.
2 The finished rolled croissant, curved slightly into a cresent.

Granary croissants with kissel (page 220) used as jam

beneath. Don't worry if the edge of the circle is uneven. Let the dough sit for 10 minutes.

10 Cut the circle into 12 even wedges. Let them rest while you slightly warm and then grease 2 baking sheets.

11 Beat the second egg in a cup with the rest of the salt. Brush the wedges with the beaten egg.

12 Roll each wedge up *loosely* towards the centre of the circle, finishing with the point almost underneath.

13 Place the rolls on the baking sheets, curving each roll into a crescent shape. Cover the croissants with polythene and leave them to rise for about 40 minutes.

14 While the croissants are rising, heat the oven to 240°C (475°F), gas mark 9.

15 Brush the croissants generously with egg again. Bake them for 10 minutes, then reduce the heat to 220°C (425°F), gas mark 7, and bake for another 5 to 10 minutes.

POTATO SCONES

A quick and easy change from bread for breakfast, these scones are particularly useful for those who find wholemeal bread too brown and chewy. Try serving potato scones with browned mushrooms (page 129). *Makes 10 medium.*

100g (4oz) plain wholemeal flour
5ml (1 tsp) baking powder
pinch of sea salt
30ml (2 tbsp) oil or 25g (1oz) soft margarine
100g (4oz) potatoes, boiled
a little skimmed milk to mix

Calories About 60 a scone. As potatoes, plain, contain only about 25 per 25g (1oz), this form of roll has fewer calories than an all-grain one.

• Suitable for diabetics
• Medium-to-high fibre
• Very low fat
• Very low salt (using low-sodium baking powder and oil or unsalted fat)

No need to peel the potatoes. If they have been cooked for the minimum of time in the minimum of water, they will have kept as much as possible of their vitamin C.

1 Heat the oven to 220°C (425°F), gas mark 7. Lightly grease a baking sheet.
2 Sift the flour, baking powder and salt into a mixing bowl.
3 Rub in the fat.
4 Use a wooden spoon to push the potatoes through a sieve into the mixture.
5 Stir in just enough milk to make a soft and pliable dough.
6 Roll out the dough to just over 1cm (½in) thick.
7 Cut it into squares or rounds. Place the scones on the baking sheet and bake them for 20 minutes. Eat them warm.

PANCAKES & WAFFLES

These can provide an interesting change. Top them with stewed fruit, rather than butter or jam, for a healthier start to the day.
.

SCOTCH PANCAKES OR DROP SCONES

Calories About 25 a scone; for apple scones, add an extra 2 a scone; for apricot scones, 1; for sultana scones, 7.

• Suitable for diabetics
• Very low salt (using low-sodium baking powder and omitting salt)
• Gluten-free (substituting millet and maize flour, half and half, for wheat flour)

Although these pancakes are fried, you need add hardly any oil if you use a cast-iron pan, which will also provide even cooking.

Another easy way to make breakfast special. You can leave half of the batter plain, and add apple, apricots or sultanas to the other half. A recipe children enjoy making. *Makes about 18, 5cm (2in) diameter.*

100g (4oz) plain wholemeal flour
10ml (2 tsp) baking powder or 2ml (½ tsp) bicarbonate of soda plus 5ml (1 tsp) cream of tartar
pinch of sea salt (optional)
1 large egg
150ml (¼ pint) skimmed milk

1 Sieve the flour with the raising agents, add the salt if you are using it. Tip the bran from the sieve back into the flour mixture.
2 Beating thoroughly but quickly, beat in the egg and half of the milk, then the rest of the milk.
3 Heat a thick-based frying pan or griddle, ideally a cast-iron one, and brush it lightly with oil.
4 Over a medium heat, drop spoonfuls of batter on the pan.
5 Cook each pancake until the top bubbles, then turn it over and cook the underside for about 1 to 1½ minutes.
6 To stop the finished pancakes from drying out, transfer them to a folded tea towel, from which they can be served.

VARIATIONS

Apple scones Add to the batter a small, finely chopped sweet apple, plus a pinch of dried cloves.
Apricot scones Simmer 2 dried apricots in boiling water for 20 minutes, chop them finely and add them to the batter.
Sultana scones Before starting to make the batter, pour boiling water over 50g (2oz) sultanas in a cup. Drain the sultanas and add them to the batter before cooking.

Calories About 130 a waffle.

- Suitable for diabetics
- High fibre

The wheat germ gives a substantial boost of proteins, B vitamins and vitamin E, as well as making the waffles tastier.

WEEKEND BREAKFAST MENU

Nutmeg waffles **130 cals**
Cottage cheese **50 cals**
Fresh fruit or apricot spread
50 cals
Decaffeinated coffee or herb tea

Total calories per person **230**

NUTMEG WAFFLES

This recipe makes light golden waffles that few people would suspect were 'good for them'. The quantity of nutmeg used sounds large, but the result is excellent. Try these waffles topped with stewed apple or with cottage cheese and strawberries. *Makes 4, 15cm (6in) diameter.*

65g (2½oz) fine plain wholemeal flour
25g (1oz) wheat germ
pinch of sea salt
5ml (1 tsp) nutmeg, freshly grated
7ml (1½ tsp) baking powder
1 egg, separated
15ml (1 tbsp) oil
225ml (8fl oz) skimmed milk

1 Heat a non-stick waffle iron and brush it lightly with oil.
2 Mix the first five ingredients well.
3 Whisk the egg white until it is stiff. This is easier with an electric whisk.
4 Beat the egg yolk with the oil and the milk.
5 Pour the milk mixture into the flour mixture, then fold in the egg white carefully. Spoon about a quarter of the batter into the waffle iron and cook it for 2 to 3 minutes on each side, or until the waffle is crisp and golden. Cook the rest of the batter in the same way.

COOKED BREAKFASTS

Many people who don't feel like a cooked breakfast during the week enjoy a more leisurely sit or brunch at weekends. Here's a selection of ideas to consider.

Bacon ✳✳✳ Grill until crisp; or try thin, lean ham instead.
Eggs ✳✳ Boil, poach or coddle.
Kidneys ✳✳ Trim off fat, then grill them.
Kippers ✳✳ Poach in a jug of boiling water or bake, rather than fry. Grilling also minimizes fat content, but I prefer to poach or bake kippers, as these methods reduce lingering aroma as well as avoiding spitting fat.
Mushrooms ✳ Sweat in 5ml (1 tsp) oil in a thick-based pan for 3 to 4 minutes. Mushrooms keep much more flavour when cooked this way than when they are grilled.
Sausages ✳✳✳ Provided the sausages are well pricked, grilling will reduce fat, but the fat content will still be high. You can make your own chicken sausages, so long as you don't expect them to taste like pork ones. Almost all bought sausages contain assorted additives.
Smoked haddock ✳✳ Choose Finnan haddie, which is usually free of artificial colouring. Poach for 8 minutes in skimmed milk; bake; or make kedgeree (page 174).
Tomatoes ✳ Brush them lightly with oil and grill; or cook like mushrooms.

✳ Balanced enough to eat every day.
✳✳ Good food value, but too rich to eat every day unless you are skipping lunch.
✳✳✳ An occasional treat – too high in fat to eat often.

APPETIZERS & BUFFET FOODS

Party nibbles and first courses catch us at our hungriest. We'll tuck into food with a will. So a good 'starter' or party snack should not fill you up. The idea suggested by the older name of appetizer is what to aim for, but not the so-called appetizer that oozes with fat from its flaky pastry or filling. Although they look small and insubstantial, vol-au-vents or fried prawns will blunt your appetite for the following meal – and do more than many a main course to increase your waistline.

Here is a selection of recipes aimed at satisfying eager tastebuds without being heavy in calories or in fat. Many are based on vegetables, which means that they tend to be crunchy or chewy – textures most people enjoy. Extra chewing can also improve digestion: it alerts the stomach to prepare for work by stimulating the production of the right digestive juices.

If you plan meals around a main course choose a complementary rather than a challenging first course. Don't, for instance, precede a delicate-flavoured fish dish with a highly spiced curried dip or ratatouille; and remember that first courses with lots of garlic should be saved for dinners where other strong flavours can hold their own afterwards.

First courses can be so interesting that they tempt you to eat two – the second instead of a main course – which is what I often do in a restaurant. The recipes in this section can be treated in exactly this way and serve a variety of purposes, not only as starters and party fare, but also as light meals or main courses, with the portions adapted for larger appetites.

These recipes have another advantage: they keep last-minute work to a minimum, so that the cook can sit down, relax, and enjoy the meal and the company. I know one particularly elegant cook who prepares six or seven interesting and complementary dishes and lays them out on a side table. Guests help themselves and then bring their plates to the beautifully set dinner table. In this way their host can enjoy the evening without having to jump up and down, clearing one course and serving the next, keeping an eye on every plate, and probably spending more time out of the room than in it. At the same time, this kind of dinner offers guests more choice in what they eat and how much. The table isn't cluttered with serving dishes, no one has to pass plates around, and everyone feels free to sit back and take part in the conversation. I've tried entertaining like this, and it's the easiest dinner party ever.

Vegetable terrine – colourful and much easier to make than it looks, a low-fat form of taramasalata, and almond bites, a good nibble for parties or for children

FINGER FOODS

If you look at the huge success of 'take-away' foods, those that people seem to enjoy most are the ones they can eat with their fingers: fish and chips, hamburgers, chicken pieces and pittas. I think most people like eating with their fingers: I do, and many children will eat things like this that they wouldn't take a knife and fork to.

Finger foods also do away with two of the problems of parties: at a buffet, they mean you aren't trying simultaneously to balance a glass, hold a plate and wield a fork, a three-handed job for which I for one have been inadequately equipped. And at dinner parties they can help to break the ice and give an informal, friendly atmosphere.

AUBERGINE CRUNCHIES

Calories About 20 to 25 a slice; as a main course for 4 people, about 240 each.

- Suitable for diabetics
- Medium fibre
- Very low salt (using low-sodium bread and replacing cheese with flaked nuts)
- Milk-free (omitting cheese)
- Gluten-free (using gluten-free bread and rice or buckwheat flour)

An example of how a vegetable dish can be high enough in protein (from the eggs, cheese and bread) to become a light main dish, without having too much fat.

An interesting buffet food, which also makes a good main dish. The aubergine crunchies must not be made too far in advance. Prepare a trayful, and bake them while your guests settle down, to serve hot in mid-party. If you are using them as a main course, they will go well with a dish such as plain pasta rings with a little soured cream and walnut topping together with a green salad – flavours that won't drown the delicate flavour of the aubergine. Keep the Mediterranean theme with a dessert such as peaches, fresh or sliced into cold, dried fig compôte.

Buy thin aubergines, so that the slices will be neater and less floppy. *Makes about 40 to 45 pieces. Serves 4 as a main course.*

45ml (3 tbsp) vegetable oil or 45g (1½oz) soft margarine
700g (1½lb) aubergines (preferably long, thinnish ones)
2 standard eggs
50g (2oz) wholemeal bread (2 fairly thin slices)
25g (1oz) Parmesan cheese, freshly grated
15ml (1 tbsp) parsley, chopped
large pinch of white pepper
1ml (¼ tsp) sea salt
25g (1oz) plain wholemeal flour

1 Heat the oven to 200°C (400°F), gas mark 6. Use the fat to grease 2 baking sheets generously.
2 Wash the aubergines, trim the ends and cut them into slices about 1cm (½in) thick. Leave the peel on – it keeps the slices firm, and you can always leave it if it turns out too chewy for your taste.
3 Beat the eggs lightly in a shallow dish.
4 Toast the slices of bread to crisp, then turn them into breadcrumbs in a food processor or electric coffee grinder, or with a rolling pin.
5 Mix the breadcrumbs, cheese, parsley, pepper and salt on a sheet of paper or a plate. Put the flour on a saucer.
6 Dip the aubergine slices in the flour, then in the eggs, then coat them thoroughly in the crumb mixture. Shake off any excess.
7 Place the slices on the baking sheets and bake them for 25 minutes, turning after about 15 minutes.

VARIATION

This dish can also be made with sliced *courgettes*.

PIZZA SQUARES

- Suitable for diabetics
- High fibre
- Very low salt (omitting salt and cheese, and using low-sodium baking powder)

Even without fish, this handy dish contains plenty of protein for a main course. Pizza purists may hate the idea of a no-yeast pizza, but this scone dough base tastes good, is quick, and is, like pizza dough, low in fat. Using cold-pressed olive oil enhances the Mediterranean character of the pizza and, as it has a good, strong flavour, you don't need to use much, so it doesn't add a lot of oiliness.

Cutting a large pizza into squares pleases not only those who eat them, each person getting less edge than with individual pizzas or quiches, but also the cook, who can make this versatile dish in about 30 minutes. Serve with a green salad. *Makes about 12 small squares, or serves 4 as a main course.*

Base

100g (4oz) plain wholemeal flour
2ml (½ tsp) bicarbonate of soda
5ml (1 tsp) cream of tartar
good pinch of sea salt
30ml (2 tbsp) cold-pressed olive oil or 25g (1oz) soft margarine or butter
a little skimmed milk for mixing the dough

Topping

100g (4oz) onion, finely chopped
100g (4oz) mushrooms or courgettes, sliced
6 fresh tomatoes or 1 400g (14oz) tin*
5ml (1 tsp) mixed dried herbs
5ml (1 tsp) fresh oregano, chopped, or 2ml (½ tsp) dried oregano
black pepper
sea salt
15ml (1 tbsp) tomato purée
1 pepper, preferably red, cut in rings
100g (4oz) Mozzarella or mature Cheddar or Cheshire cheese, grated
handful of black olives
25g (1oz) walnut pieces or pine nuts

*If the pizza is to be eaten with the fingers, drain off the juice from tinned tomatoes or cook fresh tomatoes over a slightly higher heat, for a drier result.

1 Heat the oven to its maximum temperature. Grease a rectangular baking tin, roughly 18 × 25cm (7 × 10in), with side rims at least 2cm (¾in) high.
2 Sift the flour with the bicarbonate of soda, cream of tartar and salt.
3 Fork in the fat, and enough milk to form a soft dough.
4 On a floured board, roll out the dough to fit the baking tin. Line the tin with the dough and bake for 10 minutes.
5 Meanwhile, brush a thick-based pan lightly with oil and set it on a low heat. Add the onion to the pan, put the lid on and soften the onion gently.
6 After 5 minutes, add the mushrooms or courgettes to the onion.
7 After another 5 minutes, add the tomatoes and half of the herbs. Simmer the mixture with the pan uncovered, gently breaking up the tomatoes with a fork. Season.
8 Remove the pizza base from the oven. Stir the tomato purée into the vegetable mixture. Spread the mixture over the base, then top it with the rings of pepper, the grated cheese, the olives, the nuts and the remaining herbs, in that order.
9 Return the pizza to the hot oven for 10 minutes, until the cheese has melted.

FINGER FOOD BUFFET MENU

Halved pitta bread stuffed with cold turkey in curry sauce
330 cals each
Tjatziki **45 cals**
Watercress and orange salad
120 cals

—•—

Pizza squares **115 cals each**
Waldorf dip **100 cals**
Crispy prawn fingers
30 cals each
Aubergine crunchies
20 cals each

—•—

Exotic fruit – kumquats, fresh dates, fresh figs, grapes or cherries **50 cals**
Miriam's cheesecake **230 cals**

10 Cool the pizza for a few minutes before cutting it into small squares that can be eaten with the fingers, or larger squares to be served as a main course.

VARIATION

For a really hefty pizza, add a cupful of *flaked, cooked fish*, such as *tuna*, to the topping.

CRISPY PRAWN FINGERS

Chinese magic – here without the deep frying. *Makes about 40 fingers.*

100g (4oz) white fish, cooked
100g (4oz) prawns or shrimps, peeled
1 standard egg, beaten
5ml (1 tsp) fresh root ginger, finely grated
8 water chestnuts, finely grated
10ml (2 tsp) soya sauce
15ml (1 tbsp) sherry
30ml (2 tbsp) cornflour
8 thin slices of wholemeal bread, crusts removed
15ml (1 tbsp) olive or sesame oil
40g (1½oz) sesame seeds

1 Mince or mash the fish and shellfish with the egg, ginger, chestnuts, soya sauce, sherry and cornflour, to make a smooth paste.
2 Toast the slices of bread on one side.
3 Spread the untoasted sides with the paste.
4 Grease a thick-based pan lightly with the oil, saving some for later slices. Set the pan over a low heat.
5 Dip the slices, paste side down, in the sesame seeds. Place some slices, sesame seeds down, in the pan. Press the slices down with a broad spatula. Cook them gently for 1 minute, then remove them from the pan.
6 Brush the pan with oil again and cook the rest of the slices in the same way.
7 Cut the slices into narrow fingers. Stack the fingers in rows on a serving plate, placing each row at right angles to the one beneath.

VARIATIONS

The cost of these snack fingers can be cut by omitting the shellfish and using white fish alone, but in this case you may need to use a little more salt than the soya sauce provides.
If you would like to bring out more of the sesame flavour, crush the seeds slightly in an electric coffee grinder or a mortar before using them to coat the bread.

ALMOND BITES

Cumin, celery, mint and ginger are just a few of the many flavours that combine well with the soft cheese and the toasted almond coating to make bite-sized morsels to serve at buffet meals and with drinks. These bites sound fiddly, but they are really quick to make once you have

Calories About 30 a finger.

• Suitable for diabetics
• Medium fibre
• Gluten-free (if using gluten-free bread)

These provide a high-protein first course.

Use a pastry brush to grease the pan with the minimum of oil, as the last thing you want is a greasy result.

Sesame seeds supply a soothing, jellying type of fibre, calcium, B vitamins and vitamin E, as well as oil. Crushing the seeds not only releases their flavour, it also makes it more likely that you will get the benefit of the vitamins and calcium, as, left whole, the seeds tend to pass undigested through the system.

Calories About 18 a bite.

Almond bites provide a high-protein first course.

- Suitable for diabetics
- Low fibre
- Very low fat (using low-fat cheese and half quantity of hazelnut flakes)
- Very low salt (omitting salt and soya sauce)
- Gluten-free

collected the ingredients, especially if you have a food processor to do the initial chopping. However, do not be tempted to put the soft cheese in a processor: it may come out too wet. *Makes about 40.*

225g (8oz) low- or medium-fat dry soft cheese	
50g (2oz) almond flakes	
Batch 1	**Batch 2**
1 stick of celery, 15ml (1 tbsp) parsley, 6 leaves of fresh mint (all finely chopped)	1 sheet of nori seaweed (optional)
cumin, coriander (both ground)	3 water chestnuts, 1 spring onion, 15ml (1 tbsp) parsley (all finely chopped)
pepper	5ml (1 tsp) ginger root, grated
sea salt	5ml (1 tsp) soya sauce
	pepper

1 Divide the cheese into 2 batches.
2 Toast the almond flakes in an ungreased, thick-based pan over a low heat for 2 to 3 minutes, until they are turning golden. Transfer them to a plate.
3 Cover a serving platter with *green leaves*, for example, *vine leaves*, *celery tops* or *watercress*.
4 Mix the chopped celery, parsley and mint and flavour the mixture with cumin, coriander, pepper and salt to taste. Mix with half the cheese.
5 If you are using nori, a Japanese seaweed that comes in crisp sheets, re-crisp it by passing it back and forth over a flame for a few seconds. Use scissors to cut it into tiny pieces. Mix the nori, chestnuts, onion, parsley, ginger, soya sauce and pepper with the other half of the cheese.
6 Using a wet spoon, scoop up teaspoons of each mixture, shaping each spoonful into a small round with the help of another teaspoon. Alternatively, roll into balls between the palms of your hands.
7 As each ball is made, dip it into the almonds and place it on the leafy platter.

DIPS & SPREADS

Another style of eating with your fingers. Given larger portions, by the way, these make balanced meals. They're fun, easy to make and enjoyed even by people who normally avoid salads or vegetables.

TARAMASALATA

Calories About 75 to 110 a serving.

- Suitable for diabetics
- No fibre
- Milk-free (if soya cheese is used)
- Gluten-free

This version of taramasalata has none of the heaviness associated with the usual high oil content. Bought taramasalata usually contains artificial colouring. This one, with no added colouring, is palest pink.

Only a small piece of cod's roe is needed to make a good quantity of dip, so it is far cheaper to make taramasalata than to buy it ready-made. And of course home-made taramasalata tastes far fresher than bought. I am indebted to cookery writer Nathalie Hambro for the idea of buying and freezing fresh cod's roe when it is available in the winter, so that in the summer, when you can't buy fresh roe, you will have it in the freezer, instead of having to turn to tins. *Serves 4 to 6.*

100g (4oz) chunk of smoked cod's roe
juice of 1 to 2 lemons, to taste
225g (8oz) curd cheese
paprika, to garnish

1 Peel off the skin of the cod's roe if possible. Otherwise, scoop out the roe with a teaspoon.
2 Using a wooden spoon, mash the roe with the juice of 1 lemon.
3 Work in the curd cheese with the spoon. Avoid using a blender, as the action tends to break down the texture of the roe and the cheese.
4 Taste the taramasalata and add more lemon juice if wanted. The roe is very salty, so no extra salt will be needed. Sprinkle with paprika.
5 Chill the taramasalata for about an hour. Serve it with fingers of wholemeal toast and/or crudités.

VARIATION

If you want to make your taramasalata a little redder, add *10 to 15ml (2 to 3 tsp) beetroot juice.* Reduce the amount of lemon juice, so that the taramasalata doesn't become too liquid.

HUMUS

A recipe I'm particularly pleased with, because it's just as good as humus laced with around 1000 extra calories' worth of oil. I've kept a little oil just for the flavour, but you could use chopped olives instead. *Serves 4 to 6 as a starter, 2 to 3 as part of a main course.*

100g (4oz) chick peas
25g (1oz) sesame seeds
2 cloves of garlic, crushed
juice of 1 to 2 lemons, to taste
large pinch of ground coriander
white pepper
30ml (2 tbsp) olive oil
100g (4oz) low-fat soft cheese
paprika, to garnish

1 Put the chick peas in a saucepan, cover them with water and soak them overnight; or bring them to the boil, simmer for 2 minutes, then soak for 2 hours.
2 Drain off the soaking water, checking to make sure that none of the little stones which sometimes find their way between chick peas remain. Cover the chick peas with fresh water.
3 Bring the chick peas to the boil, cover the pan and simmer for 1 to 1½ hours, until they are cooked through.
4 Toast the sesame seeds in an ungreased pan over a low heat for 2 to 3 minutes, then grind them thoroughly in an electric coffee grinder or a mortar.
5 Drain the chick peas, reserving the cooking water, and transfer them to the goblet of a blender. Add the crushed garlic, the juice of 1 lemon, the ground sesame seeds, the coriander, pepper, 15ml (1 tbsp) of the oil and enough of the cooking liquid to enable the blender to run.
6 Blend to a thick consistency. Remove the purée from the blender and stir in the soft cheese thoroughly. Check the seasoning and add more lemon juice if wanted.
7 You can serve the humus immediately, but it will taste even better if you leave it for a few hours for the flavours to blend. To serve, transfer it to a flat dish, sprinkle it generously with paprika and pour over the remaining olive oil. Provide pitta bread or crudités to scoop it up with.

Calories About 90 to 140 a serving as a starter, 180 to 280 a serving as a main course.

- Suitable for diabetics
- High fibre
- Very low fat (if oil is omitted)
- Very low salt (using home-made soft cheese and omitting salt)
- Gluten-free

Make sure the sesame seeds are well pulverized before adding them to the blender. This is important, not only to bring out their flavour, but also to help extract the calcium, B vitamins and vitamin E, as if they are left whole the seeds may simply pass undigested through the system.

VEGETARIAN PARTY MENU

Humus *115 cals*
Carrot sticks *30 cals*
Wholemeal roll or garlic bread
90 cals each
—•—
Aubergine roast *155 cals*
Green beans or broccoli
30 cals
Puréed beetroot with yogurt
and lemon juice *60 cals*
—•—
Apple strudel *240 cals*

Total calories per person *720*

Waldorf Dip

Calories About 75 to 110 a serving.

- Suitable for diabetics
- Low fibre
- Very low salt (using home-made cheese and omitting salt)
- Gluten-free

Vegetable dippers are enjoyed by many people who wouldn't touch a raw carrot otherwise, and by those who don't like cooked vegetables very much. So serve them often, for maximum goodness with minimum calories. If you want to provide other dippers, keep away from cocktail biscuits, which have a particularly high fat content. Use wholemeal toast fingers or chappatis or pitta bread.

Waldorf dip, with a selection of dippers

Too many dips depend on garlic and onion. They do add lots of flavour, but, at a buffet, many guests won't welcome the addition to their breath. And too much garlic in a dinner party starter may overwhelm following flavours, unless the main course is an equally strong-tasting dish. There are dozens of herbs, spices and other flavourings which make delicious dips when mixed with soft cheese or with soured cream. Here is one based on the same flavours as Waldorf salad. *Serves 4 to 6.*

1 red-skinned apple, 2 sticks of celery, 1 good handful of parsley (all roughly chopped)
25g (1oz) walnut pieces
juice of ½ lemon
white pepper
sea salt
nutmeg
225g (8oz) low-fat soft cheese

1 Place the chopped apple, celery and parsley in a blender with the walnuts, lemon juice and a good pinch of pepper and sea salt. Blend quickly, so that the vegetables are not puréed but remain in very small pieces. The red apple peel should give a fleck of colour here and there.

2 Grate nutmeg, to taste, into the mixture.
3 With a wooden spoon, work the mixture into the cheese. If the consistency is too stiff for dipping, add *a little apple juice* to thin. If it is too thin, add *5 to 10ml (1 to 2 tsp) rolled oats*: they will absorb liquid if you leave the dip to stand for 30 minutes or more.
4 Serve with a selection of these dippers □ Slices of carrot, cut vertically to give a long 'plank' shape □ Leaves of chicory □ Mushrooms: cut flat mushrooms into quarters, use buttons whole but without their stalks □ Thin slices of swede □ Sticks of celery, not cut too small □ Pieces of the individual leaves from a bulb of fennel □ Triangles of red or green pepper □ Very thin slices of young turnip □ Leaves from cooked globe artichokes □ Thin slices of apple, dipped in lemon juice to prevent them from browning □ Spears of cucumber, cut lengthways □ Wholemeal Melba toast □ Thin slices from large courgettes, cut across.

VARIATIONS

If you would like something a little unusual, add *30ml (2 tbsp) unsweetened dried coconut* to the Waldorf mixture.
Other good ingredients for a dip include: *tarragon*, chopped if fresh or finely powdered if dried; *fresh mint*; *finely chopped cucumber*; and, in the summer, *basil* galore.

CHICKEN LIVER PÂTÉ

A very smooth-textured, filling pâté that goes well with a light salad main course, or can be served on a main course salad platter. You can also use this mixture as a stuffing for mushrooms. *Serves 4 to 5 as a starter, 3 as a main course.*

5ml (1 tsp) oil or soft margarine
1 large onion, finely chopped
225g (8oz) chicken livers
1 clove of garlic (optional), crushed
5ml (1 tsp) mixed herbs
15ml (1 tbsp) brandy
1ml (¼ tsp) paprika
75g (3oz) smooth, low-fat soft cheese
fresh parsley, chopped, and paprika, to garnish

1 Heat the fat in a thick-based pan and add 10ml (2 tsp) water. Add the chopped onion, cover the pan and cook the onion gently for 3 minutes.
2 Trim the chicken livers of any green or black bits, then add them to the onion. Cook for a further 3 minutes.
3 Add the garlic, if used, and the herbs. Cook for a further 3 minutes.
4 Put the mixture through the finest blades of a mincer or food processor. Repeat, if necessary, until the texture is smooth.
5 Stir in the brandy, paprika and soft cheese. Chill for about an hour.
6 Serve the pâté sprinkled with chopped fresh parsley and more paprika and accompanied by wholemeal Melba toast and pitta bread and/or sticks of carrot, celery or cucumber.

VARIATION

If you like a spicier flavour, add *a little powdered nutmeg or mace* and *a dash of anchovy essence*.

Calories About 100 to 120 a serving as a starter, 160 a serving as a main course.

• Suitable for diabetics
• No fibre (except for dippers)
• Very low fat
• Milk-free (using soya cheese)
• Gluten-free

Very high in protein, with all the other well-known plus-factors of liver: a high iron content, zinc, vitamin A, vitamin D, B vitamins, vitamin E – and only about 6 per cent fat, compared with around 10 per cent fat for lamb's liver. A quarter of this recipe provides about 14g (½oz) of protein – about a quarter of an adult's average daily protein need.

Calories About 45 a serving.

- Suitable for diabetics
- Medium fibre
- Very low-fat
- Gluten-free

The yogurt provides some protein. If cucumber usually gives you indigestion, include the crushed caraway seeds, don't peel the cucumber, and chew your tjatziki thoroughly.

TJATZIKI

Tjatziki, served in Greece as an appetizer or side dish, provides a cool, light first course, ideal to precede a solid main course such as lamb casserole or chili con carne. *Serves 4.*

450g (1lb) cucumber (1 large)
225ml (8fl oz) thick, plain, low-fat yogurt
1 clove of garlic, crushed, or 5ml (1 tsp) caraway seeds, crushed
juice of 1 lemon
chives or parsley, chopped, to taste
freshly ground black pepper

1 Chop the cucumber finely – don't grate it, or the result will be too wet and you will lose the crunchiness.
2 Mix all the ingredients together and check the seasoning.
3 Serve cold but not chilled, with wholemeal toast fingers or pitta bread.

VARIATIONS

To turn tjatziki into a main dish, mix it with *hard-boiled egg* or *cooked white beans* and stuff it into wholemeal pitta bread or baked potatoes, for example.

GREEK BUFFET MENU

Taramasalata **95 cals**
Humus **115 cals**
Tjatziki **45 cals**
Stuffed vine leaves **70 cals**
Wholemeal pitta bread strips **90 cals**
Greek salad **200 cals**
—•—
Thick yogurt with honey and sliced figs or peaches **150 cals**

VEGETABLE STARTERS

Elegant, light, tasty ways to start a meal, these recipes are chosen for their handsome looks as well as for flavours that appeal to the hungry tastebud. Served in larger portions, with accompanying grain, they make good light meals that are a refreshing change from chunks of meat, without inducing any sense of sacrifice.

STUFFED VINE LEAVES

Easier than they look, because although vine leaves tear easily, they also wrap easily. As with many fiddly recipes, it's worth making a large batch and storing some in a refrigerator for a few days. *Serves 8 as a starter, 4 as a main course.*

Calories About 70 a serving as a starter, 140 a serving as a main course.

- Suitable for diabetics
- High fibre
- Very low fat
- Milk-free
- Gluten-free (substituting millet, buckwheat or rice for bulgur wheat)

The proteins in grains and pulses balance each other. You can vary this filling by substituting other grains and pulses, and still have a well-balanced main dish. This recipe also provides no fewer than 3 kinds of fibre, from the lentils, from the bulgur wheat, and from the prunes and sultanas.

50g (2oz) whole lentils
75g (3oz) bulgur wheat
8 prunes
15ml (1 tbsp) sultanas
5ml (1 tsp) oil
1 medium onion, finely chopped
2ml (½ tsp) ground nutmeg
2ml (½ tsp) dried mint
2ml (½ tsp) white pepper
juice of 1 large lemon
225ml (8fl oz) stock or water
225g (8oz) vine leaves
2ml (½ tsp) ground coriander

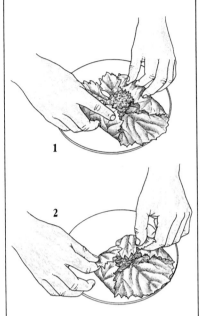

Rolling up vine leaves
1 Tuck in the sides of the leaf after placing the stuffing on it.
2 Fold the leaf carefully, starting at the widest end.

Stuffed vine leaves, served with a Greek salad

1 Wash the lentils in a sieve held under a tap, place them in a saucepan, cover them with water and bring to the boil. Put the lid on the pan and simmer for 20 minutes.

2 Place the bulgur in the sieve, rinse it under the tap and leave it to drain – it will swell up.

3 Simmer the prunes and sultanas in a little water in a covered pan for 20 minutes.

4 Heat the oil in a large, thick-based saucepan and cook the onion gently, covered, over a low heat for 10 minutes.

5 Drain the lentils. Drain the prunes and sultanas, stone and chop the prunes. Add the lentils, sultanas and chopped prunes to the onion with the bulgur, nutmeg, mint, pepper, lemon juice and stock or water. Bring to the boil, cover and simmer until the liquid has been absorbed, about 25 minutes. Check the seasoning.

6 Meanwhile, plunge bought vine leaves into boiling water for 3 to 4 minutes to remove brine, or simmer fresh vine leaves for 15 minutes to soften.

7 Place the leaves, veins upward, on a plate. Let the lentil mixture cool a little, then place about 10ml (2 tsp) of the mixture in each leaf. Starting by tucking in the sides, roll each leaf up. If a leaf tears, just patch it with half of another leaf. You can use 2 small leaves as 1.

8 Heat the oven to 180°C (350°F), gas mark 4.

9 Pack the rolled leaves tightly into a baking dish, so they can't unroll. Sprinkle them with coriander and pour over just enough water to cover. Put a plate on top to press the leaves down.

10 Bake for 1½ hours.

11 Serve the stuffed vine leaves warm or cold, with creamy herb sauce (page 32) and a Greek-style salad (page 155).

VEGETABLE TERRINE

A layered, sophisticated terrine from *nouvelle cuisine* that has caught on fast with elegant restaurants. This version is simple to make at home, and a sure way to impress. *Serves 8 as a starter, 4 as a main course.*

Lining
100g (4oz) fresh spinach leaves
Filling
225g (8oz) spinach leaves
225g (8oz) parsnips, sliced
275g (10oz) carrots, sliced
20ml (4 tsp) oil
100g (4oz) curd cheese
3 eggs
25g (1oz) soft wholemeal breadcrumbs
10ml (2 tsp) green peppercorns, crushed
5ml (1 tsp) mixed herbs
white pepper
sea salt
½ red pepper, cut in long, thin strips
5ml (1 tsp) Madras curry powder
1 long, straight courgette cut in long, thin strips
parsley or chives, to garnish

1 In separate covered saucepans, lightly cook the spinach (for the filling), the parsnips and the carrots in the minimum of liquid. For the spinach use only the water left on the leaves after washing; for the parsnips and carrots use 10ml (2 tsp) oil plus 30ml (2 tbsp) water each.
2 Boil a large saucepan of water. Grease a loaf tin. Dip the lining spinach leaves in the water for 30 to 40 seconds, drain them briefly on a rack, then use them to line the tin thoroughly, keeping back enough leaves for the top.
3 In a jug, whisk together the curd cheese, eggs, breadcrumbs, peppercorns, mixed herbs, pepper and salt.
4 Drain any liquid from the spinach for the filling, and chop it finely. Stir in about a third of the mixture in the jug, and pour it into the spinach-lined tin.
5 Put the red pepper strips with a little of the stock from cooking the carrots, or some water, into the pan in which the spinach was cooked, bring to the boil and simmer for 4 minutes.
6 Arrange the pepper strips lengthways on top of the layer of spinach.
7 Drain the parsnips. Grate them coarsely – they should be grated, not puréed – and add the curry powder. Mix the grated parsnips with another third of the egg mixture. Pour on top of the spinach and red pepper layers.
8 Place the courgette strips in the parsnip saucepan, add a little water, bring to the boil and simmer for 4 minutes. Arrange them on top of the parsnips.
9 Drain the carrots, grate them coarsely, combine with the remaining egg mixture and spread on top of the parsnip and courgette layers.
10 Heat the oven to 180°C (350°F), gas mark 4. Meanwhile, boil a kettle of water.

Calories About 115 a serving as a starter, 230 a serving as a main course.

• Suitable for diabetics
• Medium fibre
• Very low fat (substituting low-fat cheese for curd, and using egg whites only)
• Milk-free (using soya cheese)
• Gluten-free (using gluten-free breadcrumbs)

This terrine is high in vitamins and minerals from the vegetables, low in protein. Complement it with a light, high-protein dish – a main course such as Turkish chicken (page 192) if you are serving the terrine as a starter; a starter such as chicken liver pâté if the terrine is your main course.

COLD FORK BUFFET

Mushrooms à la grecque
65 cals
Chicken liver pâté **110 cals**
Wholemeal melba toast or pitta fingers **90 cals**
Vegetable terrine **115 cals**
Creamy herb or tomato sauce **50 cals**
New potato salad with radishes **170 cals**
Tjatziki **45 cals**
Carrot salad with walnut dressing **80 cals**
—•—
Fresh fruit salad **50 cals**
Walnut gateau **300 cals**

Calories About 50 to 75 a serving.

- Suitable for diabetics
- Medium fibre
- Very low fat
- Very low salt
- Milk-free
- Gluten-free

An ideal starter for a meal with a solid main course, as this dish provides, above all, a taste treat, with little protein.

Calories Leeks à la grecque, about 60 to 90 a serving.

11 Cover the top of the terrine with the reserved spinach leaves, then with kitchen foil.
12 Place the loaf tin in a roasting tin and pour boiling water from the kettle into the outer tin to a depth of half the tin. Cook the terrine for 1¼ hours, or until it is firm.
13 Chill for several hours, or overnight. Remove the terrine from the refrigerator 1 hour before you want to serve it. Immediately before serving, turn it out on a cutting board. Cut it into slices 1cm (½in) thick, using a sharp, serrated knife and holding each slice upright with a spatula until you have finished cutting it.
14 Serve 2 slices per person as a starter, arranging the slices prettily on each plate with a garnish of parsley or chives and a spoonful of creamy herb sauce (page 32), hazelnut sauce (page 31) or tomato sauce (page 29) beside them.

VARIATION

When fresh spinach is not available, *vine leaves* make the best substitute. They give a slightly smoky flavour. If you use fresh ones, simmer them for 15 minutes; if they are brined, simmer them for 3 to 4 minutes.

MUSHROOMS À LA GRECQUE

Appetizing, light and subtle in flavour, this version of mushrooms à la grecque avoids tomatoes, which can overpower the taste of the mushrooms. *Serves 4 to 6.*

10ml (2 tsp) olive oil
1 large onion, 1 large carrot (both finely chopped)
150ml (¼ pint) dry white wine
2 cloves
2 black peppercorns
2 bay leaves
1 clove of garlic (optional), crushed
2ml (½ tsp) ground coriander
2ml (½ tsp) dried thyme
450g (1lb) button mushrooms, washed but not peeled
parsley, chopped, to garnish

1 Heat the oil in a large, thick-based saucepan, and add the onion and carrot plus 15ml (1 tbsp) water. Put the lid on the pan and cook the vegetables gently for 8 minutes.
2 Add the wine and all the spices and herbs, except the parsley. Simmer, covered, for 2 minutes.
3 Add the mushrooms and cook, uncovered, for 15 minutes or until they are tender but not falling apart. Add a little more wine or stock if the mixture is getting dry.
4 Remove the bay leaves, cloves and peppercorns. Allow the mushroom mixture to cool.
5 Spoon the mixture into individual cocotte dishes, and sprinkle with the chopped parsley. Serve cold but not iced.

VARIATION

Alternatively, *leeks* can also be prepared like this. Use both the white and the green parts of the leek, cut into 5cm (2in) lengths.

Mushrooms and leeks à la grecque

Calories About 50 to 60 a serving.

- Suitable for diabetics
- Medium fibre
- Very low fat
- Very low salt (omitting salt)
- Milk-free
- Gluten-free

This is a light first course but with plenty of vegetables, so it's quite filling. It would go well with a not-very-bulky main course such as fish kebabs (page 173) or cheese soufflés (page 68).

POOR MAN'S CAVIARE

Not a bit like caviare, but something you can serve as confidently, as it tastes great. *Serves 4 to 5.*

450g (1lb) aubergines
10ml (2 tsp) oil
1 onion, ½ green pepper, 1 large stick of celery (all finely chopped)
1 clove of garlic (optional), crushed
3 tomatoes, chopped
75ml (5 tbsp) wine vinegar
10ml (2 tsp) dried oregano
5ml (1 tsp) basil
pinch of sea salt
a few black olives

1 Bake the aubergines at 180°C (350°F), gas mark 4, for 1 hour, or until they are very soft.
2 When they are cool, scrape the pulp from the skin. Throw the skin away.
3 Heat the oil in a thick-based pan and gently cook the onion, green pepper and celery, and the garlic, if used, in a covered pan for 10 minutes, until they are softening.
4 Add the aubergine pulp and everything else. Simmer the mixture, uncovered, for 20 minutes. Adjust the seasoning and chill. Serve with crudités or wholemeal pitta bread or Melba toast.

HERB PLATTER

Calories About 175 serving as a starter, 225 to 340 a serving as a main course, with a few extra for the herb sprigs.

- Suitable for diabetics
- High fibre

As either starter or main course, it is a nutritionist's dream, with complementary proteins from the cheese and the wholemeal bread, fibre from the bread and, from the herbs, vitamins and minerals unaffected by any cooking process.

A Middle Eastern-style first course that looks wonderful, with a freshness from the greenery and a down-to-earth simplicity that people are now realizing can be far more elegant than an elaborate presentation. *Serves 4 as a starter, 2 to 3 as a main course.*

---

6 each of at least 4 of these: parsley sprigs, mint sprigs, spring onions, tarragon sprigs, coriander leaves, watercress sprigs, celery leaves, fennel fronds

---

4 wholemeal pittas or chappatis

---

4 egg cups, each filled with 50g (2oz) curd cheese or small cubes of goat's cheese

Arrange the herbs decoratively on a large platter with the warmed pittas or chappatis and the egg cups containing the cheese on one side. Each person tears off a piece of bread, spreads it with curd cheese, then folds in a sprig or two of greenstuff, to eat with the fingers.

Herb platter with cubes of goat's cheese and wholemeal pitta bread

FISH STARTERS

Start a meal with protein-rich fish when you plan to go on to risotto or salad, and no one will ask, 'Where's the beef?'. Both risotto and salad provide the fibre for the meal that is missing in fish.

FISH TERRINE

A simpler version of Michel Guérard's Hure de Saumon, this can be doubled in size for an impressive party dish. It needs a loaf-shaped terrine dish of the right size to achieve the full visual impact. Pink fish, or a mixture of pink and white, makes the prettiest effect. *Serves 6 as a starter, 4 as a main course.*

350g (12oz) salmon, salmon trout, monkfish, huss or similar
50g (2oz) shelled cooked prawns
150ml (¼ pint) dry white wine
trimmings from fish
450ml (¾ pint) water
½ onion, 2 mushrooms, 1 tomato, 5cm (2in) piece of leek, ½ stick of celery (all chopped)
juice of ½ lemon
5ml (1 tsp) dried tarragon or 10ml (2 tsp) fresh tarragon, chopped
1 egg white, whisked until semi-stiff
2ml (½ tsp) white pepper
sea salt
20ml (4 tsp) gelatine
½ red pepper, 1 courgette (both cut in long, thin strips)
1 lemon
1 egg, hard-boiled and cut into dice, not too small
30ml (2 tbsp) fresh parsley, coarsely chopped
10ml (2 tsp) fresh tarragon (if available), leaves only, chopped
10ml (2 tsp) green peppercorns, coarsely ground

1 Cut the fish into long strips about 1cm (½in) wide. Place the fish strips in a large saucepan with the prawns and pour the wine over. Leave for 1 hour. Put the terrine you plan to use in the refrigerator to chill at the same time.
2 Put the fish trimmings in another saucepan with the water, the chopped vegetables, the lemon juice and the dried or fresh chopped tarragon. Bring to the boil, then simmer, covered, for approximately 20 minutes.
3 Using a fork, stir in the egg white to trap the bits of debris in the stock. Strain the stock through a cloth-lined sieve into a measuring jug. Season with pepper and salt.
4 Stir the gelatine into the warm stock until throughly dissolved. Put the jug in a refrigerator.
5 Simmer the pepper and courgette strips briefly in a very little water for 4 minutes. Drain, retaining water for stock.
6 Chop the lemon into small dice, discarding the pith between the segments as well as the peel.

Calories About 160 a serving as a starter, 240 a serving as a main course.

• Suitable for diabetics
• Very low fibre
• Very low fat
• Milk-free
• Gluten-free

A high-protein dish. If using as a main course, try a hot starter such as carrot and caraway soup (page 72) and serve with new potatoes and watercress salad (page 157). Complete the meal with a fibre-rich pudding such as apple-filled pancakes (page 226). The whole meal can be prepared in advance, and only the pancakes need to be finished at the last moment.

SIMPLE DINNER MENU

Herb platter **175 cals**
—•—
Ceviche **135 cals**
Tabbouleh **110 cals**
Green salad **100 cals**
—•—
Fresh pineapple **60 cals**

Total calories per person **580**

7 Bring the fish to the boil in the wine and simmer for 3 minutes. Drain, taking care to keep the fish strips intact, and retain the wine.
8 Dice the pepper and the courgette.
9 Remove the fish stock from the refrigerator. Make the quantity up to 500ml (18fl oz) with wine from cooking the fish. Pour a thin layer into a chilled terrine dish.
10 Sprinkle roughly a quarter of the diced lemon, egg, courgette, red pepper, chopped parsley and chopped tarragon leaves over the stock in the terrine dish. Sprinkle on a few of the green peppercorns.
11 Place a layer of fish strips and some prawns on top. Cover with a layer of the jellying stock. Put the dish in the refrigerator for about 30 minutes, or until the jelly is set.
12 Repeat the layers until all the ingredients are used. Chill the terrine until it is wanted; the flavour will improve over 24 hours.
13 To serve, dip the base of the dish in boiling water for a few seconds and turn the terrine out. Cut slices 1cm (½in) thick, using a broad spatula to hold each slice upright as you cut. As a starter, serve 2 slices per person, with a large spoonful of creamy herb sauce (page 32), pesto (page 32) or egg and lemon sauce (page 31).

VARIATION

Should you come across '*baies roses*' (*pink 'peppercorns'*), they are attractive and aromatic as a change from green ones.

Fish terrine – ideal for a cold buffet

Won ton with soya sauce. The Chinese bamboo steamer makes an attractive serving dish

Calories About 170 a serving as a starter, 340 a serving as a main course.

- Suitable for diabetics
- High fibre
- Very low fat
- Very low salt (omitting salt and most of soya sauce)
- Milk-free

A clever Chinese way of turning wheat into a main dish, with added protein from the egg and the shellfish. Highly savoury-tasting, with barely a trace of fat – something that many people allege is impossible.

WON TON
(CHINESE PRAWN WRAPLINGS)

Irresistible savoury morsels that go well with a small side portion of stir-fried beansprouts on each plate – and why not get out the chopsticks? You can cook won ton in any sort of steamer, or improvise with a wire sieve over a saucepan of water, but a flat-based steamer is best. And if you have a Chinese bamboo steamer, you can serve straight from it at table. *Serves 6 as a starter, 3 as a main course.*

Filling

4 mushrooms

225g (8oz) shelled cooked prawns or shrimps, 3 water chestnuts, 2 spring onions (all finely chopped or minced)

5ml (1 tsp) fresh ginger root, grated

10ml (2 tsp) soya sauce

5ml (1 tsp) sherry

1ml (¼ tsp) white pepper

10ml (2 tsp) peanut oil

Wrappers

1 egg, beaten

225g (8oz) plain wholemeal flour, preferably strong

60 to 75ml (4 to 5 tbsp) water

an extra egg, beaten, to seal (only about half will be used)

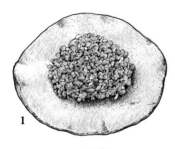

Sealing won ton
1 Place the filling in the centre of the circle of dough.
2 Having brushed the edges of the circle with egg, pull one edge of the dough over the filling, and fold the near edge of the dough over it.
3 Make small pleats along the edges to seal the dumplings.

Calories About 197 each.

• Suitable for diabetics
• Low fibre

Using mature Cheddar cheese gives more flavour for less cheese. This recipe also uses less fat and fewer eggs than most soufflé recipes – but works perfectly. A good first course for a salad meal; or use as the main course with a green salad.

1 Cut a piece of greaseproof paper to fit the base of your steamer.
2 Brush a thick-based pan very lightly with oil and set it over a low heat. Slice the mushrooms and sweat them in the pan for 3 to 4 minutes.
3 Finely chop or grind the mushrooms and mix them with the prawns or shrimps, water chestnuts, spring onions and ginger. Add the soya sauce, sherry and pepper. Leave the mixture to stand while you make the wrappers.
4 Add the first beaten egg to the flour, together with enough water to make a fairly soft dough.
5 Knead the dough lightly, then tear off walnut-size pieces and roll them out very thinly to make circles about 9cm (3½in) across.
6 Place 10ml (2 tsp) of the filling in the centre of each circle. Brush the edges of the circle with some of the other beaten egg. Fold the dumplings as shown left.
7 Place the filled won ton in rows on the greaseproof paper in the steamer. Sprinkle with the peanut oil. Cover and steam over boiling water for 10 to 15 minutes. Serve with a saucer of soya sauce to dip the dumplings in.

VARIATIONS

Won ton can also be dropped into *clear chicken* or *fish soup* 10 minutes before serving.
Cooked minced chicken can be substituted for the shellfish.
You can also use many other fillings for won ton – try the *cannelloni soft cheese and spinach* filling on page 110, for instance.

CHEESE STARTERS

The savoury flavour of cheese is especially attractive at the start of a meal, when you are hungry, and starters made with it give you the option of having a light main course, such as a salad or a vegetable main dish, without your feeling you haven't had 'a real meal'.

Here are two ways of using modest amounts of cheese to give a meal a mouthwatering start. Both are easy to make.

INDIVIDUAL CHEESE SOUFFLÉS

Don't be nervous at the prospect of making soufflés. These ones are very reliable. All you have to do is get everyone assembled *before* you put the soufflés in the oven, so they can sit down just before the soufflés are ready. A good first course for a salad meal; or serve as the main course with a green salad. *Makes 4.*

25g (1oz) soft margarine or butter
22ml (1½ tbsp) plain wholemeal flour
150ml (¼ pint) skimmed milk
15ml (1 tbsp) skimmed milk powder
65g (2½oz) mature Cheddar cheese
2 eggs and 1 extra white
cayenne pepper
white pepper
sea salt

1 Heat the oven to 200°C (400°F), gas mark 6. Grease 4 small soufflé dishes.
2 Melt the fat in a good-sized saucepan set over a low heat.
3 Stir in the flour smoothly.
4 Remove the pan from the heat. Gradually work in the milk, then the milk powder.
5 Return the pan to the heat and stir steadily until the mixture is thick and leaves the sides of the pan, after a few minutes.
6 Remove the pan from the heat, grate the cheese in and stir well.
7 Beat in the egg yolks one at a time. Season the mixture.
8 Beat the egg whites until extremely stiff and fold them lightly into the mixture.
9 Spoon the mixture into the soufflé dishes. Each one should be about three-quarters full.
10 Bake for 15 minutes. Serve immediately.

CHEESE DARIOLES

Rich-tasting, these team well with a vegetable main course. *Makes 4.*

1 large egg, separated
15ml (1 tbsp) soft margarine or butter, softened
175g (6oz) curd cheese
dab of honey
pinch of sea salt
15ml (1 tbsp) plain wholemeal flour
paprika, to garnish

1 Heat the oven to 220°C (425°F), gas mark 7. Grease 4 small cocotte dishes.
2 Beat the egg yolk with the margarine or softened butter, then beat in all the other ingredients, except the paprika.
3 Beat the egg white until stiff and fold it into the mixture.
4 Divide the mixture between the dishes. Bake for 20 minutes. Sprinkle with paprika and serve immediately.

VARIATIONS

Double the quantities, and this makes a very simple main course which goes beautifully with lightly cooked broccoli or fennel, for instance. Use larger individual dishes and cook for 30 minutes.

Another alternative is to put a layer of *lightly browned mushrooms* or *cooked, chopped spinach* at the bottom of each cocotte before filling it with the mixture.

Calories About 100 each.

• Suitable for diabetics
• Almost no fibre
• Gluten-free (using rice flour)

This recipe's main contribution, apart from its lovely texture and flavour, is protein from the cheese. Cheese darioles are almost fibre-free, so serve them with other foods that contribute fibre, such as a main course including brown rice or another whole grain. And have some vegetables or fruit in the meal.

For lower fat, you can use a skimmed-milk soft cheese, although the result won't be as creamy tasting.

SOUPS

When all cooking was done over open fires, almost every meal was a soup – something cooked in water, with flavourings. If you were poor, it was mainly 'pot herbs': vegetables like carrots, turnips and onions. If you could afford it, your soup was at least half-way to a meat casserole.

Soup is still one of the easiest and most nourishing meals. But modern soup has made one great gain, the electric blender, and one great loss, the stock pot.

As far as the gain is concerned, it's not just that you can purée ingredients without putting them laboriously through a sieve, although that has made soup one of the quickest routes to a good meal. It's also that you no longer need cook your vegetables to the mushy state when they will go through a sieve: now you can keep your vegetables fresh-tasting (and retain more of their vitamins too) by reducing cooking time to the minimum. Yet the blender can still produce a smooth texture in seconds.

The ease with which vegetables can be puréed has also encouraged the use of purées for thickening soups that have long been overpowered by eggs, butter, cream and flour in the search for 'body'. Today's soups have much more flavour of their basic ingredients.

As for the loss of the stock pot, although stock cubes are useful occasionally, there is no getting away from the fact that they taste of stock cubes. Many of us also dislike the monosodium glutamate that is in every supermarket cube (although there are stock cubes and stock powders without taste enhancers, sold in health food stores). Modern cooks simply dislike the notion of a large saucepan of stock that is permanently on the stove and needs to be reboiled daily so that it remains wholesome. Yet good stock is the key to so many soups.

The solution I recommend is to keep in the bottle department of your refrigerator a tall, thin measuring jug, with a lid, into which you empty your vegetable cooking water, chicken cooking water and any liquid left after cooking beans. Knowing that you have a special container ready to hand makes you much more inclined to keep bits of stock that would otherwise seem hardly worth saving. If you have measuring marks on the side of the jug, you can pour stock straight from it to make your soups and sauces, or to moisten casseroles. The lid helps the stock stay fresh, and stops it scenting other foods. (Unless you are prepared for the daily reboiling, though, you must use the stock within three or four days. And if you keep water from cooking potatoes or brassicas, use it the same day.)

Stock gives soup not only flavour but also extra minerals and often vitamins as well. However carefully you cook vegetables, even if you steam them, some vitamins will be lost. If you use a method where the vegetables touch water, some vitamins and

Three variations of the same soup recipe – from top to bottom: swede, carrot and caraway, and beetroot

minerals will be left in it. By using the stock, you retrieve most of that goodness.

Another benefit from using stock is that it usually contains less fat than the alternative, milk. If, when you have cooked a chicken or some lamb, you keep the stock, you can dodge vast amounts of fat (and calories) by chilling the stock, then skimming it of fat before you use it.

Stock helps a soup stay light; but sometimes you will want to use milk – in which case, the protein in skimmed milk makes your soup a useful protein dish. Bean, lentil and rice-based soups are also high enough in protein to team with a low-protein main course, such as baked potato and salad, and make a meal that comes out nicely balanced.

Then there are the meal-in-a-bowl soups, like fish chowder or minestrone, the former the equivalent in food value of meat and vegetables, and the latter with protein from beans complementing the protein from the noodles and cheese on top – and you'll team it with more protein if you eat it with wholemeal bread, to top off a meal that's a nutritionist's delight.

The common factors among the recipes in this section are that they all use as little fat as possible and the vegetables are cooked for as short a time as possible. After that, choose your recipe, feather-light as carrot and caraway soup, or solid as Scotch broth, to suit the occasion and other food. Some are deceptively substantial: borscht, for example, can certainly make a meal, but provides only a modest number of calories.

Now, how full is the stock jug? Every time the level reaches 600ml (1 pint), it's time to make soup.

LIGHT SOUPS

Choose these when you either plan a solid main course, or when you want a first course with few calories. These recipes are chosen to give you a range of methods which can often be adapted for other vegetables in season.

CARROT AND CARAWAY SOUP

A model for many light, rather than thick, vegetable soups which have a wonderful freshness, especially if you make sure the aromatic oils in the caraway or other seeds are released by thorough blending. *Serves 4.*

5ml (1 tsp) vegetable oil
1 large onion, very finely chopped
350g (12oz) carrots, finely chopped
4ml (¾ tsp) caraway seeds, crushed
900ml (1½ pints) stock
75ml (3fl oz) thick plain low-fat yogurt
cress and ground coriander, to garnish

1 Heat the oil in a thick-based saucepan. Turn the onion in the oil, cover the pan and cook the onion over a low heat for about 8 minutes, until it is soft.

Calories About 50 a serving.

- Suitable for diabetics
- Medium fibre
- Very low fat
- Very low salt (using unsalted stock)
- Milk-free (using soya yogurt)
- Gluten-free (if not using flour)

For a thicker soup, sprinkle 30ml (2 tsp) plain wholemeal flour over the carrot and caraway seeds in step 2, before adding the stock. This adds about 90 calories to the soup (23 a serving), but would make your soup a good balance to a lighter main course, such as a salad.

2 Add the carrots and the caraway seeds and stir, uncovered, over the heat for 1 minute.
3 Add the stock, increase the heat and bring the soup to the boil. Reduce the heat again, cover the pan and simmer the soup for 20 minutes.
4 Liquidize three-quarters of the soup, then return it to the pan.
5 Stir in the yogurt. Heat the soup gently but do not allow it to boil again.
6 Check the seasoning. Serve the soup garnished with cress and a sprinkle of coriander.

VARIATIONS

Following this recipe, any root vegetable can be turned into a tasty soup. For variety, try *whole coriander*, *celery seeds* or *fennel seeds* instead of caraway.
Beetroot soup Celery seeds go well with beetroot soup. Add lemon juice, to taste, at the end.
Potato soup Replace 300ml (½ pint) of the stock with skimmed milk, adding the milk after the soup has been liquidized, use soft cheese instead of yogurt, and add a very little yeast extract, to taste, at the end of cooking. You can also use potatoes half and half with other vegetables for thicker soups, if you prefer.
Swede soup Replace 300ml (½ pint) of the stock, with skimmed milk, as for potato soup.

WATERCRESS BROTH

Even those who don't count watercress as a favourite food enjoy this light, tasty broth with its beautiful fresh green colour. Serve watercress broth hot or cold, but avoid making it long in advance, as its colour and flavour – just as with fresh watercress – spoil quickly. *Serves 4.*

10ml (2 tsp) oil, soft margarine or butter
4 spring onions
2 bunches of watercress, chopped
40g (1½oz) plain wholemeal flour
1 litre (2 pints) stock
pinch of sea salt
1 egg white
125ml (4fl oz) plain low-fat yogurt
curls of carrot or cucumber, to garnish

1 Heat the fat in a large saucepan, and use scissors to chop the spring onions in finely.
2 Cook the onions over a low heat for 5 minutes, until transparent.
3 Stir in the watercress and continue cooking for 1 minute.
4 Sprinkle in the flour and stir for 1 minute. Remove the pan from the heat.
5 Work in the stock gradually and add the salt. Return the pan to the heat, bring the soup to the boil, cover, and simmer for 6 minutes.
6 Liquidize the soup in a blender, return it to the pan and check the seasoning.
7 Whisk the egg white into the yogurt, then whisk in a cup of the soup.
8 Add the yogurt mixture to the pan and reheat the soup but do not boil it again. Serve the soup garnished with curls of carrot or cucumber cut with a potato peeler.

Calories Beetroot soup, about 70 a serving; potato soup, 120; swede soup, 70.

Calories About 95 a serving.

- Suitable for diabetics
- Medium fibre
- Very low fat
- Very low salt (omitting added salt)

Watercress is one of the most mineral-packed foods, with iron and calcium in substantial amounts – as well as vitamin A, several B vitamins, vitamin C and vitamin E in quantity.

Calories About 75 to 115 a serving.

• Suitable for diabetics
• Low fibre
• Very low fat (using low-fat smetana)
• Very low salt (using 45ml [3 tbsp] smetana and omitting salt)

If using soured cream, keep the rest of the meal low in fat – for instance, serve a fish dish or risotto as the main course.

CUCUMBER-DILL SOUP

With its rich, smooth character, this Russian-style soup is equally good hot or cold. *Serves 4 to 6.*

10ml (2 tsp) soft margarine or butter
1 large onion, finely chopped
2 20cm (8in) cucumbers
1 large potato, washed but not peeled
750ml (1¼ pints) light stock
15ml (1 tbsp) white wine vinegar
few sprigs of fresh dill
150ml (5fl oz) smetana or soured cream
white pepper
pinch of sea salt (optional)

1 Heat the fat and cook the onion gently, covered, for 8 minutes, without letting it brown.
2 Meanwhile, peel the cucumbers and use a potato peeler to cut a few long strips to use as garnish. Chop the remainder into 1cm (½in) chunks.
3 Dice the potato.
4 Add to the onion pan the cucumber chunks, potato dice, stock, vinegar and dill.
5 Bring the soup to the boil, then simmer it, uncovered, for 20 minutes.
6 Liquidize the soup, reheat it if serving hot, stir in the smetana or soured cream and season to taste. Do not boil again after adding smetana or cream. Garnish the soup with the thin curls of cucumber.

GAZPACHO

Every region of Spain has its own recipe: this one blends a recipe from Andalusia with one from Catalonia, and I think you'll like it. If the tomatoes are not particularly juicy, you may need to thin the soup with a little water. *Serves 4.*

Calories About 75 a serving, with an extra 10 a serving for the garnish.

• Suitable for diabetics
• Very low fat (omitting olive oil)
• Very low salt (using unsalted breadcrumbs)
• Milk-free
• Gluten-free (using gluten-free breadcrumbs)

Purists may prefer to peel the tomatoes and pepper as well as the cucumber. Others will want to keep the peel, for the sake of convenience and fibre – and it's no problem to chew. If you don't enjoy salad, this is an excellent way of getting the goodness of vegetables into your system pleasurably.

30ml (2 tbsp) soft wholemeal breadcrumbs
1 clove of garlic
15ml (1 tbsp) hazelnuts, toasted
15ml (1 tbsp) olive oil
4 tomatoes
1 red pepper, seeds removed
½ cucumber, peeled (unless it is very young and tender-skinned)
1 medium onion, cut in chunks
15ml (1 tbsp) wine vinegar
To garnish
¼ cucumber, 1 green or red pepper, spring onions, parsley, mint (all chopped very finely)

1 Put all the ingredients except the garnishes in the goblet of a blender and blend until smooth.
2 Chill the gazpacho well before serving, when you may want to dilute it with very cold mineral water. Serve with small bowls of the garnishes.

Fish consommé garnished with consommé cubes

Calories About 85 a serving. Very few calories, but a good many minerals.

- Suitable for diabetics
- No fibre
- Very low fat
- Milk-free
- Gluten-free

FISH CONSOMMÉ

You could use this same recipe to make a good stock for a thicker soup. But why not stop now and enjoy the consommé as it is, light and refreshing? *Serves 4.*

about 450g (1lb) fish trimmings, including some from smoked fish, such as Finnan haddie
1 carrot, 1 onion, 1 stick celery (all chopped)
3 peppercorns
1 bay leaf
450ml (¾ pint) water
300ml (½ pint) dry white wine
1 egg white, whisked until semi-stiff
parsley, chopped, egg pancake strips (page 85) or consommé cubes (page 84), to garnish

1 Place all the ingredients except the egg white and the garnish in a large saucepan. Bring the stock slowly to the boil, then cover the pan and simmer gently for about 40 minutes.
2 Stir in the egg white. This forms a scum in the liquid which holds particles of fish and other debris, so when it is strained out the soup is left clear.
3 Strain the soup through a sieve lined with cloth.
4 Check the seasoning – if the flavour is weak, boil again to evaporate some of the liquid, or add some vegetable stock if you have it.
5 Garnish with slices of carrot from the sieve, chopped parsley, egg pancake strips or consommé cubes.

Calories About 50 a serving.

- Suitable for diabetics
- Low fibre
- Very low fat
- Milk-free
- Gluten-free

A typically delicate Japanese broth. It contains considerable protein value from the miso – soya bean paste, which also has a high salt content – and beancurd. The bonito fish flakes add some minerals.

MILK-FREE LUNCH MENU

Leek and oatmeal soup **60 cals**

—•—

Gravad lax **230 cals**
Tabbouleh **110 cals**
Wholemeal bread **120 cals**
Green beans **20 cals**

—•—

Stuffed pears **140 cals**

Total calories per person **680**

Calories About 60 a serving.

- Suitable for diabetics
- Medium fibre
- Very low fat
- Very low salt (using unsalted stock and omitting added salt)
- Gluten-free (substituting millet flakes for oats)

VARIATIONS

The soup will set lightly without the addition of gelatine if you want to serve it chilled.
Add *20ml (4 tsp) gelatine* per 600ml (1 pint) of soup for fish aspic, to coat cold fish, or to chop to form a bed for buffet savouries.

MISO SOUP

This is what the Japanese eat for breakfast, with plain rice, a little fish or vegetable and perhaps a raw egg which is semi-cooked by stirring it into the very hot rice. *Serves 4.*

900ml (1½ pints) water*
10cm (4in) piece kombu seaweed*
7ml (½ tbsp) bonito flakes*
1 small carrot, thinly sliced
75g (3oz) red miso
2 mushrooms
100g (4oz) beancurd (tofu), cut in 2cm (¾in) squares
1 spring onion, cut diagonally in 5mm (¼in) slices

*Alternatively, use 900ml (1½ pints) chicken or vegetable stock

1 Bring the water and kombu to the boil, stir and simmer, uncovered, for 4 minutes; then remove the kombu and discard it. Add the bonito flakes, bring to the boil and remove from the heat immediately. When, after a few minutes, the flakes sink, drain them off.
2 You now have the basic Japanese stock, 'dashi'. Add the carrot slices to it and simmer until they are tender, about 8 to 10 minutes.
3 Soften the miso with a little of the dashi, then whisk it into the rest of the dashi in the pan.
4 Slice the mushrooms, add them to the soup and simmer for 2 minutes.
5 Add the beancurd and the spring onion. Avoid stirring once the curd has been added, as it is fragile. Simmer for just 20 to 30 seconds and serve.

VARIATIONS

You can replace the beancurd with: *shredded cooked chicken*; more *mushrooms* briefly sweated in 5ml (1 tsp) oil; some *cooked brown rice*; *shredded cooked spinach*; some quick-cooking *wholemeal noodles* (to be simmered for 8 to 9 minutes before the spring onion is added).

LEEK AND OATMEAL SOUP

A light Irish broth which brings out the full flavour of the leeks. *Serves 4.*

350g (12oz) leeks
600ml (1 pint) stock
5ml (1 tsp) soft margarine or butter
15ml (1 tbsp) rolled oats
white pepper
pinch of sea salt
15ml (1 tbsp) parsley, chopped, to garnish

Oatflakes have more thickening power than flour, and give a special, slightly viscous, texture to the soup. This is soothing to the digestion and, if you like the effect, you can use oatflakes rather than flour in other soups, with no loss of food value.

1 Wash the leeks thoroughly, chop both white and green parts into 2cm (¾in) chunks, then rinse again.
2 Heat the stock with the fat and, when it comes to the boil, add the rolled oats and the leeks. Cover the pan and simmer the soup for 30 minutes.
3 Liquidize half of the soup, then return it to the pan and reheat it. Season the soup and serve it sprinkled with the parsley.

VARIATION

For a thicker soup, *a little yogurt* or *smetana* can be stirred into each bowlful just before serving.

SUBSTANTIAL SOUPS

Soups that are a meal in themselves – a big bowlful, served with interesting bread or crispbread – can be either simply filling (but not particularly high in calories, and so suitable for extra-hungry days or for slimmers) or they can provide the kind of protein you'd get from a main course. Fish chowder or Scotch broth come into this category.

Pick the one that suits you; your choice will depend on whether you're planning a salad meal, and want a solid soup to counteract the chill of a cold day, or whether you want a simple one-course meal, without worrying that anyone's going short of protein.

Borscht – a colourful soup to warm up a cold winter's day

Calories About 95 a serving.

- Suitable for diabetics
- Gluten-free

Some borscht recipes stew the vegetables for hours. In this one they are only lightly cooked, as if you use a blender there is no need to reduce them to the mushy state required before they will go through a sieve. The lemon juice keeps the colour bright, as well as adding vitamin C.

HOT FORK BUFFET

Borscht *95 cals*
Pirozhki *280 cals*
Cannelloni *330 cals*
Kedgeree *200 cals*
Green salad *100 cals*
Watercress salad *90 cals*

—•—

Glazed fruit tart *145 cals*
Fresh fruit *50 cals*

Calories About 150 a serving, with an extra 5 calories a serving if you add sherry. You can lower the fat content to almost zero by replacing the hard cheese with cottage cheese. The bread can be omitted, as this version is solid enough with onions to hold up the cheese on its own. The calorie count will then work out at about 70 a serving.

- Suitable for diabetics
- Medium fibre
- Very low fat (substituting cottage cheese for hard cheese)
- Milk-free (omitting cheese)
- Gluten-free (substituting split-pea flour for wheat flour, and using gluten-free bread)

BORSCHT

A beautiful red soup to warm up a cold day, or a cold main meal. This version is far simpler to make than many. *Serves 4.*

15ml (1 tbsp) oil
225g (8oz) raw beetroot, 2 onions, 2 carrots, 1 small parsnip (all roughly diced)
1 bay leaf
pinch of allspice
900ml (1½ pints) boiling water
5ml (1 tsp) vegetable concentrate
juice of 1 lemon
white pepper
pinch of sea salt
125ml (4fl oz) thick plain low-fat yogurt or smetana
15ml (1 tbsp) parsley, chopped, to garnish

1 Heat the oil in a large saucepan, and turn in it the diced vegetables with the bay leaf and allspice.
2 After 8 minutes, add the boiling water and the vegetable concentrate. Cover the pan and simmer the soup for 30 minutes.
3 Remove the bay leaf. Add the lemon juice. Season to taste. Blend all or three-quarters of the soup, heat again to serve hot or chill to serve cold.
4 Stir in the yogurt or smetana just before serving, leaving a swirl of white on the surface. Sprinkle with the parsley. Do not let the soup boil after the yogurt or smetana has been added.

FRENCH ONION SOUP

An old favourite that is still delicious. For the best onion tang, make it with a mixture of sharper shallots and milder onions. Add a tablespoonful of sherry on chillier nights. *Serves 4.*

2 large onions
4 shallots
2 cloves
15ml (1 tbsp) oil or butter
5ml (1 tsp) clear honey
15ml (1 tbsp) plain wholemeal flour
1 litre (2 pints) stock
1 bay leaf
pinch of sea salt
5ml (1 tsp) yeast extract (preferably low-salt variety)
4 medium-thick slices wholemeal bread
40g (1½oz) Edam or Gruyère cheese, grated

1 Slice the onions and shallots thinly, leaving 1 larger piece. Stick the cloves into this piece.
2 Heat the fat, add the onions and shallots, cover the pan and cook over a low heat for 15 minutes. Dribble over the honey, stir it in and cook for another 5 minutes, until the onions are golden-brown.

3 Add the flour and stir it in for 1 minute.
4 Remove the pan from heat and gradually stir in the stock.
5 Return the pan to a medium heat, stir the soup until it comes to the boil, then reduce the heat, add the bay leaf and simmer the soup, uncovered, for 15 minutes. Add the salt and the yeast extract.
6 Cover the bread slices with the grated cheese and put each slice, cut in quarters, in a soup bowl.
7 Remove the bay leaf and cloves from the soup. Pour the boiling soup over the bread in the bowls and serve.

VICHYSSOISE

Vichyssoise usually drips with cream and butter, which often hide instead of heightening the delicate flavours. As well as being fresh-tasting, this version is creamy-smooth and a lovely pale green. *Serves 4.*

10ml (2 tsp) oil
3 shallots, chopped
175g (6oz) potatoes, washed but not peeled
450g (1lb) leeks, both white and green parts, sliced
450ml (¾ pint) water
450ml (¾ pint) skimmed milk
30ml (2 tbsp) skimmed milk powder
2ml (½ tsp) white pepper
pinch of sea salt
75ml (3fl oz) smetana or soured cream
grating of nutmeg

1 Heat the oil in a thick-based saucepan. Turn the chopped shallots in the oil, then cover the pan and cook the shallots gently until they are transparent (about 10 minutes), keeping the lid on so they don't stick or brown.
2 Dice the potatoes. Add the potatoes and the sliced leeks to the shallots and continue to cook, adding 15ml (1 tbsp) water if the vegetables seem likely to dry out or become brown.
3 After 3 minutes, add the water and bring to the boil, then simmer, covered, for 20 minutes, or until the potatoes are tender.
4 Transfer the soup to the goblet of a blender and liquidize it, adding some of the milk to help the blender work, and the skimmed milk powder to thicken the soup. Add remaining milk.
5 Season the soup with the pepper and salt, and when it has cooled slightly, stir in the smetana or soured cream. Check the seasoning again.
6 Chill the soup, and grate a little nutmeg on top before serving.

LORNA'S BUTTERBEAN TARRAGON SOUP

Many bean soups are too 'beany': this one may baffle eaters as to what its base is, for the main impression is of a fresh, lemony flavour. Highly recommended, this recipe was developed by my mother-in-law, who manages to whip up some wonderful flavours with no apparent effort. *Serves 4.*

Calories About 190 a serving.
• Suitable for diabetics
• Medium fibre
• Very low fat (using low-fat smetana)
• Gluten-free

Using the whole of a potato and leek doesn't spoil the look of the soup, saves the cook time, reduces waste and increases the amount of minerals and vitamin C (in which the green part of the leek is much richer).

Calories About 160 per serving.
• Suitable for diabetics
• High fibre
• Very low-fat (substituting low-fat yogurt for cream or smetana)
• Gluten-free

Provides 8g (⅓oz) of protein per serving, about one seventh of an adult's average total daily need.

175g (6oz) butterbeans

10ml (2 tsp) tomato purée

5 to 7ml (1 to 1½ tsp) dried tarragon, to taste

juice of ½ lemon

white pepper

pinch of sea salt

2ml (½ tsp) dried mixed herbs

75ml (3fl oz) soured cream or smetana

1 Soak the butterbeans overnight, or cover them with water, bring them to the boil, simmer for 2 minutes, then soak for 2 hours.
2 Discard the soaking water, cover the beans with fresh water and bring them to the boil.
3 Put the lid on the saucepan and simmer the beans for about 45 minutes, or until they are very tender.
4 Blend the beans in an electric blender, adding enough of the cooking liquid to give a thin purée.
5 Add the tomato purée, tarragon, some of the lemon juice, pepper, salt and mixed herbs, and blend again.
6 Return the soup to the saucepan and reheat it. Check the seasoning: you will probably need all of the lemon juice and even a little more to give the best, fresh taste.
7 Stir in the soured cream or smetana. Heat the soup to serve but do not boil it again.

MINESTRONE

A meal-sized soup – and if you cook beans in batches so you often have some ready-cooked in the refrigerator, an ideal recipe when you don't feel like cooking. You can vary the vegetables, and complete the meal with another Italian favourite – fresh grapes or figs. *Makes 4 enormous servings.*

Calories About 195 a serving.

- Suitable for diabetics
- High fibre
- Very low fat
- Milk-free (omitting cheese)
- Gluten-free (omitting pasta)

Wholewheat pasta adds extra fibre and only takes a minute or two longer than white pasta to cook. By cooking the tomatoes and cabbage for the minimum of time, you retain the tomatoes' sweetness, a fresher green for the cabbage, and more of the vitamins of both.

100g (4oz) haricot beans, dry weight

10ml (2 tsp) oil

1 small onion or shallot, 2 small carrots, 2 sticks celery, 1 leek (all cut in rough chunks)

1 clove of garlic (optional), chopped

1 litre (2 pints) water, including bean-cooking water

50g (2oz) wholewheat macaroni or noodles

¼ small cabbage, cut in chunks

3 tomatoes

freshly ground pepper

pinch of sea salt

15 to 30ml (1 to 2 tbsp) tomato purée

25g (1oz) Parmesan cheese, grated

25g (1oz) parsley, coarsely chopped

1 Soak the beans in water overnight, or cover them with water, bring to the boil, simmer for 2 minutes, then soak for 2 hours.
2 Discard the soaking water, cover the beans with fresh water and simmer in a covered pan for about 1 hour, or until just tender.

3 Heat the oil in a large saucepan. Add the onion or shallot, carrots, celery, leek and garlic if using. Cover the pan and cook the vegetables over a low heat for about 8 minutes.
4 Pour the beans into a measuring jug, and add water to make up the level to 1500ml (2½ pints). Add to the vegetables in the large pan. Simmer, covered, for 30 minutes.
5 Add the macaroni or noodles, cabbage and tomatoes. Season with pepper and salt. Simmer for 10 minutes.
6 Check the seasoning and add tomato purée to intensify the flavour, and also to thicken the soup if necessary – remember, the purée is already salted.
7 Serve with grated Parmesan and chopped parsley on top of each bowl.

FINNAN CHOWDER

A simple but impressive one-pot meal that needs little preparation or watching. In larger quantities, it is an ideal dish for a party. *Serves 4 to 6.*

5ml (1 tsp) oil or butter
1 large onion or 3 large shallots, chopped
225g (8oz) Finnan haddie
225g (8oz) white fish fillet
350g (12oz) potatoes, washed but not peeled
black pepper
pinch of sea salt
pinch of nutmeg
25g (1oz) skimmed milk powder
5ml (1 tsp) cornflour
125ml (4fl oz) thick plain low-fat yogurt or low-fat soft cheese
25g (1oz) parsley, chopped

1 Heat the fat in a large saucepan. Add the chopped onion or shallots and soften them, covered, over a low heat for about 8 minutes, but do not allow them to brown.
2 Meanwhile remove the skin and any bones from the fish, and chop it into soup spoon-sized chunks.
3 Arrange the fish on top of the onions, mixing up the yellow and white pieces.
4 Cut the potatoes into slices about 5mm (¼in) thick, and lay the slices on top of the fish. Season with the pepper, salt and nutmeg.
5 Add the milk powder and sufficient water to reach to the top of the potatoes. Bring the soup to the boil. Cover and simmer very gently for about 30 minutes, until the potatoes are tender but not breaking up.
6 Stir the cornflour into the yogurt or soft cheese, stir the mixture gently into the soup in the saucepan, simmer for 1 minute, check the seasoning and, just before serving, stir in the parsley.

VARIATIONS

You can add a variety of vegetables to the chowder, laying them above the potato: *courgette slices*, *peas* and *mushrooms* would be particularly suitable. Add 10 minutes before the end of cooking. Alternatively, pour your chowder over a generous chopping of *watercress* at the bottom of each bowl.

Calories About 160 to 210 a serving.

- Suitable for diabetics
- Low fibre
- Very low fat
- Gluten-free

Because the smoked fish is salty, the chowder won't need more than an additional pinch of salt.

Calories About 300 a serving. Letting the stock get cold so that fat can be skimmed off makes the process of preparing the soup longer, but if it's done the night before the meal, it's easy to organize. It greatly reduces the fat content and can cut the calories in the soup by at least 100 a serving.

• Suitable for diabetics
• Medium fibre
• Very low salt
• Milk-free
• Gluten-free (substituting rice for barley)

Unlike many Scotch broth recipes, this one doesn't cook the vegetables for hours along with the meat and barley – so they and their vitamins don't get cooked to pieces. If you make this soup in advance, you will get a better flavour by only going as far as step 4, and adding the remaining vegetables 15 to 20 minutes before serving.

SCOTCH BROTH

A complete main course; follow it with fresh fruit. *Serves 4 to 6.*

700g (1½lb) scrag end of lamb or mutton
6 peppercorns
1 litre (2 pints) water
50g (2oz) pot or Scotch barley
2 carrots, 2 turnips, 2 onions, 1 leek, 2 sticks celery (all diced)

1 Place the meat and peppercorns in a saucepan with the water. Bring slowly to the boil, then cover the pan and simmer for 3 hours. Chill for several hours or overnight.
2 Skim off the fat. Remove the meat and reserve it, discarding the bones and the peppercorns.
3 Bring the stock to the boil with the barley. Cover the pan and simmer for 20 minutes.
4 Add the diced carrots. Simmer for another 20 minutes.
5 Add the diced turnips, onions, leek and celery. Simmer for a further 20 minutes.
6 Check that the barley is tender, return the reserved meat to the pan, re-heat thoroughly, check the seasoning and serve.

LENTIL SOUP

Calories About 190 a serving; add a few extra a serving for the spicy variation.

• Suitable for diabetics
• High fibre
• Very low fat
• Very low salt (omitting salt)
• Milk-free
• Gluten-free

A quarter of this recipe, or 1 good serving, provides over 13g (½oz) of protein, almost a quarter of an adult's average daily protein need. So you can confidently follow this soup with a salad or vegetable main course.

Simple, quick, comforting and appetizing. A more spicy, Middle Eastern variation, is also given. *Serves 4.*

225g (8oz) split red lentils
5ml (1 tsp) oil
1 onion or 2 shallots, chopped
1 bay leaf
1050ml (1¾ pints) water or stock
2ml (½ tsp) ground coriander
2ml (½ tsp) white pepper
good squeeze of lemon juice
pinch of sea salt
45ml (3 tbsp) parsley, chopped

1 Wash the lentils in a sieve under a tap, picking them over for black bits.
2 Heat the oil in a thick-based saucepan over a low heat. Add the chopped onion, or shallots for more flavour, and the bay leaf. Cover the pan and cook for 5 minutes.
3 Add the lentils, the water or stock and the coriander and pepper. Bring the soup to the boil, then cover the pan again and simmer for about 20 minutes.
4 Liquidize the soup, return it to the pan, season it with lemon juice and salt and reheat it. Serve with the parsley stirred in.

VARIATION

For a spicy, Middle Eastern-style soup, at step 2, add to the onion and cook for 1 minute over the heat, 15ml (1 tbsp) of the following spice mixture, ground in a coffee grinder (ready-ground won't be quite so aromatic): *2ml (½ tsp) black peppercorns, 1ml (¼ tsp) coriander seeds,*

1ml (¹/₄ tsp) cinnamon; 1ml (¹/₄ tsp) cloves; 1.6ml (¹/₃ tsp) cumin seeds, 1ml (¹/₄ tsp) grated nutmeg, 2ml (¹/₂ tsp) paprika and the seeds from 3 cardamom pods. With this, you may also like to add *2 cloves of crushed garlic* to the pan. When you add the stock add *1 dried lime* or *half a scrubbed lemon,* which you later liquidize with the soup. Omit the lemon juice, pepper and coriander of the original recipe.

CHAWANMUSHI
(JAPANESE STEAMED EGG SOUP)

A set soup that is one of the very few dishes the Japanese eat with a spoon! There will always be some liquid in it from the mushrooms and meat. *Serves 4.*

900ml (1½ pints) stock
pinch of sea salt
5ml (1 tsp) soya sauce
5ml (1 tsp) honey
8 mangetout pods or 4 sprigs of chervil
3 mushrooms
75g (3oz) raw chicken, sliced very thinly
4 eggs, beaten
grated lemon zest, to garnish

Calories About 130 a serving.

Makes a filling first course, so follow it with a light main course such as a vegetable stir-fry or salad, with brown rice to keep the Eastern mood and also to provide the meal with fibre.
• Suitable for diabetics
• Low fibre
• Milk-free
• Gluten-free

Chawanmushi – more filling than it looks

1 Bring the stock to the boil with the salt, soya sauce and honey. Add the mangetout pods if using, and leave them in the hot stock for a couple of minutes to blanch.
2 Slice the mushrooms very thinly. Divide the chicken and mushroom slices between 4 soup bowls or mugs.
3 Remove the mangetout pods from the stock. Stirring all the time, pour the hot stock on to the beaten eggs.
4 Pour the egg-stock over the chicken and mushrooms in the bowls. Steam, covered with a cloth, gently for 15 minutes, placing chervil or mangetout on top of the bowls half-way through. Garnish with the lemon zest and serve.

SOUP TRIMMINGS

If you dress soups up just a little, you will have something that people enjoy much more. This is a good example of how food that looks good is far more satisfying. I don't know why, perhaps it's something to do with soul food. Trimmings naturally make soups a little more filling, too.

ALMOND BALLS

Calories About 35 to 50 a serving.

- Suitable for diabetics
- Low fibre
- Very low salt (using low-salt bread)
- Milk-free
- Gluten-free (using gluten-free breadcrumbs)

This recipe replaces some of the ground almonds in the traditional version with wholemeal breadcrumbs, keeping the fat content down. Both almonds and breadcrumbs, as well as egg, provide small amounts of protein.

Adapted from a recipe used for the Jewish Seder festival, these almond balls make an unusual soup trimming, especially good in fish soups and consommés. *Makes enough for 4 to 6 servings.*

25g (1oz) wholemeal breadcrumbs
3 drops of almond essence
25g (1oz) ground almonds
grated zest of ¼ lemon
1 small egg white

1 Mix the breadcrumbs, almond essence, almonds and lemon zest.
2 Whisk the egg white until it is stiff and fold it in lightly.
3 Lightly brush a thick-based pan with oil, and set it on a medium heat.
4 Drop teaspoonfuls of the mixture on the hot pan.
5 Cook the almond balls for 2 to 3 minutes each side until they are brown on both sides, remove them and drop them into soup just before serving.

VARIATION

Add *2ml (½ tsp) dried herbs* to the breadcrumbs.

CONSOMMÉ CUBES

Calories About 20 a serving.

- No fibre
- Very low fat
- Milk-free
- Gluten-free

Easy to do if you steam the custard standing in the soup – and definitely adds class to any kind of thin soup. *Makes enough for a few cubes in each of 4 bowls.*

1 egg
15ml (1 tbsp) soup or stock
few drops of soya sauce
few drops of clear honey

1 Whisk all the ingredients together in a small, flat-based cocotte dish.
2 Sit the dish in simmering water (or above your soup on an improvised stand, such as a pottery egg cup) for 15 to 20 minutes, until the savoury custard is solidly set.
3 Remove the dish from the heat, cool the custard slightly, turn it out, then cut it into small cubes to float in consommé.

EGG PANCAKE STRIPS

Thin ribbons of pancake look very pretty floating on top of a bowl of soup. And they can be made in advance. This recipe makes delicious pancakes which can be served with savoury fillings (page 000), as well as with soup. *Makes about 10 paper-thin, not very large pancakes.*

1 small egg or ½ larger egg
150ml (¼ pint) skimmed milk
100g (4oz) plain wholemeal flour
5ml (1 tsp) soya sauce
150ml (¼ pint) stock

1 Using an electric beater if possible, beat the egg and milk into a well in the flour, until the batter is smooth and airy. If you don't have an electric beater, beat for 2 to 3 minutes with a whisk or a wooden spoon.
2 Add the soya sauce and enough of the stock to make a thin batter. If you have time, leave the batter to rest for half an hour. Beat it quickly again when you are about to use it.
3 Grease a thick-based pan, preferably cast-iron, very lightly with oil and set it on a medium heat.
4 Pour the batter into a jug, then tip just enough into the hot pan to cover its base when you twirl the pan with the other hand. Immediately tip any excess batter back into the jug. If the batter is too thick, thin it with water.
5 Cook the pancake for about 45 seconds on each side. Transfer the pancake to a wire rack to cool, to avoid sticking. Cook the other pancakes in the same way.
6 Use one or two pancakes to make the soup garnish: roll each one up loosely and cut it in very thin strips across, to make ribbons. Drop 1 or 2 pieces per person in the soup.
7 Keep the remaining pancakes, wrapped in kitchen foil in a refrigerator, to use with savoury fillings another day. They will keep for two or three days. Or, for longer-term storage, you can freeze them.

Calories About 40 a pancake.

• Suitable for diabetics
• High fibre
• Very low fat
• Very low salt (omitting soya sauce and using unsalted stock)

An attractive way of adding a little substance, with some protein, fibre and B vitamins, to a consommé.

GRAINS, PASTA & PULSES

When you plan a meal, you probably start by deciding on a main course. The recipes in this section are chosen to widen your choice beyond meat and fish.

In fact, grains and pulses are the staple foods of the world, and every country has delicious main course recipes for them. They range from elegant Japanese sushi – flavoured rice shapes with dozens of toppings and stuffings – to Italian pasta, Mexican tortillas with beans, Russian blini pancakes and even the humble sandwich, if well made.

This chapter offers a selection of traditional favourites. Many of them use meat or fish in small amounts, almost as flavourings – and in some cases I've given both meat and non-meat versions. But they don't depend on meat or fish to be 'solid' enough, in taste and food value, for a main course – except psychologically. For many of us a meal without meat or fish, however satisfying, doesn't seem quite right. Just as for Chinese people a meal without rice, no matter how rich and exotic it is, isn't complete. It's all in the mind!

If you or your family feel like this, you'll find plenty of recipes here with just enough meat or fish to do the trick. Start with familiar tastes like pasta or pancakes, then explore the less familiar – stuffed vine leaves or pease pudding, for instance. You can be confident that either grains or pulses will provide enough protein for a main course – and when combined with each other in dishes such as lentil and cheese savoury, or with dairy foods, as in gnocchi or pancakes, you get a particularly high quality of protein. Plan to use about 50 to 75g (2 to 3oz) weight of uncooked grains or pulses per person (depending on their appetite) as the basis of a main course.

Don't imagine that grains mean food that is over-heavy, branny, very chewy or boring. Look through these recipes and you'll see the huge variety of ways that these foods can be served.

You can roughly count about 95 calories per 25g (1oz) of uncooked grain or pulse. So a main course cooked with a 50g (2oz) helping has just 190 calories – plus whatever you add. That's less than all but fish and poultry portions. Both grains and pulses provide vitamins, iron, zinc, potassium, chromium and assorted trace elements.

Apart from considerable savings on housekeeping bills, grain and pulse meals open up extra variety in meals, tastes and textures. As their protein sources are far lower in fat than almost all meat, it seems a shame not to use them more. These proteins

Top to bottom: tagliatelle with smoked salmon sauce; black-eyed bean casserole and tabbouleh with mint and parsley

also have another advantage over meat, fish and dairy foods. Both grains and pulses are rich in fibre, the two foods providing different kinds of bulk that seem to complement each other. Grain fibre is associated with faster transit of food through the body, easing digestion, and bean fibre (along with oat fibre) with normalizing blood fat and sugar levels.

Will grains, pasta and pulses make you fat? A look at amply fed Asians who tuck into bowls of rice and noodles twice daily should answer that question – they are far slimmer than us. Pasta's notoriety for adding inches is due mainly to the butter and cream that we, but not the Italians, tend to pile upon the pasta. The same applies to beans. If you don't add much fat, it's almost impossible to eat that many calories: you'll feel too full.

GRAINS

Once you start using grains in cooking, you can widen your choice by using the full range. Here are recipes for 7 of the 'big 8': buckwheat, millet, wheat and bulgur wheat, maize, rice, oats and barley. Rye is mainly useful for bread, although rolled rye flakes can be made into muesli and porridge.

You can only take full advantage of the food values of grains – in terms of fibre, protein, vitamins and minerals – if they are unrefined, because so high a proportion of nutrients is contained in the grain shoot and coating lost from the white versions.

BARLEY WITH ALMONDS

Calories About 170 a serving.

• Suitable for diabetics
• High fibre
• Very low fat (omitting, or reducing quantity of, almonds)
• Very low salt (using unsalted stock and omitting salt)

Pot or Scotch barley is less refined than pearl barley.

So simple, and yet so tasty, this is one recipe where I do use butter, or half butter, as it seems to suit the flavours. Most of us find it hard to accept this kind of dish as a main course, yet, in food value, the almonds and barley both provide protein, as well as B vitamins and fibre. *Serves 4 as a side dish.*

10ml (2 tsp) unsalted butter, or 5ml (1 tsp) each butter and oil
100g (4oz) pot barley
40g (1½oz) flaked almonds
750ml (1¼ pints) stock
a little pepper and sea salt
good pinch of ground nutmeg (optional)

1 Melt the butter in a thick-based saucepan, toss in the barley and half of the almonds.
2 Add the stock, stir, bring to the boil, cover and simmer.
3 Cook over a low heat for about 45 minutes, checking occasionally that the liquid has not all been absorbed.
4 Uncover and cook for 20 minutes more. Season.
5 Toast remaining almonds in an ungreased pan over a low heat for 2 to 3 minutes, sprinkle them on top of the barley and partly stir them in.

VARIATION

To turn this into a barley risotto, add some *cooked, shredded chicken* or *sliced mushrooms* with the stock, and some *sliced courgettes* and *peas* about 8 minutes before the end of cooking.

Barley risotto – a variation of barley with almonds

Calories About 95 a serving.

- Suitable for diabetics
- High fibre
- Very low fat
- Very low salt (omitting salt)
- Milk-free
- Gluten-free

Buckwheat is one of the most useful grains for a gluten-free diet, as in most recipes buckwheat flour is a better substitute for wheat flour than rice or maize flour.

Apart from the usual value of a whole, unrefined carbohydrate, buckwheat is particularly noted as a source of rutin, a vitamin-like substance, used by herbalists to improve the strength of the capillary cell walls and hence circulation. Like other grains, buckwheat has plenty of fibre.

KASHA

A quick-to-cook change from rice or noodles, kasha is a traditional staple food of Russia. You can buy buckwheat ready-toasted but you can also toast your own, as in this recipe. The results have a dark brown colour that shouldn't put you off. It tastes as good, or better, next day, and can be eaten cold with milk and a little salt as a breakfast cereal. *Serves 4 as a side dish.*

100g (4oz) buckwheat

5ml (1 tsp) oil

pinch of sea salt (optional)

1 Rinse the buckwheat in a sieve under the tap, and remove any black bits.
2 Place it in a thick-based pan with the oil, and stir over a low heat for a few minutes until it turns a light brown.
3 Add 300ml (½ pint) of boiling water (to barely cover the grain).
4 Cover and simmer for 15 minutes, when all the liquid should have been absorbed and the grains fluffed up into separate pyramid shapes.
5 Remove the lid and allow the buckwheat to dry out over a very low heat for a few minutes.

BUCKWHEAT AND MUSHROOM STUFFING

A traditional filling for pirozhki – crescent-shaped patties (page 104) – but also useful for stuffing peppers, marrows or tomatoes before baking them in a covered casserole for about an hour at medium heat. A little stock (about 2cm [¾in] deep) will prevent the vegetables from drying out. This stuffing is an alternative to those that depend on a lot of oil or high-fat mince. *Fills a batch of pirozhki or 4 peppers.*

5ml (1 tsp) oil, soft margarine or butter
50g (2oz) buckwheat
150ml (¼ pint) boiling water
1 large onion or 4 shallots, finely chopped
50g (2oz) mushrooms, finely chopped
1 hard-boiled egg, chopped (optional)
2ml (½ tsp) mixed dried herbs, including sage
30ml (2 tbsp) smetana, or soft cheese, or thick yogurt

1 Brush the saucepan lightly with some of the fat, and put in the buckwheat. With a wooden spoon, turn it over a low heat for a few minutes, until it starts browning.
2 Add 150ml (¼ pint) boiling water, return to the boil, cover and simmer for 15 minutes. Remove the lid and simmer for 5 minutes more. Cool.
3 Meanwhile, soften the onions (or the shallots, which give more flavour) in the remaining fat in a covered pan for 10 minutes. Add the mushrooms and continue cooking for 5 minutes.
4 Mix together the cooked buckwheat, onion-mushroom mixture, egg (if using), herbs and smetana. Check seasoning.
5 Use as stuffing.

VARIATIONS

You can make this recipe using *bulgur wheat* instead, if you prefer: it will cook in the same time.

BLINI

Traditional Russian buckwheat pancakes, grey-brown in colour, to wrap around savoury fillings. Guests pick up the blinis in their fingers and top them with, or fold them around, one of the suggested fillings. *Makes 8, enough for 4 as a starter or 2 to 3 as a main course.*

50g (2oz) buckwheat flour
50g (2oz) plain wholemeal flour
50ml (1 tsp) micronized yeast
large pinch of sea salt
1 large egg
5ml (1 tsp) honey
150ml (¼ pint) warm skimmed milk
about 75ml (3fl oz) warm water

Calories About 340 in total.

• Suitable for diabetics
• Very low fat (omitting egg yolk and using yogurt)
• Very low salt (omitting egg white)
• Milk-free (using soya yogurt)
• Gluten-free (using buckwheat)

Non-dairy product users can substitute mushroom sauce (page 30) for the mushrooms and curd cheese, using about half the amount of stock.

Calories About 60 per blini. Allow, per batch of filling, about 130 for the mushrooms, about 140 for the chicken livers, about 180 for the onions, about 250 for the herrings, and about 215 for the soft cheese.

• Suitable for diabetics
• High fibre
• Very low fat (omitting egg yolk)
• Very low salt (omitting added salt)
• Milk-free (using soya milk or water to mix)

The fillings are all suitable for diabetics. The mushrooms and onions have medium fibre but the others have no or little fibre. All the fillings are very low fat, except the herrings and caviare. The mushrooms and onions have very little salt, as has the soft cheese, if unsalted. The chicken livers are milk-free.

If you wish to use fresh or large-particle dried yeast, rather than micronized yeast, follow the instructions for yeast preparation in Yeast baking, pages 235–43.

pages 235–43.

VEGETARIAN LUNCH MENU

Watercress broth **95 cals**
—•—
Vulgur bulgur **330 cals**
Lightly cooked cabbage **30 cals**
—•—
Baked apples **120 cals**

Total calories per person **575**

Calories About 90 a serving.

- Suitable for diabetics
- Medium fibre
- Very low fat
- Very low salt (if added salt is omitted)
- Milk-free

Because it has been partially pre-cooked, bulgur wheat is not as unprocessed as other grain, nor as fibre-rich, since it is dehusked. However, it is still a valuable food, particularly when you are in a hurry.

Calories About 330 a serving. Calories depend on the vegetable chosen – allow an average of about 40 per 100g (4oz).

1 Mix the flours, yeast and salt in a large jug.
2 Separate the egg, and add the yolk to the mixture with the honey and warm milk, and enough of the warm water to make a thickish batter.
3 Cover the jug and leave it in a warm place for about 45 minutes.
4 Beat the egg white until stiff, then fold it into the mixture.
5 Heat a thick-based pan, preferably cast-iron, and brush very lightly with oil.
6 Pour enough batter from the jug to make pancakes about 10cm (4in) in diameter. Cook each pancake over a very low heat until it bubbles on top, then turn it and cook the other side until it is browning.
7 Transfer the cooked blini on to a plate that has been kept warm above a pan of simmering water. Serve as quickly as possible.

Fillings for blini Choice of:
Mushrooms Slice and sweat 225g (8oz) mushrooms in a thick pan, lightly brushed with oil, over a low heat until they are just dry. Then mix them with a few spoonfuls of smooth low-fat soft cheese.
Chicken livers Either use chicken liver pâté (page 58), or sauté 225g (8oz) chicken livers with a finely chopped onion in a thick-based pan, lightly brushed with oil, for about 8 minutes. Then mince the livers.
Onions Chop 3 onions fairly finely, turn them in 10ml (2 tsp) oil in a thick-based pan, over a low heat. Add 10ml (2 tsp) water, cover and sweat for 8 minutes. Remove the lid, and continue cooking for a few minutes to evaporate any liquid. Mix with smooth low-fat soft cheese or thick yogurt, and season with a little nutmeg.
Herrings Chop about 225g (8oz) smoked herring or any other smoked fish, or put through a mincer on a medium cutter. Mix with some lemon juice and a little low-fat soft cheese, and season with dill and parsley.
Soft cheese Mash 225g (8oz) low-fat soft cheese or cottage cheese with any favourite fresh herbs. Add a crushed clove of garlic, if liked.

BASIC BULGUR

One of the quickest-cooking grains. Much quicker to cook than brown rice, it is rivalled only by buckwheat and wholewheat pasta. *Serves 4 as a side dish.*

100g (4oz) bulgur wheat
generous 300ml (½ pint) water or stock
pinch of sea salt

1 Rinse the bulgur wheat in a sieve under a running tap. Put the bulgur and seasoning in a saucepan, add the liquid and bring to the boil.
2 Cover the saucepan, turn the heat to the lowest setting and simmer for 10 to 15 minutes, until the grains are tender. Check after 10 minutes that the water is not evaporating too fast. If it is, add a little more.

VULGAR BULGUR

A simple but successful risotto, ready in less than half the time taken by one made with brown rice. When I do cookery demonstrations, I usually include this recipe as an example of how quickly you can make something appetizing and well balanced. A recipe to keep in mind for a quick, economical all-in-one meal with the least effort and least washing up. *Serves 4 generously.*

- Suitable for diabetics
- High fibre (if using peas, sweetcorn or broad beans as vegetables)
- Very low fat (if hazelnuts are replaced with extra vegetables or cooked pulses)
- Very low salt (omitting soya sauce and salt)
- Milk-free

Protein comes from the wheat, nuts and any peas, beans or sweetcorn. Provides some cereal and some vegetable fibre.

225g (8oz) bulgur wheat
1 large onion, finely chopped
100g (4oz) hazelnuts, whole
5ml (1 tsp) oil
600ml (1 pint) stock
15ml (1 tbsp) soya sauce
5ml (1 tsp) dried herbs
about 225g (8oz) of one, or a mixture, of: peas, sweetcorn kernels, sliced mushrooms, sliced courgettes, any cooked diced or sliced vegetables
large pinch of pepper
pinch of sea salt if necessary

1 Rinse the bulgur wheat in a fine-meshed sieve under a tap.
2 Turn the onions and nuts in the oil in a large, thick-based saucepan for 8 minutes, with the lid on.
3 Add the bulgur, stock, soya sauce and herbs.
4 Simmer with the lid on for 10 to 15 minutes, until the bulgur is almost tender.
5 Add the prepared vegetables and stir in. Cook for a further 5 minutes, by which time the vegetables should be just tender or, if using cooked vegetables, hot.
6 Add pepper, and salt if liked (although the soya is very salty).

TABBOULEH

Lebanese cracked wheat salad – to serve as a side dish, or as a main course if part of a salad selection, such as shredded carrot with toasted almonds, sweetcorn and green beans, kidney beans and peppers, or cheese cubes with watercress, all adding to the wheat protein in the tabbouleh. The one thing you must have to make this successfully is a large bunch of parsley. *Serves 4.*

Calories About 110 a serving.

- Suitable for diabetics
- High fibre (parsley is very high in fibre)
- Very low fat (halving quantity of oil)
- Very low salt (omitting salt)
- Milk-free

This method speeds preparation by using boiling water and a sieve, so that the water can easily be drained off. However, you do lose a little food value into the soaking water. If you have more time, simply soak the wheat in enough cold water to cover, so it all gets absorbed.

This is a good salad for those who would never otherwise touch parsley, which is particularly rich in minerals, including iron, and in fibre and vitamin C.

75g (3oz) bulgur wheat
50 to 75g (2 to 3oz) parsley, coarsely chopped
3 good sprigs of mint leaves, ½ bunch of spring onions, both finely chopped
1 clove of garlic, crushed
15ml (1 tbsp) cold-pressed olive oil
juice of 1 lemon
black pepper
pinch of sea salt

1 Place the bulgur wheat in a large sieve, and rinse under the tap.
2 Place the sieve over a bowl, and pour over enough boiling water to cover. The wheat grains will swell up, becoming tender and edible in about 20 minutes.
3 In the bowl that you choose to serve the tabbouleh, combine all the ingredients, except the bulgur wheat. Check that the bulgur is tender.
4 Drain it by lifting the sieve and pressing down the bulgur to remove any excess water.
5 Mix the bulgur and the ingredients in the serving bowl. Let the mixture stand for at least 15 minutes before serving.

TORTILLAS

A Mexican staple food – a cornmeal pancake in which any number of savoury mixtures can be wrapped, from chili beans to omelettes, although it is also eaten on its own. It's an attractive pale yellow in colour. Here are two methods, one made on the same principle as regular pancakes, which I prefer both for its lightness and the ease of making; the other a more authentic rolled-out version for which you need strong wholemeal flour. The second method produces a much more solid result. *Serves 4 when filled.*

Calories About 150 a serving. The second version has about 180 a serving.

- Suitable for diabetics
- High fibre
- Very low fat (using egg white only)
- Very low salt (omitting salt)
- Milk-free (second version only)

When you buy cornmeal, check that it's the unrefined rather than the degerminated kind. Refining removes much of the B vitamins. The snag about unrefined cornmeal is that it easily becomes rancid; buy it from a shop that has a rapid turnover and keep it in a cool place or in a refrigerator.

Tortillas with spicy bean sauce (page 30) and avocado pear

Method 1
Makes 9 tortillas about 15cm (6in) wide

50g (2oz) fresh, unrefined cornmeal
50g (2oz) plain wholemeal flour
15ml (1 tbsp) cornflour
pinch of sea salt
1 egg
225ml (8fl oz) skimmed milk
5ml (1 tsp) corn oil

1 Sift the cornmeal, flour, cornflour and salt into a bowl.
2 In a large jug, beat the egg until fluffy.

3 Beat the skimmed milk and oil into the beaten egg, then add the flour mixture, stirring well.
4 Heat a pan, preferably cast-iron, well. Brush with the oil. Turn the heat to a low setting.
5 Tipping the pan with one hand, pour in enough batter to cover the base.
6 Cook over the lowest heat for about 1 minute, until the edges of the tortilla curl and the base colours. Turn it over and cook the other side. Stack the tortillas to keep warm on a plate in the oven, or on a rack, to cool for later.
7 After the first tortilla, you won't need to regrease the pan, thanks to the small amount of oil beaten into the batter, and the thick-based pan.

Method 2
Makes 8 tortillas, about 15cm (6in) wide

100g (4oz) unrefined fresh cornmeal

100g (4oz) strong plain wholemeal flour

1 small egg

about 15ml (1 tbsp) cold water

about 15ml (1 tbsp) oil

1 Mix together the flours and salt.
2 Beat the egg with the water until blended.
3 Mix the egg mixture into the flour with enough extra water to make a firm dough.
4 Divide into 8 balls. Roll out as thinly as possible to make roughly shaped circles about 15cm (6in) in diameter.
5 Brush them with the oil, and cook in an ungreased thick-based pan over a low heat for a few minutes each side, until they brown.

Fillings Fill tortillas with bean sauce (page 30) or with any savoury mixture, such as tuna fish and salad, stir-fried vegetables, chicken and salad, chicken liver pâté and salad, and tofuburger and salad. The authentic 'tastes' that traditionally go with tortillas include avocado, sweetcorn and beans.

CORN COCOTTES

A kind of sweetcorn soufflé, which lifts sweetcorn from a side dish to a light main course, it is particularly quick and easy to make. I like to use red pepper, to give little flecks of colour, and plenty of paprika on top. *Serves 4.*

225g (8oz) sweetcorn kernels

2 eggs, separated

25g (1oz) wholemeal breadcrumbs

50g (2oz) low-fat soft cheese

5ml (1 tsp) dried basil

pinch of pepper

good pinch of paprika

pinch of sea salt

breadcrumbs or bran to coat the cocottes

a few strips of green or red pepper

Calories About 130 a cocotte.

• Suitable for diabetics
• High fibre
• Very low salt (using unsalted cheese and omitting salt)
• Milk-free (using soya cheese)

1 If you are using frozen sweetcorn, thaw it by steaming it for a few minutes.

2 Place the corn in a blender with the egg yolks and blend briefly to a pulp, but not a purée.

3 Tip the mixture into a bowl, stir in the breadcrumbs, low-fat soft cheese, basil, pepper, paprika and salt.

4 Boil a little water in a wide saucepan (a 3cm [1¼in] approximate depth of water).

5 Grease 4 cocottes and scatter a few breadcrumbs or a little bran in them.

6 Beat the egg whites until stiff. Fold them gently into the mixture and then divide it between the cocottes, arranging strips of pepper on top.

7 Sit the cocottes in the saucepan of water, cover with greased foil or paper, and steam for about 20 minutes, until the soufflés have risen. Nicest if eaten immediately, they will soon sink slightly, but will still be enjoyable.

Mock Duck

Don't be put off by this apparently daunting list of ingredients. This is one of the simplest recipes to put together. The result is a type of savoury bread pudding – to eat with a fork or with your fingers. Serve it as a side dish to mop up casserole juices, or on its own with a complementary vegetable such as broccoli, and with mushroom sauce (page 107). *Serves 4.*

10ml (2 tsp) oil
350g (12oz) onions
25g (1oz) chopped walnuts
generous 5ml (1 tsp) dried sage, 10 allspice berries, 5ml (1 tsp) dried thyme, all ground to a powder
225g (8oz) wholemeal breadcrumbs
225ml (8fl oz) stock or skimmed milk
50g (2oz) medium oatmeal
1 small egg
2ml (½ tsp) white pepper
25g (1oz) currants
30ml (2 tbsp) parsley, chopped
large pinch of salt
juice of ½ lemon
½ green or red pepper, fairly finely chopped
15ml (1 tbsp) any wine (optional)
10ml (2 tsp) sesame seeds, to garnish

1 Heat oven to 190°C (375°F), gas mark 5.

2 Heat the oil in a pan and soften the onion in the oil for about 8 minutes, then add the chopped walnuts, and pulverized spices. Continue to stir over a low heat for 2 minutes.

3 Meanwhile, place all the other ingredients in a bowl. Stir in the onion mixture and mix well.

4 Transfer to a well-greased 18cm (7in) diameter cake tin; the mixture should be at least 5cm (2in) deep. Sprinkle the sesame seeds on top.

Calories About 320 a serving.

• Suitable for diabetics
• High fibre
• Very low fat (omitting or reducing quantity of walnuts and the egg yolk)
• Very low salt (using no-added-salt breadcrumbs and unsalted stock)
• Milk-free (using stock)
• Gluten-free (using gluten-free breadcrumbs and millet flakes instead of oats)

The kind of recipe that would have been written off as fattening stodge a few years ago. Now, the protein and fibre value of grain is recognized and used as here, with the odd egg and some nuts, it adds up to good food value.

Bake for 1 hour until lightly browned.
5 Mark into portions a few minutes after removing from the oven.

GLAMORGAN SAUSAGES

A sausage in shape only, but just as savoury. Pile in the herbs, otherwise they won't be noticeable. If you want, you can, of course, add meat – such as minced cold cooked lamb or lean beef. *Makes 8; serves 3 to 4.*

5ml (1 tsp) oil
1 pink onion or 4 shallots, finely chopped
25g (1oz) rolled oats
100g (4oz) Cheshire cheese, finely grated
75g (3oz) wholemeal breadcrumbs
1 large egg
2ml (½ tsp) each thyme, rosemary and sage
grating of nutmeg
large pinch of pepper
large pinch of mustard powder

1 Heat the oil in a pan and soften the onion in the oil over a low heat for about 8 to 10 minutes.
2 Mix the onion with all of the other ingredients.
3 Shape the mixture into sausages.
4 Grill under medium-to-high heat for a few minutes on each side, or bake at 220°C (425°F), gas mark 7, for 15 to 20 minutes.

BASIC MILLET

Millet's main attraction, to my eyes, is its colour – a delicate creamy-yellow when cooked – which makes a refreshing change from the brown tones of most grains. However, this historic grain – it's mentioned in the Bible; the Romans liked it – is a good foil for spicy dishes, and popular with those who like milk puddings. Unlike most grains, it tends to lose the distinctness of the grains even when cooked for the minimum of time to become tender. So don't feel you've failed if your millet looks mushy, although it should not be wet. *Serves 4 as a side dish.*

100g (4oz) millet
scant 600ml (1 pint) water, or mixture of water with skimmed milk or stock
pinch of sea salt

1 Wash the millet in a sieve under the tap, picking out any black grains.
2 Bring the liquid to the boil, add the millet and salt.
3 Turn the heat to minimum, cover the pan and simmer for 15 to 20 minutes, until all the water has been absorbed.
4 If you want to be sure your millet is as dry as possible, add only 450ml (¾ pint) liquid at first, then check the pan after about 12 minutes and add more liquid if the grain is sticking at the base.

Calories About 100 a sausage.

- Suitable for diabetics
- High fibre

Calories About 80 a serving.

- Suitable for diabetics
- High fibre
- Very low fat
- Very low salt
- Milk-free
- Gluten-free

Millet has a high protein and fibre content.

MILLET 'N' MUSHROOM BURGERS

These can be served in burger buns with all the usual trimmings. *Makes 8; serves 4.*

5ml (1 tsp) oil
225g (8oz) mushrooms
15ml (1 level tbsp) plain wholemeal flour
15ml (1 level tbsp) soya flour
5ml (1 scant tsp) vegetable concentrate
10ml (2 tsp) soft margarine
150ml (¼ pint) stock
225g (8oz) cooked millet, drained if necessary
5ml (1 tsp) Worcestershire sauce
25g (1oz) wholemeal breadcrumbs, for coating
8 burger buns

1 Heat the oil in a thick-based pan, slice the mushrooms and sweat them in the oil over a low heat.
2 Mix the flour and soya flour in a small saucepan, then add just enough water to make a smooth paste. Stir in the vegetable concentrate, margarine and stock. Bring the mixture to the boil.
3 Simmer for 2 minutes, then add the mushrooms. Cook for a few minutes until thick.
4 Add the cooked, dry millet (see basic millet method, step 4). Stir in the Worcestershire sauce. This should make a fairly firm mixture.
5 Shape into 8 large burgers and coat with the breadcrumbs.
6 Grease a thick-based pan, heat well, then reduce the heat to low-to-medium. Cook each side of the burgers for a few minutes. Alternatively bake for 20 minutes in a preheated oven, at 190°C (375°F), gas mark 5.
7 Serve in burger buns with all the usual trimmings.

BASIC BROWN RICE

If you haven't tried it, do. Although it may seem chewy and strange at first, after a while white rice seems insipid by comparison. Long grain rice is the most useful and easiest to cook to perfection – and brown rice does not go mushy. *Serves 4.*

175g (6oz) long grain brown rice
450ml (¾ pint) water

1 Rinse the rice in a sieve under a running tap, picking out any unappetizing bits.
2 Boil the water in a pan with a close-fitting lid.
3 Tip in the rice, reboil, cover, then simmer over the lowest heat for 40 to 50 minutes.
4 Check after 30 minutes in case the water is evaporating or the rice is getting too dry. If so, add a very little more water.
5 By the end of the cooking time, the water should have been completely absorbed, and the rice dry and fluffy. If it is still a little wet, remove the lid and stir the rice for a few minutes over the lowest heat to steam off excess moisture.

Calories About 260 a serving.

- Suitable for diabetics
- High fibre
- Very low fat (omitting, or reducing quantity of, oil and almonds)
- Milk-free (using soya yogurt)
- Gluten-free

One of the best and most economical ways of turning a grain into a popular main meal, with the added protein of nuts and yogurt.

Sushi, ready for rolling in a bamboo mat (left of picture) and rolled and sliced (right of picture). The filling shown is smoked fish with chopped spring onion and slivers of cucumber

BIRYANI

A vegetarian risotto with a difference – a really interesting taste that will cheerfully make a basis for a main dish coupled with tjatziki (page 59), mango chutney and green beans. The lime juice makes a delicious difference. If you must have meat or fish, add a handful of peeled prawns or cubed cooked meat at step 5. Finish with fresh fruit for dessert. *Serves 4.*

450ml (¾ pint) water
175g (6oz) long grain brown rice
10ml (2 tsp) oil
4 medium onions or 8 shallots (or a mixture of the two), sliced
½ small fresh chili pepper, deseeded and finely chopped
2 cloves of garlic, crushed (optional)
5ml (1 tsp) fresh ginger root, grated
5ml (1 tsp) curry powder
large pinch of cinnamon
large pinch of turmeric
300ml (10fl oz) plain low-fat yogurt
15ml (1 tbsp) honey
50g (2oz) sultanas
25g (1oz) almonds, chopped
juice of ½ lime

1 Boil the water and add the rice. Bring the water back to the boil, cover and simmer for 45 minutes. Check after 30 minutes and if the rice has dried out, add a little extra water. By the end of the cooking time, all the water should have been absorbed.
2 Meanwhile, heat the oil and soften the onions in a saucepan over a low heat for about 8 to 10 minutes.
3 Add the chili, the garlic (if using) and all the spices. Cook for a few minutes, then remove from the heat.
4 Heat the oven to 180°C (350°F), gas mark 4.
5 Into the onions, stir the cooked rice, yogurt, honey, sultanas and half of the almonds.
6 Transfer the mixture to a casserole dish. Bake, covered, for 30 minutes.
7 Uncover, stir in the lime juice, sprinkle the remaining almonds on top and bake without the lid for another 10 to 15 minutes.

SUSHI

Visitors to Japan love the beautiful arrangement of food in the sushi bars (like our sandwich bars), where flavoured rice, moulded into cork shapes, is topped with raw fish. Sushi is also the basis of many hors d'oeuvre and lunchboxes, and is always beautifully arranged with a variety of shapes, garnishes and fillings. *Serves 4.*

Calories About 310 a serving (using smoked mackerel); about 295 a serving (using smoked salmon); about 285 a serving (using prawns). Deduct 20 calories a serving if not using wine.

Nori, like other seaweeds, is a rich source of minerals and its saltiness reduces the amount of salt required in the rice.

175g (6oz) brown rice, preferably round grain
450ml (¾ pint) water
1 10 to 12cm (4 to 5in) piece kombu seaweed
125ml (4fl oz) distilled vinegar or white wine
10ml (2 tsp) mild-flavoured honey
2ml (½ tsp) sea salt
Fillings
a few spring onions
50g (2oz) sesame seeds
½ cucumber
2 eggs, beaten with 5ml (1 tsp) soya sauce
75g (3oz) smoked mackerel, cut in very thin long strips or the same weight of trimmings of smoked salmon or any smoked fish, or the same weight of shelled prawns
2 sheets of nori (paper-thin seaweed)
a little horseradish sauce, or wasabi (Japanese horseradish)

1 Wash the rice in a sieve under the tap. Bring to the boil with the kombu in the water, then cover tightly and simmer over lowest heat for 40 minutes, by which time all the water should have been absorbed. Discard the kombu.
2 Remove the rice from the heat and let it stand while you boil together the vinegar or white wine, honey and salt.
3 Remove from the heat, pour it over the hot rice, fanning it to cool, and mix in the liquid with a spatula.
4 Divide the rice roughly in half.
5 To prepare the fillings, slice spring onions lengthways into very thin strips. Cut very thin lengths of cucumber the same length as a width of nori sheet. Toast the sesame seeds briefly over a low heat. Make the beaten eggs into an omelette, remove from the pan when still very soft

and roll up into a cylinder. Cut into strips 1.5cm (½in) wide.

6 Put a bamboo mat on the table, top with a sheet of nori which you have crisped by holding it close to a hot plate or flame for a few seconds (avoid scorching it).

7 Put about half of the rice in a tightly packed layer on the bottom two-thirds of nori.

8 In the centre of the rice, running across it, arrange a few slices of spring onion and cucumber lengths, then a strip of omelette or smoked fish or both. Dab with a little horseradish.

9 Roll up the sheet of nori tightly, away from you, using the bamboo mat to help you. The spare end of the nori should be rolled last, to fold over and hold the roll. Leave the roll in the bamboo mat for a few minutes to settle, then remove the mat.

10 Using a very sharp knife, cut the roll carefully, diagonally, into 2.5cm (1in) thick slices to serve, with slices of spring onion and cucumber.

11 Shape the other half of the rice into another roll; or into 5 or 6 balls of rice, compressed tightly with your hands around either a cube of smoked fish, or a prawn, or a chunk of omelette, all dabbed with horseradish. Roll the balls in the sesame seeds, or dip one side only in the seeds. The balls can also be pressed into triangular shapes. Serve with a crisped nori sheet that has been rolled up and cut into very thin shreds with scissors, together with slices of spring onion and cucumber.

RICE AND LAMB STUFFED AUBERGINES

A rice-based stuffing that can be adapted for use with other vegetables. When using brown rice, it's important to cook the stuffing separately, since it takes so long to cook that any vegetable in which it was baked would have disintegrated before the stuffing was tender. *Serves 4.*

4 small aubergines or 2 large
100g (4oz) lean lamb, minced
1 medium onion, finely chopped
1 clove of garlic, crushed (optional)
25g (1oz) pine nuts or hazelnuts, chopped
1ml (¼ tsp) ground cinnamon
2ml (½ tsp) dried rosemary, powdered in your fingers
2ml (½ tsp) ground allspice
100g (4oz) cooked brown rice
2 tomatoes, roughly chopped
10ml (2 tsp) tomato purée
pinch of black pepper
pinch of sea salt
50g (2oz) strong-flavoured cheese, grated (optional)

1 Heat the oven to 180°C (350°F), gas mark 4.

2 With a knife, score a line through the skins of aubergines, circling them. Place on a baking sheet, and bake for 30 minutes for small aubergines, 45 minutes for large.

3 Meanwhile, place the minced lamb in a fairly large, ungreased, thick-based pan over a low heat and cook until the fat runs out. Spoon it away.

Calories About 260 a serving.

- Suitable for diabetics
- High fibre
- Very low fat (using very lean lamb and omitting cheese)
- Very low salt (omitting salt and cheese)
- Milk-free (omitting cheese)
- Gluten-free

One of the shortest routes to cutting fat intake while increasing fibre (here from grain, vegetables and nuts) without sacrificing full flavour, is to make a little meat go a long way by coupling it with other protein foods like rice, nuts and cheese.

4 Add the onion to the pan and cook for 8 minutes. Add the garlic (if using) and, after another few minutes, the nuts, cinnamon, rosemary and allspice, for a minute.
5 Add the rice, chopped tomatoes, tomato purée, pepper and salt. Cover the mixture and simmer gently for about 20 minutes.
6 Take the aubergines from the oven and, with a knife, cut a deep slit in each one. The flesh inside will be soft enough to scoop out about half of it. Mash the scooped-out flesh with the rice mixture.
7 Stuff the filling into the aubergines and stack them, slit side up, in a casserole. Put any extra filling around them, and a little stock if the filling looks dry.
8 Bake for about 30 to 40 minutes. Serve 1 small aubergine per person, or cut large ones in half, crossways. If liked, sprinkle with grated cheese 10 minutes before the end of the cooking time.

ALMOND-RICE STUFFED VINE LEAVES

Less trouble than they look, these stuffed vine leaves are a handy and unusual meal to offer guests. There are few shopping requirements, especially if you have access to a vine! Serve hot with a vegetable dish that won't compete, such as stelk (page 143), or serve cold with two or three salads, plus pitta or wholemeal bread. *Serves 4 as a main course, 6 as a starter.*

Calories About 300 a serving as a main course; about 200 as a starter.

- Suitable for diabetics
- High fibre
- Very low fat (substituting cooked chick peas for the almonds)
- Very low salt (using fresh vine leaves and unsalted stock)
- Milk-free
- Gluten-free

This recipe produces the same savoury taste as bought vine leaves, without their oil and salt.

**36 fresh vine leaves
or about half of a bought 225g (8oz) packet of brined vine leaves**

10ml (2 tsp) olive oil

2 onions, finely chopped

450g (1lb) cooked brown rice (about 175g [6oz] raw)

50g (2oz) almonds, chopped

50g (2oz) currants

7ml (1½ tsp) ground allspice

30 to 45ml (2 to 3 tbsp) chopped dried dill leaves

30ml (2 tbsp) lemon juice

300ml (½ pint) stock or water

1 Blanch the vine leaves in simmering water for 5 minutes if brined, or for 15 minutes if fresh. Drain them and let them dry.
2 Heat the oil in a pan and soften the onions in the oil for about 8 minutes, then add the almonds.
3 Mix into the rice with all the other ingredients except the vine leaves. Add a little stock or water to moisten, so it is easier to form the mixture into balls with your fingers.
4 Lightly grease a shallow casserole with a lid.
5 Fill the leaves by placing each one vein side up on a board, trimming off any stalk. Make a cork-shape of the filling near the wide end of each leaf, rolling and folding in the sides. Broken or small leaves can be patched. (This amount of mixture should fill about 32 leaves, allowing 4 for patching.)
6 Wedge the filled leaves into the casserole so that they don't unroll.
7 Heat the oven to 180°C (350°F), gas mark 4.
8 Pour the rest of the stock over the dish, cover with a plate so that the

leaves don't unroll and then with a lid or with foil to stop the stock evaporating too quickly. Bake for about 45 minutes.
9 Serve warm or cold.

SAVOURY PANCAKES

Many people tend to think of pancakes as a sweet, rather than as a main course. As a result, they eat them only on Shrove Tuesday – or as crêpes Suzette. Here are savoury pancakes you don't need to feel bad about, and can enjoy often. Prepare the fillings before you cook or reheat the pancakes. *Makes 10 in a 20cm (8in) diameter pan.*

100g (4oz) plain wholemeal flour
1 egg
300ml (½ pint) skimmed milk
pinch of sea salt
a little ground nutmeg
10ml (2 tsp) olive oil

1 Place all ingredients in a blender and liquidize for 1 minute.
2 Brush a thick-based, preferably cast-iron, pan (with an 18 to 20cm [7 to 8in] diameter base) very lightly with oil. Heat thoroughly. By adding oil to the batter, you should not need to re-oil the pan more than once or twice while making the whole batch.
3 Transfer the batter to a jug. Tipping the pan with one hand, swirl the batter around, pouring in just enough to cover the base very thinly. (Pour too little batter rather than too much: it is easier to pour a little more than to avoid a thick pancake if you have poured too much. If you have, quickly tip the excess back into the jug.)
4 Cook the pancake over a medium-low heat for about 1 minute until the edges are curling slightly. Turn it over and cook the other side.
5 Cool the pancakes on a cake or grill rack, so they don't stick together. When cool, stack, wrap in foil or polythene and store them in the refrigerator for several days. To reheat, simply place each pancake in an ungreased, heated pan for half a minute on each side. To keep pancakes hot for immediate use, transfer them, when cooked, to a plate resting on top of a saucepan of simmering water.
6 Fill the pancakes with any of the chosen fillings (below) and serve immediately. They can be treated in various ways: rolled; folded into envelopes to make square packets; folded in four, to make cornets; or stacked, to make a 'cake', by layering pancakes with filling, then cutting the 'cake' in wedges to serve.
7 Alternatively, wedge the rolled, filled pancakes into a lightly greased flat oven dish, cover them with a sauce, such as wholemeal cheese sauce (page 28), tomato sauce (page 29) or creamy herb sauce (page 32) and then cover with foil. Bake in an oven pre-heated to 190°C (375°F), gas mark 5 for 40 minutes, then remove the foil and cook for a further 10 minutes.

Fillings Choice of:
Vegetable Cook chopped vegetables in a wholemeal white sauce (page 27).
Ratatouille (page 133).
Poor man's caviare (page 63).

Calories About 60 a pancake. For fillings, see relevant recipes. Spinach: about 30 per 100g (4oz); cheeses: cottage, about 50 per 50g (2oz); curd, 70 per 50g (2oz); skimmed milk soft cheese, about 45 per 50g (2oz); quark, about 60 per 50g (2oz).

• Suitable for diabetics
• High fibre (depending on filling chosen)
• Very low fat (using egg white only)
• Very low salt (omitting egg white and salt and sparing milk from allowance)

This recipe adds the value of wholemeal flour to pancakes, while reducing the fat content by using skimmed milk. The pancakes can still be made wafer-thin; they taste just as good and are just as versatile.

Savoury pancakes rolled cornet style and filled with mixed vegetables in wholemeal white sauce

Bean sauce (page 30).
Waldorf dip (page 57).
Mushrooms in soured cream (page 142).
Chopped cooked spinach, with half of its weight of low-fat soft cheese, flavoured with rosemary and nutmeg.

PALATSCHINKEN

This recipe has layers like lasagne, but is made with pancakes, and is very tasty. *Makes 10 small pancakes, or 8 large; serves 2 to 3 generously.*

100g (4oz) plain wholemeal flour
300ml (½ pint) skimmed milk
1 egg
Filling
450g (1lb) spinach
45ml (3 tbsp) sour cream, soft cheese or smetana
black pepper
pinch of sea salt
good grating of nutmeg
300ml (½ pint) mushroom sauce (page 107)
50g (2oz) strong-flavoured cheese, grated

Calories About 50 to 60 per pancake. Pancake and filling, about 440 a serving (excluding sauce – see page 107).

• Suitable for diabetics.
• High fibre
• Very low fat (using low-fat soft cheese)

For those on very low fat diets, pancakes can be made quite satisfactorily using the white of egg only. They have less flavour but in this recipe the filling compensates for it. Low-fat soft cheese can be used to replace the grated cheese on top.

1 Follow steps 1 to 5 from savoury pancakes (page 102) to make the pancakes.

2 Simmer the spinach briefly in the water left on the leaves after washing. Stir in the cream or soft cheese and the seasoning.

3 Grease a cake tin. Put a pancake on the bottom. Cover it with quarter of the spinach, then a pancake, then quarter of the mushroom sauce, then another pancake and so on.

4 Heat the oven to 180°C (350°F), gas mark 4.

5 Sprinkle the cheese on top of the layers, and bake for about 40 minutes until it browns. To serve, cut in wedges like a cake.

VARIATIONS

Any lasagne filling can be used in this way: for instance, *cooked haricot beans mixed with tomato sauce* (sauce recipe page 29); *aubergine roast* (page 139).

PIROZHKI

These little savoury patties are an essential part of zakuski, the Russian way of serving meals as a smorgasbord table. Traditionally served with a soup like bortsch, and salads such as cucumber-dill, herring-apple or hard-boiled egg, they make an interesting change from flans and pies. For another example of how to use this type of low-fat pastry, see recipe for kulebyaka (Russian fish pie), page 175. Not only is it far healthier, it requires less skill than 'rubbed in' and flaky pastries. *Makes about 40, very small; serves 4 to 5.*

Calories About 255 to 320 a serving. For fillings, see relevant recipes. Curd cheese, about 145 per 100g (4oz).

Pirozhki, served with sliced hard-boiled egg, cucumber and dill

• Suitable for diabetics
• High fibre
• Very low fat
• Very low salt (omitting salt and egg white)
• Milk-free (using water only to mix)

If you wish to use fresh or larger particle dried yeast, rather than micronized yeast, follow the instructions for yeast preparation in Yeast baking, pages 235–43.

pages 235–43.

Wrappers

275g (10oz) strong plain wholemeal flour
5ml (1 tsp) micronized yeast
35g (1¼oz) soft margarine or butter
150ml (¼ pint) half and half water and skimmed milk
1 egg
pinch of sea salt
some beaten egg for brushing

1 Mix together the flour and yeast.
2 Warm the fat and the liquid slightly, add to the flour with the egg and salt, and mix to make a fairly soft dough.
3 Knead on a floured board for 8 to 10 minutes.
4 Cover with a plain polythene bag and leave the dough in a draught-free place for about 45 minutes, by which time it will have risen well. Meanwhile, prepare the chosen filling (below).
5 Divide the dough into 2 pieces, rolling them out, one at a time, until very thin indeed on a well-floured board.
6 Heat the oven to 200°C (400°F), gas mark 6. Grease the baking sheets.
7 Using a pastry cutter or an upturned glass about 7.5cm (3in) in diameter, dipped in flour, cut out circles of dough.
8 Brush each circle with the beaten egg, place 5ml (1 tsp) filling in the centre and fold over to make a pasty shape, curving the folded edge, if liked, to make a 'canoe' shape. Press the edges together to seal.
9 Place rows of filled pirozhki on the greased baking sheets, and leave in a warm place while you fill the remainder.
10 Brush them all with egg, and bake for 10 to 15 minutes, until golden.

VARIATION

Although this recipe sounds very time-consuming, the circles can be filled quite quickly. When you don't have time, make patties in triangular shapes, big enough for one patty per person.

Fillings Choice of:
Buckwheat and mushroom stuffing (page 90).
Chicken liver pâté (page 58)
Curd cheese mixed with chopped herbs, such as chives, basil and parsley, with a pinch of powdered cumin or coriander.
Humus mixed with chopped chives (page 56).

PASTA

Before embarking on this book, I had rarely cooked pasta, while recognizing that it was one of the best-established, most popular ways of using a grain as a main meal. I found a pasta machine more trouble than it was worth, but produced good results easily using a rolling pin and strong wholemeal flour. Home-made pasta and freshly made bought pasta both cook in 3 to 6 minutes after being fed gently into boiling water. Dried wholemeal pasta takes from 10 to 15 minutes, depending on the shape – the packet usually gives instructions.

In all cases, boil a very large saucepan of water, say 3 to 3.5 litres (6 to 7 pints). Although most recipes instruct you to add salt to the water, this is not necessary. The water must be boiling energetically before the pasta is put in it.

INFORMAL PARTY MENU

Borscht **95 cals**
Pirozhki **280 cals**
Cucumber salad with dill **80 cals**
Carrot and walnut salad **80 cals**
Herring and apple salad **200 cals**
—•—
Coffee éclairs **200 cals**

Total calories per person **935**

When your pasta is cooked, drain it through a sieve and let it dry out a little before adding any sauce. Large strips of pasta, such as cannelloni and lasagne, should be looped over the edge of a saucepan to dry off.

Dried wholewheat pasta is now widely available and, if you live in a city, so is fresh wholewheat. Both are good, but the advantage of making your own is that you save a lot of money, although it has no more food value than bought pasta. It's worth noting that pasta wheat has a particularly high protein content. Pasta is not fattening unless your sauce is laden with butter and cream. When someone casually chooses between a tomato-sauced and a cheese-sauced pasta dish in a restaurant, they may think that both mean the same in food value – or not think at all, apart from a possible spasm of guilt about 'calories'. Well, it's the amount of butter and cream in the sauces that makes the difference between two pasta dishes that may be equally delicious, but in one case won't widen your waistline and will provide good food value, while in the other is not only extremely high in calories, but also in fat and indigestion potential. The six suggestions in this chapter all belong to the first category: they get pasta on your side. If you want to add richness, simply add a *little* butter or cream – but you may find you prefer to taste the ingredients.

BASIC PASTA

Serves 4

Calories About 135 a serving.

- Suitable for diabetics
- High fibre
- Very low fat
- Very low salt (omitting salt and egg white)
- Milk-free

225g (8oz) strong plain wholemeal flour
pinch of sea salt
1 extra-large egg
about 60 to 75ml (4 to 5 tbsp) cold water

1 Place the flour in a shallow bowl, and stir in the salt.
2 Break the egg in the centre, and add 45ml (3 tbsp) water.
3 Work the mixture together, adding enough extra water to make a soft, but not sticky dough.
4 Turn the mixture on to a lightly floured board and knead for about 5 minutes.
5 Cover with a cloth or upturned bowl, or a sheet of polythene, and leave for 30 minutes.
6 Roll out the dough very thinly indeed, first with a rolling pin, then by holding the dough down in the centre with the flat of one hand while stretching it, by pulling the edges gently, with the other.
7 Cut into the required shapes, and place them on a well-floured board or a lightly oiled rack to dry off (about 40 to 60 minutes).
8 To cook, bring a large saucepan of water to the boil, plunge the pasta in and cook for 3 to 6 minutes until just tender.

Shapes There is a wide choice of pasta shapes. Among them:
Lasagne With scissors, cut the dough into strips about 4cm (1½in) wide and about 15cm (6in) long.
Cannelloni Using scissors, cut the dough into oblongs about 12.5 × 10cm (5 × 4in).
Tagliatelle Sprinkle dough well with flour, roll up very loosely, and cut into thin ribbons with a sharp knife or scissors, then unroll it immediately and hang it on a clean teacloth over the back of a chair, or on a baking rack, to dry. If your dough is at all sticky, the strands won't

unroll without tearing, and you'll have to cut the ribbons laboriously with scissors.

Ravioli After step 6, when the sheet of dough is rolled, place teaspoonful of your chosen filling (such as chicken and mushroom, page 108) in rows at about 5cm (2in) spacing over one half. Fold the other half over, draping it loosely over the fillings. Cut out with a pastry 'wheel' cutter, or with a small, preferably fluted, biscuit cutter, taking in as little dough as possible around each ravioli. The ravioli don't have to be square although it makes them look more professional.

Tortelloni or **capelletti** These 'little hats' start out like ravioli: rows of spoonsful of filling. Now cut between them to make 5cm (2in) squares. Fold each square once to make a triangle enclosing the filling. Seal the edges well. Wind the triangle round your finger, then squeeze the ends together to make a shape like a bishop's hat. If the ends won't stay sealed, dab them with a little beaten egg.

Farfalletti These little bows are easy to make with a fluted square cutter or a pastry wheel. Cut small rectangles about 3cm (1½in) long by about 1cm (½in) wide. Pinch the centres together firmly before leaving them to dry.

SMOKED SALMON SAUCE

Adapted from one of Nathalie Hambro's recipes. *Serves 3 to 4.*

100g (4oz) smoked salmon, slices or trimmings, cut into strips about 1 × 4cm (½ × 1½in)
150ml (¼ pint) low-fat soft cheese or quark mixed with smetana or sour cream
30ml (2 tbsp) fresh parsley, chopped
grating of nutmeg
paprika, to garnish

1 Mix the first two ingredients and let them stand for at least an hour.
2 Add the parsley and nutmeg. You won't need salt because smoked salmon is salty.
3 Stir into very hot pasta, and garnish with paprika.

MUSHROOM SAUCE

Serves 4 to 5

225g (8oz) mushrooms, thinly sliced
5ml (1 tsp) unsalted butter or oil
1 clove of garlic (optional), crushed
10ml (2 tsp) cornflour
150ml (5fl oz) plain low-fat yogurt
freshly ground black pepper
pinch of dried marjoram or basil
a little sea salt

1 Sweat the mushrooms and the garlic in the butter or oil over a low heat while the pasta is cooking.
2 When the juices have almost evaporated (after about 5 minutes), stir together the cornflour and yogurt, and add to pan. Stir over a low heat

Calories About 350 in total.

- Suitable for diabetics
- Low fibre
- Gluten-free

Calories About 170 in total.

- Suitable for diabetics
- Medium fibre
- Very low fat
- Very low salt (omitting salt and sparing yogurt from milk allowance)
- Milk-free (using soya yogurt)
- Gluten-free

while it thickens, then simmer for 2 minutes, very gently. Remove from the heat.

3 Season with pepper, herbs and a little sea salt.

BLUE CHEESE SAUCE

Serves 2 to 3

50g (2oz) Gorgonzola or other blue cheese

100g (4oz) cottage cheese

1 clove of garlic, crushed

60ml (4 tbsp) thick plain low-fat yogurt, smetana or quark

45ml (3 tbsp) fresh parsley, chopped

1 Blend the first three ingredients by hand or machine to smoothness.
2 By hand, work in the yogurt, smetana or quark and parsley.

GREEN AND WHITE SAUCE

Serves 4 to 5

10ml (2 tsp) oil

225g (8oz) onions, thickly sliced

90ml (6 tbsp) water

15ml (1 generous tbsp) plain wholemeal flour

300ml (½ pint) skimmed milk

175g (6oz) peas or broad beans, fresh or frozen, uncooked

60ml (4 tbsp) thick plain low-fat yogurt or smetana

sea salt, to taste

white pepper

1 Soften the onions in the oil, with the water, over a low heat in a covered, thick-based pan, for 15 minutes, without them browning.
2 Add the flour to the pan, stir it in and remove the pan from heat.
3 Work in the milk smoothly. Return the pan to the heat, stirring all the time as the mixture thickens. Simmer for 5 minutes.
4 Add the peas or beans. Simmer for 3 to 6 minutes.
5 Remove the pan from the heat, stir in the yogurt or smetana and the seasoning and stir the sauce into the pasta.

Tomato sauce
Use the recipe from page 29 as a sauce for spaghetti or tagliatelli.

CHICKEN AND MUSHROOM CANNELLONI

Roll out your pasta dough until it is almost thin enough to see through. You can then omit the awkward step of boiling the sheets of pasta before filling them, provided your cooking sauce is wet enough to pass on moisture to the cannelloni during baking. *Fills 8 cannelloni generously; serves 4.*

Calories About 640 in total.

- Suitable for diabetics.
- Low fibre
- Gluten-free

Calories About 395 in total.

- Suitable for diabetics
- High fibre
- Very low fat
- Very low salt (omitting salt and sparing milk from allowance)
- Gluten-free (substituting maize or pea flour for the wheat)

LUNCH MENU

Carrot and caraway soup
50 cals

—•—

Chicken and mushroom cannelloni **430 cals**
Green salad **100 cals**

—•—

Coffee almond ice **150 cals**

Total calories per person **730**

Calories About 150 for each cannelloni (pasta and filling); allow an extra 130 a serving for the sauce.

- Suitable for diabetics
- Medium fibre

Chicken liver is a particularly useful ingredient for a low-fat diet. Although it gives richness of flavouring and texture, it contains only 7 per cent fat – less than lamb's liver – and considerably less than almost any red meat. It has one drawback: intensive farming can mean that it carries residues of drugs used for intensive rearing of livestock. If you are concerned, look for an appropriate supplier.

½ basic pasta mix (page 106), rolled out paper-thin and cut with scissors into 8 or 9 pieces

Filling

4 chicken thighs

225g (8oz) chicken livers, washed and trimmed

100g (4oz) mushrooms, caps and stalks, sliced

5ml (1 tsp) oil or butter

1 egg

50g (2oz) curd cheese

1ml (¼ tsp) white pepper

Sauce

stock from cooking chicken plus 300ml (½ pint) stock or water

25g (1oz) soft margarine

50g (2oz) plain wholemeal flour

50g (2oz) curd cheese

good pinch of white pepper

pinch of sea salt

25g (1oz) Parmesan cheese, to sprinkle on top

Chicken and mushroom cannelloni

1 Simmer the chicken thighs in 300ml (½ pint) water for 30 minutes.

2 Add the chicken livers and cook for a further 10 minutes. Remove the meat, retaining the stock.
3 Cook the mushrooms in the fat in a thick-based pan for about 6 to 7 minutes, until brown and fairly dry.
4 Bone the chicken, and mince the chicken, chicken livers, and mushrooms on the finest blade.
5 By hand, stir in the egg and curd cheese. Season. Chill the mixture until needed.
6 Place a cylinder of mixture across the centre of each cannelloni, roll up the dough and make a row of filled cannelloni in a greased ovenproof dish, with the joins in the dough downwards.
7 Heat oven to 190°C (375°F), gas mark 5.
8 Measure the chicken cooking liquid and make up to about 600ml (1 pint) with other stock or with water plus vegetable concentrate.
9 Melt the fat over a gentle heat and stir in the flour. Remove the pan from the heat.
10 Stir in the stock gradually, to make a smooth mix. Return the pan to the heat and stir steadily until it thickens. Simmer for 6 to 7 minutes.
11 Remove from heat, add the curd cheese and season.
12 Pour the sauce, which should be fairly thin, over the cannelloni. Sprinkle them with Parmesan cheese. Bake them for about 40 minutes.

CHEESE AND HAZELNUT CANNELLONI

Traditionally made with ricotta and walnuts but here the walnuts are replaced by hazelnuts. It has an excellent texture as well as flavour. *Makes 8 cannelloni; serves 4.*

½ basic pasta mix (page 106), rolled out paper-thin and cut with scissors into 8 to 9 pieces

Filling

25g (1oz) whole hazelnuts

100g (4oz) spinach, cooked, drained and chopped

225g (8oz) curd and cottage cheese, mixed half and half, *or* ricotta

5ml (1 tsp) dried tarragon

good grating of nutmeg

pinch of pepper

Sauce

225g (8oz) tomatoes, fresh or tinned

225ml (8fl oz) smetana or mixture of thick plain low-fat yogurt and sour cream, half and half

10ml (2 tsp) cornflour

5ml (1 tsp) mixed dried herbs, including basil

good pinch of pepper

pinch of sea salt

25g (1oz) Parmesan cheese

1 Toast the hazelnuts in an ungreased, thick-based pan over a low heat for a few minutes to bring out the flavour. Chop them fairly finely, but don't grind or grate them.

Calories About 100 each cannelloni; about 195 a serving. Allow an extra 105 a serving for the sauce.

• Suitable for diabetics
• High fibre
• Very low fat (halving quantity of nuts and using yogurt only)
• Very low salt (using unsalted pasta, soft cheese and fresh tomatoes, and omitting salt and Parmesan cheese)

The protein comes from soft cheese, nuts and the wheat in the pasta, and the fibre from the unrefined wheat, spinach, tomatoes and nuts.

2 Mix with the spinach and soft cheese, adding tarragon and seasonings.
3 Chill until needed.
4 Heat the oven to 190°C (375°F), gas mark 5.
5 Arrange the filling in cylinders along the centre of each piece of dough. Fold the dough over, place the filled cannelloni in a baking dish, with the joins in the dough downwards.
6 For the sauce, stir everything together, chopping up the tomatoes.
7 Check the seasoning. If the sauce is very thick, thin it a little with tomato juice, water or stock.
8 Pour it over the cannelloni, sprinkle with Parmesan cheese, and bake for about 30 minutes.

VARIATIONS

Many other savoury mixtures can obviously be used to stuff pasta. The two requirements are that they should be heat-stable and fairly firm. You can flavour *low-fat soft cheese* with *a variety of herbs* (*chopped basil* and *chives* are an obvious choice), or use different nuts or other vegetables, such as *finely chopped raw fennel*, *red pepper*, *sweated mushrooms* or *grated raw celeriac*.

MUSHROOM AND SPINACH LASAGNE

It's surprising how little lasagne pasta you need to make this dish, which is tasty hot or cold. If you start with a layer of lasagne at the bottom of the dish, it makes a much neater 'bottom' when you cut the lasagne to serve it. It's important to let the pasta dry off well before using it. *Serves 4.*

Calories About 240 a serving.

• Suitable for diabetics
• High fibre
• Very low fat (using low-fat sauce (page 28) and low fat cheese, instead of Cheddar)

100g (4oz) wholewheat lasagne
Mushroom layers
175g (6oz) mushrooms
5ml (1 tsp) oil
15ml (1 tbsp) plain wholemeal flour
15ml (1 tbsp) soya flour
5ml (1 scant tsp) vegetable extract
150ml (¼ pint) stock or water
Spinach and cheese layers
225g (8oz) fresh spinach (or 175g [6oz] frozen)
15ml (1 tbsp) soft margarine or butter
25g (1oz) plain wholemeal flour
300ml (½ pint) skimmed milk
1 bay leaf
½ onion
25g (1oz) strong-flavoured Cheddar cheese
pinch each of pepper and sea salt
good grating of nutmeg

1 Bring a large pan of water to the boil.
2 Heat the oven to 200°C (400°F), gas mark 6.
3 Plunge the lasagne into the boiling water, and set the timer for 10 minutes.

4 Meanwhile, set mushrooms to sweat in the oil in a thick-based pan for about 8 minutes.
5 Prepare spinach by cooking it lightly for about 5 to 7 minutes in only the water left on leaves from washing, or from defrosting it, over a low heat. Drain any excess water and retain, then chop the spinach very finely.
6 Make the sauce for the mushroom layers. Mix the wholemeal and soya flour to a smooth paste with a little of the stock or water, then stir in the remaining flour with the vegetable concentrate. Bring the mixture to the boil and simmer for 2 to 3 minutes. Add to the mushrooms, cook together for 1 to 2 minutes, then remove from the heat.
7 Make the sauce for the spinach and cheese layers, by melting the fat in a saucepan, stirring in the flour smoothly, then removing the pan from the heat while you work in the milk. Add the bay leaf and the half onion and return to the stove. Stir continually over a moderate heat until the mixture boils and thickens. Reduce heat and simmer for 4 to 5 minutes.
8 Remove from the heat, stir in the cheese, seasoning and nutmeg. Remove the bay leaf.
9 Pour half of this mixture over the spinach and mix together.
10 When the lasagne has cooked for 10 minutes, check that it is just tender but still has 'bite'. If it is not ready, cook it for 1 to 2 minutes longer. Drain and drape the lasagne over the side of the pan to dry off.
11 Using a greased rectangular or square dish, place a layer of pasta in the base, then pour in about half of the mushroom sauce. Top with the pieces of lasagne. Then add a layer of spinach and cheese sauce, followed by another layer of lasagne, then one of mushroom sauce. Continue, ending with a layer of lasagne.
12 Pour over the retained half of the cheese sauce, chopping the cooked onion into the sauce.
13 Bake for 30 minutes, until it bubbles.

VEGETABLE MACARONI

A cross between a pasta dish and a vegetable casserole, this recipe is versatile enough to suit whatever vegetables you have. I find that including sweetcorn, broad beans or peas adds 'body' and colour. An all-in-one meal, with your vegetables built in, but don't over-cook them. *Serves 4.*

5ml (1 tsp) oil
1 large onion, chopped
450g (1lb) mixed vegetables, such as peas, green beans, carrots, courgettes, broad beans, sweetcorn, leeks, broccoli, parsnips, etc.
1 clove of garlic, crushed (optional)
½ red pepper, chopped
400g (14oz) tin tomatoes, or 6 fresh tomatoes
black pepper
100g (4oz) wholewheat macaroni or other pasta
75g (3oz) strong-flavoured cheese, or Parmesan, grated

1 In a large saucepan, soften the onion in the oil over a low heat for about 8 minutes, covering the pan to prevent the onion from sticking.
2 Meanwhile, boil a 1cm (½in) depth of water in another pan and add all the mixed vegetables, except the red pepper and tomatoes.

Calories About 240 a serving. If using cheese sauce to make the macaroni cheese, deduct 250 for the omitted cheese, but add the relevant number of calories for the cheese sauce (page 28). For the low-fat version, allow about 190 a serving.

• Suitable for diabetics
• High fibre (using peas, broad beans, leeks or sweetcorn)
• Very low fat (using cottage cheese or tomato sauce, page 29) instead of cheese
• Very low salt (using tomato sauce instead of cheese)
• Milk-free (with tomato sauce instead of cheese)

For a very low fat meal, replace the hard cheese with cottage cheese and sprinkle some additional mixed dried herbs on top.

This dish provides protein not only from the pasta but also from the cheese and from any beans, peas or sweetcorn. (The last three are particularly rich in vegetable fibre).

VEGETARIAN MENU

Miso soup **60 cals**

—•—

Vegetable macaroni **240 cals**
Watercress **20 cals**
Creamy herb sauce **50 cals**

—•—

Rhubarb fool **195 cals**

Total calories per person **565**

Calories About 200 a serving. If using eggs, add 20 to 40 calories a serving.

• Suitable for diabetics
• High fibre
• Very low fat (using all low-fat cheese)
• Milk-free (using soya milk and soya cheese)

If eggs are used, this becomes a less 'lean' dish, but has more protein. It already has a considerable amount of protein from the wheat in the semolina, the milk and the cheese, so serve it with light dishes, such as salad and fruit.

3 Simmer for 5 minutes, until they are just tender.
4 Add the garlic and red pepper to the onion, cook for 1 to 2 minutes longer, then add the tomatoes, minus juice, and seasoning. Simmer uncovered for about 5 minutes. Remove from heat. Add the cooked vegetables.
5 Boil a large panful of water to cook the pasta in.
6 Heat oven to 200°C (400°F), gas mark 6.
7 Cook the pasta for 10 to 11 minutes, until just tender. Drain well.
8 Combine the pasta with the vegetable mixture.
9 Sprinkle half of the cheese in the bottom of the casserole dish. Add the pasta and vegetable mixture. Top with the remaining cheese. Bake for 15 minutes, until the cheese is melting.

VARIATION

If you want to turn this into a macaroni cheese, simply swop the cheese for _300ml (½ pint) cheese sauce_ (page 28) in step 9.

GNOCCHI ALLA ROMANA

Top cookery writer Rose Elliot said it all when she remarked of this dish that it was 'difficult to believe it's made from semolina, which people associate with dull school puddings'. It's very 'more-ish' as it sizzles its way from the oven. Team it with green salad and a Waldorf salad, and follow with a light dessert, such as fruit fool. _Serves 3 to 4._

600ml (1 pint) skimmed milk
100g (4oz) wholewheat semolina
1 bay leaf
1 shallot, finely chopped
1ml (¼ tsp) white pepper
1ml (¼ tsp) paprika
pinch of sea salt
pinch of cloves, ground
75g (3oz) cheese, ideally 25g (1oz) each of mature Cheddar, Parmesan and curd cheese
2ml (½ tsp) rosemary, crushed and chopped or celery seeds, crushed

1 Bring all the ingredients, except the cheese and rosemary or celery seeds, to the boil in the top of a double boiler or in a pan over a larger pan of simmering water. Stir steadily until the mixture thickens smoothly.
2 Cook over a low heat, stirring often, for about 15 minutes.
3 Remove the pan from the heat, discard the bay leaf and add half of the cheese.
4 Wet a large shallow pottery or porcelain baking dish, and pour the mixture, which will be fairly stiff, into it. Smooth the top with a wet spoon and place the dish in the refrigerator for at least 1 hour.
5 Heat oven to 190°C (375°F), gas mark 5.
6 The cold mixture should be very stiff. Cut into circles or squares with a biscuit cutter and place shapes, overlapping if they are thinner than 1cm (½in), on a lightly greased flat baking dish.
7 Sprinkle the gnocchi with the remaining cheese, sprinkle the crushed rosemary or celery seeds on top, and bake for 30 minutes.

PULSES

Types of beans and pulses

Split red lentils

Chick peas

Black-eyed beans

Kidney beans

Mung beans

Aduki beans

Split yellow peas

Butterbeans

Flageolet beans

Haricot beans

Rosecoco beans

Pulses comprise beans, peas and lentils, and attract cooks by their variety of shapes and colours, and their extraordinarily good value for money. A 500g (18oz) packet of beans or lentils will form the basis of a main dish for 8 people.

But many cooks lose their enthusiasm because they find it difficult to incorporate bean and lentil dishes into their usual repertoire. If the family are used to meaty main dishes, beans and lentils served as main courses can arouse protest, even though they are just as satisfying and nourishing.

It's often best to start with bean dishes that are familiar to everyone and those not thought of as 'beany', such as minestrone, chili con carne, lamb and lentil stew, lentil soup, pease pudding and baked beans.

To start with, simply use more beans and less meat in casseroles, so that the meat becomes a flavouring rather than the main ingredient. You'll gradually discover which beans you prefer, but to start with, I recommend these four:

Split red lentils They need no soaking, cook in 20 to 25 minutes, are an attractive colour and taste familiar and appetizing.

Chick peas They can be overcooked without going mushy, and their flavour, whether puréed in humus, added to a casserole, soup or a stir-fry vegetable dish, is particularly appealing to me.

Black-eyed beans These are the only sizeable beans that need no soaking, so they are useful when you are in a hurry. The taste is undistinguished, but the beans easily absorb other flavours, and cook in 35 to 40 minutes.

Kidney beans Most people seem to like these both in salads and hot dishes, and they add colour.

Other beans worth considering are:

Butterbeans Most people are familiar with them, and won't find them strange. They have a pleasantly floury texture, and are particularly good in salads, soup and dishes like butterbean bobottie (page 118).

Flageolet beans These are a beautiful pale green. They break up easily, so overcooking should be avoided. They are usually expensive, and look their best in salads. If using other ingredients, toss these with dressing before adding the beans to avoid stirring and breaking them more than necessary.

Haricot beans These are versatile and accept flavour well in salads, soups, casseroles and oven-baking.

Rosecoco beans Among the most attractive, these beans have pink skins speckled with darker patterns. Use them wherever you might use kidney or haricot beans. (Pinto beans are also speckled.)

Although the recipes that follow name particular beans, you can usually substitute another type. This is more a demonstration of the variety of cooking methods available.

Basic method for cooking beans

1 Rinse beans or lentils in a sieve under cold water to wash them. Check for small foreign objects, such as seeds or stones, and remove.

2 Soak all types except split red lentils, mung beans and black-eyed beans by:

Overnight method Covering generously with cold water and leaving to soak for 8 to 12 hours *or*

2-hour method Placing the pulses in a saucepan and covering well with water. Bring them to the boil, simmer for 3 minutes, then turn off the heat and leave for 2 hours.

3 Change the water, covering the beans generously. This is partly because fresh water avoids the little bits of residual dust that have drifted into the soaking water, and partly because it is thought that doing so creates less likelihood of the beans causing wind.

4 Bring to the boil. Members of the kidney bean family have been found to be capable of causing stomach upsets and serious illness if they are eaten without thorough cooking, which inactivates natural irritants in them. So these beans should boil energetically for at least 10 minutes before being simmered.

5 When it is boiling well, cover the pan and reduce the heat to the lowest setting.

As you might expect, smaller beans should become tender with shorter cooking. Split red lentils take the shortest time at 20 to 25 minutes, and other small pulses, such as all the lentil family, mung beans, aduki beans and the unusual black-eyed beans, should be tender in 35 to 40 minutes. The longer beans have been kept in a dry place, the longer they will take to rehydrate, so cooking time will vary somewhat. Larger beans take from about 50 minutes to 1½ hours, but soya beans take even longer – up to 2½ hours.

Generally, I prefer large beans for cooking, plus the split red lentils, and use small beans and whole lentils mainly for growing beansprouts, (see page 312). Small beans too easily become mushy when cooked to tenderness, and seem to have too high a proportion of skin to contents. But the dish for which they *are* ideal is dhal – the much-spiced, semi-purée dish of India.

Beans provide a good background for herbs and spices. The flavourings that I find especially useful are: tarragon – which gives a fresh, lemony 'lift' to bean dishes; fennel and dill seeds (crushed) and fronds – which couple a distinctive, almost buttery flavour with traditional carminative, or wind-dispelling, properties; bay leaf – boiled with beans to give depth of flavour; cinnamon – particularly for white beans; marjoram – which gives an aromatic sweetness; cumin – in spicy bean dishes; parsley – used by the handful, rather than the sprig.

In most cases, these herbs are best not added until near the end of preparation. Long cooking will only drive off their aromatic oils which hold most of the flavour. Bay leaves are the exception.

50g (2oz) of raw pulses form a good serving per person, and provide roughly 12g (½oz) of protein when cooked – much more for soya beans, and often increased by other ingredients in the recipe, such as breadcrumbs, yogurt or cheese. A typical recipe providing 12g (½oz) of protein would give over a quarter of an average adult woman's daily protein need, and just under a quarter of a man's. Unlike meat, this comes with almost no fat attached, and with plenty of fibre. Like meat, beans provide a variety of B vitamins, as well as minerals.

INFORMAL PARTY MENU

Dhal **220 cals**
Brown rice **160 cals**
Tjatziki **45 cals**
Red pepper salad **80 cals**
Mango chutney **40 cals**
Spiced shrimp **115 cals**

— • —

Sliced fresh fruit **60 cals**

Total calories per person **720**

Calories About 220 a serving.

DHAL

You don't have to like Indian food to enjoy dhal, and this recipe is just to start you off experimenting with all the seasonings and pulses that make every dhal special. This version is spicy, but not hot. Serve with chappatis, or pitta bread, tjatziki and rice or spinach for a satisfying main course; it goes equally well with baked potatoes and salad, or makes an unusual pasta sauce. *Serves 4.*

- Suitable for diabetics.
- High fibre
- Very low fat
- Very low salt (especially using unsalted tomato puree and oil)
- Milk-free
- Gluten-free

A classic, low-fat protein dish. One serving provides about a quarter of an adult's daily protein needs, together with fibre, B vitamins and minerals.

The oven-cooking method allows all the liquid to be retained and any nutrients that may have dissolved into it during cooking.

225g (8oz) whole or split lentils, or mung beans, or yellow split peas
5ml (1 tsp) turmeric
4 cardamom pods, crushed
2 bay leaves
5cm (2in) length of fresh ginger root, grated
2ml (½ tsp) chili powder
15ml (1 tbsp) soft margarine or butter or oil
1 clove of garlic, crushed
10ml (2 tsp) cumin, ground
15ml (1 tbsp) coriander, ground
45ml (3 tbsp) chopped parsley
30ml (2 tbsp) wine vinegar
30ml (2 tbsp) tomato purée

1 Heat the oven to 180°C (350°F), gas mark 4.
2 Wash the pulses in a sieve under the tap. Place in a casserole with a well-fitting lid, cover with water by 3cm (1½in). Put in the oven and set the timer for 1 hour.
3 After 20 minutes, add the turmeric, 2 of the crushed cardamom pods, bay leaves, ginger, chili powder and fat.
4 At the end of the hour, the lentils should be swollen and almost tender.
5 Combine the garlic, remaining crushed cardamom, coriander and cumin thoroughly. Add to the lentil mixture, with extra water if needed, to make a thick, soupy texture. Heat for about 15 minutes until the lentils are completely soft. Check the seasoning: add the chopped parsley, wine vinegar and tomato purée.

VARIATION

For a smooth dhal, finish by putting the mixture in the blender for 20 seconds.

LENTIL AND CHEESE SAVOURY

Homely, easy and, to my taste, very satisfactory. Because of the tomatoes, it's also an attractive red-orange to please those who complain that beany foods are boringly brown. It's tasty hot or cold. *Serves 4.*

175g (6oz) split red lentils
450ml (¾ pint) water
2 onions, thinly sliced or chopped
10ml (2 tsp) oil, soft margarine or butter
125g (5oz) strong-flavoured Cheddar cheese, grated
4 Weetabix or similar wholewheat cereal biscuits, crumbled
5ml (1 tsp) dried mixed herbs
3 tomatoes, roughly chopped
30ml (2 tbsp) tomato purée

1 Wash the lentils in a sieve under the tap. Bring to the boil in the water, and simmer, covered, for 15 to 20 minutes. Check occasionally, adding more water if the mixture is too dry. (By the end of cooking time the liquid should have all been absorbed, and the lentils moist and soft.)

Calories About 340 a serving.

- Suitable for diabetics (replacing Weetabix with unsugared Shredded Wheat)
- High fibre
- Very low fat (using all cottage cheese)
- Gluten-free (using millet flakes or puffed rice instead of wheat cereal)

Although wholewheat biscuits do contain a small amount of sugar (6 per cent), in the context of a pattern of eating that is low in sugar, this adds up to a tiny amount per day. The recipe provides about a third of an adult's daily protein needs. It isn't particularly low fat, thanks to all the cheese.

Lentil and cheese savoury garnished with basil

2 Heat the oven to 180°C (350°F), gas mark 4.
3 While the lentils are cooking, brown the onions in the fat.
4 Mix the onions, grated cheese, crumbled biscuits and herbs together. Add the lentils (draining off any excess fluid), tomatoes and the tomato purée.
5 Tip the mixture into a greased shallow baking tin about 18cm (7in) in diameter and bake for about 30 minutes until sizzling.

VARIATION

If, for any reason, the mixture is a little sloppy, add *another crumbled wheat biscuit*.

PEASE PUDDING

Calories About 220 a serving.

Traditionally, you might have added an egg to this mixture, which was then wrapped in a cloth and boiled in a cauldron of meat. However, I think this simple method produces a really delicious result. The carrot helps to keep the attractive colour. This way of enjoying split peas, and of getting protein, fibre and vitamins in the process, is due for a revival. It goes well with lightly cooked fennel and baked potatoes. *Serves 4.*

- Suitable for diabetics
- High fibre
- Very low fat
- Very low salt (using unsalted stock cube for vegetable concentrate)
- Milk-free
- Gluten-free

225g (8oz) yellow split peas

1 carrot, finely chopped

300ml (½ pint) water or stock

5 to 10ml (1 to 2 tsp) green peppercorns, ground, or 1ml (¼ tsp) ground white or black pepper

5ml (1 tsp) vegetable concentrate

good pinch of nutmeg

dab of mild French mustard (optional)

1 Wash the split peas in a sieve under the tap, then soak them overnight or by the 2-hour method (page 114). Drain.
2 Place them in a saucepan with the carrot and 300ml (½ pint) water or stock.
3 Bring to the boil, cover and simmer for about 45 to 60 minutes until tender (different batches of peas seem to vary).
4 When the peas are tender, most of the water should have been absorbed. If not, drain and keep the liquid for stock. Mash the peas with a fork or a potato masher. Alternatively, if you prefer a very smooth purée, use a vegetable mill or food processor.
5 Into the peas, stir the pepper, vegetable concentrate and nutmeg, and the mustard, if wanted. Check the seasoning.

BUTTERBEAN BOBOTTIE

Calories About 295 a serving.

- Suitble for diabetics
- High fibre
- Very low fat (omitting topping)
- Very low salt (omitting salt and egg whites, and using low sodium bread)
- Milk-free (using soya milk)
- Gluten-free (using gluten-free bread)

A mildly curried, succulent way of cooking beans. Travel writer Angela Humphery searched out an authentic recipe for the meat version of this in its country of origin, South Africa. I loved it – and adapted it. It is an excellent example of how a slightly sweet, savoury taste can be achieved without adding anything but fruit. You can add 450g (1lb) minced lean lamb if you like. *Serves 4.*

550g (1¼lb) cooked butterbeans (about 225g [8oz] raw weight)

5ml (1 tsp) oil

2 onions, finely chopped

30ml (2 tbsp) curry paste, medium-hot

2 thin slices of wholemeal bread

30ml (2 tbsp) water

1 apple, small

1 banana

15g (½oz) sultanas

10ml (2 tsp) no-added-sugar apricot jam, or 2 dried apricots, chopped

10ml (2 tsp) wine vinegar

1 clove of garlic, crushed

good pinch of sea salt

Topping
1 large or 2 small eggs

30ml (2 tbsp) semi-skimmed milk

a few almond flakes, to garnish

1 bay leaf

1 Heat the oven to 180°C (350°F), gas mark 4.
2 Drain the cooked beans.
3 Heat the oil in a pan and cook the onions in the oil for about 8 minutes. Add the curry paste, cook for a further minute, then add the beans and cook for another minute.
4 Soften the bread in the water. Grate the apple and mash the banana.
5 Remove the onion-bean mixture from the heat, add the grated apple, mashed banana, sultanas, jam, vinegar, garlic, salt and softened bread. Stir well.
6 Transfer the mixture to a lightly greased pie dish. Beat the egg or eggs with the milk, and tip over the mixture. Place the nuts and bay leaf on top. Bake for 30 minutes.

VARIATIONS

Haricot or other *fairly soft-skinned beans* can be used instead of butterbeans.

BLACK-EYED BEAN CASSEROLE

An adaptable recipe, suited to all kinds of beans and vegetables; there are many delicious changes that can be rung. It makes a complete meal if you serve a mixed salad with it. Meat fans can add cubed cooked meat at step 5, if wished. *Serves 4.*

225g (8oz) black-eyed beans
1 bay leaf
5ml (1 tsp) olive oil
2 onions, chopped roughly
1 clove of garlic (optional), crushed
3 sticks of celery, chopped
2 carrots, sliced thickly
2 potatoes, unpeeled, cut in chunks
1 turnip, roughly chopped
5ml (1 tsp) green peppercorns, ground
10ml (2 tsp) black treacle
45ml (3 tbsp) tomato purée
large pinch of dried marjoram
2ml (½ tsp) rosemary, ground
50g (2oz) strong-flavoured Cheddar cheese, grated
pinch of sea salt

1 Wash the beans in a sieve under the tap, then barely cover with water, add a bay leaf and bring to the boil. Cover and simmer for about 30 minutes.
2 Meanwhile, heat the olive oil in a pan and soften the onions in the olive oil for about 8 minutes.
3 Add the garlic, if using, for 2 minutes, then the remaining vegetables. Cover and sweat them for about 8 minutes.
4 Transfer the onions, garlic and vegetables to a casserole, stir in the pepper, treacle, tomato purée, marjoram, rosemary and seasoning. Remove the bay leaf from the beans.
5 Add the beans to the vegetables, plus enough of the cooking water to

Calories About 330 a serving.

• Suitable for diabetics
• High fibre
• Very low fat
• Very low salt (replacing tomato purée with mashed tomatoes and the Cheddar cheese with unsalted soft cheese, and omitting salt)
• Gluten-free

The beans provide protein, fibre, B vitamins and a selection of useful minerals, all with very little fat.

VEGETARIAN MENU

Gazpacho **75 cals**
— • —
Black-eyed bean casserole
330 cals
Mixed salad with fennel
100 cals
— • —
Walnut gateau **200 cals**

Total calories per person **705**

completely cover, adding a little extra stock or water if there isn't enough.

6 Cook, tightly covered, over the lowest heat for about 1 hour, or until vegetables are just tender.

7 Remove the lid, sprinkle on the cheese and brown under a hot grill.

VARIATION

If preferred, this casserole can be baked for 1 hour at 180°C (350°F), gas mark 4. If can also be made with other beans, such as *chick peas* or *haricots*. However, these must be pre-soaked and then cooked for 1½ hours before they are added to the vegetable mix at step 5.

TOFU BURGERS

The best way I know to eat tofu – apart from in miso soup (page 76). Serve with more soya sauce and green vegetables. *Serves 4.*

350g (12oz) tofu (beancurd)
75g (3oz) rolled oats
1 large carrot, grated
1 onion, finely chopped
5ml (1 tsp) fresh ginger root, grated finely
5ml (1 tsp) dried mixed herbs, including basil or oregano
22ml (1½ tbsp) soya sauce, to taste
about 25g (1oz) wheat germ

Calories About 150 a serving.

- Suitable for diabetics
- Medium fibre
- Very low fat
- Milk-free
- Gluten-free (replacing oats and wheat germ with millet flakes and soya sauce with tomato purée)

Tofu burgers served with broccoli and soya sauce

Tofu has one of the lowest ratios in any plant food of fat and calories to protein: 25g (1oz) contains only about 20 calories. Two burgers provide about 8g (⅓oz) protein, about the same as a 50g (2oz) all beef, no-added-cereal burger, but only about the same number of calories as one meat burger, which can be as much as 20 per cent fat.

1 Heat the oven to 190°C (375°F), gas mark 5.
2 Making sure the tofu is well drained (keep the liquid for stock), mix all the ingredients to a firm blend.
3 Let the mixture stand for a few minutes. Shape into 8 burgers, and dip each one in the wheat germ.
4 Bake on a greased tray for 15 to 20 minutes.

VARIATION

I think the flavour is improved by cooking the onion and carrot lightly in 5ml (1 tsp) oil for a few minutes before adding to the other ingredients. *A stick of celery, finely sliced*, can also be added.

TOFU QUICHE

Beancurd, with its low-fat high-protein balance, is used here to replace milk and eggs. *Serves 4.*

¾ mix of wholemeal shortcrust pastry (page 257)
1 onion, finely chopped
5ml (1 tsp) oil
50g (2oz) mushrooms
225g (8oz) tofu (beancurd), well mashed
150ml (¼ pint) water*
1 carrot, grated
30ml (2 tbsp) parsley, chopped
5ml (1 tsp) soya sauce
10ml (2 tsp) sesame seeds

*If you use shrink-wrapped firm tofu, you will need all of this liquid, but if you use the type packed in a long-life carton, you will need only about half or two-thirds of this amount, including any liquid from the carton.

Calories About 160 a serving.

A dairy-free quiche filling with a substantial protein content but with far less fat than the conventional egg, milk and cheese fillings.

• Suitable for diabetics
• Medium fibre
• Very low fat
• Very low salt (omitting salt in pastry and soya sauce)
• Milk-free

1 Line a 20cm (8in) flan tin with the pastry. If you have time, leave the pastry case in a refrigerator for 15 minutes or so. Heat the oven to 200°C (400°F), gas mark 6. Place greaseproof paper or kitchen foil in the pastry shell and weight it with a few dried beans. Bake for 15 minutes.
2 Soften the onion in 5ml (1 tsp) oil in a covered pan for 5 minutes.
3 Slice the mushrooms, add them to the onion and continue to cook, uncovered, for another 5 minutes.
4 Remove the onion and mushroom mixture from the heat and mix it with the tofu, water, carrot, parsley and soya sauce.
5 Pour the mixture into the shell, sprinkle with sesame seeds and bake at 180°C (350°F), gas mark 4, for 40 minutes, until the flan is lightly browned.

CHICK PEA WEDGES

Calories About 280 a serving.

I find chick peas one of the most tempting pulses to keep in my kitchen. Here's another way of handling them – the coconut and lime juice transform the wedges into something rather special. The protein in the chick peas is complemented by the eggs and breadcrumbs, so this makes an adequate main dish. Balance it with an apple dessert – the flavours are complementary. *Serves 6.*

- Suitable for diabetics
- High fibre
- Very low fat (omitting egg yolks)
- Very low salt (using low sodium bread, egg yolks only, coconut or mustard powder and omitting salt)
- Milk-free
- Gluten-free (using gluten-free breadcrumbs)

Don't forget that lemon and lime juice are rich in vitamin C; the juice of half a large lemon can provide about 14mg, while limes contain about half as much.

175g (6oz) chick peas
1 bay leaf
1 large onion, finely chopped
1 carrot, grated
1 stick celery, finely sliced
10ml (2 tsp) oil
7ml (1½ tsp) curry powder
75g (3oz) wholemeal breadcrumbs
2 eggs
10ml (2 tsp) desiccated coconut or mild wholegrain mustard
juice of 1 small lemon or lime (or, preferably, a mixture of the two)
2ml (½ tsp) marjoram
2ml (½ tsp) white pepper
good pinch of sea salt

1 Wash the chick peas in a sieve under the tap, removing any little stones or sticks. Soak them overnight or by the 2-hour method (page 114).
2 Change the water and cover chick peas with fresh water. Add a bay leaf and boil for 10 minutes, then simmer for 1 to 1½ hours until very tender, in a covered pan.
3 Heat the oil in a thick-based pan and soften the onion, carrot and celery in the oil, covered, for 10 minutes.
4 Mix all the other ingredients in a bowl, with the onion mixture.
5 Drain the chick peas, reserving the liquid. Mash with a fork or potato masher until the mixture is fairly floury.
6 Add to the other ingredients with just enough cooking liquid to make a moist, but not soggy, mixture.
7 Grease a thick-based, fairly small pan, about 20cm (8in) in diameter, and heat. Tip the mixture in and level it off with a spatula. Cook over a low-to-medium heat for a few minutes, then cut twice at right-angles to make 4 wedges. Use a slice to turn each wedge over, and cook for a few minutes on the other side.

BAKED BEANS

These are like the ones the cowboys eat – you can add tomato if you like. They're dark and slightly treacly; make them a main course dish with baked onions and a green salad – fennel goes well with the flavour.
Serves 2 as a main course; 4 as a side dish.

Calories About 120 a serving as a side dish; about 240 as a main dish. If using tomato purée, add about 5 calories a serving.

- High fibre
- Very low fat (halving quantity of oil)
- Very low salt (replacing tomato purée with tomato sauce or omitting altogether)
- Milk-free
- Gluten-free

Haricot and butter beans are both particularly good sources of iron and zinc, although iron from vegetable foods is poorly absorbed compared with iron from animal foods. Taking vitamin C at the same time can help absorption, so a green salad including watercress, parsley or green peppers goes well with it.

100g (4oz) haricot or butterbeans
15ml (1 tbsp) walnut oil
30ml (2 tbsp) black treacle
15ml (1 tbsp) vinegar, not malt
1 onion, cut in quarters
2ml (½ tsp) dried mixed herbs
pinch each of cinnamon and cloves, ground
black pepper
juice of ½ lemon
30 to 45ml (2 to 3 tbsp) tomato purée (optional)

1 Rinse the beans in a sieve under the tap. Soak them overnight or by the 2-hour method (page 114). Drain.
2 Add all the other ingredients except the lemon juice and tomato purée. Stir in just enough water to cover. Bring to the boil and transfer to a casserole with a well-fitting lid.
3 Cover tightly, bake at 130°C (250°F), gas mark ½ for 5 to 6 hours. Stir occasionally, and add a very little water or stock if the beans are drying out.
4 When the beans are tender, stir in the lemon juice, to taste. Add the tomato purée, if liked, and check the seasoning.

LENTIL MOUSSAKA

I find this as good as meat moussaka: if wished, 100g (4oz) or more of lean minced lamb (raw) can be blended in at step 3, but omit the oil as even the leanest meat provides enough to moisten the cooking. *Serves 4.*

225g (8oz) cooked whole lentils (about 75g [3oz] raw weight)
450g (1lb) aubergines (2 medium), sliced under 1cm (½in) thick
15ml (1 tbsp) oil
175g (6oz) onions, thickly sliced or chopped
1 clove of garlic, crushed
5ml (1 tsp) dried thyme
2ml (½ tsp) cinnamon, ground
400g (14oz) tin tomatoes, or 6 fresh, chopped
2 eggs, beaten
150ml (¼ pint) plain low-fat yogurt
2ml (½ tsp) freshly ground nutmeg
1ml (¼ tsp) black pepper
pinch of sea salt
15g (½oz) Parmesan cheese, grated

1 If you are starting with raw lentils, soak them overnight or by the 2-hour method (page 114), then simmer them in just enough fresh water to cover, for about 45 minutes or until very tender.
2 Place the aubergine slices on a baking tray brushed with a little of the oil, and grill for 5 minutes.
3 Cook the onions in the remaining oil for about 10 minutes in a covered pan over a low heat. Then add the garlic, thyme and cinnamon, for a further minute's cooking.
4 Add the tomatoes, uncover the pan and simmer for about 5 minutes. Add the drained lentils.
5 Heat the oven to 180°C (350°F), gas mark 4.
6 Stir the lentil mixture again. In a fairly shallow ovenproof dish, arrange layers of slices of grilled aubergine alternating with the lentil mixture, finishing with the aubergine.
7 Mix together the eggs, yogurt, nutmeg and pepper. Pour over the contents of the casserole.
8 Sprinkle the Parmesan on top, and bake for 30 to 40 minutes.

Calories About 210 a serving. If using meat, add about 50 to 75 calories (depending on the fat-to-meat ratio of the meat used).

• Suitable for diabetics
• High fibre
• Very low fat (halving the quantity of oil, and using egg whites only)
• Very low salt (using fresh tomatoes, omitting salt and Parmesan cheese and if milk can be spared from allowance)
• Milk-free (using soya yogurt and omitting cheese)
• Gluten-free

By simply grilling the aubergine instead of using the conventional method of salting the slices and letting the juice drain off, you avoid a substantial amount of added salt, the loss of the drained-off nutrients and an extra preparation stage. I don't notice any bitterness in the aubergines as a result.

GREEK LUNCH MENU

Greek tomato salad **200 cals**
—•—
Lentil moussaka **210 cals**
Green beans **15 cals**
—•—
Greek lemon cinnamon pudding **180 cals**

Total calories per person **605**

VEGETABLES

Freshness, colour, crisp and crunchy textures, a sense of sharing nature's vitality – they are all wrapped up in vegetables. Today there is more choice of vegetable varieties and there are longer seasons – in the shops at any rate – than ever before. This section aims to help you make the most of the opportunities.

Although certain vegetables do seem to have a natural affinity with particular dishes (think of fennel and fish, or red cabbage and rabbit or lamb), I am convinced that the way to make the most of vegetables is to buy not primarily to suit your menu, but what looks best when you're out shopping. Then decide what to make with them. This section offers a variety of ideas for how to get the best flavour from vegetables. And you will find that the cooking methods that give you the most flavour also give you the greatest food value. Some of that flavour, for instance, comes from minerals, so any cooking method that retains the maximum of minerals also conserves flavour.

How you keep vegetables will have considerable influence on how much you enjoy them, and benefit from eating them. If possible, keep your vegetables in the refrigerator. Cold and dark protect them from two of the main villains that speed up loss of vitality. Shops with chilled displays are preferable, while supermarket lights hasten vitamin loss.

For the same reasons, don't prepare vegetables hours in advance and then keep them in water. By protecting them from air, heat and water until shortly before they are served, you'll retain more flavour as well as more vitamins. Chop or slice vegetables just before cooking and cook all vegetables in as large chunks as practical, to minimize the surface area through which vitamins and minerals can leach out. If you must do some advance preparation, leave till the last moment those vegetables, such as mushrooms, celeriac, potatoes and Jerusalem artichokes, which discolour badly if the cut surfaces are long exposed to the air. The addition of salt to vegetable cooking water can increase the loss of minerals; if you keep the produce's own flavour intact by minimal cooking, you will find that you often don't need salt anyway.

Apart from heat and light, the other enemy of vegetable flavour and goodness is water. Flavour, vitamins and minerals can all dissolve in it so you'll find very little used in the vegetable recipes in this chapter. (When you do have a few spoonfuls of vegetable cooking water left over – except for brassica water, which should be used the same day – add them automatically to your stock jug. You won't only be preserving food value that would otherwise be thrown away; to have stock on hand is one of the best ways of guaranteeing flavour in your cooking.)

Top to bottom: mangetout peas, asparagus and broccoli

PREPARATION & COOKING

The most important message in this section is to avoid overcooking vegetables or keeping them hot. They lose flavour, colour and texture, as well as food value, as a result.

Steaming, pressure cooking and microwave cooking can all keep vegetables away from contact with water. Tests on the two latter methods have shown that in spite of many people's considerable distrust of such gadgets, the very short cooking time and water-free conditions do keep vitamin levels high – as high as steaming.

The main disadvantage of steaming is that it takes so long. I prefer what's often called 'the conservative method'. This means heating to boiling point a very small amount of water in a pan with a tight-fitting lid, adding the prepared vegetables, covering and cooking over a low-to-medium heat for a few minutes. This method creates steam as the water boils and most of the vegetables don't actually touch the water at all. Cooking times range from 5 minutes for shredded or thinly sliced soft vegetables to 25 minutes for potatoes, but different batches take different times. Home-grown vegetables, obviously superior in fresh-ness, take as little as half as long to cook. To test whether your vegetables have reached the required degree of tenderness, prod them with a sharp knife.

With root vegetables, I find that a teaspoon of oil or fat added to the pan with the water at the start brings out flavours much better than a dollop of butter added to the vegetables when they are served. And this way you add much less fat.

The amount of vitamin C in your vegetables will vary considerably with the variety, storage time and method of cooking. Because of this uncertainty, be generous in your use of vegetables so you don't run the risk of running short.

The fibre in vegetables is a different type from that in grain: for instance it is less bulk-forming. Your meals need to contain some of both types.

All vegetables are valuable sources of minerals. Two of particular interest are calcium and potassium. Calcium, richest once again in the leafy greens, is important for maintaining bone strength throughout life. If you don't want to eat quantities of milk products (the richest source), dark green vegetables are your back-up. To absorb calcium you need vitamin D, which is absorbed through the action of sunshine on your skin, or which can be obtained by eating oily fish, such as herrings.

Potassium pairs with sodium in controlling body fluid levels. Western meals are far higher in sodium, from added salt, than in potassium, which is often neglected and lost in refining. Anyone concerned with reducing sodium level, or who takes diuretic drugs which cause potassium loss, is wise to take potassium from unsalted vegetables and vegetable juices rather than in tablets, which irritate the digestive tract. The richest vegetable source of potassium is parsley, but potatoes, leafy greens, mushrooms, celeriac, cauliflower and beetroot are also good sources.

In general, it's better not to peel vegetables unless the skin is tough or damaged. The skin and layer just under it tend to be richest in fibre and in some nutrients. However, farming sprays and lead pollution can contaminate them. If possible, use organically grown produce.

COOKING SUGGESTIONS FOR SELECTED VEGETABLES

	Basic cooking methods	Special points	Herbs and spices*
LEAVES			
Broccoli	Use conservative method; split the stalks if thick, and cook upright.	Goes well with cheese and pasta; good with shapeless dishes like grain risottos, owing to its elegant shape and colour.	Crushed caraway seed, coriander.
Cabbage	Use conservative method.	Dark green leaves are the most nutritious. Cabbage balances spicy dishes well.	Nutmeg, paprika, or toasted crushed celery or caraway seeds.
Spring greens	Use conservative method or stir-fry (page 138). Split thick stems.	As cabbage.	
Spinach, spinach beet	Beet: use conservative method or stir-fry (page 138). Spinach: don't add water other than any left on the leaves after washing. Don't chop until after cooking.	Has particular affinity with pasta, pancakes, fish, cheese, soufflés, Chinese and Middle Eastern food.	Nutmeg, cinnamon, both added after cooking; sesame seeds, toasted and crushed, to garnish.
Kale	Use conservative method.	Traditional ingredient of colcannon: add chopped cooked kale to potatoes (as for stelk, page 143), beating to a pale green fluff. Can also be sautéed in patties like bubble-and-squeak.'	Mace, crushed celery seeds, paprika.
Swiss chard	Cook thick, juicy stems separately, by the conservative method, as for heads of celery.	Use leaves as a green vegetable. They are best served unchopped, like spinach beet, or stir-fried (added a minute or two later than the stems).	Touch of mixed spice, garlic, nutmeg.
Sorrel	Used more as a flavouring than on its own.	Adds 'tang' when substituted for up to a quarter of another vegetable, in soups, vegetable purées or soufflés.	With its sharp lemony taste, it needs no extra flavouring.
Chinese leaves	Use conservative method or stir-fry. Cut slices across head, and don't separate the leaves unless stuffing.	Use for stuffing or to line terrine dishes. (Blanch to soften, then drain.) Lightly cooked, Chinese leaves make a handsome bed for rice, kebab and poultry dishes.	Nutmeg, paprika. Also goes well with soya sauce, root ginger, garlic.
Watercress	Principal vegetable for food value, best in salads, but also good cooked like spinach. Mix in small amounts with other vegetables or use in soups and soufflés.	Adds colour and tang to other vegetables and reduces the need for salt owing to flavour and peppery taste. Goes well with potatoes, nuts (particularly walnuts) and pulses.	
STEMS, STALKS AND FLOWERS			
Asparagus	Trim stems, cut off hardened white ends (use for stock) and split thick ones. Cook standing upright in about 5cm (2in) of water to prevent tops becoming mushy before the stems are tender. Slender, homegrown asparagus takes about 14 minutes; thick, shop-bought asparagus about 45 minutes.	Serve alone as a hot first course with egg and lemon sauce (page 31) or creamy herb sauce (page 32). Has a tonic effect on the kidneys.	If serving with creamy herb sauce, add tarragon, parsley and/or crushed toasted sesame seeds to the sauce.
Seakale	Cook as for Chinese leaves or Swiss chard, or asparagus.	Serve long stalks as a first course like asparagus or with the leaves on as a side dish for a main course.	As for asparagus.
Celery	Either slice across and use conservative method or stir-fry, or trim the heads, cut in halves or quarters lengthways and follow cooking instructions for carrots and parsnips (page 130). The latter method is only suitable for celery grown with no grit between the leaves.	A natural partner for cheese, fish and any kind of game, celery adds flavour, avoiding need for salt. Celery leaves taste just as good as the stalks and can be eaten in the same way; otherwise use them for garnishing, for salads and for flavouring stock.	Lovage, the 'celery herb' or crushed celery seeds intensify celery flavour. Fennel seeds or dill weed complement it.
Fennel	Slice and quarter bulbs vertically (use fronds as well) and cook using conservative method. Alternatively, use raw in salads.	A natural partner for fish, pasta and beans.	

Most herbs and spices are best added to vegetables just after cooking, so that they are heated, releasing the aromatic oils that produce most of their flavour, but not cooked so long that the oils are driven off. Seeds like caraway, cumin or celery give more flavour when crushed.

Continued overleaf

	Basic cooking methods	Special points	Herbs and spices*
Leeks	Discard only the coarsest part of the green leaves and white parts. Slit in half or in quarters vertically and rinse well. Cook using conservative method.	Makes a refreshing change from chopped and sautéed onions and is a natural partner to barley, cheese, potatoes, chicken and walnuts.	A little sage, coarsely ground black pepper, basil.
Cauliflowers	All but the coarsest outer leaves can be used. Cook by conservative method, in 1cm (½in) depth water and cut a deep cross in base. Alternatively, break into large florets, including chopped base, and cook in a few spoonfuls water.	A natural partner for cheese or lamb. Use with cheese sauce or any pasta sauce as a light main meal.	Paprika to garnish, ground coriander, nutmeg. Ground caraway or fennel seeds, sprinkled on before browning under grill, will help dispel wind.
Sprouts	As cauliflower florets, cut crosses in the bases and cook for 5 to 8 minutes.	As cauliflower, or purée with equal quantity of potato, and a little milk, pepper, nutmeg and sea salt.	
TUBERS, BULBS AND ROOTS			
Jerusalem artichokes	Peeling is unnecessary – fortunately, as the knobbly skin makes it a chore. Artichokes discolour once they've been cut, so either prepare immediately before cooking or keep them in a shallow dish of water and lemon juice until you're ready to cook them. Discard only the hard tips. Follow beginning of recipe for artichoke chips (page 137)	Best known in Palestine soup – follow same procedure as for carrot and caraway soup (page 74), replacing the carrots with half artichokes and half potatoes. The unique and delicate flavour of artichokes means they are best served plain as a side vegetable. Eat them cautiously as they are notorious wind-raisers.	Generous amount of parsley, cloves, fennel seed (crushed).
Beetroot	Don't cut or peel raw beetroot: the colour and flavour will leak out. Twist off the roots, scrub the beetroot gently and steam them or cook them like carrots and parsnips (page 130) for about 25 minutes, or bake them in the oven like jacket potatoes.	Far tastier and also far cheaper than bought cooked or pickled types. Can be dressed with creamy herb sauce made with yogurt (page 32), and with chives and lemon juice. Sweet, but not as high in calories as people fear: 28 per 100g (4oz).	Chives, dill, lemon juice.
Onions, spring onions and shallots	Bake (page 132) or boil in 2cm (½in) depth water for 20 to 30 minutes, depending on onion size. See also pickled onions and salads.	Large, sweet and bland onions are best for baking or boiling; shallots give tangier flavour, although they don't smell strong, and are better for salads; spring onions are indispensable for Chinese or Japanese cooking.	Black pepper, nutmeg, cloves (stick them in an onion for easy retrieval), cautious amount of sage, oregano.
Swedes	Prepare and cook as in carrots and parsnips (page 130). Serve in small chunks, or mashed alone.	Swedes complement strong-flavoured dishes such as game, lamb and grilled mackerel, and provide good colour too.	Generous amounts of parsley, black pepper and a little allspice.
Turnips	As swedes. Buy young turnips, which are delicious raw or cooked alone.	Young turnips, whole if neat and small, or in quarters if larger, go well in parsley sauce with lamb, or poultry.	As swede, plus nutmeg.
Kohlrabi	Cook as for swedes or turnips. Peeling is not necessary if you choose kohlrabi no bigger than a tennis ball.	Use as turnips and swedes. Attractive purple colour of some specimens, unfortunately, disappears during cooking.	As swede or turnip.
Carrots	Use conservative method; but equally good steamed whole for about 1 hour, or stir-fried. Prone to absorb farm chemicals, so peel unless organically grown or very young.	Along with onions, the most useful vegetable, for colour, versatility and flavour. Cooked or shredded raw, they suit almost any meal.	A touch of ginger (root or ground), nutmeg, marjoram, tarragon.
Celeriac	Needs scrubbing, then peeling if tough. Keep peelings for stock. Discolours when cut, so toss immediately in lemon juice diluted with a little water. Best for salads, but good cooked as for carrots and parsnips (page 130) or served with carrots in chunks or puréed.	As celery, it purées well, to go with dry main courses, such as kebabs.	
Parsnips	Peel if blemished. Cook as in carrots and parnips (page 130) or Jerusalem artichoke chips (page 137).	Ideal alternative to potatoes. Although they taste sweet and starchy, parsnips provide only about 50 calories per 100g (4oz).	Generous amounts of parsley and black pepper, touch of curry powder, coriander, caraway seeds, nutmeg or mace.
Salsify and Scorzonera	Trim and scrub but don't peel, cook as in carrots and parsnips (page 130).	Serve as a first course, cut in short lengths, with a little curd cheese and with flaked almonds on top.	Parsley, rosemary, lemon, thyme.

	Basic cooking methods	Special points	Herbs and spices*
Yams and sweet potatoes	Cook as in carrots and parsnips (page 130), or Jerusalem artichoke chips (page 137).	Sweet potatoes are much sweeter than yams, resembling chestnuts in flavour. Both vegetables suit spiced and curried dishes.	Cinnamon, nutmeg, chopped nuts.
FRUITS			
Marrows, squashes and courgettes	Peel only if the skin is tough. Keep away from water, apart from a few spoonfuls, as in carrots and parsnips (page 130). Cut in large chunks and cook for only 6 to 8 minutes. Best flavour is achieved by tossing cooked chunks in a barely oiled pan for 1 to 3 minutes.	Goes well with rich-tasting dishes, such as sunflower slices (page 142), lamb, herrings and other oily fish and game. Useful for kebabs, as it cooks so quickly and actually benefits from being slightly 'singed'.	Tarragon, rosemary, pepper.
Vegetable spaghetti marrow	Cook whole, covered with water, for 30 to 45 minutes until tender (when pierced with skewer).	The inside of a vegetable spaghetti marrow has long strands, which can be carefully scooped out and used just as the name suggests. It makes an excellent 'bed' for savouries, or can be eaten in a pile with sauce, like pasta.	Nutmeg, basil, rosemary.
PULSES			
Broad beans	Even the pods of very young beans can be eaten. Use conservative method, and if serving in pods, cut in diagonal slices.	They have about 4% protein and 50 calories per 100g (4oz). Use to 'beef up' light protein meals like stir-fried vegetables (page 138) or stuffed vine leaves (page 61). They are also good added to pasta sauces.	Garlic, winter or summer savory, pepper, parsley.
Green beans	Use conservative method. Also good in stir-fried vegetables.	A very versatile vegetable, they go with almost any main course.	Paprika, red pepper, toasted almond flakes, pinch of chili powder.
Mangetout or sugar peas	The flat peapods are so tender you eat them whole. Remove the wiry stalks and tips, and any string between them. Use conservative method or stir-fry (page 138).	Eat with the fingers, sprinkled with a pinch of sea salt, and serve with a side dish of creamy herb sauce (page 32). Goes with almost any main course that won't overwhelm their delicate flavour.	Black pepper.
Peas	Use conservative method, for not more than 4 to 5 minutes. Frozen peas are good just thawed, without cooking, or if adding to a recipe, do so from frozen and allow only 2 to 3 minutes' cooking.	Should be thought of more as an extension of protein food, although they will be moderately rich in vitamin C if very fresh, or frozen and not overcooked. High in fibre.	Black pepper, mint.
MISCELLANEOUS			
Sweetcorn	Cobs need to be very fresh to be sweet. Plunge them, complete with husk, into a 2.5cm (1in) depth of boiling water, cover and simmer for 5 to 10 minutes. Peel off the husk and 'silky' threads. Cobs can also be brushed with oil, then grilled under a medium heat for about 10 minutes, turning 3 times. Barbecued cobs can be wrapped in foil (they can also be baked in foil) to keep moisture in and avoid scorching.	Ideal for adding colour, protein, fibre and flavour to many dishes, particularly other vegetables and grain ones such as rice, which may be delicious but lack visual appeal. If using frozen sweetcorn, add frozen to recipes and allow only 2 to 3 minutes' cooking. Grilled sweetcorn on the cob with toasted ground sesame seed mixed with salt makes a good first course.	Sesame seed, pinch of chili powder, mild mustard.
Globe artichokes	Cut stalk close to body, and soak heads upside down in water. Plunge into a large pan with enough boiling water to cover, and simmer for about 30 minutes. Drain upside down for a few minutes.	Serve as a course on their own, hot with egg and lemon sauce (page 31), or cold with creamy herb sauce (page 32), or with oil and lemon dressing.	
Mushrooms	Do not peel or soak, or discard the stems. Rinse under a tap, scrubbing them gently with a soft brush. Brown, without adding water, in a thick-based pan lightly brushed with oil, for about 5 to 8 minutes.	My favourite vegetable for adding body, in spite of mushrooms' minimal calorie count, to small amounts of meat in a casserole or pie. Add them 10 to 20 minutes before the end of cooking time. Mushrooms complement almost any food, adding a year-round flavour and touch of luxury.	Marjoram, tarragon, black pepper, garlic, coriander and my favourite, cumin.

LIGHT VEGETABLE DISHES

Use these recipes as 'models', adapting them for other vegetables. An occasional meal of three of these dishes, without any meat, can be very refreshing. Try red cabbage, Greek spinach and Jerusalem artichoke chips; or carrots with parsnips, baked onions and Greek spinach.

CARROTS AND PARSNIPS

Root vegetables are sometimes bland, but cooked in this manner they really keep their flavour. *Serves 4.*

225g (8oz) carrots, cut in 1cm (½in) chunks
225g (8oz) parsnips, cut in 1cm (½in) slices
5ml (1 tsp) oil, soft margarine or butter, according to taste
60ml (4 tbsp) water

1 Heat all the ingredients in a thick-based saucepan over a medium-to-high heat until the liquid sizzles.
2 Cover the pan with a tight-fitting lid, turn the heat to minimum and cook for about 20 minutes.
3 By now, the water should have almost evaporated and the vegetables should be tender but firm.

VARIATIONS

Use the same method for *turnips, swedes, leeks, Jerusalem artichokes* or *celeriac*. The cooking time will vary a little with the size of slice and whether the vegetables are young or old, fresh from the garden or bought in a shop. So prod them with a knife every now and then to see whether they are done.

RED CABBAGE

Even better the next day. A natural partner for lamb dishes and grains, especially buckwheat. If you feel like a really light yet filling meal, try a plate of this with a baked onion (page 132) and a little cottage cheese. For a larger meal, use generously to balance small portions of lamb or game. *Serves 5 to 6.*

1 red cabbage, about 700g (1½lb)
1 large onion, chopped
2 large cooking apples, peeled and chopped
10ml (2tsp) margarine or oil
juice of 1 to 2 lemons
2 cloves
4 peppercorns
10ml (2 tsp) honey
sea salt, to taste

Calories About 55 a serving.

- Suitable for diabetics
- Medium fibre
- Very low fat (omitting fat)
- Very low salt (using unsalted fat)
- Milk-free (using oil or dairy-free fat)
- Gluten-free

A pressure cooker can be used for this recipe, taking about 5 minutes and needing a little less liquid. It will keep the nutrients in just as well.

The small amount of added fat enhances the flavour of the vegetables, without increasing the fat content nearly as much as would a good dollop of butter on top of the vegetables when they are served.

Calories About 70 to 80 a serving.

- Suitable for diabetics
- Medium fibre
- Very low fat
- Very low salt (omitting salt)
- Milk-free
- Gluten-free

If you feel like a really light yet filling meal, try a plate of this with a baked onion (page 132) and a little cottage cheese. For a larger meal, use generously to balance small portions of lamb or game.

Red cabbage, its brightness kept with lemon juice

1 Boil a large kettle of water.
2 Meanwhile, shred the cabbage finely into a large heatproof bowl.
3 Pour the boiling water over the cabbage and leave for 1 minute. Drain.
4 Heat the oil in a large saucepan and cook the onion gently, covered, for about 8 minutes. Add the apples, the drained cabbage and all the other ingredients, except for half of the lemon juice.
5 Stir, bring to the boil, cover and simmer over the lowest heat for about 1¼ hours. Remove the cloves and peppercorns. Check the seasoning and add the reserved lemon juice if you feel the dish needs it.

AUBERGINES WITH SESAME

A Japanese style of serving vegetables – although simple, it brings out the flavour well. *Serves 4 to 5.*

2 large aubergines
30ml (2 tbsp) sesame seeds
4 spring onions, chopped fairly finely
1ml (¼ tsp) paprika
30ml (2 tbsp) soya sauce
15ml (1 tbsp) water
5ml (1 tsp) sherry
2ml (½ tsp) honey

1 Heat the grill. Brush the grill pan lightly with oil.

Calories About 65 to 75 a serving.

• Suitable for diabetics
• Medium fibre
• Very low fat (reducing sesame seeds to 10ml [2 tsp])
• Milk-free
• Gluten-free (using tamari instead of soya sauce)

Sesame seed is usually thought of as a pretty garnish only, but its protein, oil, fibre and calcium content should be appreciated. Sesame makes an important contribution to the Japanese diet. The seeds must be crushed to release both flavour and food value.

2 Cut the aubergines in slices 2cm (¾in) thick, and place them on the grill pan.
3 Grill the slices at a medium to high heat for 5 minutes on each side.
4 Meanwhile, toast the sesame seeds in an ungreased, thick-based pan over a low heat until they start to 'jump' and change colour a little. Then crush three-quarters of them in a pestle and mortar or coffee grinder. Mix the crushed sesame seeds with the whole ones.
5 Stir the crushed seeds, spring onions, paprika, soya sauce, water, sherry and honey in a saucepan set over a fairly low heat for about 2 to 3 minutes, until the mixture is hot.
6 Arrange the grilled aubergine slices on a serving dish. Spoon the sesame seed mixture over them.

VARIATIONS

You can substitute *halved courgettes* or *tomatoes* for the aubergines.

BAKED ONIONS

One of the easiest and most delicious vegetable dishes. Make a meal of one, with cottage cheese and some cress. *Serves 4.*

4 large onions, unpeeled
10ml (2 tsp) any fat or oil
150ml (¼ pint) stock
Cottage cheese or Cheddar cheese, grated, to taste
black pepper or paprika, to taste

Calories About 50 a serving. If using cheese, add about 25 calories per 25g (1oz) for cottage cheese, 85 per 25g (1oz) for Cheddar cheese.

Baked onions with cottage cheese and paprika

- Suitable for diabetics
- Medium fibre
- Very low fat (unless using Cheddar cheese)
- Very low salt (using unsalted cheese)
- Gluten-free

A great dish for slimmers. Use instead of baked potatoes to cut calories.

Onions, like garlic, have been shown to encourage blood fat levels to fall after rich meals.

Calories About 190 a serving.

- Suitable for diabetics
- Medium fibre

Protein comes from the mushrooms, wheat, milk, watercress and eggs. Watercress, a true superfood, is particularly rich in carotene (for making vitamin A), folic acid (a B vitamin), vitamin E, iron, calcium and fibre, as well as a range of other B vitamins and minerals.

Calories About 75 a serving as a main dish; 40 to 50 a serving as a side dish.

1 Heat the oven to 150°C (300°F) gas mark 2.
2 Cut the roots from the onions but do not peel them. Sit them in a baking dish, brush them with the oil and pour stock around them.
3 Bake for about 1½ hours, depending on size. To test whether an onion is done, squeeze it gently between a finger and thumb; it should give slightly.
4 To eat, cut back the brown skin and sprinkle the tops with a little cottage cheese or grated Cheddar cheese plus black pepper or paprika.

WATERCRESS AND MUSHROOM SOUFFLÉ

This soufflé is really easy to make and people like it. Provided you can get your guests to table a few minutes before your soufflé is ready, you should have no problems with it. *Serves 4.*

25g (1oz) soft margarine
100g (4oz) mushrooms
1 clove of garlic (optional), crushed
50g (2oz) plain wholemeal flour
300ml (½ pint) skimmed milk
good pinch of sea salt
10ml (2 tsp) mild mustard
generous pinch of ground nutmeg
1 bunch watercress, including stalks, finely chopped
3 eggs, separated, and 1 extra white

1 Heat the oven to 190°C (375°F), gas mark 5. Grease 4 individual soufflé or casserole dishes, or 1 larger soufflé dish, lightly with oil.
2 Melt the margarine in a large saucepan set over a low heat. Slice the mushrooms and add them to the pan with the garlic if you are using it. Cook them, uncovered, for about 4 to 5 minutes.
3 Stir in the flour.
4 Remove the pan from the heat and smoothly work in the milk.
5 Return the pan to a moderate heat. Stir the mixture constantly until it boils. It should become thick enough to form a ball.
6 Remove the pan from the heat again. Add salt, mustard, nutmeg and watercress.
7 Beat in one egg yolk at a time.
8 Beat the egg whites until they are stiff. Fold them into the mixture.
9 Divide the mixture between the greased soufflé dishes.
10 Bake individual soufflés for 20 to 25 minutes, until they have risen and are beginning to brown. If you use a single larger soufflé dish, bake for 30 minutes. Serve immediately.

RATATOUILLE

The taste of the Mediterranean, without the oil that tends to swamp restaurant versions. One of the vegetable dishes I am happy to treat as a main course, especially if it is served with pancakes or plain rice. *Serves 4 as a main course, 6 to 7 as a starter or side dish.*

• Suitable for diabetics
• Medium fibre
• Very low fat
• Very low salt (omitting salt)
• Milk-free
• Gluten-free

Peppers, especially green ones, have more vitamin C than oranges.

10ml (2 tsp) oil or soft margarine
2 large onions, sliced
1 green pepper, sliced
1 large aubergine, cut in small chunks
4 courgettes or ½ small marrow, cut in small chunks
275g (10oz) tomatoes, chopped
2 cloves of garlic, crushed
large pinch of basil
freshly ground black pepper
pinch of sea salt
30ml (2 tbsp) parsley, chopped

1 Heat the fat in a large saucepan set over a low heat, add the sliced onion and cook, covered, for about 10 minutes, or until it is transparent.
2 Add the pepper and the aubergine and cook, still covered, for another 5 minutes.
3 Add the courgettes and tomatoes, cover the pan again, and simmer the mixture gently for 30 minutes.
4 Mix the garlic and basil with the pepper and salt. Add to the mixture in the pan and simmer for 5 minutes more.
5 By now the mixture should be fairly wet and the vegetables should have blended into each other. If not, simmer for 10 minutes longer.
6 Stir in the parsley.
7 Serve hot, as a pancake filling, a topping for baked potatoes or a side dish; or cold, as a first course with wholemeal bread.

CARROT RING

A light main course or a good side dish. The vegetables keep their lovely fresh colours. *Serves 4.*

Calories About 130 to 140 a serving. Add about 10 extra calories a serving if using almonds.

• Suitable for diabetics
• High fibre (especially if using peas)
• Gluten-free

Provides vegetable fibre and some protein, especially if using peas, and the meal should also contain some cereal fibre, for instance from a side dish of buckwheat or rice. A useful main course to follow a substantial starter like chicken liver pâté (page 58), cheese soufflés (page 68) or fish terrine (page 65).

5ml (1tsp) oil or butter
1 medium onion, finely chopped
700g (1½lb) carrots, peeled and roughly sliced
75ml (3fl oz) chicken or other stock
scant 5ml (1 tsp) honey
100g (4oz) peas or courgettes cut in slices
15ml (1 tbsp) flaked almonds or some leaves of fresh tarragon or chervil, to garnish
2 eggs
50g (2oz) curd cheese
10ml (2 tsp) fresh tarragon, chopped, or 5ml (1 tsp) dried tarragon
1ml (¼ tsp) pepper
good grating of nutmeg
good pinch of sea salt

1 Heat the oil or butter in a saucepan set over a low heat. Add the chopped onion and cook it, covered, for 10 minutes.
2 Add the carrots. Stir them over the heat for 2 minutes, then add the stock and the honey. Cover the pan again and cook over a low heat for 20 minutes, checking after 10 that the carrots have not dried out.

Carrot ring with creamy herb sauce (page 32)

3 Now add the peas or courgettes and cook for a further 5 minutes.
4 Drain any excess water (keeping it for stock), and put the vegetables through the coarse cutter of a mincer, vegetable mill or food processor.
5 Heat the oven to 190°C (375°F), gas mark 5.
6 Grease a 1050ml (1½ pint) ring mould thoroughly, and sprinkle it lightly with your choice of flaked almonds, tarragon leaves or fronds of chervil, which will give the carrot ring a decorative garnish when it is turned out. If you like, arrange the garnish to make a symmetrical pattern in the mould.
7 Whisk together the eggs, curd cheese, tarragon, pepper, nutmeg and sea salt.
8 Stir into the vegetable mixture. Spoon the mixture into the mould, being careful not to dislodge your decorations. Tap the mould firmly on a wooden board to shake the mixture down well. Cover the mould with kitchen foil.
9 Place the mould in a baking tin and pour hot water into the tin to reach half-way up the mould. Bake for about 40 minutes, until the ring is firm.
10 Turn the carrot ring out carefully, as it is fairly fragile. Serve with a small bowl containing creamy herb sauce (page 32) or cheese sauce (page 28), placed in the centre of the ring.

Calories About 170 to 225 a serving.

• Suitable for diabetics
• Medium fibre

A way of keeping soufflés lower in fat, without any sacrifice of flavour, by using egg whites rather than yolks. Match with a starter or dessert that is high in fibre.

VEGETARIAN DINNER MENU

Spring rice salad **200 cals**

— • —

Vegetable soufflé **200 cals**
Artichoke chips **20 cals**

— • —

Miriam's cheesecake **230 cals**

Total calories per person **650**

Calories About 28 each; about 112 a serving.

• Suitable for diabetics
• Medium fibre
• Very low fat (omitting egg yolk)
• Very low salt (omitting salt)
• Milk-free
• Gluten-free (using potato or rice flour)

VEGETABLE SOUFFLÉ

A light, appetizing main dish that works beautifully. Vary the vegetables according to what's in your refrigerator. Drained leftover stir-fried vegetables, with their note of ginger, are excellent. Don't purée the vegetables, just chop into pieces roughly 5mm (¼in) long. *Serves 3 to 4.*

25g (1oz) soft margarine or butter
22ml (1½ tbsp) plain wholemeal flour
150ml (¼ pint) skimmed milk
50g (2oz) mature Cheddar cheese, grated
1ml (¼ tsp) paprika
1ml (¼ tsp) pepper
pinch of sea salt
1 egg, separated, and 2 extra whites
175g (6oz) lightly cooked vegetables, shredded

1 Heat the oven to 190°C (375°F), gas mark 5.
2 Grease well a soufflé or casserole dish big enough for the mixture to fill it only two-thirds full. If you have to use a smaller dish, make a collar for it from a double band of greaseproof paper or baking parchment. Use string to fasten the collar round the dish so that is rises about 10cm (4in) above the rim. Grease the inner surface of the collar thoroughly.
3 Melt the fat in a large saucepan, set over a low heat, then stir in the flour smoothly.
4 Remove the pan from the heat and gradually work in the milk.
5 Return to a gentle heat, and stir steadily as the mixture thickens. Cook until it is thick enough to leave the sides of the pan in a ball as you stir.
6 Stir in the cheese and the seasoning. Beat in the egg yolk. Stir in the vegetables.
7 Beat the egg whites until they are very stiff. Using a metal spoon or spatula, fold them into the vegetable mixture.
8 Pour the mixture into the soufflé dish and bake for 35 minutes. Serve at once.

LATKES

The easy way to make potato pancakes – no grating and no soaking, and another example of blender magic. Makes tender, tasty little pancakes. I have given small quantities, because this batter won't keep. If not used within 30 minutes, it turns dark and needs to be thrown away. If you don't need all the mix at once, turn it into pancakes and chill or freeze until wanted. Serve plain or with apple sauce or cottage cheese. Eat with the fingers. *Makes 12; serves 3.*

225g (8oz) potatoes
1 egg
generous 15ml (1 tbsp) plain wholemeal flour
pinch of sea salt
½ small onion, roughly chopped
good pinch of mixed dried herbs (optional)

1 Chop the potatoes. Place all the ingredients in the goblet of a blender and blend until smooth.

2 Heat a thick-based pan, preferably cast-iron, and brush it with oil or butter.
3 From the blender goblet, pour on small pats of the mixture to make 5cm (2in) diameter pancakes. Reduce the heat to fairly low and cook them on each side for 3 or 4 minutes.

VARIATIONS

Add *a pinch of celery seed, crushed caraway seed* or *cumin seed* to mix. By omitting the soaking of grated potatoes common in latke recipes, you retain more nutritional value, and I find the results just as tasty and light.

GREEK SPINACH

This has been included simply to illustrate how to cook spinach with no water added other than that lingering on the leaves after washing. It's delicious. *Serves 4.*

½ clove of garlic (optional)
450g (1lb) fresh spinach leaves
25g (1oz) pine nuts (optional)
1 lemon

1 Rub a large saucepan with garlic, if you like the flavour.
2 Wash the spinach thoroughly, then place it immediately, with the water still dripping off the leaves, in the saucepan.
3 Cook uncovered on a medium-to-high heat until you hear it sizzling, then reduce the heat to minimum, cover the pan and continue to cook for about 6 minutes until the spinach is just tender and a brilliant green. (The time needed may be a little longer or shorter, depending on the thickness of the spinach stems, and also on the shape of the saucepan.) Stir in pine nuts if you are using them.
4 Serve immediately with wedges of lemon, to be squeezed over the spinach.

JERUSALEM ARTICHOKE CHIPS

This method works just as well with parsnips, potatoes and turnips. *Serves 2.*

225g (8oz) Jerusalem artichokes, scrubbed but not peeled.

1 Heat a few tablespoons of water in a tightly lidded pan. Add the whole artichokes, cover the pan again and cook the vegetables over a low heat for about 15 to 20 minutes, until tender.
2 Heat the oven to 220°C (425°F), gas mark 7. Grease a baking sheet fairly generously.
3 Remove the vegetables from the pan, saving the liquid for stock.
4 Cut the artichokes into long thick pieces.
5 Spread the artichoke pieces on the baking sheet. Bake them for about 10 to 15 minutes, until they have a roasted appearance. Turn them once during baking.

Calories About 40 a serving.

- Suitable for diabetics
- Medium fibre
- Very low fat
- Very low salt
- Milk-free
- Gluten-free

The fame of spinach as a superfood has been much jibed at in recent years. It's true that most of the iron cannot easily be absorbed, but here, teamed with lemon juice, it offers you the best chance of doing so, as the vitamin C in the juice helps iron absorption. I still think spinach is in the top league for food value, because it contributes so much carotene (for making vitamin A), B vitamins, vitamin C and vitamin E, as well as a surprisingly high level of protein, calcium and assorted minerals.

Calories About 20 a serving using Jerusalem artichokes; 63 using parsnips, 90 using potatoes; 16 using turnips.

- Suitable for diabetics
- Medium fibre
- Very low salt
- Milk-free
- Gluten-free

Deep frying won't hurt anyone occasionally, but it's a method of the past, partly because it's expensive to replace oil with every use, while straining and storing large amounts are not practical for occasional use. What is more, oil that has been re-used several times for deep frying at high temperatures is suspected of breaking down with new chemical compounds forming that may be unhealthy.

Stir-Fried Vegetables

Calories About 125 a serving as a side dish; about 225 a serving as a main dish.

- Suitable for diabetics
- Medium fibre
- Very low fat
- Very low salt (omitting salt and soya sauce)
- Milk-free
- Gluten-free

You don't need a wok to benefit from this Chinese method of cooking vegetables. The vegetables retain both crunchiness and more vitamins because they have not suffered long cooking in water. This makes a good main dish to follow a substantial first course such as chicken liver pâté (page 58) or, accompanied by a little plain rice, on its own, to provide a low-calorie meal.

Stir-fried vegetables with cashew nuts

One of my favourite quick meals. Cashew nuts go perfectly with it, although almonds are good too. Substitute other vegetables for the ones used here, but keep an eye open for good colour mix. *Serves 4 as a side dish, 2 as a main dish.*

15ml (1 tbsp) oil
1 2.5cm (1in) length of root ginger, cut in slivers
1 clove of garlic (optional), crushed
1 large carrot, thinly sliced
about 100g (4oz) cauliflower, broken into very small florets
175g (6oz) spring greens or cabbage, chopped into 2.5cm (1in) lengths
large pinch of chili powder
5ml (1 tsp) clear honey
10ml (2 tsp) soya sauce
150ml (¼ pint) well-flavoured stock
10ml (2 tsp) wine vinegar
5ml (1 tsp) sesame seeds, crushed
pinch of sea salt
5ml (1 tsp) cornflour
100g (4oz) beanshoots, rinsed under a tap
50g (2oz) cashew nuts, whole or in pieces, toasted under a low grill for a few minutes

CHINESE SUPPER MENU

Crispy prawn fingers **180 cals**
— • —
*Stir-fried vegetables with
cashew nuts* **225 cals**
Won ton **170 cals**
Brown rice **100 cals**
— • —
Sliced fresh fruit **60 cals**

Total calories per person **735**

Calories About 155 a serving.

• Suitable for diabetics
• Medium fibre
• Very low fat (omitting egg yolk)
• Very low salt (using low-salt yeast extract and cheese, and omitting salt and egg white)
• Gluten-free (using gluten-free breadcrumbs)

A fairly low-protein main course, this would go well with a high-protein first course, like humus (page 56) or taramasalata (page 55), served with dippers such as pieces of pitta bread and raw vegetables.

1 Heat the oil in a large frying pan or wok. Add the ginger and garlic and cook, uncovered over a medium heat, for 30 seconds. Add the carrot and continue to cook, stirring, for 2 to 3 minutes.
2 Add the cauliflower and cook for another 2 to 3 minutes, then the spring greens or cabbage and cook for a further 2 to 3 minutes (about 7 to 8 minutes' cooking in total). Stir in the chili powder.
3 Combine the honey, soya sauce, stock, vinegar, sesame seeds, sea salt and cornflour.
4 Pour this mixture over the vegetables, cover the pan and simmer for 3 minutes.
5 Add the beanshoots and cook for 1 more minute.
6 Serve with the cashew nuts sprinkled on top.

SUBSTANTIAL VEGETABLE DISHES

Some people will never accept that a vegetable can make a main course – then they'll happily tuck in to cauliflower cheese. Here are some more to build into your repertoire of familiar standards. Presentation is important, hence the use of moulds, which give a professional look to the meal and more confidence to the person eating it for the first time.

Note how light some of these dishes are in calories, and remember that you don't need a lot of protein at every meal.

AUBERGINE ROAST

There is a very 'meaty' feeling to this recipe so it's a good one when you want a light, meatless meal to serve to the carnivorous. *Serves 4.*

about 225g (8oz) aubergine (1 medium)
3 sticks of celery
1 medium onion or 3 shallots
10ml (2 tsp) butter
1 tomato, chopped
2ml (½ tsp) mixed dried herbs
5ml (1 tsp) ground allspice
2ml (½ tsp) yeast extract
1 egg
50g (2oz) wholemeal breadcrumbs
15ml (1 tbsp) wheat germ
225g (8oz) low-fat soft cheese, smooth or cottage
pinch each of pepper and sea salt

1 Heat the oven to 220°C (425°F), gas mark 7. Thoroughly grease a loaf tin, ring mould or other attractively shaped mould.
2 Put the aubergine, celery and onion or shallots through the fine blade of a mincer, or mince them in a food processor.
3 Melt the butter in a large, thick-based saucepan, set over a low heat. Add the minced vegetables and the chopped tomato, cover the pan and sweat the mixture for about 10 minutes, until the liquid has disappeared

and the onion is fairly soft. Add the herbs and the allspice.

4 Remove the vegetable mixture from the heat. Mix in the yeast extract and then the egg, breadcrumbs, wheat germ and soft cheese. Add the seasoning.

5 Pour the mixture into the greased mould. Bake for 30 minutes, or until firm. Turn the roast out. The texture of this dish is fairly dry, so serve it with tomato sauce (page 29) or a puréed vegetable.

WINTER PIE

Use whatever vegetables are in season, including some root vegetables. *Serves 4.*

1 mix of millet-cheese topping (page 262)
700g (1½lb) mixed vegetables, roughly chopped
150ml (¼ pint) cider or stock
sprig of thyme or 2ml (½ tsp) dried thyme
100g (4oz) quark or other low-fat soft cheese
30ml (2 tbsp) mature Cheddar cheese, grated
10ml (2 tsp) sesame seeds

1 Heat the oven to 190°C (375°F), gas mark 5.

2 Bring the vegetables to the boil in the cider or stock with the thyme, then simmer, covered, over a low heat for 8 minutes. Drain, reserving any liquid for stock.

3 Transfer the vegetables to a shallow ovenproof casserole and stir in the quark.

4 Spoon the millet mixture on top, sprinkle with the cheese and the sesame seeds and bake for 30 minutes.

COURGETTE BAKE

Not grand fare, but tasty. You can use other quick-cooking vegetables, such as mushrooms or leeks, in the same way. *Serves 5.*

5ml (1 tsp) oil
4 large courgettes, sliced
30ml (2 tbsp) water
175g (6oz) wholemeal bread, fresh or stale
450ml (¾ pint) skimmed milk
2 eggs
100g (4oz) mature Cheddar cheese
pepper, to taste
about 5ml (1 tsp) dried rosemary, powdered in your fingers
about 2ml (½ tsp) mild mustard
1 egg, hard-boiled and sliced
paprika to garnish

1 Heat the oven to 190°C (375°F), gas mark 5.

2 Brush a thick-based pan with the oil, heat it and add the sliced courgettes. Add the water, cover and cook over a low heat for 5 to 6 minutes, until the courgettes are tender, but still crunchy.

Calories About 240 a serving. Allow an extra 14 a serving if using cider.

- Suitable for diabetics
- High fibre
- Gluten-free

Calories About 210 a serving.

- Suitable for diabetics
- High fibre
- Gluten-free (using gluten-free breadcrumbs)

A surprisingly high level of protein, adding up the contributions from bread, milk, eggs and cheese.

3 Soak the bread in the milk until it is soft. Alternatively, mix the bread and milk in a blender, and transfer to a bowl.
4 Beat in the eggs and crumble in the cheese in small nuggets.
5 Season the mixture well, adding more rosemary or mustard to taste.
6 Pour a third of this mixture into an ovenproof dish. Place the sliced hard-boiled egg on top, then half of the courgettes.
7 Repeat the layers of bread mixture and courgettes, then top with the last third of the bread mixture.
8 Sprinkle paprika generously on top and bake for 35 minutes.

MUSHROOM FLAN

My enthusiasm for mushrooms shows throughout this book: here's another way of getting their flavour at its best. *Serves 4.*

1 mix of wholemeal shortcrust pastry (page 257)
175g (6oz) mushrooms, roughly sliced*
10ml (2 tsp) oil or soft margarine
15ml (1 tbsp) plain wholemeal flour
15ml (1 tbsp) soya flour
150ml (¼ pint) stock or water
pinch of mixed herbs
5ml (1 tsp) vegetable concentrate
25g (1oz) chopped walnuts
1 Weetabix or similar wheat cereal biscuit

*If you use a large flan tin, you may need 225g (8oz) mushrooms, with the remaining ingredients staying the same.

1 Heat the oven to 200°C (400°F), gas mark 6.
2 Line a 20cm (8in) flan tin with the pastry. Pinch the edges decoratively. If you have time, place the prepared tin in a refrigerator, for the pastry to rest, while you prepare the filling. But if you are in a hurry, you can bake the flan case straight away.
3 Sweat the mushrooms, uncovered, in the oil or margarine for about 6 minutes, until most of the liquid has disappeared.
4 Meanwhile, in a saucepan, mix the wholemeal and soya flour with enough of the stock or water to make a smooth paste. Stir in the remaining stock and heat the mixture to boiling point. Simmer for 4 to 5 minutes.
5 Remove the pan from the heat and flavour the mixture to taste with the herbs and the vegetable concentrate (you'll need a little more if using water rather than stock). Stir in the walnuts and the cereal biscuit. Add this mixture to the mushroom pan and simmer for 2 minutes more.
6 Place greaseproof paper or kitchen foil in the pastry shell and weight it with dried beans or pasta. Bake for 15 minutes.
7 Remove the pastry case from the oven and pour in the mushroom mixture. Return the filled case to the oven and bake for 5 minutes, or until the pastry is crisp and the mixture well heated.

VARIATIONS

Use *sliced fennel*, *leeks*, or *onions* instead of the mushrooms, allowing about *275g (10oz)* of each.

Calories About 270 a serving. If using an extra large tin, add 4 calories for extra mushrooms; if using fennel, leeks or onions, add 10 calories each.

• High fibre
• Very low salt (using oil, unsalted vegetable concentrate and shredded wheat instead of Weetabix)
• Milk-free (using oil and dairy-free fat for pastry)

The inescapable high fat content of shortcrust pastry is here balanced to some extent by the low-fat filling. When making up any flan or quiche recipe, the fat can be reduced by using skimmed milk and a little less cheese than specified, and by omitting one egg yolk from the recipe.

VEGETARIAN MENU

Humus **115 cals**
with and toast dippers **80 cals**

— • —

Courgette bake **215 cals**
Mushroom sauce **115 cals**
Carrots and watercress
100 cals

— • —

Dutch apple ice **105 cals**

Total calories per person **730**

Calories About 110 a serving if using yogurt and egg white. Add another 45 a serving if using soured cream.

- Suitable for diabetics
- Medium fibre
- Gluten-free (using rice flour)

Mushrooms should not be peeled, just washed with a soft brush under running water. The stalks are just as good as the caps.

Served on a bed of spinach, this makes a good low-calorie main course. Mushrooms are not rich in vitamin C, so a green salad or fresh fruit should accompany the meal.

MUSHROOMS IN SOURED CREAM

An easy way of turning rice, pasta or a flan into a treat. *Serves 4.*

25g (1oz) soft margarine or butter
1 onion, finely chopped
450g (1lb) mushrooms, caps and stalks, washed but not peeled
2ml (½ tsp) Worcestershire sauce
15ml (1 tbsp) plain wholemeal flour
5ml (1 tsp) paprika
freshly ground black pepper
150ml (¼ pint) smetana, soured cream or yogurt mixed with 1 egg white
cumin, to taste

1 Heat the fat in a fairly large saucepan set over a low heat, add the onion and cook it, covered, for about 10 minutes, until it is transparent.
2 Add the mushrooms (button mushrooms whole and others in quarters) with the Worcestershire sauce.
3 Cook for 3 minutes. Stir in the flour and the peppers. Remove the pan from the heat.
4 Stir in the smetana, soured cream or yogurt mixed with egg white.
5 Place the saucepan containing the mushroom mixture over another saucepan of boiling water. Cook very gently, stirring steadily and not allowing the sauce to come to the boil, until it thickens. Continue to cook for another 5 minutes.
6 Add cumin to taste. Serve over rice, bulgur wheat, pasta or in a pastry case, such as a choux ring (page 257).

SUNFLOWER SLICES

Leeks have a slightly buttery taste even when unbuttered – take advantage of their flavour in this filling and simple savoury that's ideal for a lunch-box as well as for serving at home. *Serves 3.*

50g (2oz) sunflower seeds
5ml (1 tsp) oil
2 leeks, both white and green parts, finely chopped
1 carrot, grated
75g (3oz) wholemeal breadcrumbs
1 egg
2ml (½ tsp) vegetable concentrate
45ml (3 tbsp) parsley, chopped
pinch each of thyme, marjoram and basil
juice of ½ lemon
a little stock or water, to bind

Calories About 200 a serving.

- Suitable for diabetics
- Medium fibre
- Very low salt (using unsalted or low-salt vegetable concentrate, low-sodium bread and egg yolk only)

For maximum value, use the green as well as the white parts of the leeks, since the tops are much richer in vitamin C. Sunflower seeds are similar to nuts in terms of food value, but much higher in protein and vitamin E, as well as containing B vitamins and fibre. Because of their high oil content, even though it's of the polyunsaturated kind, sunflower slices are too high in fat and calories to be eaten in large amounts.

1 Stir the sunflower seeds in an ungreased thick-based pan set over a low heat for 2 to 3 minutes to brown a little.
2 Heat the oil, add the leeks and carrot, cover the pan and soften the vegetables for about 8 to 10 minutes.
3 Heat the oven to 180°C (350°F), gas mark 4. Grease a small loaf tin.

Sunflower slices – good for lunch-boxes

4 Mix all the ingredients together, checking the seasoning and adding enough of the stock or water to make a moist mix.
5 Transfer the mixture to the tin. The mix is fairly solid, so if you have to use a tin that is too large for the quantity, the mixture can simply be stacked at one end of the loaf tin and will stay there while it is being cooked.
6 Bake for 40 minutes. Cut in slices to serve.

STELK

One of many Irish ways of making potatoes good enough for a meal on their own. This dish is also made with chives, when it is known as champ. *Serves 4 as a side dish, 2 as a main course.*

Calories About 140 a serving as a side dish; about 280 a serving as a main dish.

- Suitable for diabetics
- Medium fibre
- Very low fat (using low-fat cheese)
- Very low salt (using unsalted cheese)
- Gluten-free

Make a meal of this with a complementary vegetable such as carrots with parsnips (page 130).

450g (1lb) potatoes
1 bunch of spring onions, both white and green parts, chopped in 1cm (½in) lengths
150ml (¼ pint) skimmed or semi-skimmed milk
white pepper
pinch of sea salt
100g (4oz) curd cheese

1 Boil or steam the unpeeled potatoes. Drain them, keeping any water for stock.

2 Simmer the spring onions in the milk for about 5 minutes.
3 Strain off the milk, and use some or all (depending on the type of potatoes) to mash the potatoes to a smooth mix.
4 Add back the spring onions. Season the mixture.
5 Serve each helping with a dollop of curd cheese, to be stirred in at table.

VARIATION

You can use this mix as the basis of bubble-and-squeak. Add some *cooked chopped cabbage*, then spread a layer of the mixture on a lightly oiled, hot, thick-based pan set over a low heat. Cook for several minutes on each side, until it is well browned. Serve cut into wedges, with a dollop of curd cheese per person.

GNOCCHI ALLA PIEMONTESE

How to cook potatoes to get a completely different dish, with these delicately flavoured dumplings. Take care not to overcook them, or they'll tend to break up. *Makes about 20; serves 4.*

450g (1lb) floury potatoes
1 egg
about 50g (2oz) plain wholemeal flour
sea salt
25g (1oz) Parmesan cheese, grated
parsley, chopped
75ml (3fl oz) soured cream or smetana or quark
10ml (2 tsp) fresh basil, chopped, or 5ml (1 tsp) dried basil
grating of nutmeg

1 Boil the unpeeled potatoes for about 20 to 25 minutes, until they are well done.
2 Take them out, reserving the water. Peel the potatoes and mash or sieve them.
3 Add the egg, flour and salt. Knead to make a soft dough.
4 Bring the potato water back to the boil with extra water to make a full pan. Heat the oven to 220°C (425°F), gas mark 7.
5 Pinch off pieces of the dough and roll them into walnut-sized balls.
6 Drop the gnocchi into the boiling water. Reduce the heat so that the water simmers gently.
7 Cook the gnocchi for 3 minutes, by which time they will have risen to the surface. Lift them out with a slotted spoon and transfer them to an ovenproof casserole.
8 Mix the Parmesan, parsley and soured cream, smetana or soft cheese, thin the mixture with a little milk if it is too thick, then spoon it over the dumplings. Sprinkle with the basil and nutmeg.
9 Briefly heat the gnocchi through in the hot oven.

BAKED POTATOES

Stop thinking of potatoes only as a side dish and make a meal of them, treating them as a versatile base in the same way as pasta, pancakes or rice. *Serves 4.*

Calories About 210 a serving. If using soured cream, add about 15 calories a serving.

• Suitable for diabetics
• Medium fibre
• Very low fat (omitting Parmesan and using low-fat smetana or quark)
• Very low salt (omitting egg white, salt and Parmesan)

This is best with a high-protein first course that has a contrasting texture, such as herb platter (page 64), and if it is served with a generous mixed salad.

herb platter (page 64)

SUNDAY LUNCH MENU

Poor man's caviare with wholemeal toast **90 cals**
— • —
Roast chicken or game **200 cals**
Baked potatoes **150 cals**
Carrots and parsnips **55 cals**
Broccoli or green vegetables **30 cals**
Gravy **40 cals**
— • —
Apple strudel **240 cals**
Natural low-fat yogurt **60 cals**

Total calories per person **865**

Calories Potatoes contain only about 25 per 25g (1oz). Even a really huge baked potato weighing about 275g (10oz) has only 250 calories. For the calorie count for the fillings, see the relevant recipes.

• Suitable for diabetics
• High fibre (if skins are eaten)
• Fat, salt, milk and gluten content depends on filling used (see relevant recipes)

A 225g (8oz) baked potato contributes about a tenth of the average adult daily protein need, and an eighth of the estimated fibre need. Potatoes are particularly rich in potassium, the element that balances sodium in controlling body fluid. Potato-based diets are very effective in encouraging the dispersion of excess fluid.

Baked potatoes with tjatziki (page 59) and sweetcorn stuffings

4 potatoes, small for use as a side dish, large as a meal base

Toppings

cottage cheese with chives, parsley or other chopped herbs

yogurt with chopped herbs

humus (page 56) with chopped salad

Waldorf dip (page 57)

mushrooms in soured cream (page 142)

pesto sauce (page 32) and salad

creamy herb sauce (page 32)

flaked smoked fish and grated cucumber

tjatziki (page 59)

sweetcorn and chopped celery with toasted, crushed sesame seed dhal (page 115)

beansprouts with creamy herb sauce (page 32)

red cabbage (page 130)

ratatouille (page 133)

any kind of salad with a favourite dressing

1 Heat the oven to 220°C (425°F), gas mark 7.
2 For crunchy-skinned potatoes, just scrub, prick with a fork to avoid the

occasional burst and place them on the oven rack. For softer skins, wrap the potatoes in kitchen foil or brush them lightly with oil, then prick.

3 Bake for about 50 minutes to 1½ hours, depending on size. You can speed up baking by putting a metal skewer through the potatoes, so that the heat is conducted to the centres. To test whether a potato is done, pierce it with a skewer; if the skewer goes in easily, the potato is cooked through.

4 Prepare the filling while the potatoes are baking, so they can be stuffed when they are ready. Cut a slit or cross in the top of the potato and squeeze the sides of the potato so that the top is pushed open. Push the flesh aside with a fork to make room for the filling, or remove some potatoes to mash with the filling.

PASTI

A main dish from the home of pasta, but rather lighter and more delicate. With a sauce and a salad, it's a complete meal. *Makes about 15; serves 4 to 5.*

Pasti – spinach and cheese dumplings – with almond topping

Calories About 215 to 270 a serving.

- Suitable for diabetics
- Medium fibre
- Gluten-free (using gluten-free breadcrumbs)

Eggs, cheese and wheat contribute the protein. Balance with a crunchy-textured, vitamin-rich salad.

VEGETARIAN LUNCH MENU

Watercress and pear salad **100 cals**
Carrot salad with walnut dressing **80 cals**

— • —

Pasti **270 cals**
Creamy herb sauce **50 cals**
Mixed salad **100 cals**

— • —

Baked apples **120 cals**

Total calories per person **720**

5ml (1 tsp) oil

1 clove of garlic (optional)

175g (6oz) fresh spinach, cooked, well drained and finely chopped, or frozen chopped spinach

about 5ml (1 tsp) dried rosemary, pulverized

about 1ml (¼ tsp) each marjoram, thyme, white pepper

3 eggs, separated

175g (6oz) cottage cheese

75g (3oz) Parmesan or mature Cheddar, grated

50g (2oz) wholemeal breadcrumbs

good pinch of sea salt

75g (3oz) plain wholemeal flour

1 Heat the oil in a saucepan set over a low heat. If you are using garlic, stir it in the oil for a few minutes.
2 Add the spinach and all of the herbs. If you are using frozen spinach, add it frozen.
3 Cook the mixture for several minutes, stirring occasionally. Remove from the heat.
4 Add the egg yolks to the spinach, then stir in the cottage cheese, grated cheese, breadcrumbs and salt. The mixture should be fairly firm – if not, add some more breadcrumbs.
5 Beat the egg whites until they are stiff. Fold them into the spinach mixture.
6 Bring a wide saucepan of water to the boil.
7 Place the flour in a bowl. Using a tablespoon, scoop up golf ball-sized rounds of the mixture. Drop them into the flour, turning them carefully just to coat them lightly. Drop them into the boiling water.
8 Bring the water back to the boil, then slightly reduce the heat under the saucepan. Cook the pasti balls for 10 minutes. Lift the balls out in a slotted spoon.
9 Place them in a heatproof dish and keep them warm until they are needed. Serve with mushroom sauce (page 107) or creamy herb sauce (page 32). Alternatively, sprinkle them with *greated cheese* and *flaked almonds*, and brown the topping quickly in a hot oven.

SALADS

Calories
As most salad ingredients are very low in calories, calorie counts have been given only for those ingredients that have a high calorific value. Otherwise, you can assume that most of the ingredients discussed yield between 10 and 50 calories for each 100g (4oz), to which should be added the calories for any chosen dressing.

Extra ingredients
Ingredients that turn a salad into a main meal:
Broad beans or peas, using about 50g (2oz) raw weight
Cheese, soft or hard
Cooked beans – larger types go best with salads
Cooked brown rice
Cooked fish, especially smoked
Cooked grains, such as barley
Cooked meat, in cubes or chunks
Cooked poultry, in cubes or chunks
Cooked wholewheat pasta
Cubes of toasted bread
Hard boiled eggs or slices of cold rolled-up omelette
Nuts, if you add about 40 to 50g (1½ to 2oz) per person
Sprouted wheat grains
Sunflower seeds (as with nuts)
Sweetcorn (as for broad beans and peas)

Vitamin content
As well as being rich in vitamin C, vegetables are a treasure house of other vitamins. Vitamin A, in the form of carotene, is richest in yellow vegetables and fruit – apricots, yellow melon, carrots, pumpkin, tomatoes, peaches – and in dark-green leafy vegetables, which are also sources of vitamins E and K. Vitamin E is also found in oily avocados, nuts and seeds. Bear in mind too that the potassium in vegetable produce will help balance your body fluids, which are inundated with sodium from many modern foods. Iron, folic acid (a B vitamin), calcium and magnesium, as well as assorted essential trace elements, are substantially supplied to you by vegetables, especially leafy, green vegetables, which are also richest in vitamin C. Watercress, parsley and other greens can truly be called 'superfoods'.

Green salad – endive, corn salad, and iceberg lettuce – with fresh basil, dill and chives.

For every person whose eyes light up at the thought of a crisp and interesting salad, there are two who wince. Except on the hottest summer days, when they might down the odd lettuce leaf, they see salad as 'rabbit food', the slimmer's penance. In my view, people who loathe the idea of a salad are very like those who claim not to like scent: they just haven't yet met the right one. I hope this section will encourage them to look a little further. To enjoy salads, you don't have to like lettuce, tomatoes, cucumber or any other vegetable usually considered as a raw salad ingredient. Most of the vegetables you more often see cooked will make delicious salads – including paper-thin slices of Brussels sprouts and crisp and sweet young turnips.

I don't buy lettuce or cucumber in winter, not only because they are then at their most expensive, but also because I enjoy eating seasonally. That way, the arrival of each newcomer to the greengrocer is an event to be enjoyed, and you eat everything at its sweetest and best, not when it's been dragged out of its natural timing.

This section is less a collection of recipes than a reminder of what each season offers, and of all the many salad ingredients whose potential you may not have realized.

As well as tasting good and doing you good, salads are a boon for busy people. Although it takes time to wash and cut the vegetables, you'd probably spend more time on even a simple cooked meal. If you are tired in the evening, a salad is easier on you and on your digestion than a session of cooking that may leave you too weary to eat. With good presentation, and by including some 'solid' ingredients, salads can be made into tempting main meals.

My own favourite meal-makers with salad are nuts or cheese. Both have protein, but also a high fat content so use modest portions. Both seem to blend beautifully with vegetables. Toast peanuts, almonds, cashews, hazels, brazils, pecans, pines, walnuts or pistachios lightly in an ungreased pan for 2 to 3 minutes, and chop them in small pieces to bring out salad flavours. Sunflower seeds have similar food value to almonds, and make a tasty and economical change. On the same principle, cold-pressed oils, from walnuts or peanuts for instance, add a special taste. Caesar dressing, here without its raw egg but with Parmesan, gives a salad the savoury tang of cheese; or you could stir in grated hard cheeses, cubed feta, sliced Mozzarella, blue cheese dressing or cottage cheese.

Salads don't have to be mixed. The most subtle flavours come from one or two vegetables, with a complementary dressing. Nor do the ingredients have to be raw. Some vegetables, such as mangetout, benefit from being plunged in boiling water for a few minutes.

For very low fat dressings, omit oil from these recipes and increase the quantity of yogurt or cottage cheese. Adding low-fat yogurt or cottage cheese to dressings dilutes the startlingly high fat (and therefore calorie) content, and increases the protein.

Calories About 525 in total.

- Suitable for diabetics (in small amounts)
- No fibre
- Very low salt (omitting salt)
- Milk-free (using soya yogurt)
- Gluten-free

DRESSINGS

The following dressing suggestions can be adapted or varied by the addition of herbs or mustard, for example.

OIL AND LEMON DRESSING

Salad oil is a very personal matter. Two oils to bear in mind, however, are the highly polyunsaturated oils, such as safflower or sunflower, which are best used in salads as they are not tolerant of high heat in cooking, and the cold-pressed oils, which are both more natural and tastier than clear, refined versions.

60ml (4 tbsp) any favourite oil
30ml (2 tbsp) lemon juice
15ml (1 tbsp) wine vinegar
125ml (4fl oz) plain low-fat yogurt
10ml (2 tsp) apple juice
pinch of fruit sugar or very small dab of honey
black pepper
½ clove of garlic, crushed (optional)
pinch of sea salt

Place all the ingredients in a screwtop jar and shake well.

VARIATION

Add any favourite *chopped herbs* to vary the flavour. A *little mustard* can be added to give the dressing more tang.

CAESAR DRESSING

Ideal for green salads and for any salad to which you want to add a little extra tang.

60ml (4 tbsp) olive, walnut or any favourite oil
30ml (2 tbsp) lemon juice
30ml (2 tbsp) Parmesan cheese, finely grated
1 large or 2 small spring onions, finely chopped
pinch of dry mustard powder
1 clove of garlic, crushed
black pepper, to taste
Worcestershire sauce, to taste
small pinch of sea salt

Place all the ingredients in a screwtop jar and shake well.

VARIATION

For a different texture, add *100g (4oz) cottage cheese* to the other ingredients. You might also like to add *a little orange juice*.

Calories About 565 in total; about 660 in total for the cottage cheese variation.

- Suitable for diabetics (in small amounts)
- Almost no fibre
- Gluten-free

WALNUT DRESSING

My favourite dressing for winter salads made with cabbage, celeriac or carrots.

60ml (4 tbsp) unsweetened apple juice
25g (1oz) walnut pieces
150ml (¼ pint) plain low-fat yogurt, preferably thick
about 1ml (¼ tsp) mixed spice or ground cinnamon, to taste

1 Blend the apple juice and nuts together. If you do not have a food processor or liquidizer, mix them by hand, after grating or chopping the nuts coarsely.
2 Stir in the yogurt, by hand, to retain its thickness.
3 Add spice to taste.

BLUE CHEESE DRESSING

Blue cheese fans (and I am one) tend to like this on most salads, but it has a special affinity with cucumber, watercress, celery, and with bean salads.

150ml (¼ pint) plain low-fat yogurt
50g (2oz) blue cheese, grated or crumbled
10ml (2 tsp) lemon juice
small pinch of mustard powder
black pepper, to taste

Mix all the ingredients by hand (mechanical processing will break down the yogurt texture). Grated cheese gives a smoother texture.

SPRING SALADS

By spring any winter-harvested, stored vegetables are getting old and stringy and the year's early crops will not have yet arrived. This is the least interesting time for home-grown salads, although many ingredients are available from other, warmer areas. Make use of home-grown beansprouts at this time of year.

WATERCRESS

For freshness and food value, watercress is the star of the season (see also page 157).

Serving suggestion
Serve the watercress in large sprigs with thin slices of orange from which the pith has been removed. Wider orange slices can be halved or quartered. Sprinkle whole black olives over the watercress and orange salad.
Dressing Add oil and lemon dressing or Caesar dressing with cottage cheese just before serving, otherwise the watercress will go limp.
Herbs Chives and caraway seeds bring out the flavour of watercress.

Calories About 240 in total.

• Suitable for diabetics
• Low fibre
• Very low salt
• Gluten-free

To reduce the calorie content, halve the quantity of walnuts.

Calories About 260 in total.

• Suitable for diabetics
• No fibre
• Gluten-free

Danish-type blue cheese is substantially lower in fat than Stilton.

Calories Black olives: about 80 per 100g (4oz).

Although watercress is high in iron, nutritionists point out that the body does not absorb the mineral very efficiently from this or other greens. Iron absorption improves, however, if vitamin C is present, supplied here by both watercress and oranges.

BROCCOLI AND CAULIFLOWER

Calories Flaked almonds: about 565 per 100g (4oz).

Both of these vegetables are good raw in salads if very fresh and young. Otherwise, break or cut them vertically into long spears and place them in a pan holding 1cm (½in) boiling water. Then cover and simmer over medium heat for 6 to 8 minutes (young vegetables cook more quickly). You can use all of the cooked stalk, discarding only the woody ends of the vegetables.

Serving suggestion (1)
Lay cooked sprigs or spears of cauliflower or broccoli parallel on a flat dish and sprinkle toasted flaked almonds over them.

Serving suggestion (2)
Cut small sprigs of cauliflower or broccoli across and dice the stalks. Toss the vegetable with toasted flaked almonds and carrots cut in matchstick strips. Add a generous amount of coarsely chopped parsley.

Dressing For both serving suggestions, use blue cheese or Caesar dressing with or without cottage cheese.

BUFFET MENU

Game pie **115 cals**
Cold chicken with curry sauce
330 cals
Radish and potato salad
170 cals
Spring onions **10 cals**
Watercress and pear salad
100 cals
Mushroom salad **90 cals**
Wholemeal rolls **90 cals each**
——•——
Rhubarb fool **195 cals**

RADISHES

Calories Potatoes: about 75 per 100g (4oz).

Use whole when young and tender, sliced when older and drier. Radishes are too hot to make a salad on their own, or to mix well with other tangy ingredients such as cauliflower, watercress or onions.

Serving suggestion
Slice the radishes thinly across and serve with potatoes that have been cooked in their skins, then peeled (unless they are new potatoes) and cut in cubes about the same size as the radishes. Sprinkle over a generous amount of finely chopped parsley.
Dressing Use oil and lemon or Caesar dressing.
Herbs Dill makes a useful accompaniment for radishes.

VARIATION

If using radishes for dipping, keep enough of the leaves to use as a handle. For dip suggestions, see pages 55–9.

SPRING ONIONS

A main meal style of salad, especially if using blue cheese or Caesar cottage cheese dressing.

By adding cooked brown rice to what is usually a salad accompaniment, you can make a main-meal salad that has plenty of springtime zest.

Serving suggestion (1)
Mix together equal quantities of spring onions, sliced diagonally across, sliced radishes, coarsely chopped parsley and cooked brown rice (see page 97). Add a little diced red pepper for colour.
Dressing Use oil and lemon, walnut or blue cheese dressing.
Herbs Add fresh mint, if it is available, or caraway seeds.

Serving suggestion (2)
Combine spring onions with parsley and bulgur wheat to make tabbouleh (page 92).

Spring rice salad – a combination of spring onions, radishes, brown rice and parsley, garnished with chopped red pepper

Chick peas add protein and another kind of fibre, making this a useful contribution to the protein of a main meal. The chick peas can be sprouted, rather than cooked, if preferred.

MANGETOUT

Also known as snow peas, mangetout are tender young peas that are eaten pod and all. Often included in Chinese stir-fry vegetable dishes, they are also good in salads, after having been cooked for 3 to 4 minutes in 1cm (½in) of boiling water. This way they retain their bright-green colour and crisp texture.

Serving suggestion (1)
Trim the mangetout, then cook and immediately drain them.
Dressing Use an oil and lemon dressing or a Caesar dressing with cottage cheese.
Herbs Sprinkle over chopped chives or spring onions.

Serving suggestion (2)
Trim, cook and drain the mangetout. Serve with about half the amount again of cooked, drained chick peas and, to complement the shape and colour of the mangetout, slices of cucumber that have been cut in half.
Dressing Use an oil and lemon dressing or a Caesar dressing with or without cottage cheese.

SUMMER SALADS

Green salads belong to summer for, although lettuce is on sale all year round, it has more flavour and there are more varieties in summer. Almost any greenstuff can be mixed to make a delicious salad, provided the leaves are dry so that the dressing will coat them.

LETTUCE

The basis for many summer salads, lettuce can be mixed with a variety of other summer vegetables or served on its own with a dressing.

Serving suggestion (1)
To make one of the most attractive and tasty salads I've ever had, simply cut an iceberg lettuce into wedges.
Dressing Spoon blue cheese dressing over the centre of each wedge.

Serving suggestion (2)
Tear any kind of lettuce and some young spinach leaves into large shreds. Mix in some cucumber that has been diced, sliced or cut in matchsticks.

A simple summer salad – iceberg lettuce wedges with a blue cheese dressing

VARIATIONS

Small amounts of *young, pale dandelion leaves* will give a slightly bitter flavour to a green salad. For a sharp, lemony tang, add *a few sorrel leaves*, torn in small pieces. *Sliced or torn bunches of watercress, chopped celery, spring onions, green peppers, courgettes* and *generous amounts of parsley* are all good in green salads.

GREEN BEANS

Although green beans can be eaten raw, they are actually crunchier and greener after they have been plunged into a pan containing about 1cm (½in) of boiling water, covered, for 4 to 5 minutes.

Serving suggestion
Arrange any kind of cooked whole green beans on a plate or, if desired, slice them in matchstick lengths.
Dressing Pour over an oil and lemon, Caesar or blue cheese dressing.
Herbs and seasoning Use chopped basil, coarsely ground black pepper, chopped chives, savory or paprika.

VARIATIONS

Toasted flaked nuts are a suitable accompaniment for all green beans. Or you could serve them with *diced new potatoes, finely chopped onion, carrots* that have been diced, coarsely shredded, or cut in strips or *young turnips*, cut in matchsticks or very thin slices.

TOMATOES

Unlike green salads, tomato salads often improve if made at least an hour before they are wanted, so that the flavours have time to blend.

Serving suggestion (1)
For a plain tomato salad, thickly slice some unpeeled tomatoes and sprinkle with chopped basil and a little crushed garlic.

Serving suggestion (2)
To make a Greek salad, combine sliced tomatoes, chunks of cucumber, onions, black olives and cubes of feta cheese.
Dressing Pour over an oil and lemon dressing with garlic added.

Serving suggestion (3)
To make salade niçoise, combine chunks of tomatoes, cooked cubed potatoes, sliced onion, pieces of tuna fish, black olives and anchovies.
Dressing Pour over an oil and lemon dressing.

VARIATION

To a salade niçoise, lightly cooked *green beans* can also be added.

POTATOES

New potatoes can be steamed or conservatively cooked very lightly in their skins, then dressed and served while still warm. Skinning is optional with young and tender potatoes. Waxy varieties suit salads best.

Calories Potatoes about 75 per 100g (4oz); nuts: about 140 per 100g (4oz)

SUPPER MENU

Iceberg wedges **85 cals**

—•—

Carrot ring with creamy herb sauce **190 cals**
Green beans or broccoli **30 cals**

—•—

Mrs Beeton's figgy pudding **250 cals**

Total calories per person **555**

Calories Black olives: about 80 per 100g (4oz); feta cheese: about 190 per 100g (4oz); potatoes: about 75 per 100g (4oz); cooked rice or pasta: about 130 per 100g (4oz); tuna: 290 per 100g (4oz).

Greek salad and salade niçoise both contain enough protein for a main meal. Both are salty (from olives, cheese or anchovies), so don't add too much of these ingredients, and don't add salt to the dressing.

Calories Potatoes: about 75 per 100g (4oz); cooked chicken: about 120 per 100g (4oz); shellfish: about 110 to 120 per 100g (4oz); fish: 100 to 150 per 100g (4oz), depending on type.

A salad ingredient that turns a salad into a meal. Without the usual mayonnaise, potatoes are not particularly high in calories.

Serving suggestion

Lightly cook some new potatoes, then skin them if necessary. Very small potatoes can be left whole. Otherwise they should be cubed or sliced.
Dressing Use an oil and lemon dressing, creamy herb dressing (page 32) or cold curry sauce (page 198).
Herbs Fresh mint, coarsely chopped parsley, dill, caraway seeds, chives and any fresh, chopped herbs are suitable for potato salad.

VARIATIONS

Sliced radishes, chopped spring onions or *onions finely chopped* will give a tang to potato salad. You could also add *roughly chopped cucumber, sliced celery, chopped red or green pepper* or *cubed cheese*. Potatoes provide body for a main-meal salad of *cubed cooked chicken, shrimps, prawns* and other *shellfish* or *cold cooked fish*, especially the smoked varieties.

BROAD BEANS

Only the youngest, most tender beans are suitable for eating raw.

Calories Broad beans: about 50 per 100g (4oz); sweetcorn: about 75 per 100g (4oz).

Broad beans and peas (below) both provide enough protein, eaten in 150g (6oz) portions, to supply over ⅛th of an adult's daily protein needs. They also have more fibre than most vegetables.

Serving suggestion

Shell some broad beans. If they are old enough to need light cooking, try dressing and serving the beans while they are still slightly warm.
Dressing Use an oil and lemon or Caesar dressing with cottage cheese.
Herbs Sprinkle over chopped fresh mint, savory or basil.

VARIATIONS

Mix with *lightly cooked new potatoes*, cut in pieces of about the same size as the broad beans, *sweetcorn kernels* or *young turnips*, cut in paper-thin slices. Or you could make a bean salad by adding *cooked dried beans*, such as *haricot beans*, and *lightly cooked green beans* cut in short lengths.

COURGETTES

Slice raw courgettes very thinly or cut lightly cooked courgettes in 1cm (½in) chunks.

Serving suggestion

Combine raw or cooked courgettes with shredded carrot or with raw or lightly cooked peas.
Dressing Use an oil and lemon or Caesar dressing.

PEAS

Calories Peas: about 50 per 100g (4oz); cooked rice or pasta: about 130 per 100g (4oz); sweetcorn: about 75 per 100g (4oz).

Delicious raw when fresh and sweet, peas should be lightly cooked if they are starchier through longer storage. Frozen peas can be used after thawing without further cooking. Keep peas away from vinegar and lemon juice, which spoil their colour and taste.

Serving suggestion

Combine peas with cooked brown rice or wholewheat pasta, sweetcorn kernels or diced cucumber, diced red or green pepper and finely

chopped spring onions or onion.
Dressing Stir chopped herbs into plain low-fat yogurt.
Herbs Chives, parsley, thyme, marjoram or basil all go well with peas.

AUTUMN SALADS

Now is the time to abandon lettuce and tomatoes, even though they are still on sale, in favour of the autumn crops of mushrooms, apples, young root vegetables, grapes and peppers.

MUSHROOMS

Low in vitamin C, so include some richer source in the meal.

It's not necessary to peel mushrooms or to discard the stalks. Simply clean them with a soft brush under the cold tap and trim the stalks. As soon as they are brushed or cut, mushrooms will start to brown unless immediately tossed in a little lemon or orange juice.

Serving suggestion
Arrange thick slices of mushroom on a plate. Pour over oil and lemon dressing or Caesar dressing with or without cottage cheese.
Herbs and seasoning Use cumin, coarsely ground black pepper or parsley.

VARIATIONS

Mustard and cress or *small sprigs of watercress*, including the finely sliced stalks, will add colour to a mushroom salad. For a more filling salad, add *roughly chopped hard-boiled eggs*.

WATERCRESS

Calories Nuts: about 140 per 100g (4oz); cooked brown rice: about 130 per 100g (4oz).

A useful salad ingredient in the spring, watercress comes into its own again in autumn (see also page 151). To maximize the short life of watercress, place it in a closed polythene bag or box in the refrigerator after rinsing it in water and shaking off the excess.

Serving suggestion
Using whole sprigs and finely chopped stems, arrange a bed of watercress on a serving plate. Peel, halve and de-pip a few firm pears and place them, flat side up, on the bed of watercress.
Dressing Spoon blue cheese or Caesar dressing into the pear centres.
Herbs Use coriander for this dish.

VARIATIONS

Grate over any kind of *roasted nuts* or add *cooked brown rice* or *small pieces of orange*.

PEPPERS

Calories Walnuts: about 525 per 100g (4oz).

Raw green peppers have more vitamin C, weight for weight, than oranges.

One of the most versatile salad ingredients, peppers add colour as well as a distinctive texture and flavour to rice, bean, tomato, pasta and other salads. Sliced in rings, diced or cut in strips, peppers make an attractive garnish. Discard the seeds, which can be quite hot.

LUNCH MENU

Leafy green salad **100 cals**

— • —

Tabbouleh **110 cals**
Mushroom salad **80 cals**

— • —

Trifle **150 cals**

Total calories per person **440**

Autumn pepper salad with courgette and cheese cubes, and slices of fresh pear

Serving suggestion
Dice or cut in strips a few red or green peppers and mix them with cubes of unpeeled courgette. Add cottage cheese or small cubes of hard cheese.
Dressing Use an oil and lemon or Caesar dressing.
Herbs Stir in some parsley or tarragon.

VARIATION

The addition of *a few chopped walnuts* or *small chunks of firm pears* will give your pepper salad a totally different flavour.

WINTER SALADS

Although winter might seem to be the worst time for salads, many root vegetables are at their best in cold weather. An infinite variety of winter salads can be put together with almost any vegetables you have available, if they are shredded coarsely or finely. Such a salad is easily transformed into a main course by adding cooked brown rice, cooked beans, cooked pasta, hard-boiled eggs, shredded cheese or larger helpings of nuts.

WHITE CABBAGE

A colourful and tasty alternative to that other salad made with shredded white cabbage – coleslaw.

Serving suggestion
Shred together white cabbage, carrots, a green or red pepper or a red-skinned apple. Stir in mustard and cress or beansprouts and some raisins, sultanas or currants.
Dressing Almost any type of dressing will do.
Herbs Garnish the salad with coarsely chopped parsley or ground toasted sesame seeds.

VARIATION

You can use *Chinese leaves* instead of white cabbage for this recipe.

RED CABBAGE

Raw red cabbage is best mixed with other ingredients in a salad, as, on their own, the chewy leaves can have too strong a flavour. Discard the thick, woody ribs at the base of the leaves.

Serving suggestion
Finely shred and mix together equal quantities of red cabbage and white or Savoy cabbage. Mix with some baked or boiled chestnuts that have been peeled and halved or some whole, lightly toasted hazelnuts.
Dressing Use a walnut or oil and lemon dressing.

CELERY

Use the leaves as well as the stems of this adaptable salad vegetable, which has a particular affinity with rice, pasta, beans and cheese.

Serving suggestion (1)
Chop some celery in 1cm (½in) lengths and mix it with cubes of marrow or courgette. Unlike courgettes, marrows have to be peeled. Add some diced green or red peppers.
Dressing Use a blue cheese dressing or a Caesar dressing with or without cottage cheese.
Herbs Caraway seeds or fennel seeds go well with celery.

VARIATIONS

Add *mustard and cress* or *chopped watercress* or, for a different texture, some *toasted peanuts* or *chestnuts* that have been baked or grilled then peeled and halved. The addition of *cooked brown rice, beans, whole-wheat pasta* or *diced potatoes* will give you a main-meal salad.

Serving suggestion (2)
To make a Waldorf salad, one of the classic salad combinations, mix together equal quantities of celery, sliced in 1cm (½in) widths, and 1cm (½in) cubes of unpeeled, red-skinned apple, which have been tossed in lemon or orange juice. Add a few coarsely chopped walnuts.
Dressing Use an oil and lemon, walnut or blue cheese dressing.
Herbs Garnish with chopped chives or sliced pink onions.

---

n spite of the whiteness, these cabbages still have lenty of vitamin C. However, shredding reduces it y about 20 per cent, hence the advantage of dding peppers, cress or other greens to the salad.

Calories Hazelnuts: about 380 per 100g (4oz); hestnuts: about 170 per 100g (4oz).

s high in vitamin C as green cabbage varieties.

Calories Toasted peanuts: about 570 per 100g 4oz); pasta: about 130 per 100g (4oz), cooked eight; chestnuts: about 170 per 100g (4oz); otatoes: about 75 per 100g (4oz); walnuts: about 25 per 100g (4oz).

lot high in vitamin C. You gain more by using the aves as well as the stems.

VEGETARIAN MENU

Humus with pitta strips
215 cals

— • —

Gnocchi alla Romana **200 cals**
Waldorf salad **150 cals**
Green salad **100 cals**

— • —

Sliced peaches in liqueur
80 cals

Total calories per person **745**

CARROTS

An ideal winter salad vegetable, carrots complement and enhance many salads, adding colour and crunch. Finely shred coarser, older carrots and cut sweeter, juicier carrots in rings and chunks.

Serving suggestion (1)
Shred the carrots coarsely or finely depending on their age.
Dressing Use walnut or oil and lemon dressing.
Herbs Garnish with chervil, parsley, chives or thyme.

Serving suggestion (2)
To make a German winter salad plate, grate equal quantities of large carrots, celeriac, beetroot and swede. Toss the celeriac in lemon juice. Don't peel or cut the raw beetroot before shredding, otherwise the colour will leak. Arrange the vegetables in separate heaps around a serving plate.
Dressing Use without dressing or with a Caesar dressing with cottage cheese. You could also try an oil and lemon dressing to which a little honey has been added.
Herbs Garnish with parsley, dill, caraway seeds or celery seeds.

Cutting up carrots
Young carrots can be cut into thin matchstick strips (**1**), coarsely grated (**2**) or cut in rings (**3**), as preferred.

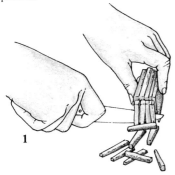

1

2

LEEKS

When preparing leeks, discard only the coarsest green parts.

Serving suggestions (1)
Trim and wash the leeks, then lightly cook them whole in a small amount of water. Leave them to cool.
Dressing Serve with an oil and lemon dressing.

Serving suggestion (2)
Wash the leeks and slice them very thinly across. Add some cooked and drained red kidney beans and a generous amount of coarsely chopped parsley.
Dressing Any dressing suits this salad, and it can also be served with mustard.
Herbs Use savory or thyme.

3

Calories Beetroot: about 45 per 100g (4oz).

Not nearly as high in calories as its sweetness might lead you to expect.

BEETROOT

Avoid the beet you can buy ready-vinegared. Baby beet can be steamed or cooked in 2cm (¾in) of water for about 25 minutes. Large beet may need as long as 60 to 80 minutes' cooking by the same method, or it can be baked in the oven. Young beetroot are delicious shredded raw. Wear a large apron as stains are hard to remove from clothes.

Serving suggestion
If the beetroot is young, lightly cook it, and simply serve it whole. An older, cooked beet should be sliced thickly.
Dressing Use an oil and lemon or walnut dressing.
Herbs Garnish with chopped chives, chopped dill or finely chopped onions.

German winter plate salad of grated swede, carrot, celeriac and beetroot, served with Caesar dressing made with cottage cheese.

Not high in vitamin C, but lemon juice in the dressing will add some

CHICORY

Divide chicory into spears or cut it in slices about 2cm (¾in) thick.

Serving suggestion
Thickly slice the chicory and mix it with half-segments of apple that have been tossed in lemon juice. Just before serving, add chunks of beetroot that has been cooked in its skin. If you add the beetroot before tossing the salad, it will stain everything pink.
Dressing Use an oil and lemon dressing to which a dab of mild French mustard has been added.

CHINESE LEAVES

Dirt rarely penetrates the tight head of this vegetable, so you don't have to separate the leaves when cleaning it. Chinese leaves can be an inexpensive substitute for chicory.

Serving suggestion
Slice the Chinese leaves finely across and arrange them on a serving plate with wedges of orange.

FISH &
SHELLFISH

Not only is fish delicious, it's also the original healthy convenience food. When you are tired or busy, think fish. You can cook most kinds in under 10 minutes, and take many straight from freezer to cooker. Refrigeration has made fish widely available in excellent condition, and it seems to lose far less flavour in freezing than other foods. So if you've been put off fish by flabby, overcooked, over-sauced and tired dishes, please take another look.

The two enemies of tasty fish are time and water. Fish must never be kept or cooked for too long a time. Unless it is frozen, fish should be fresh enough to smell of sea and fresh air, not of fish. Overcooking makes fish flabby and tasteless.

The second pitfall is water. Fish may live in it, but they shouldn't be cooked in water alone. The flavour can just float away. When fish is poached, it should be in a well-flavoured stock.

As with vegetables, the best fish to buy is the one that happens to be in top condition the day you go shopping (unless you order fish for a special occasion).

Food value
Fish is far superior to meat in food value. Like meat, it is high in protein, but the protein in fish is not accompanied by considerable amounts of highly saturated hard fat, as it is in meat.

White fish is extremely low in fat, and even in oily fish, the oil is soft and includes some highly polyunsaturated fatty acids. Oily fish is also the main food source of vitamin D, as well as providing large amounts of vitamin A. These are particularly useful in late winter, when vitamin D production from sunlight on skin, and vitamin A from eating leafy greens, orange vegetables and fruit, may be lower than usual.

Seafoods – fish, shellfish and 'sea vegetables' – are the most reliable source of minerals, including iodine, zinc, and a wide variety of others. Fish where the bones are eaten, such as sardines, whitebait or sprats, are a rich source of calcium. Shellfish are even richer in minerals, particularly in zinc, than other fish. Although they have a low fat content, they have a fairly high level of some cholesterol-type substances, and for this reason some diets for heart patients restrict their use. However, few people are likely to have access to shellfish often enough for this to be a worry, and it is not even known whether this form of cholesterol can be harmful in large amounts. The only people who really have to steer clear of shellfish are those who have

Snapper grilled over a barbecue

allergic reactions to it – and such reactions are fairly common – and those with a tendency to gout, which can be aggravated by the high level of purines in shellfish.

Fish enjoys yet another advantage over most meat: it has not been subjected to the intensive farming methods widely used for cattle and pigs. If you eat fish rather than intensively farmed meat you will avoid the hormone growth promoters, antibiotics and other aids to intensive farming which may leave residues in the meat you buy.

Smoked fish

Smoked fish comes in more and more variety. It has advantages and snags. The advantages are that it has already been cooked, and can be eaten immediately, whether in the form of smoked salmon or as humbler smoked mackerel. It also has a special flavour from the smoking, and can be used in small amounts with blander types of white fish to give dishes a lift.

The disadvantages are that it is very salty, and that it is often artificially coloured. Because of its high salt content, smoked fish needs to be diluted with other ingredients, and no extra salt need be added to recipes in which it appears (such as those for taramasalata, page 55, or the fish terrines, pages 65 and 177). The dyes aren't questionable only on health grounds. They can mean that the fish won't have as much of the characteristic flavour of smoking. Colourings have to be declared on the labels of packed fish, but with unpackaged fish it's hard to find out which have been dyed. In general, smoked haddock, kippers and mackerel are likely to be dyed. To avoid colouring, choose Finnan haddie, Arbroath smokies (smoked whiting or small haddock), Manx kippers, which are much paler, or smoked trout, which is less often coloured.

PREPARATION & COOKING

Ask the fishmonger to gut the fish for you.

If you buy fish wrapped in polythene, remove the polythene when you get home and replace it with a wrapping of greaseproof paper or kitchen foil.

Fish tails and heads can be removed or left on: in general, leaving fish intact during cooking helps keep them moist and tasty. If you want to remove the head before cooking, cut it off just behind the gills, using a sharp knife.

Boning oily fish, such as trout and salmon, is easy. Put the gutted fish, top side up, on a board, and press down firmly along the backbone, flattening the fish out. Turn it over, and you'll be able to pull the backbone, and the larger bones attached to it, neatly away from the fish.

To fillet a flat fish, such as a plaice, cut along the middle of the backbone from head to tail with a sharp knife. Then, holding the knife as flat as possible, separate the flesh on one side of the backbone from the bones. Do the same on the other side of the backbone. Turn the fish over and repeat, to produce 4 fillets.

1

2

Filleting flat fish
1 First cut along the backbone from head to tail.
2 Then separate the flesh on one side of the backbone from the bones. Do the same on the other side of the backbone. Turn the fish over and repeat both steps to produce 4 fillets.

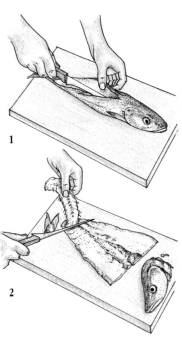

Filleting round fish
1 Cut along the middle of the backbone from head to tail and remove one fillet from one side of the fish.
2 To remove the remaining fillet, lay the fish skin side down, cut off the head and tail, and cut away the backbone.

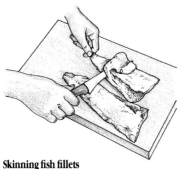

Skinning fish fillets
Put the fish skin side down on a board and, with a sharp knife, saw gently between the flesh and skin, working from the tail.

A round fish (whiting, for example) yields 2 fillets. Cut along the middle of the backbone. Insert the knife between the flesh and the bone and gradually remove the fillet from the bones, working downwards. Remove the fillet from the other side, as shown.

Skinning fish fillets only requires a sharp, narrow-bladed knife. Put the fish, skin down, on a board. Starting at the tail, cut a little of the flesh away from the skin, then, keeping the knife blade at about a 45° angle, cut with a sawing movement along the surface of the skin. Hold the fish by the skin of its tail. The flesh will curve over as you work.

Most of the simple basic cooking methods described in the following pages can be adapted to suit a variety of fish. A fish is cooked when the flesh is opaque, and a fork will easily pierce the inner flesh.

Baking Can be used for almost any fish. Bake oily fish, such as herrings, mackerel or kippers, whole and uncovered on a barely greased baking sheet. They will have even more flavour if they are stuffed before baking (see the recipe for grilled mackerel on page 171). White fish or any kind of fish that is in fillets or steaks must be protected against drying out. Either bake the fish with liquid, such as fish stock, cider or tomatoes, basting occasionally; or wrap the fish, or piece of fish, and seasonings such as lemon juice, herbs, mushrooms, a little wine or stock, parsley, tomatoes, yogurt, or onion slices, in parcels of kitchen foil.

Bake at 180°C (350°F), gas mark 4. The thickness of the fish serves as a rough guide to the length of baking time: for fish 2.5cm (1in) thick, allow about 20 minutes; 5cm (2in) thick, 30 minutes; 8cm (3in) thick, 35 to 40 minutes. Always check fish before you think it will be done, to avoid overcooking.

Grilling My own favourite way of cooking fish. I include cooking on a griddle, barely greased, and barbecuing, which follow the same principles. All three methods keep the flavour of the fish, sealing in the juices and cooking the flesh so quickly that the inside stays moist.

Grilling suits oily fish particularly well. The intense dry heat of the grill causes some of the fat layer under the skin to melt into the fish and this keeps the inside moist. At the same time, the richness of the fish is tempered as fat drains out of fish like herrings and mackerel.

But white fish too is delicious grilled, especially if it is marinated first. Coriander fish kebabs (page 173) are a good example of this method. Marinating adds flavour to the fish and helps it to stay moist during cooking; marinated fish also shrinks less.

Brush the grill or griddle lightly with oil and heat it thoroughly before you start cooking.

Whole fish should be gutted and cleaned, and can then be stuffed if you want. Cut 2 or 3 diagonal slashes from backbone to belly almost to the bone, to let heat and marinades penetrate. The smaller the fish, the closer it can be to the grill – sardines as close as 5cm (2in). Larger fish are best kept 10 to 15cm (4 to 6in) from the grill so the outside doesn't overcook before the inside is done. Whole fish should be turned once during grilling. Very small fish, such as sardines, need only 2 to 4 minutes' grilling on each side, a fish the size of a mullet or a whiting will take about 5 minutes on each side, and even a 1.5kg (3lb) carp will take only about 10 minutes each side.

Split fish and fish steaks keep their moisture better if they are grilled with skin and bone intact. Fresh-water fish, such as carp and pike, will need basting with their marinade often during cooking, other types just once. Unless the fish is very thick, it will cook in 8 to 10 minutes, and does not need turning. Fairly thick fish fillets are best for grilling. If you leave the skin on, turn the fish briefly for a few minutes at the end of cooking to crisp the skin side. A good way to ensure that fillets stay moist is to put two fillets flesh to flesh, with some seasoning such as herbs or lemon in between, then grill as though the fillets were a thick steak.

Barbecuing over charcoal or wood chips produces the best flavours of all. Make sure the fire has died down before you start to cook the fish, or it may burn. Secure the fish between metal grids to prevent pieces falling in the fire as they soften with cooking. Barbecued kebabs are only practical with firm-fleshed fish, such as huss, scallops, monkfish, sea bass or similar types.

Poaching Only suits whole white or oily fish, most famously salmon, although it doesn't suit mackerel or raw herring. The liquid used is generally a flavoured stock, known as court bouillon. There are many variations of seasoning for this, so don't be hidebound by the exact number of peppercorns in a recipe. Once you've tried the recipes, perfect your own favourite. This is mine.

900ml (1½ pints) water
1 carrot, 2 sticks of celery, 1 onion (all roughly chopped)
1 bay leaf
3 sprigs of parsley
22ml (1½ tbsp) wine vinegar
1 clove
4 peppercorns, crushed
pinch of sea salt

1 Bring all the ingredients to the boil in a large saucepan, cover the pan and simmer the court bouillon for about 20 minutes.
2 Strain and use as poaching liquid.

Fish to be served hot should be slowly brought to the boil in a cold court bouillon, then simmered for about 5 minutes per 450g (1lb). If you don't have a fish kettle with a rack to put the fish on, make a cradle of thick foil strips to go under the fish so that you are able to lift it out of the pan gently.

Fish you plan to serve cold is brought to the boil in the same way, but as soon as the stock boils energetically, turn off the heat, cover the pan and leave the fish in the liquid until it is cold. This stops it drying out.
Steaming Suitable for fish steaks and whole fish up to 1.5kg (3lb) in weight. Steaming suits white fish better than oily, and fish on the bone better than fillets. Chinese bamboo steamers come in large sizes and are very useful if you like to steam whole fish. Flavour the fish well (see the recipe for Chinese steamed fish, page 174) and place it in the steamer above simmering water.

Alternatively, you can steam it sitting on a thin layer of herbs, particularly fennel fronds, rosemary sprigs or celery and oregano. Cover tightly.

Again, the thickness of the fish gives a rough time guide: for fish 2.5cm (1in) thick, allow 6 to 8 minutes; 5cm (2in) thick, 10 to 15 minutes; 8cm (3in) thick, 18 to 25 minutes. Check a few minutes before you expect the fish to be cooked, to avoid overcooking.

Some kinds of whole fish will be difficult to remove from the steamer intact. Either wrap the fish in cheesecloth before steaming, so that you can lift it out easily, or find a plate that just fits inside your steamer and, when the fish is done, remove the steamer from the saucepan, put the plate inside the steamer right up against the fish and invert the steamer so that the fish drops gently in one piece on to the plate.

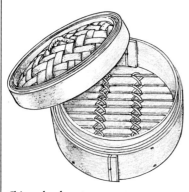

Chinese bamboo steamer

Chinese steamed sea bass

METHODS FOR SHELLFISH

COCKLES

Can be cleaned and cooked in any way used for mussels (page 168), or steamed open, then included in any fish chowder (page 81) or fish terrine (pages 65, 177) or eaten as a first course with salad dressing and bread and butter.

CRABS

Are almost always sold cooked. The brown and white meat are equally good to eat. Use crab for fish cocktails, mixed with white fish in fish cakes (page 172), cold with salad, in luxurious sandwiches or served dressed in the shell.

To dress crab, wash it well, lay it on its back and twist off the claws and legs. Break off the apron-shaped flap by pushing it up. Push the body and shell apart with your fingers. Scoop out the meat from inside the shell. Discard the stomach bag and any spongy, waxy bits. Crack the shell of each claw and extract the meat. Extract the meat from the legs. Mix the body, shell and leg meat together. Wash the shell, polish it with a little oil, then pile the meat back in, garnishing it with the claws and some lettuce and parsley. Be careful not to overwhelm the delicate flavour of the crab with strong sauces: egg and lemon sauce (page 31) and creamy herb sauce (page 32) both suit it.

If you acquire a live crab, cook it in the same way as lobster (below) if it is hard-shell. Soft-shell crabs are cooked and eaten shell and all. Brush the crab with butter and lemon juice, then grill it, cook it on a griddle or barbecue it for about 10 minutes.

LOBSTER

One fair-sized lobster will serve 2 people, and is equally good served hot or cold. Controversy continues about whether a lobster suffers less if it is gradually heated to death in cold water brought to the boil, or if it is plunged in boiling water. You'll have to decide for yourself. In either case, when the water has come to the boil, cover the pan and simmer for 20 to 25 minutes. Then remove the lobster. When it is cool enough to handle, slit the underside of the shell with strong scissors. Remove the dark vein that runs along the body and the hard sac near the head. Crack the claws. Cut the lobster in half lengthways with a large, strong knife and flatten it out.

You can serve the lobster at this point, perhaps accompanied by a dish of egg and lemon sauce (page 31). But I prefer grilled lobster. Kill and prepare the lobster as above, then place it on a rack about 5cm (2in) from a pre-heated grill, the flesh side towards the heat. Brush with butter, margarine or oil and grill on a medium heat for about 10 minutes. Serve sprinkled with paprika, garnished with lemon wedges and accompanied by egg and lemon sauce (page 31) and parsley.

MUSSELS

These need to be eaten very fresh, but if in any doubt about their origin, I keep them for a day in clean salty water so they can clean themselves out a bit: mussels' health very much reflects that of the water they come from. They are like little filters. You need about 450g (1lb) weight of shells per generous serving. Discard any mussels that don't close tightly when you touch them. Wash the mussels under running water, scrubbing the shells and pulling off any wiry beards. Place them in a casserole with a few tablespoons of wine and some chopped parsley and chives and bake in a very hot oven until the shells open – about 5 to 10 minutes. Or simmer them with wine, parsley and chives in a large saucepan on top of the stove, again for 5 to 10 minutes. Discard any mussels that have not opened. Mussels steamed or baked open can be eaten hot from the shell, or removed from the shell when cold and eaten with salad, or added to fish soup.

To make moules à la marinière, for 4: bring to the boil in a large pan 300ml (½ pint) dry white wine, 2 sticks of celery, 2 onions and 4 shallots, all finely chopped, a crushed clove of garlic and a handful of chopped parsley. Simmer for 5 minutes, then add 1.5 to 2kg (3 to 4lb) cleaned mussels, cover the pan and simmer for another 5 minutes or so, until the mussels open. Discard any closed mussels. Add a little oil or butter if wanted, and season with pepper. Serve the mussels in heated bowls, with their cooking liquid. Always avoid overcooking mussels, as this makes them rubbery.

OYSTERS

People do cook them, but then they lose their special qualities of taste and texture. Their texture and scent of the sea are 'love it or hate it', but if you love it, acquire the skill of opening oysters without cutting

---

LUNCH MENU

Herb platter with curd or goat's cheese **175 cals**

—•—

Moules marinière **160 cals**

—•—

Gooseberry crumble **195 cals**

Total calories per person **530**

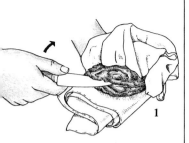

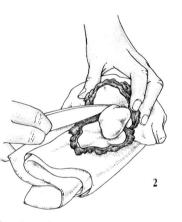

Opening oysters
1 Wrap one hand in two thicknesses of cloth and press down on the shell, flat side up, with your palm. Insert a wide-bladed strong knife into the shell through the hinge, and prise the two halves of the shell apart by twisting the knife blade, as shown.
2 Gently cut the oyster from its moorings, top and bottom.

yourself. Like most people, I have never had enough practice at this, but the approved method which practice is claimed to make perfect is to wrap your left hand (if right-handed) in two thicknesses of clean cloth, and put each shell, flat side up, under your palm, pressing down on the worktop. Then insert a wide-bladed, stubby but strong kitchen knife between the two halves of the shell through the hinge. Holding the top shell down with your hand curved over it, prise the halves open by twisting the knife. Remove the top half of the shell and gently cut the oyster from its moorings top and bottom. If you don't own an oyster dish, which has hollows to keep the shells upright and avoid spilling their liquor, settle each shell into a bed of crushed ice as you open it.

To eat an oyster, squeeze lemon juice on it, lift it in your fingers and tip the contents of the shell, oyster and liquid, into your mouth. Between oysters, eat thin slices of wholemeal or rye bread sparingly spread with butter.

PRAWNS

Treat like scallops (below). They keep their size and flavour better if they are cooked in the shell.

SCALLOPS

One of the great treats. Allow only 2 to 3 good-sized ones per person as a main course, as they are very rich. To prepare them, shell if necessary, then cut out and discard the dark veins that run along the sides. It is usually best also to cut off the coral and cook it separately, but if you are intending to barbecue the scallops, leave the coral on.

Scallops taste wonderful grilled, cooked on a griddle or barbecued. You can just brush them lightly with oil and lemon juice before grilling on a medium-high setting. Or marinate them first for at least an hour in the mixture given in the recipe for coriander fish kebabs (page 173). Beware of overcooking: scallops only take about 3 to 4 minutes to cook, and if they are left longer they get tough. Add the corals to the grill or griddle half-way through the cooking time. Barbecue the corals with the scallops.

Although scallops have plenty of flavour of their own, tarragon does complement them particularly well, and this can be used to replace other herbs in the marinade. Serve on a bed of rice, or with salad in pitta bread.

SCAMPI AND LARGE PRAWNS

Remove the shells. Remove the black veins from the backs. Only the tails and meat from the claws of scampi are usually eaten. Grill scampi or large prawns on a greased baking tin – to catch the juices – simply brushed with a mixture of a very small amount of oil, 5ml (1 tsp) soya sauce and a crushed clove of garlic. Grill for about 8 minutes, about 10cm (4in) from a high heat, turning once. They can also be grilled on a skewer, as ingredients of a kebab. Cut them in pieces if they are very large. Serve grilled scampi or prawns on a bed of rice with leafy greens such as spinach or fennel. Any extra can be used in fish cocktails or mixed with a green salad.

TRADITIONAL FISH DISHES

This section covers special ideas for baking, grilling and steaming fish as well as a variety of ideas for mixing fish with other ingredients, from rice to potatoes. As fish lacks fibre, serve it with high-fibre food.

HAZELNUT TROUT IN AN OVERCOAT

This recipe is elegant enough for a party, and makes the fish go much further. It can be adapted to other types of fish, although the moistness of trout is ideal. Salmon trout has a more exciting flavour than its freshwater relative. *Serves 5 to 6.*

1 mix of yeast pastry (page 259), with a little egg reserved for glazing
15ml (1 tbsp) brandy (optional)
1 × 900g (2lb) trout or 2 × 450g (1lb) trout, gutted
Stuffing
75g (3oz) hazelnuts, toasted
100g (4oz) sultanas, well washed
15ml (1 tbsp) parsley, chopped, or fronds of fennel
good squeeze of lemon juice
1ml (¼ tsp) nutmeg
good grinding of pepper
about 15ml (1 tbsp) flaked hazelnuts or flaked almonds, to garnish

1 Make the yeast pastry, adding the brandy, if you are using it, with the egg. Cover the pastry and set it aside while you prepare the trout.
2 Wash the trout (they are naturally slimy; that doesn't mean they aren't fresh) under a tap, and place it slit down on a wooden board. Cut off the head and tail, and press down firmly along the backbone until you feel it give. This loosens the bone, and when you then turn the fish over you should be able to extract the backbone and the large bones joining on to it fairly easily.
3 On a large, lightly greased baking sheet, roll out the pastry thinly into a shape that will wrap your fish.
4 Place the fish on the pastry, skin down.
5 Pile hazelnuts, sultanas, parsley or fennel, lemon juice, nutmeg and pepper into the empty space in the fish.
6 Heat the oven to 200°C (400°F), gas mark 6.
7 Close the fish over the filling and encase both in the pastry. Seal the edges and trim the pastry, making decorative shapes with the trimmings such as small fishes or leaves, if you like. Brush the 'overcoats' with the reserved egg and sprinkle with the nuts. Bake large fish for 35 to 40 minutes, smaller fish for 25 to 30 minutes, reducing the heat to 190°C (375°F), gas mark 5, for the last 10 minutes, or for even longer if you find that the pastry is browning too rapidly.
8 Serve cut in diagonal slices.

Calories About 375 to 450 a serving. If using flaked almonds, add about 5 a serving.

• Suitable for diabetics (halving quantity of sultanas)
• Medium fibre
• Very low fat (using white fish)
• Milk-free (using water only in pastry)

This recipe adds fibre (from the pastry casing, the nuts and the sultanas) to the fish. The very small amount of fat in the pastry keeps the fish moist.

Trout is, in theory, an oily fish but it contains only about 4 per cent fat. It is low in vitamins compared with some fish, but relatively high in protein.

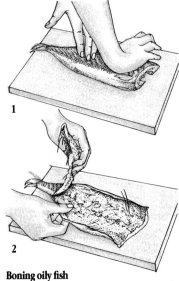

Boning oily fish
1 With the head removed, place the fish slit side down on a board and press firmly on the backbone with your hand to loosen the bone.
2 Turn the fish over and remove the backbone and any large bones attached to it.

VARIATIONS

You can use *herring* instead of trout, substituting *apple slices* for the sultanas in the filling. In fact almost any moist fish can be used, in fillets if you dislike boning. You could even, for instance, encase a slice from a big *tuna fish*.

GRILLED MACKEREL WITH GOOSEBERRY SAUCE

The tang of this combination of Chinese-style stuffing and very English sauce suits the richness of the fish. The fibre in the gooseberries helps to make up for the lack of it in the fish. *Serves 4.*

4 small mackerel, boned, or 4 steaks from large mackerel
soya sauce, for brushing
Stuffing
60ml (4 tbsp) wholemeal breadcrumbs
30ml (2 tbsp) soya sauce
5ml (1 tsp) ginger root, grated
juice of ½ lemon
10ml (2 tsp) sherry
1 egg
Sauce
225g (8oz) gooseberries
15ml (1 tbsp) honey
2 sprigs of sweet cicely (if available)

1 Heat the grill. Brush the rack with oil.
2 Mix the stuffing ingredients and divide the stuffing between the fish, packing it well into the cavities. Secure the openings with toothpicks if necessary. If using steaks, remove the bones and stuff the centres, or make 2 deep slits through the flesh and stuff these.
3 Cut diagonal slits across the side of each fish. Brush the fish with soya sauce.
4 Grill the stuffed mackerel at a medium-to-high setting for about 6 minutes on each side, until they are cooked through.
5 Meanwhile, cook the gooseberries with the honey, and the sweet cicely if available, in the minimum of water. Fresh gooseberries will take about 15 minutes to cook to the right consistency. They will probably burst and 'purée' themselves naturally; otherwise they can easily be mashed them with a fork.
6 Serve the mackerel accompanied by the hot gooseberry sauce.

GRILLED HUSS, KABAYAKI STYLE

So easy, and makes unexciting fish (or eel, which some people find off-putting) mouthwateringly savoury, the outside firm, the flesh moist. This method comes from Japan, where mirin is used rather than sherry, and the fish used for kabayaki is eel. This dish is much eaten at midsummer. *Serves 4.*

Calories About 410 a serving.

• Suitable for diabetics (halving quantity of honey)
• Low fibre
• Milk-free
• Gluten-free (using gluten-free breadcrumbs and tamari instead of soya sauce)

Sweet cicely can be difficult to find, so it's worth growing it, as it is extremely useful when cooking fruit. It seems to reduce the sharpness of fruit, so that less sugar is needed, even for gooseberries and rhubarb which are often sour.

GLUTEN-FREE DINNER MENU

Mixed salad **100 cals**
—•—
Grilled mackerel with gooseberry sauce **410 cals**
Greek spinach **40 cals**
Potatoes, boiled or baked, **150 cals**
—•—
Fresh fruit salad **60 cals**

Total calories per person **760**

Calories About 210 a serving.

- No fibre
- Very low fat (unless using eel)
- Milk-free
- Gluten-free

Mature silver eels are very rich in fat, so choose the spring and summer elvers and eels or use huss, the much neglected dogfish which is very tasty and low in fat.

Calories Makes 10 at about 85 calories each (using white fish); about 100 calories each (using salmon).

- Suitable for diabetics
- Medium fibre
- Very low fat (omitting fat and egg yolks, and using white fish)
- Very low salt (omitting salt and egg whites)
- Gluten-free (using gluten-free breadcrumbs)

Don't reach for the frying pan whenever you see a burger or patty shape in a recipe. Although you can finish such dishes in very little fat in a cast-iron pan, you can also usually grill them or cook them in the oven instead.

700g (1½lb) huss (dogfish) or eel, cut in 5cm (2in) lengths
45ml (3 tbsp) soya sauce
45ml (3 tbsp) dry sherry

1 Heat the grill. Lightly grease a baking sheet.
2 Boil the soya sauce and the sherry together for 2 to 3 minutes, to thicken.
3 Put the fish chunks on the baking sheet and, using a pastry brush, paint them with the sauce mixture.
4 Grill on a high heat for 3 minutes, paint the fish again and grill for 2 minutes more.
5 Turn the fish pieces over, paint, grill for 3 minutes, paint and grill again for 2 minutes.
6 The fish surface will be brown and shiny. Serve with any extra sauce poured over.

NUTMEGGY FISH CAKES

Really worth making, because they are so much better than bought ones. *Makes about 10 medium-size.*

225g (8oz) white fish or salmon, cut in chunks
450g (1lb) potatoes, unpeeled
1 onion, finely chopped
10ml (2 tsp) soft margarine or butter
2 eggs
150ml (¼ pint) skimmed milk or water
2ml (½ tsp) ground nutmeg
good pinch of chili pepper
30ml (2 tbsp) parsley, chopped
large pinch of white pepper
10ml (2 tsp) lemon juice
pinch of sea salt
50g (2oz) wholemeal breadcrumbs, dried in the oven

1 Boil or steam the potatoes for about 25 minutes.
2 Meanwhile, soften the onion in the margarine or butter in a covered pan over a low heat for 15 minutes.
3 Mash the potatoes thoroughly with the onion, then beat in the eggs, reserving about 30ml (2 tbsp) egg for coating.
4 Cook the fish very gently for about 8 minutes in the milk or water in a covered pan.
5 Shred the fish, removing any odd bones, and mix it with the potatoes and all of the other ingredients except the reserved egg and the breadcrumbs. Chill the mixture for at least an hour.
6 With your hands, pat the mixture into about 10 fish cakes.
7 Dip the fish cakes into the reserved egg, then the breadcrumbs, patting the crumbs on firmly.
8 Either sauté the fish cakes in a very little oil in a thick-based pan, or grill them on a lightly greased oven tray under a medium to hot grill, in either case for 4 to 5 minutes each side.

DINNER PARTY MENU

Vegetable terrine **115 cals**
Tomato or creamy herb sauce
50 cals
—•—
Coriander fish kebabs **200 cals**
Rice **160 cals**
Watercress, orange and black olive salad **120 cals**
Stuffed pears **140 cals**

Total calories per person **785**

CORIANDER FISH KEBABS

An excellent dinner party dish; although it needs advance preparation, it's simple, quick and fun to serve. The red wine in the marinade gives a delicate pale pink colour. Use a chunky fish. Monkfish is ideal, but swordfish, tuna or halibut would be good. *Serves 4.*

700g (1½lb) monkfish (or similar), cut in large chunks
1 large onion, cut in eighths
8 small mushrooms
8 very small (cherry) tomatoes or chunks of courgette or marrow
Marinade
juice of 1 lemon (about 30ml [2 tbsp])
1 clove of garlic, crushed (optional)
5ml (1 tsp) mild mustard
5ml (1 tsp) ground coriander
30ml (2 tbsp) red wine
15ml (1 tbsp) cold-pressed olive or other oil
freshly ground black pepper
pinch of sea salt

Calories About 200 a serving, depending on the fish chosen.

Suitable for diabetics
No fibre
Very low fat (halving quantity of oil)
Milk-free
Gluten-free

Coriander fish kebabs

1 Combine the marinade ingredients in a bowl. Use *dry cider* or *white wine* instead of red wine if you don't want a pink colour. Stir the fish and the onion thoroughly into the marinade, and leave for at least 1 hour and up to 24. There will be a good deal of marinade left over, ideal for making a variation on mushrooms à la grecque (page 62).
2 Heat the grill or barbecue. Brush the rack lightly with oil.
3 Use 4 long skewers or 8 shorter ones. Thread the skewers with the fish chunks, mushrooms, tomatoes or courgette chunks and the onion broken into thin pieces. Grill on a high heat for about 5 minutes on each side.
4 Serve with a plain grain, such as brown rice, or with wholemeal pitta bread.

CHINESE STEAMED FISH

How to take the 'bland and tasteless' slur away from steamed fish: this way it's full of flavour. Suitable for any type of fish except herring or mackerel, which are too rich for this treatment. *Serves 3 to 4.*

1 fish, about 550g (1¼lb) when gutted
Stuffing
10ml (2 tsp) ginger root, grated
4 to 5 spring onions, roughly chopped
10ml (2 tsp) soya sauce
2ml (½ tsp) white pepper
5ml (1 tsp) oil, preferably peanut or sesame

1 Wash and dry the fish.
2 Mix the ginger, half of the spring onions, the soya sauce and the pepper. Stuff the mixture into the fish.
3 Boil water in the bottom half of a steamer. Place the fish in the top of the steamer and dribble the oil over it. Cover tightly.
4 Steam the fish over simmering water for 10 minutes, then sprinkle it with the remaining onions and steam for a further 5 to 8 minutes, until it is cooked.

VARIATION

If you dislike fish with bones, place the same filling between *2 fillets of fish*, or on top of *single thin fish steaks*, which will need only about 8 to 10 minutes to cook.

KEDGEREE

This version is generous with the fish, so you don't end up eating your way through mounds of rice to find shreds of it. *Serves 4.*

100g (4oz) long grain brown rice
225g (8oz) Arbroath smokies or Finnan haddie, in large flakes
2 eggs, hard-boiled and chopped
10ml (2 tsp) soft margarine or butter
paprika, to taste and to garnish
freshly ground black pepper
15ml (1 tbsp) parsley, chopped

Calories About 120 to 190 a serving.

- Suitable for diabetics
- Very low fibre
- Very low fat
- Milk-free
- Gluten-free (using tamari instead of soya sauce)

Balance this mainly protein dish with complementary flavours that also provide fibre and freshness such as spinach, brown rice or baked potatoes. Keep the oriental mood by starting the meal with won ton (page 67) or carrot and caraway soup (page 72).

Calories About 200 a serving.

- Suitable for diabetics
- Medium fibre
- Very low fat (omitting egg yolks and halving quantity of fat)
- Milk-free (using dairy-free margarine)
- Gluten-free

Arbroath smokies and Finnan haddie are usually free from the colouring standard in ordinary smoked herrings and haddock, and have a subtler and, to my taste, better flavour.

1 Wash the rice in a sieve under a tap, and place it in a saucepan with 300ml (½ pint) water. Bring to the boil, cover and simmer over the lowest heat for 30 minutes.
2 Add the fish, chopped eggs, margarine or butter, paprika and black pepper. Stir together.
3 Replace the lid and continue simmering for 10 to 15 minutes. By this time the rice should be tender and the mixture quite dry. If it is too dry, add a little water.
4 Stir in the parsley and serve.

VARIATION

100g (4oz) toasted peanuts can be used to replace the fish.

KULEBYAKA
(RUSSIAN FISH PIE)

A good party piece. Traditionally made with buckwheat, but check whether you like buckwheat first. If not, use rice. I like even better the egg and mushroom filling which I have noted as a variation – with that slice of smoked salmon on top. The rosemary makes all the difference. *Serves 4 to 5.*

1 mix of yeast pastry (page 259)
50g (2oz) buckwheat or long grain brown rice
10ml (2 tsp) oil
1 onion, chopped
175g (6oz) white fish, such as haddock, skinned and boned, in chunks
15ml (1 tbsp) white or red wine
generous 5ml (1 tsp) fresh rosemary, finely chopped
scant 5ml (1 tsp) mixed herbs
50g (2oz) mushrooms (optional), chopped
5ml (1 tsp) oil or butter (optional)
10ml (2 tsp) lemon juice
good pinch of white pepper
30ml (2 tbsp) parsley, chopped
100g (4oz) smoked haddock or 75g (3oz) smoked salmon, in thin slices
a little egg, beaten (reserved when making the pastry), to glaze

1 Check the buckwheat or rice using the basic methods (pages 89 and 97).
2 Soften the onion in 5ml (1 tsp) oil in a covered pan, set over the lowest heat, for 8 minutes.
3 Add another 5ml (1 tsp) oil, then the fish, and cook for 5 minutes.
4 Remove the pan from the heat, add the wine, rosemary and mixed herbs and mash everything together roughly with a fork.
5 If using mushrooms, sweat them in another 5ml (1 tsp) oil, or butter, in a thick-based pan over a low to medium heat, uncovered, for 5 minutes, until they are browning.
6 Mix well the buckwheat or rice, the fish mixture and the mushrooms. Add the lemon juice, pepper and parsley.
7 Roll out the pastry on a greased baking sheet into a square about 25cm (10in) across. Keep any excess pastry for another dish.

alories About 280 to 350 a serving.

Suitable for diabetics
High fibre
Very low salt (replacing sauce with low-fat ariation, page 28)
Milk-free (using soya milk)
Gluten-free (replacing flour with cornflour or ce flour)

sing more vegetables than usual improves the alance of this dish. Peas and broad beans are as ch in protein as dried pulses, and both they and reen beans provide good sources of fibre, which is kind of pie otherwise lacks.

y using a mixture of white and smoked fish, you dd interest and reduce the amount of salt that is sually required.

RUSSIAN MENU

Blini with onions and soft cheese **300 cals**

—•—

Kulebyaka (fish pie) **280 cals**
Mushrooms in soured cream **110 cals**
Beetroot, apple and chicory salad **80 cals**

—•—

Dutch apple ice **105 cals**

Total calories per person **875**

8 Place half of the mixture in the centre of the pastry, arranged in the shape of a square with the sides facing the corners of the pastry square. Top with half of the slices of smoked fish. Repeat the layers.
9 Fold the edges of the pastry over the filling like an envelope. If there is any more spare pastry (I usually have a little over), use scissors to cut it into fish shapes to decorate the pie.
10 Cover the pie with a cloth or polythene and let it prove for 20 minutes.
11 Heat the oven to 200°C (400°F), gas mark 6.
12 Brush the pie generously with the beaten egg and bake it for 20 to 25 minutes, until it is golden.

VARIATION

Replace the white fish with *2 hard-boiled eggs, chopped*, and increase the quantity of mushrooms to 175g (6oz). This version is particularly good with salmon slices. Vegetarians can replace the fish layers with layers of either *Cheshire cheese, sliced very thinly*, or any *lightly cooked vegetables.*

Calories About 290 to 365 a serving for the egg variation; about 310 to 385 if substituting cheese for fish.

SEASONED FISH

Six dishes with special spicing, although none are 'hot'. If you like to be just a little adventurous, try them. They're very simple to make.

MEDITERRANEAN SQUID

When you see squid at the fishmongers, it's hard to believe they are ever going to taste delicious – never mind so easily. Take the plunge, and this economical meal can become part of your regular repertoire. You don't need to worry about the squid being tough if you treat it like this: it's octopus that's more inclined to be rubbery. *Serves 4.*

Calories About 270 a serving.

- Suitable for diabetics
- Low fibre
- Very low fat (halving quantity of oil)
- Milk-free
- Gluten-free

Many people are put off squid by over-oily dishes in Mediterranean resorts. But, like other seafood, it's a good source of protein, complete with a selection of vitamins and minerals.

700g (1½lb) squid (2 smallish)
15ml (1 tbsp) olive oil
1 large onion, cut in half-rings
1 clove of garlic (optional), crushed
pinch of chili powder
450g (1lb) tomatoes, roughly chopped
22ml (1½ tbsp) tomato purée
150ml (¼ pint) dry wine
2ml (½ tsp) honey
generous paprika, to taste
black pepper
pinch of sea salt
2ml (½ tsp) basil, or 5ml (1 tsp) fresh leaves, chopped (optional)
15ml (1 tbsp) parsley, chopped

1 Hold the tentacles of a squid with one hand, the other end in the other hand, and pull it gently apart.
2 Inside the 'bag' end you'll find a long, thin, almost transparent piece of what looks like plastic, but is in fact a 'pen'-shaped quill of bone. Take it out and throw it away.
3 Hold the squid under a cold water tap and rub and pull off the filmy

outer skin. Cut the squid's body into rings 1 to 2cm (½ to ¾in) wide.
4 Cut the tentacles into 2cm (¾in) lengths and add them to the rings.
5 Remove the ink sac intact from the remaining head part, if possible. If not, forget it. Put the ink sac in a cup. Throw the head away.
6 Prepare the second squid in the same way.
7 Heat the oil in a pan, add the squid and the onion and shake the pan to coat them with oil. Cook over medium heat until they are lightly browning. At this stage, you may get an unpleasant whiff of ammonia – don't worry.
8 Add the garlic, chili powder, tomatoes, tomato purée, vermouth or wine and honey, plus the contents of the ink sacs if retained.
9 Simmer, covered, over a low heat for 15 to 30 minutes, until the squid is tender.
10 Season the sauce with paprika, black pepper and sea salt, adding a little basil if liked. Taste, and if it lacks flavour add a little more tomato purée and basil. This sauce should be fairly thick. If it is too runny, remove the squid and boil the sauce for some minutes to reduce it. Return the squid to the sauce to reheat it.
11 Serve the dish with a lavish amount of parsley on top.

FISH TERRINE

A very pretty way of serving fish, especially if you have a long, not too deep terrine. Buy your courgettes to fit your terrine, and pick straight ones. This recipe may look complicated, but it's not tricky. It's important to season generously, or the result is bland. *Serves 5 to 6*

Fish terrine (much easier than it looks) with tarator hazelnut sauce (page 31)

Calories About 160 to 190 a serving.

• Suitable for diabetics
• Medium fibre
• Very low fat (substituting yogurt for smetana, omitting fat) if you don't use Cheshire cheese variation
• Gluten-free (using gluten-free breadcrumbs)

This terrine avoids the pitfalls of double cream and many egg yolks. It brings out the taste of the fish. Serve it with a creamy herb sauce (page 32), tarator hazelnut sauce (page 31) or pesto (page 32), plus a garnish of greenstuff.

450g (1lb) white fish, filleted and skinned
10ml (2 tsp) mixed herbs
2 pinches of 5-spice powder
10ml (2 tsp) brandy
juice of 1 small lemon
1ml (¼ tsp) pepper
pinch of sea salt
100g (4oz) fine wholemeal breadcrumbs
about 45ml (3 tbsp) skimmed milk to moisten breadcrumbs
45ml (3 tbsp) smetana or soured cream
10ml (2 tsp) soft margarine or butter, melted
3 egg whites, stiffly beaten
2 long thick courgettes, about 225g (8oz)
4 slices smoked salmon (large trimmings will do well)
about 100g (4oz) or 75g (3oz) red Cheshire cheese, grated
a few slices of courgette or some almond flakes, to garnish

1 Mince the fish on the finest blade of a mincer or purée it in a food processor.
2 Add the herbs, 5-spice powder, brandy, lemon juice, pepper, sea salt and breadcrumbs moistened sparsely with the skimmed milk. Mix well.
3 Stir in the smetana or soured cream and the melted fat.
4 Beat the egg whites until stiff and fold them into the mixture.
5 Grease a long terrine or 2 × 450g (1lb) loaf tins thoroughly and arrange a few decorative courgette slices or flaked nuts along the base. Tip in half of the mixture.
6 Heat the oven to 180°C (350°F), gas mark 4.
7 Blanch the courgettes, whole and unpeeled, in boiling water for 4 minutes. Drain.
8 Trim the courgettes so that, laid end to end, they make a neat cylinder along the terrine.
9 Wrap each one in two thicknesses of smoked salmon, and press it up to half its depth into the fish mixture, making a central cylinder. Or, if using cheese, halve the courgettes lengthways and sandwich the halves with the cheese, before placing them in the terrine mixture.
10 Tip in the rest of the fish mixture. Tap the terrine or tins firmly on a wooden board to shake the mixture down, rather than flattening it with a spoon, which would take the air out of the beaten whites.
11 Cover the top of the dish with kitchen foil and sit it in a baking tin. Pour into the outer tin hot water to half the depth of the terrine. Bake for 1 hour. The fish should be fairly firm when you prod it.
12 Chill the terrine for at least 2 hours.
13 To serve, dip the base of the dish for a few seconds in boiling or very hot water and turn the terrine out. Cut 2 slices per person as a starter, 3 thicker ones as a main course, holding each slice upright with a broad spatula as you cut.

VARIATION

If you like, you can cover the terrine with *aspic*. Heat *150ml (¼ pint) well-flavoured stock* and dissolve in it *5ml (1 tsp) gelatine*. Chill until tepid, then add *5ml (1 tsp) sherry or port*. When the aspic becomes syrupy, spoon it over the fish terrine turned out on a serving dish. Excess aspic will set around the terrine. Chop it up roughly before serving.

SPICED SHRIMP

Just delicious – and if prawns and shrimps are expensive, mix them half and half with cubed white fish. *Serves 4.*

450g (1lb) prawns or shrimps, peeled
20ml (4 tsp) tarragon vinegar
20ml (4 tsp) ground coriander
1 clove of garlic, crushed
20ml (4 tsp) ground ginger
15ml (1 tbsp) honey
5ml (1 tsp) 5-spice powder

1 If you are using large prawns, de-vein them and split them down the back to make flat x-shapes.
2 Place all of the ingredients in a bowl and stir well. Leave the mixture to marinate for at least 2 hours, and up to 24.
3 Heat a thick-based pan or wok thoroughly, and brush lightly with oil.
4 Add the contents of the bowl and stir-fry over a fairly high heat for 3 to 4 minutes.

LIGHTLY CURRIED FISH

Not hot, but an interesting variation for white fish – and you can use inexpensive kinds, such as coley (which whitens on cooking). Very quick after the initial marinade. *Serves 4 to 5.*

700g (1½lb) white fish, filleted, with the skin on or off, to taste*
60 to 75ml (4 to 5 tbsp) plain low-fat yogurt
10ml (2 tsp) curry powder
2ml (½ tsp) ground cumin
pinch of turmeric
2ml (½ tsp) ground coriander
juice of 1 lemon
1cm (½in) piece of fresh ginger root, finely grated
1 clove of garlic (optional), crushed
4 shallots, roughly chopped
10ml (2 tsp) oil
1ml (¼ tsp) white pepper
pinch of sea salt
15ml (1 tbsp) parsley, chopped, to garnish

*If you prefer your fish to stay in separate pieces, rather than flake together, leave the skin on.

1 Cut the fish into 8 pieces, and place it in a flat dish.
2 Mix the yogurt, curry powder, cumin, turmeric, coriander, half of the lemon juice, the ginger, and the garlic if using. Spread this mixture over the skinned side of the fish pieces. Leave the spiced fish for at least 1 hour in a refrigerator, to allow the flavours to blend.
3 In a large, wide saucepan, covered, sauté the shallots in the oil, until they are soft – about 10 minutes. Add the fish pieces and shake the pan to spread the juices around.

Calories About 110 a serving using shrimps; about 120 in total using shrimps and white fish half-and-half.

- Suitable for diabetics
- No fibre
- Very low fat
- Milk-free
- Gluten-free

Shellfish are particularly rich in minerals, especially iodine, zinc and iron. Although they are low in fat, they are often high in cholesterol.

Calories About 115 to 175 a serving.

- Suitable for diabetics
- No fibre
- Very low fat
- Milk-free (using soya yogurt)
- Gluten-free

4 Cover the pan again and simmer for 5 minutes. Turn the fish over, taking care not to break up the pieces, and simmer for 4 to 5 minutes more, when it will be done. Season with pepper and salt, and add more lemon juice to taste.

5 Strew chopped parsley thickly over the dish before serving.

CEVICHE
(LIME-MARINATED RAW FISH)

Don't turn over the page at the mention of raw fish. It is no more raw than smoked salmon by the time you eat it. Use the freshest fish – and feel confident that this recipe is tried and tested. *Serves 4 to 6.*

450g (1lb) monkfish or shark, boned and shredded (or use salmon)
350g (12oz) mixed fresh lemon and lime juice (say, 4 lemons and 2 limes)
1 chili pepper, deseeded and finely sliced
1 onion, sliced
1 large tomato, chopped
15ml (1 tbsp) oil, preferably sesame
large pinch of oregano
15ml (1 tbsp) wine vinegar
wedges of lemon or lime, to serve
wholemeal bread, thinly sliced, to serve

Calories About 90 to 135 a serving. If using salmon, add 45 to 70 a serving. Allow 60 to 70 calories for each slice of wholemeal bread.

- Suitable for diabetics
- High fibre (if eaten with wholemeal bread)
- Very low fat (omitting half the oil)
- Milk-free
- Gluten-free (served with gluten-free bread)

Gravad lax, served here with fennel and mustard sauce

Fish does not lose much value in cooking, so the main advantage of this style of recipe is the flavour, plus the generous amount of vitamin C in the citrus juice.

The marinade will keep for a few days in the refrigerator.

Calories About 155 to 230 a serving.

• Suitable for diabetics.
• No fibre
• Gluten-free (serving with gluten-free bread)

Salmon is one of the oiliest fish, yet its average fat content of 4 to 10 per cent is still lower than that of most meat. The fat content varies according to the time of year and is mainly unsaturated rather than hard. Like most oily fish, salmon includes some highly polyunsaturated fatty acids, which may be particularly useful to health.

1 Place the fish in a glass bowl and cover it with the citrus juice. Refrigerate, covered, for 4 hours.
2 Combine the chili pepper, onion, tomato, sesame oil, oregano and vinegar in a bowl. Cover the bowl and leave the mixture until the fish is ready, for the flavours to blend. Do not chill it.
3 Drain the juice from the fish (keep the juice to marinate another batch of fish if you want). Mix in the chili blend.
4 Serve the ceviche with citrus wedges and thinly cut wholemeal bread.

GRAVAD LAX
(DILL-PICKLED SALMON)

Scandinavian dill-pickled salmon, 'gravad lax', uses dill and pepper to give the fish a very attractive flavour. Curing salmon in this way isn't difficult, but the result is impressive. Curing with honey pre-dates the arrival of sugar in northern Europe. *Serves 4 to 6.*

450 to 700g (1 to 1½lb) salmon tail
30ml (2 tbsp) clear honey
22ml (1½ tbsp) rock salt
5ml (1 tsp) green or pink peppercorns, crushed
good bunch of fresh dill, including stalks, chopped
30ml (2 tbsp) brandy
Sauce
creamy herb sauce (page 32)
5 to 10ml (1 to 2 tsp) mild Dijon or wholegrain mustard, to taste
lemon juice, to taste
wholemeal bread, thinly sliced, to serve

1 Ask the fishmonger to remove the bone, or do it yourself like this: cut a deep slit along the belly next to the bone. Open out the fish, slit down, on a work surface. Press the top ridge flat gently with your palm. This loosens the bone: turn the fish over again and you can lift out the bone with minimum disturbance to the flesh. Complete the cut through the fish so that it is divided lengthways into 2 halves.
2 Dry the fish surface with kitchen paper.
3 Put one half skin down in a flat china or glass dish.
4 Mix together the honey, salt, peppercorns, dill and brandy.
5 Rub the mixture into the surfaces of both pieces of fish, using most on the skinless side. Keep a little of the mixture aside.
6 Spread the reserved mixture on top of the fillet in the dish. Cover it with the second fillet, skin side uppermost. Put kitchen foil over the dish and weight it heavily – this is important. A brick or a large tin of food makes a suitable weight.
7 Place the dish in the refrigerator. Turn the fish, top to bottom, twice a day, for 3 to 4 days.
8 Gravad lax is usually served with a mustard sauce: add to creamy herb sauce (page 32) mild Dijon or wholegrain mustard, to taste, plus a little lemon juice. Serve cold.
9 Wipe the marinade off the gravad lax and slice the fish thinly. Serve accompanied by the mustard sauce and very thinly cut wholemeal bread.

GAME, POULTRY & MEAT

Choosing leaner meat is one of the simplest ways of improving your diet. There is a lot of fat in a small quantity. So, each time you dodge enough fat to fill a matchbox, you're making a worthwhile cut in a form of food that most of us eat far more of than we need for health. At the same time, you're freeing about 200 calories which would be better consumed in foods most of us eat too little of, such as high-fibre cereals.

This section concentrates on meat that is naturally lower in fat and on delicious recipes that avoid added fat or that actively reduce fat.

Poultry is the obvious choice, especially as it's available and economical. You'll enjoy it far more, though, if you take the trouble to find a supplier whose birds have not been intensively reared. The meat has more flavour, is usually less fatty and won't leave you with an aftertaste of anxiety about residues of farming drugs or food poisoning that often affect mass-reared birds through their food. This is particularly important when you want to buy chicken or turkey livers, as it's the liver which tends to collect drug traces.

Game is free from such problems, and has other advantages too. Firstly, it's just as low in fat, and the fat is of a more useful kind than that in farmed meat. It's less saturated, richer in the polyunsaturated and essential fatty acids. Secondly, the flavours are richer, which means that smaller portions are more satisfying.

What about duck? It is certainly high in fat, so I've suggested cooking methods which extract a startling amount of the fat, leaving you with the tasty meat. I've also included lamb recipes that follow the same principle.

You won't find recipes for beef or pork here. This is partly because recipes abound elsewhere, and partly because neither meat is particularly helpful when you are restyling your eating patterns. Lean pork is almost a contradiction in terms, unless you come across wild boar. Beef can certainly be lean, but one reason why farm-reared beef is getting leaner is because of the common usage of hormone implants. I personally find plenty of variety in meals without using either pork or beef and, although I wouldn't frown at their use, I think it's a good trend to move towards other, leaner meats and fish.

When you are cooking lean meat, marinades become part of daily life. They have a wonderful effect on tenderness, moistness and flavour, and they are simple to prepare. The marinade also shortens the cooking time required, reducing the risk of the

Pigeon with black grapes, garnished with tarragon and parsley

meat's becoming too dry. Usually the wine and herbs from the marinade are also used in the cooking, or they can be added to the stock jug to make a particularly good soup.

Roasting and grilling are the best methods of bringing out the flavour in meat and, if you want to cook beef or pork, I recommend these methods also for maximum fat reduction.

Roasting is to my mind the best way of retaining the distinctive flavour of game such as pheasant, quail or wild duck (which, in contrast to farmed duck, is lean). With the very leanest meats, such as rabbit, hare and venison, casseroling is preferable, as it keeps them constantly moist.

Several of the recipes can be used as models, and adapted to other kinds of meat. The lamb curry, for instance, can be made substituting chicken or turkey for the lamb. The rabbit with prunes can be made with pigeons or grouse instead of rabbit. The general principles to follow in adapting are that the new meat should have the same level of flavour – delicate like chicken or rich like pigeon; and a similar fat content – for instance, use goose instead of duck, but not wild duck instead of farmed duck.

ROASTING CHART

Type of meat	Time	Oven temperature	Tips
Chicken	15 to 20 minutes per 450g (1lb) plus 10 minutes extra	200°C (400°F), gas mark 6	Remove flaps of fat from inside bird. Cover bird with foil and cook on its side, turning breast-up and removing foil at half-time. No basting is then needed.
Duck	15 to 20 minutes per 450g (1lb) plus 15 minutes extra	200°C (400°F), gas mark 6	Prick skin all over, immerse bird in boiling water for 1 minute, drain and dry off before roasting on rack over deep tin. Pour off surplus fat during cooking.
Goose	15 to 20 minutes per 450g (1lb)	190°C (375°F). gas mark 5	Allow a generous portion per person. Roast on rack, as for duck, pouring off surplus fat.
Grouse	Total time 25 to 40 minutes	220°C (425°F), gas mark 7	Serve very slightly underdone. Allow 1 grouse per person (some people eat breast only). Young birds only should be roasted; casserole older ones. Watch out for lead pellets.
Lamb	20 to 25 minutes per 450g (1lb)	180°C (350°F), gas mark 4	Serve slightly pink on inside. Allow 10 minutes extra per 450g (1lb) for stuffed joints. Roast on rack, as for duck. Garlic slivers and rosemary can be inserted into skin, to flavour, before roasting.
Mallard (wild duck)	Total time 35 to 45 minutes	190°C (375°F), gas mark 5	A 550g (20oz) bird will serve 3 to 4. Far less fatty than duck, and needs no rack. Paint generously with plum sauce (page 208) before roasting, and serve with more sauce. Watch out for lead pellets.
Partridge	Total time 25 to 30 minutes	190°C (375°F), gas mark 5	Start on its side, turn breast-up after 10 minutes. Watch out for lead pellets.
Pheasant	Total time 1 hour	As for partridge	As for partridge
Pigeon	Total time 20 to 25 minutes	As for partridge	As for partridge
Poussin	Total time 15 to 25 minutes	200°C (400°F), gas mark 6	Start with bird on its side, turn breast-up at half-time. Sit bird on piece of bread while roasting.
Quail	Total time 15 to 20 minutes	190°C (375°F), gas mark 5	Allow 1 to 2 birds per person.
Rabbit	Total time 45 to 60 minutes	180°C (350°F), gas mark 4	Young rabbits only should be roasted. Tie legs firmly under body.
Turkey	See page 198	See page 198	See page 198. Cover with foil, removing foil 30 minutes before end of cooking time.
Venison	15 to 20 minutes per 450g (1lb) plus 15 minutes extra	190°C (375°F), gas mark 5	Roast only large pieces of saddle, leg or haunch. All venison benefits from marinating.

GAME

Game benefits from being well hung and from being marinated, to bring out the flavour and to make the flesh more tender. It does have one drawback – lead pellets – so watch out for them.

GAME PIE

Calories About 325 a serving.

• Suitable for diabetics (occasionally)
• High fibre
• Very low salt (using unsalted butter and breadcrumbs, and omitting salt)
• Milk-free

Simply a lower-fat version of something you may well have dismissed as too complex or fattening to make at home.

An impressive dish, especially if you decorate the top with care. *Serves 8.*

150ml (¼ pint) red wine
30ml (2 tbsp) wine vinegar
2 cloves
450g (1lb) hare, off the bone
1 onion, finely chopped
1 stick of celery, finely chopped
5ml (1 tsp) oil
75g (3oz) mushrooms, chopped
100g (4oz) wholemeal breadcrumbs
1 small apple, grated
5ml (1 tsp) sage, powdered or crumbled
2 eggs
zest of 1 lemon
2ml (½ tsp) ground mace
pinch of sea salt
225g (8oz) chicken, chopped or roughly minced
1 mix of hot water pastry (page 258)
25g (1oz) plain wholemeal flour
5ml (1 tsp) gelatine or agar (optional)

1 Mix together the wine, wine vinegar and cloves, pour over the hare and marinate in the refrigerator for about 2 days.
2 Cook the onion and celery in the oil in a covered pan for about 10 minutes, then add the mushrooms and cook, uncovered, for a further 3 to 4 minutes.
3 Combine the vegetables, breadcrumbs, grated apple, sage, one of the eggs, lemon zest, mace and salt. Stir in the chicken.
4 Roll out enough pastry to fit a fairly deep pie, cake or loaf tin, preferably one with a removable base or springform device. Make sure that the pastry is not more than about 5mm (¼in) thick and that the corners are not too solid.
5 Pack half of the vegetable and chicken mixture in the tin.
6 Drain and chop the hare, then dip the pieces in the flour. Pack on top of the chicken mixture.
7 Heat the oven to 200°C (400°F), gas mark 6.
8 Place the remaining chicken mixture on top of the pie.
9 Roll out the remaining pastry to make a lid for the pie. Use some of the second egg to seal the edges and to glaze the pie lid. Trim the pastry edges decoratively and cut a hole in the centre of the lid. Make decorative shapes for the lid from any remaining pastry. Brush the pie with egg once more.

10 Bake for 30 minutes, then reduce the heat to 160°C (325°F), gas mark 3, and cover the pie with foil to avoid over-browning.

11 After about 1 hour, push a skewer through the hole in the pie lid to test the meat for tenderness. When the meat is tender, remove the pie from the oven and unmould it. Brush the sides with egg, then bake for another 5 minutes.

12 Serve hot or cold. If you intend serving the pie cold, make 150ml (¼ pint) stock, using trimmings from the hare or chicken and the hare marinade. Add to the hot stock 5ml (1 tsp) gelatine or agar. If you use gelatine, just stir to dissolve it; if you use agar, boil the stock with the agar for 2 minutes. Cool the stock until it starts to gel. When the pie is almost cold, spoon the stock in through the hole in the lid. Refrigerate until wanted.

VARIATIONS

You don't have to use hare for the middle layer of your game pie. Any *available game meat* will do.

If you use a fairly large tin, you may find that your pie casing is too big for your filling. You can increase the volume of filling by making a top layer of *sliced raw mushrooms, onions* or *peeled chestnuts*.

HARE WITH MUSTARD AND DILL

Hare has a much stronger and more unusual flavour than rabbit. It's meaty, and small amounts can be satisfying. *Serves 4.*

450 to 550g (1 to 1¼lb) saddle of hare or hare joints
150ml (¼ pint) red wine
30ml (2 tbsp) wine vinegar
2 shallots, chopped
1 bay leaf
1 sprig of fresh rosemary or 5ml (1 tsp) dried rosemary
2 sprigs of fresh thyme or 5ml (1 tsp) dried thyme
15 to 22ml (1 to 1½ tbsp) mild wholegrain mustard
20ml (4 tsp) oil or butter
150ml (¼ pint) stock
1ml (¼ tsp) black pepper
15ml (1 tbsp) plain wholemeal flour
125ml (4fl oz) smetana or thick plain low-fat yogurt
15 to 30ml (1 to 2 tbsp) fresh dill, chopped

1 Place the hare in a flat dish, and pour the wine and wine vinegar over it. Add the chopped shallots, bay leaf, rosemary and thyme. Marinate the hare in the refrigerator for between 12 and 48 hours.

2 Lift out the hare and pat it dry. Use a pastry brush to coat it thoroughly with the mustard, then brown it in the oil or butter for 2 to 3 minutes.

3 Transfer the hare to a large saucepan or casserole, add the stock, the marinade (from which you have removed the bay leaf) and the pepper. Bring to the boil, cover and simmer for about 1½ hours, or until the meat is very tender and coming away slightly from the bones. How long this takes will depend a good deal on the age of the hare.

4 Lift out the hare and slice or cut it into serving pieces, placing them on a warmed serving dish in a warm oven.

Calories About 270 a serving.

• Suitable for diabetics
• Very low fibre
• Very low salt (using oil and milk allowance as yogurt)
• Gluten-free (replacing flour with cornflour)

Hare meat is extremely rich in iron, with a low fat content – averaging 6 to 8 per cent.

5 Strain the cooking liquid into a bowl or the type of gravy boat that has a deep spout from which you can pour off the lower liquid while leaving the fat on top. Leave the stock for 2 to 3 minutes to allow the fat to separate off, then, if it is in a bowl, either spoon off the fat or remove it with a special fat-lifting brush. Measure 300 ml (½ pint) stock into a saucepan.

6 Mix the flour with the smetana or yogurt, add to the hot stock and stir until it boils. Simmer for 5 to 6 minutes. Remove from the heat. If the sauce is lumpy, blend it in a liquidizer with half of the dill, keeping the other half to add after blending. Otherwise, add all of the dill to the pan. Spoon the sauce over the meat.

RABBIT WITH WINE AND APRICOTS

Rabbit with wine and apricots, served with wholewheat spaghetti (page 106) and watercress and orange salad

Farmed rabbit can be a little insipid, but not when it is prepared using this method, which can be applied equally successfully to wild rabbit. Try it cold – if you have any left over. *Serves 4.*

Calories About 295 a serving.

- Suitable for diabetics
- Medium fibre
- Very low fat
- Very low salt
- Milk-free (using oil)
- Gluten-free

Rabbit is similar to the light meat of chicken in that it has only about 4 per cent fat, in contrast to the average 8 per cent fat in lean rump steak, for instance. The apricots add some fibre to this dish, but you can add a little cereal fibre, too, by serving it with rice, wholewheat pasta, bulgur wheat or barley, as well as a salad rich in vitamin C: watercress complements rabbit well.

| 150ml (¼ pint) red wine |
| 22ml (1½ tbsp) wine vinegar |
| 1 or 2 cloves of garlic, lightly crushed |
| 1 bay leaf |
| 450g (1lb) rabbit, boned and cut into 2.5cm (1in) cubes |
| 50g (2oz) dried apricots |
| 25g (1oz) oil or butter, or a mixture |
| 2ml (½ tsp) wholegrain mild mustard |
| 1ml (¼ tsp) black pepper |

1 Mix together the wine, wine vinegar, garlic and the bay leaf and marinate the rabbit and apricots in the mixture overnight, in the refrigerator.
2 Brown the rabbit in the heated fat. Simmer gently, covered, for about 20 minutes.
3 Add the apricots and the rest of the marinade, bring to the boil, cover the pan tightly and simmer for about 30 minutes, or until the rabbit is tender.
4 Add the mustard and pepper, check the seasoning and serve.

RABBIT WITH PRUNES

Equally good for family feasts or entertaining, this dish is best served with rice, potatoes or barley to soak up the juices. *Serves 4.*

Calories About 300 a serving. Add a few extra per serving, if using mushrooms.

- Suitable for diabetics
- Low fibre
- Very low fat (halving quantity of fat)
- Very low salt (using oil)
- Milk-free
- Gluten-free (replacing flour with cornflour)

Rabbit tastes so rich that it's difficult to believe how much lower in fat it is than most other meats.

| 350ml (12fl oz) red wine |
| 45ml (3 tbsp) wine vinegar |
| 9 peppercorns |
| 2 bay leaves |
| 3ml (¾ tsp) dried thyme |
| 6 cloves |
| 1 small rabbit, cut in 8 pieces |
| 8 large prunes |
| 30ml (2 tbsp) oil or 25g (1oz) soft margarine |
| 25g (1oz) plain wholemeal flour |

1 Mix together the wine, wine vinegar, peppercorns, bay leaves, thyme and cloves. Pour the marinade over the rabbit and the prunes and leave in the refrigerator for between 24 and 48 hours.
2 Place the rabbit pieces in a large, heavy casserole or saucepan and brown them in the oil or margarine.
3 Sprinkle over the flour, add the prunes, the marinade (strained to remove the spices) and enough water to bring the liquid two-thirds up the rabbit.
4 Cover the pan and simmer for about 1 hour, or until the rabbit is tender.
5 Check the seasoning before serving.

VARIATION

Add *100g (4oz) mushrooms, quartered*, 20 minutes before the end of cooking.

DINNER MENU

Stuffed vine leaves **70 cals**
— • —
Rabbit with wine and apricots
300 cals
Green vegetables **40 cals**
Rice or noodles **160 cals**
— • —
Christine's banana ice **210 cals**

Total calories per person **780**

RABBIT PIE

Everyone seems to like this substantial pie. You can make it with chicken, pigeon breasts or turkey instead of rabbit, but remember that it needs generous flavouring. *Serves 6.*

Calories About 375 a serving.

- High fibre
- Very low salt (using unsalted breadcrumbs, stock and butter for the pastry, and omitting salt and egg white)
- Milk-free (using dairy-free fat for pastry)

½ mix of hot-water pastry (page 258)
about 450g (1lb) rabbit, boned and cut in chunks
glass of dry white wine or cider (optional)
50g (2oz) plain wholemeal flour
good grating of nutmeg
pinch of sea salt
100g (4oz) mushrooms
1 large onion, sliced
1 good sprig of fresh sage or generous 5ml (1 tsp) dried sage
50g (2oz) wholemeal breadcrumbs
45 to 75ml (3 to 5 tbsp) stock
egg, beaten, to glaze
150ml (¼ pint) stock (optional)
5ml (1 tsp) gelatine (optional)

1 If you are using farmed or frozen rabbit, improve the flavour by marinating it in a glass of wine or cider overnight.
2 Heat the oven to 200°C (400°F), gas mark 6. Grease an 18cm (7in) diameter cake tin with a detachable base. Or, if you are concerned about extracting the pie intact at the end, line the tin with foil, leaving the ends sticking up so that you can lift the pie out. Grease the foil.
3 Use three-quarters of the pastry to line the tin.
4 Dip the rabbit pieces in the flour mixed with nutmeg and salt. Slice the mushrooms.
5 Fill the pie with layers of rabbit pieces, sliced mushrooms, and sliced onion and sage. Sprinkle each layer with a few breadcrumbs and a spoonful of stock. Pack the filling tightly.
6 Roll out the remaining quarter of the dough to make a lid. Cut a hole in the centre. Press the lid into place on top of the pie, pinch the edges to seal them, then knock them up into a frill. Decorate the pie with shapes cut from the pastry trimmings.
7 Brush the pastry lid with a little of the egg. Bake the pie for 20 minutes, then reduce the heat to 180°C (350°F), gas mark 4, and bake for 1 hour longer. Cover the pie with greaseproof paper or kitchen foil and bake it for another 30 minutes, making almost 2 hours in all.
8 Remove the pie from the oven and take it from the tin. Brush it twice with egg and return it to the oven for 5 to 10 minutes.
9 Serve the pie hot, with vegetables and gravy, or cold. If you want a cold pie with jellied stock, pour warm stock with a little gelatine dissolved in it through the central hole when the pie has half cooled and refrigerate the pie until it is wanted.

PIGEON WITH GRAPES

Calories About 365 a serving.

A model method for casseroling small birds. Since there is a high proportion of bone to meat on a pigeon, you may prefer to use only the pigeon breasts in this recipe. *Serves 2.*

- Suitable for diabetics
- Low fibre
- Very low salt (omitting salt and using oil)
- Gluten-free (replacing flour with cornflour)

Pigeon is not the leanest type of game but as it's a very 'solid' meat, unusually high in protein and rich in flavour, you can serve fairly small portions.

DINNER MENU

Watercress broth **95 cals**

—•—

Pigeon with black grapes
365 cals
Kasha **95 cals**
Green beans **30 cals**

—•—

Fresh fruit salad **60 cals**

Total calories per person **645**

15ml (1 tbsp) oil, soft margarine or butter
2 wood pigeons, plucked and cleaned
1 large onion, finely chopped
15ml (1 tbsp) almonds, skinned and halved
15ml (1 tbsp) plain wholemeal flour
300ml (½ pint) well-flavoured stock
1 bay leaf
2 peppercorns
2 cloves (optional)
100g (4oz) black grapes, halved and stoned
1ml (¼ tsp) white pepper
large pinch of sea salt
45ml (3 tbsp) smetana or soured cream

1 Heat the fat in a large saucepan and brown the pigeons, turning once, over a high heat for 2 to 3 minutes.
2 Put the pigeons aside, add the onion and almonds to the pan and cook for a few minutes, then sprinkle on the flour and remove the pan from the heat.
3 Work in the stock smoothly, return the pan to the heat and, stirring constantly, bring the sauce to the boil.
4 Return the pigeons to the pan and add the bay leaf, peppercorns and cloves.
5 Cover the pan and simmer very gently for about 1 hour.
6 Add the grapes and continue cooking for about 5 minutes.
7 Add the seasoning and check it. Just before serving, remove the pan from the heat and stir in the smetana or soured cream.

VENISON IN THE PINK

Juniper, the berry used to spice gin, has long been considered complementary to venison. Here, red port, red vinegar and beetroot team up to give you a lively but not strident pink dish. *Serves 4.*

about 450g (1lb) venison, cut in 4 pieces
125ml (4fl oz) port
125ml (4fl oz) red wine vinegar
125ml (4fl oz) water
15ml (1 tbsp) oil
1 onion, sliced
1 raw beetroot, cut in chunks
3 to 4 sticks of celery, roughly chopped
1 carrot, roughly chopped
10 juniper berries
4 black peppercorns
1 sprig of fresh rosemary or 2ml (½ tsp) dried rosemary, crumbled
1 bay leaf

1 Place the venison in a flat dish and pour over it the port, wine vinegar and water. Leave in the refrigerator for 24 to 48 hours. Drain, reserving the marinade.

Calories About 350 a serving.

- Suitable for diabetics
- Medium fibre
- Very low fat
- Milk-free
- Gluten-free

Very low in fat, venison is better casseroled, in my view, so that it stays moist without the need for basting fat or rich sauces.

Match it with baked potatoes, kasha (page 89) or, for a low-calorie dish, plenty of lightly cooked green vegetables. Fennel and celery also go well with venison.

2 Heat half of the oil in a large saucepan or casserole set over a high heat. Add the meat and brown it briefly, then remove it from the pan.
3 Reduce the heat to very low. Add the onion to the pan, cover it and cook for 5 minutes.
4 Add the remaining oil, then the beetroot, celery and carrot and cover the pan tightly. Cook over the lowest heat for about 8 to 10 minutes.
5 Add all the spices and herbs to the pan, stir, then return the browned meat to the pan.
6 Pour over the reserved marinade, plus extra stock, water or wine, if necessary, to cover the meat and vegetables completely (how much you need will depend largely on the size and shape of the pan or casserole.
7 Bring to simmering point, then cook over a low heat for at least 1½ hours, although older meat may take up to an hour longer. Luckily, venison does not break up or spoil with long cooking, provided it is well covered with liquid. Check the seasoning.
8 Remove the bay leaf before serving.

VENISON IN PORT

Venison can be young and tender or old and tough with a much stronger flavour. Both are very lean, and benefit from marinading. Make sure the meat is covered with liquid throughout cooking, so that it can't dry out. *Serves 4.*

alories About 355 a serving.

enison in the pink, accompanied by fennel

- Suitable for diabetics
- Low fibre
- Very low fat
- Very low salt
- Milk-free (using soya yogurt)
- Gluten-free (replacing flour with cornflour)

Venison has 35 per cent protein and only 6 per cent fat, a far more desirable balance than that of pork chops, for instance, which average less protein and twice as much fat, even if you cut off all the visible fat and grill them.

DINNER MENU

Aubergine crunchies **220 cals**
— • —
Turkish chicken **255 cals**
Tjatziki **45 cals**
Bulgur wheat **90 cals**
— • —
Fresh fruit **50 cals**

Total calories per person **660**

Calories About 255 a serving.

- Suitable for diabetics
- No fibre
- Very low fat
- Very low salt (if milk allowance permits)
- Gluten-free

Yogurt seems to tenderize meat. Serve this dish with plain brown rice and a generous cucumber and yogurt salad or plain green vegetables, and you have a good balance of flavour and food value.

To reduce fat, skin the chicken before cooking it with the spices.

---

4 good-sized venison cutlets
125ml (4fl oz) port
125ml (4fl oz) red wine vinegar
125ml (4fl oz) water
10ml (2 tsp) oil
225g (8oz) mixture of onions and shallots, sliced
15ml (1 tbsp) plain wholemeal flour
1 bay leaf
5ml (1 tsp) green peppercorns, ground
Dijon mustard, to taste
30ml (2 tbsp) thick plain low-fat yogurt

1 Place the cutlets in a flat dish and pour over them the port, wine vinegar and water. Leave in the refrigerator for 24 to 48 hours. Drain the cutlets and reserve the marinade.
2 Brown the cutlets briefly in the oil, then set them aside.
3 Add the onions and shallots to the oil, cover the pan and soften them for about 8 minutes. Sprinkle on the flour, stir it in and remove the pan from the heat.
4 Work in the marinade from the meat and add the bay leaf and peppercorns.
5 Return the cutlets to the pan, adding a little more water, stock or wine if necessary so that the mixture is covered by liquid.
6 Cover the pan tightly, bring to the boil and simmer for about 1¼ hours, or bake for 1¼ hours at 180°C (350°F), gas mark 4.
7 Check that the meat is tender. Stir in the mustard and yogurt just before serving.

POULTRY

Here are some interesting ways of serving what's become the best meat bargain.

TURKISH CHICKEN

Chicken joints baked in a crusty coating that gives them a spicy tang. *Serves 4.*

1 small roasting chicken, quartered, or 4 chicken joints
300ml (½ pint) plain low-fat yogurt
15ml (1 tbsp) tomato purée
zest of 1 lemon, grated
juice of 1 lemon
1 clove of garlic, crushed
5ml (1 tsp) ground ginger, or 7ml (1½ tsp) root ginger, finely grated
5ml (1 tsp) turmeric
1 to 2ml (¼ to ½ tsp) chili powder, to taste
10ml (2 tsp) garam masala
black pepper
paprika, to garnish

Turkish chicken – served with green beans

1 Place the chicken pieces skin side down in a shallow baking dish.
2 Mix together all the other ingredients except the paprika and spoon the mixture over the meat, ensuring that it is thoroughly coated.
3 Marinate overnight or for up to 24 hours, in the refrigerator, turning the chicken at least once.
4 Bake at 180°C (350°F), gas mark 4, for 1½ to 2 hours, basting occasionally, until the meat is tender. If the chicken becomes too brown, turn the oven down slightly or cover the baking dish loosely with foil.
5 Just before serving, sprinkle with paprika.

SAVOURY CHICKEN BALLS

Calories About 300 a serving.

This Japanese dish is a typical oriental way of making meat carry over for another meal, ideally matched with plain rice or noodles and with stir-fried or plain vegetables. *Serves 3.*

- Suitable for diabetics
- Low fibre
- Very low fat (if chicken is skinned)
- Very low salt (omitting soya sauce)
- Milk-free
- Gluten-free (replacing soya sauce with tamari)

450g (1lb) chicken, finely minced
1 egg
1 spring onion, finely chopped
60ml (4 tbsp) plain wholemeal flour
450ml (¾ pint) water
30ml (2 tbsp) soya sauce
22ml (1½ tbsp) mirin or dry sherry
5ml (1 tsp) honey

1 Thoroughly mix the chicken, the egg and the onion with 30ml (2 tbsp) of the flour. Shape the mixture into 12 balls.
2 Sieve the rest of the flour (retaining the bran left in the sieve for another use) and roll the balls of chicken mixture in it.
3 Bring the water to the boil and when it is bubbling energetically drop the chicken balls into it. Simmer for 4 minutes, uncovered.
4 Add the remaining ingredients to the pan, stir gently, cover the pan and simmer for 6 to 7 minutes.

CHICKEN MOUSSE

Creamy but not too bland, this mousse is too soft to slice but can be unmoulded to make a handsome dinner or buffet dish. It sets quickly enough for same-day use. Serve with cold curry sauce (page 198) or mango chutney (page 266). *Serves 6.*

15ml (1 tbsp) fresh tarragon, finely chopped, or 7ml (1½ tsp) dried tarragon
150ml (¼ pint) plain low-fat yogurt
10ml (2 tsp) cornflour
1 egg, separated
1 large carrot, diced
2 sticks of celery, finely sliced
125ml (4fl oz) chicken stock
75g (3oz) peas
generous 10ml (2 tsp) gelatine
15ml (1 tbsp) lemon juice
10ml (2 tsp) wine vinegar
225g (8oz) cooked chicken, chopped or coarsely minced
225g (8oz) quark or other low-fat soft cheese
15ml (1 tbsp) dry wine (optional)
large pinch of sea salt
1ml (¼ tsp) white pepper
bay leaf or sprig of tarragon, to garnish

1 Stir the tarragon, yogurt, cornflour and egg yolk together in the top of a double boiler or in a basin over simmering water. Do not allow the mixture to boil.
2 When the mixture thickens, remove it from the heat and leave it to cool.
3 Simmer the carrot and celery in the stock for about 8 to 10 minutes. Then add the peas and remove the pan from heat. After a minute sieve

Calories About 130 a serving. Add a few extra if using wine.

- Suitable for diabetics
- Medium fibre
- Very low fat (omitting egg yolk and doubling quantity of cornflour)
- Very low salt (omitting salt and using unsalted quark)
- Gluten-free

Avoid overcooking the vegetables for this recipe. Otherwise they'll lose colour and flavour, not to mention crispness, as well as more vitamin C. This method retains some of the goodness lost in cooking the vegetables, as the cooking liquid is returned to the mousse.

Balance by serving with green salad and rice or bean salad for fibre.

the stock into a cup, retaining the vegetables in the sieve.
4 Add the gelatine to the cup and dissolve well.
5 Stir together in a large bowl the yogurt mixture, cooked vegetables, dissolved gelatine, lemon juice, wine vinegar, chicken, the soft cheese and the wine, if using. Season. Let the mixture cool to lukewarm.
6 Beat the egg white stiffly and fold it into the chicken mixture.
7 Rinse a mould with water and arrange a bay leaf, sprig of tarragon or other decorative herb on its base.
8 Pour the mousse into the mould. Chill for at least 1 hour before serving. To turn the mousse out, dip the mould in boiling water for a few seconds.
9 Serve the mousse with a spoon as, although it's quite firm, it won't slice neatly.

VARIATIONS

Any cold, cooked meat can be served like this. With chicken, the colour is attractively pale; with other meats, there is more contrast and a stronger flavour. If using *lamb*, substitute fresh or dried *rosemary* for the tarragon.

CHICKEN TERRINE

One of the prettiest dishes I've ever made, and much easier than the long details might suggest. *Serves 4 to 5 as a main course, 6 to 7 as a starter.*

350g (12oz) chicken, boned and chopped
2 egg whites
30ml (2 tbsp) lemon juice
50g (2oz) shelled shrimps or prawns, finely chopped
100g (4oz) low-fat soft cheese
125ml (4fl oz) smetana or thick plain low-fat yogurt or soured cream
5ml (1 tsp) ground coriander
2ml (½ tsp) white pepper
large pinch of sea salt
15ml (1 tbsp) whisky or wine (optional)
about 8 large spinach leaves to line the terrine
1 large carrot
1 large or 2 small courgettes
1 red pepper

1 Place the chicken, egg whites and lemon juice in a blender or food processor and blend them to a smooth paste.
2 Stir in the shrimps or prawns, then the cheese, smetana, coriander, seasoning and whisky. Chill the paste while you prepare the terrine dish.
3 Dip the spinach leaves in boiling water for about 40 seconds, then drain them. Grease a terrine dish or a 900g (2lb) loaf tin and line it with some of the leaves, holding back enough leaves to cover the top.
4 Chop the carrot, courgette and pepper in long, very thin pieces. Cook each vegetable in a separate saucepan in a little water, allowing 5 minutes for the carrots and 3 minutes each for the others. Drain, keeping the water for your stock jug.
5 Put a quarter of the chicken mixture in the dish, smoothing it down to

Calories About 160 to 200 a serving as a main course. If using soured cream, add about 40 per serving. About 100 to 130 as a starter, with an extra 25 for soured cream. If using whisky, add a few extra per serving.

- Suitable for diabetics
- Very low fibre
- Very low fat (using yogurt)
- Gluten-free

This type of terrine was a discovery of *nouvelle cuisine*, a sophisticated feast for palate and eye that just happens to be well balanced too. This terrine is very low in fat, and yet tastes very meaty. Serve it with a high-fibre starter or dessert that has a contrasting, crunchy texture, such as herb platter (page 64) or glazed fruit tart (page 217). A watercress and orange salad will complement the terrine as well as supplying vitamin C.

Chicken terrine, served with creamy herb and tomato sauces (pages 32 and 29) and with chicory

make a thin layer. Then tap the dish firmly a few times on a wooden board to shake the mixture down well and eliminate air pockets.

6 Make a single layer of the carrot strips on top of the chicken mixture. Add another quarter of the chicken mixture, then a layer of the courgette strips, then chicken, then the pepper strips, then the remaining chicken.

7 Heat the oven to 150°C (300°F), gas mark 2. Boil a kettle.

8 Fold the retained spinach over the top of the mixture and cover with kitchen foil. Put the dish in a roasting tin and pour in boiling water from the kettle to half-fill the tin.

9 Bake the terrine for about 45 minutes. To check that it's cooked, peel back a corner of foil and leaf: the chicken mixture should be firm and white.

10 Chill the terrine for at least 5 hours.

11 To turn it out, invert a serving dish over the terrine dish, and, holding the 2 dishes firmly together, turn the terrine dish upside down. A firm tap should dislodge the terrine.

12 Using a very sharp serrated knife, cut 2cm (¾in) thick slices, holding each slice upright with a broad spatula until you have finished cutting it. Serve with cold tomato sauce (page 29) or creamy herb sauce (page 32).

VARIATION

You can vary the vegetable layers depending on the season, but try to use *vividly coloured vegetables* to contrast with the chicken mixture. *Green beans*, *peas*, *leeks* or *fennel* would make successful substitutes.

TARRAGON CHICKEN WITH LEMON

The lemony flavour of tarragon complements chicken well. There's enough sauce in this dish to make rice, barley or bulgur wheat the ideal accompaniment. Provide a contrasting texture with a fresh mushroom and parsley salad or lightly cooked broccoli. *Serves 4.*

Calories About 265 a serving.

- Suitable for diabetics
- Low fibre
- Very low fat (if chicken is skinned)
- Very low salt (using cornflour to stabilize yogurt and if milk allowance permits)
- Gluten-free

Just as rich-tasting as recipes crammed with butter, cream and oil.

10ml (2 tsp) corn or walnut oil
4 chicken quarters, each cut in half
1 onion, finely chopped
1 clove of garlic, crushed (optional)
15ml (1 tbsp) fresh tarragon, chopped, or 5ml (1 tsp) dried tarragon
300ml (½ pint) stock
1 egg white or 15ml (1 tbsp) cornflour
300ml (½ pint) plain low-fat yogurt
juice of ½ lemon, to taste

1 Heat the oil in a thick-based pan and brown the chicken pieces.
2 Remove the chicken, add the onion, and the garlic if using, and cover the pan.
3 Cook over a low heat until the onion is soft, then add the tarragon and stock. Bring to the boil.
4 Return the chicken pieces to the pan. Cover and simmer for about 25 minutes, until the chicken is tender.
5 Stir the egg white or cornflour thoroughly into the yogurt and add the mixture to the pan. Stir gently over a low heat until the sauce thickens. Simmer for 2 minutes.
6 Season to taste with the lemon juice.

JAPANESE CHICKEN

My favourite flavour for chicken, especially for the part of chicken people often ignore, the wings. *Serves 4.*

Calories About 230 a serving.

- Very low fat (if chicken is skinned)
- No fibre
- Milk-free
- Gluten-free (using tamari instead of soya sauce)

A method of making meat taste delicious and savoury without adding any fat. Match with a high-fibre dish such as plain rice, noodles or other pasta, and a salad rich in vitamin C, such as spinach or watercress with peppers, or a dark green vegetable.

1 chicken, cut in 4 pieces, or 12 to 16 chicken wings, according to size
½ lemon, roughly chopped
60 ml (4 tbsp) sake, mirin or dry sherry
10 ml (2 tsp) clear honey
30 ml (2 tbsp) root ginger, grated
5 ml (1 tsp) ground ginger
2 cloves of garlic, crushed (optional)
1 onion, finely chopped
45 ml (3 tbsp) soya sauce, preferably the pale variety

1 Place the chicken pieces in a flat casserole.
2 Mix all the other ingredients and pour them over the chicken, adding a little water if necessary so that the marinade comes at least half-way up the chicken. Leave in the refrigerator to marinate for several hours or overnight. Turn the chicken at least once.
3 Heat the oven to 160°C (325°F), gas mark 3. Cook the casserole, uncovered, for about 1 hour, basting occasionally, until the chicken is tender. Serve.

Calories About 260 a serving. For the sauce alone, about 290 for the whole recipe.

- Suitable for diabetics
- Low fibre
- Very low fat (if chicken is skinned)
- Very low salt (omitting salt and using milk allowance for yogurt)
- Gluten-free (replacing flour with cornflour)

For this recipe use only a good-quality fresh, not frozen, chicken and not one that has been mass-farmed. These off-putting warnings are necessary because of the prevalence of food-poisoning organisms in chicken feed in some mass-farming establishments. Such organisms thrive during thawing and are killed only by very thorough cooking. But when you have found a good chicken supplier this recipe will come into its own.

LUNCH MENU

Cold chicken with curry sauce
330 cals
Mushroom salad **80 cals**
Spring rice salad **200 cals**
Mango chutney **40 cals**
—•—
Crêpes Suzette **260 cals**

Total calories per person **910**

Calories About 140 to 170 for a 100g (4oz) serving.

- Suitable for diabetics
- No fibre
- Very low fat (if turkey is skinned)
- Very low salt
- Milk-free
- Gluten-free

10-MINUTE CHICKEN WITH COLD CURRY SAUCE

When first told this method, I was sure it would leave me with a half-raw chicken. Instead, it produces the tastiest, moistest poached chicken ever. Don't keep the cold curry sauce for this dish alone: it suits many cold meats and even vegetable and salad dishes. *Serves 4.*

| 1 1.2kg (2½lb) chicken |
| 30ml (2 tbsp) tarragon vinegar |
| 1 onion, roughly chopped |
| 2 or 3 peppercorns |
| 1 bay leaf |
| *Sauce* |
| 15ml (1 tbsp) oil or butter |
| 1 onion, very finely chopped |
| 5ml (1 tsp) plain wholemeal flour |
| scant 30ml (2 tbsp) curry powder |
| generous 5ml (1 tsp) tomato purée |
| 75ml (3fl oz) water |
| 2ml (½ tsp) sea salt |
| 5ml (1 tsp) honey |
| 15ml (1 tbsp) dried apricots, puréed, or no-added-sugar apricot jam |
| 150ml (¼ pint) smetana or thick plain low-fat yogurt |
| juice of 1 lemon, to taste |

1 Prepare the sauce first. Heat the fat and sauté the onion gently, covered, for about 12 minutes, until it is transparent but not brown.
2 Stir in the flour and curry powder and cook, uncovered, for a few minutes longer.
3 Add the tomato purée, water, sea salt, honey, apricot purée or jam and bring the mixture to the boil. Simmer, covered, for 5 minutes.
4 Remove the pan from the heat, allow the mixture to cool a little, then liquidize it. Cool it well before stirring in the smetana or yogurt and lemon juice to taste.
5 Place the chicken and the accompanying ingredients in a thick-based pan with a well-fitting lid. Bring to the boil, cover and boil for 10 minutes.
6 Turn off the heat and leave the chicken in the pan until cold.
7 Serve the chicken cold, carved in neat pieces, with the sauce.

FESTIVE TURKEY

Cooking a large turkey can be tricky, because while the bird has to be cooked through the very lean breast must not be allowed to dry out. Both the methods given here work well. Serve the turkey with chestnut stuffing (page 207), cooked separately. *Serves 8 to 10.*

| 1 4 to 4.5kg (8 to 10lb) turkey |
| 300ml (½ pint) stock |

Turkey is one of the leanest meats, the meat alone averaging just over 2 per cent fat, and the meat with the skin still only 7 per cent, about half as much as chicken, which is itself low in fat.

Calories About 215 to 270 a serving. Add a few extra if using breadcrumbs rather than rice.

• Suitable for diabetics
• Medium fibre
• Very low salt (using rice and omitting salt)
• Milk-free
• Gluten-free (using rice)

Don't make gravy for this sort of roast. The meat needs no moistening, and the juices are too fatty even after most of the fat has been discarded. Instead, serve it with a crisp watercress and orange salad and plain brown rice, noodles or baked potatoes.

DINNER MENU

Mushrooms à la grecque
65 cals

— • —

Swedish duck **250 cals**
Baked potatoes **150 cals**
Watercress and orange salad
90 cals

— • —

Gooseberry crumble **195 cals**

Total calories per person **750**

---

1 Heat the oven to 220°C (425°F), gas mark 7.
2 Wash and dry the turkey, removing any bag of giblets from inside.
3 Place the bird and cover with foil in a large roasting tin, breast down. Pour the stock around the bird.
4 Roast by one of the following methods.

High temperature
Up to 3kg (6lb): 1 to 1½ hours; 3 to 7kg (6 to 15lb): 2 to 2½ hours; 7 to 9kg (15 to 20lb): 3 to 3½ hours, reducing the heat to 180°C (350°F), gas mark 4, after 1 hour.

Low temperature
When the turkey has been in the oven 10 minutes, reduce the heat to 180°C (350°F), gas mark 4, and allow: 20 minutes per 450g (1lb) for birds up to 5.5kg (12lb) and 15 minutes per 450g (1lb) for birds over that weight.

5 About 45 minutes before the estimated end of cooking time, turn the bird over, so that the breast is upwards. If the stock has evaporated, add a little more.
6 About 30 minutes before the end of cooking time, remove the foil so that the skin can brown.
7 Test if the turkey is cooked by piercing the thickest part of the thigh with a skewer. If the juice that comes out is colourless or cream-coloured, the turkey is done. If the juice is reddish, cook a little longer on the low heat.

SWEDISH DUCK

The Chinese method of rinsing duck in boiling water, then wind-drying it to give a crisper, less fatty bird, is here combined with a Scandinavian stuffing. *Serves 4 to 5.*

1 medium duck
100g (4oz) prunes, stoned and roughly chopped
225g (8oz) eating apples, peeled and roughly chopped
a good squeeze of lemon juice
5ml (1 tsp) lemon zest, grated
pinch of ground cardamom
50g (2oz) wholemeal breadcrumbs or cooked brown rice
black pepper
sea salt

1 Tie a piece of non-synthetic string tightly around the duck under its wings so that you can hang it up. Prick the duck with a sharp knife in the fattiest parts.
2 Pour a kettleful of boiling water over the duck and hang the bird up to dry. This should take about 2 to 12 hours. You can use a fan heater or hair drier if you are in a hurry.
3 Heat the oven to 230°C (450°F), gas mark 8.
4 Mix all the remaining ingredients and stuff the duck with the mixture. If possible, make cuts between the skin and flesh on the breasts and insert some of the stuffing under the skin.
5 Roast the duck for 20 minutes on a rack so that fat can drain off. Don't baste the duck. Pour away the fat and reduce the heat to 180°C (350°F), gas mark 4, and cook for about 1¼ hours more. The duck should now be tender inside and crisp outside. Serve.

CRISPY DUCK

I love the Peking duck served in Western restaurants, although I have learned that the authentic Peking duck method of plain roasting produces different results. The restaurant method allows preparation well in advance and, I think, gives a better flavour. Crispy duck is traditionally served wrapped in Peking doilies (page 209) spread with plum sauce (page 208) and strips of cucumber and spring onion. *Serves 4 to 5.*

1 duck approximately 1.5kg (3lb) (exact size does not matter)
Marinade
60ml (4 tbsp) soya sauce
60ml (4 tbsp) mirin or dry sherry
10 to 15ml (2 to 3 tsp) 5-spice powder
15ml (1 tbsp) honey
600ml (1 pint) stock

1 Prick the skin of the duck with a sharp knife, then place the duck in a bowl and pour over the marinade ingredients.
2 Transfer the duck and the marinade to a saucepan and simmer for about 1½ to 2 hours, until the duck meat is almost falling off the bones.
3 Lift out the duck, and chill it. Reserve the liquid.
4 Heat the grill very high. Cut the duck into quarters. Place on a rack over a grill tray (to catch the fat) and grill them skin side down then skin side up, for about 5 minutes each side, until the skin is crisp and brown.
5 To serve, cut the skin in pieces and pull the flesh off the bones. Place the flesh and the skin on a hot serving dish.

MEAT

Several of the recipes in this section can be adapted for similar cuts from other animals. Lamb varies a great deal in fat content – look out for the leanest and trim it ruthlessly. One benefit of this meat is that it's almost always sold young, so it is usually very tender. But don't neglect mutton, if you can find it, for casseroles and curry.

BARBECUED SPARE RIBS

A barbecue-flavoured meal that you can eat with your fingers. *Serves 4.*

900g (2lb) lean breast or ribs of lamb
15ml (1 tbsp) olive oil
2 cloves of garlic, crushed (optional)
pinch of pepper
5ml (1 tsp) root ginger, finely chopped
1 medium onion, finely chopped
10ml (2 tsp) clear honey
45ml (3 tbsp) soya sauce
30ml (2 tbsp) dry sherry
75ml (3fl oz) stock

Calories About 230 a serving.

• Suitable for diabetics (occasionally)
• High fibre, when accompanied by doilies and plum sauce
• Milk-free

You'll be impressed by how thick a layer of fat you'll find floating on the duck cooking liquid, which is why duck cooked by this method is so light and appetizing. Chill the duck cooking liquid to allow you to skim the fat more easily. In true Chinese style you can then use the liquid as stock to cook a panful of finely shredded cabbage, which you can eat with or after the duck. Otherwise, use the stock as the basis for a delicious soup.

CHINESE MENU

Won ton with soya sauce
170 cals
Crispy duck **230 cals**
Peking doilies **105 cals**
Plum sauce **30 cals**
Cucumber and spring onion slivers **10 cals**
Fish consommé with pancake strips **85 cals**
Brown rice **160 cals**
Mangetout or green beans **30 cals**
Fresh fruit **50 cals**

Total calories per person **870**

Calories About 490 a serving.

• Suitable for diabetics (halving quantity of honey or omitting it altogether)
• Low fibre
• Milk-free
• Gluten-free (replacing soya with tamari sauce)

A method of cooking ribs that avoids too much frying. Choose lean ribs, and trim off visible fat.

Crispy duck, served in paper-thin Peking doilies spread with plum sauce, with slivers of spring onion and cucumber

1 Cut the lamb into single-boned pieces.
2 Cook the olive oil, garlic, pepper, ginger and onion gently together for 5 minutes.
3 Add the lamb ribs, honey, soya sauce and sherry. Raise the heat and stir-fry for 2 to 3 minutes.
4 Add the stock, reduce the heat to low and simmer, covered, until the meat is tender. Turn the ribs occasionally.
5 Heat the grill to medium. Place the meat on a baking tray and dry it off under the grill for 6 to 8 minutes. Serve.

LAMB WITH LENTILS

Cold-weather comfort, this dish is even warmly coloured from the yellow swedes, orange lentils and carrots and red tomatoes. Serve the lamb with finely cut ribbons of dark green or crinkly Savoy cabbage, very lightly cooked. *Serves 5 to 6.*

700g (1½lb) lamb, boned and cubed, or 900g (2 lb) stewing lamb chops
2 large onions, sliced
25g (1oz) plain wholemeal flour
400g (14oz) tomatoes, fresh or tinned
1ml (¼ tsp) black pepper
1 bay leaf
300ml (½ pint) stock
3 carrots, peeled and roughly chopped
2 small turnips, cut in chunks
100g (4oz) other vegetables, such as swede, celery or leeks, cut in chunks
50g (2oz) split red lentils, rinsed in a sieve
5ml (1 tsp) fresh rosemary, chopped, or 2ml (½ tsp) dried rosemary
2ml (½ tsp) mixed dried herbs
pinch of sea salt (if using fresh tomatoes)

1 Cook the lamb cubes in a large, thick-based pan until the fat runs out and the meat browns.
2 Spoon off any liquid fat, add the onions to the pan and cook over a low heat, covered, for 5 minutes.
3 Add the flour, tomatoes, pepper, bay leaf and stock. Bring the mixture to the boil, cover the pan tightly and simmer for 1 hour.
4 If you have time, refrigerate the mixture and remove congealed fat when the casserole is cold. If you haven't time to do this, cool it for as long as possible and skim off as much fat as possible from the casserole.
5 Add the carrots, turnips and other vegetables, stir in the lentils and herbs and cook for a further 30 minutes, or until the lamb is very tender.
6 Check the seasoning and serve.

LAMB KEBABS

Delicious served with wholemeal pitta bread (page 236), rice or baked jacket potatoes, and a salad such as tjatziki (page 59) or watercress. *Makes 8 or 9 short kebabs; serves 3 to 4.*

Calories About 320 to 390 a serving.

- Suitable for diabetics
- High fibre
- Milk-free
- Gluten-free

A meat-stretcher, with the lentils adding fibre as well as low-fat protein. You can double the lentils and reduce the meat by 100 to 225g (4 to 8oz).

MIDDLE EASTERN MENU

Humus 115 cals
Wholemeal pitta bread 90 cals
—•—
Lamb kebabs 260 cals
Bulgur wheat 90 cals
Mixed green salad 100 cals
—•—
Fresh fruit 50 cals

Total calories per person 705

Calories About 130 each (if making 8); about 115 each (if making 9).

Lamb kebabs served on a bed of brown rice and accompanied by tjatziki (page 59)

- Suitable for diabetics
- Medium fibre
- Very low fat
- Very low salt
- Milk-free
- Gluten-free

Kebabs are among the best and most enjoyable ways of presenting meat or fish at their leanest while making both go further.

1 large onion, cut in 8 equal pieces

1 clove of garlic, crushed (optional)

2 large sprigs of fresh rosemary or 10ml (2 tsp) dried rosemary

60ml (4 tbsp) dry wine

juice of 1 lemon

150ml (¼ pint) plain low-fat yogurt

450g (1 lb) lean lamb, boned and cut in 2.5cm (1in) cubes

12 small mushrooms, washed but not peeled

2 courgettes, washed and cut in 1cm (½in) slices

1 Mix together the onion, garlic if using, rosemary, wine, lemon juice and yogurt, and add the lamb cubes. Soak the lamb in the mixture overnight in the refrigerator or for at least 3 hours at room temperature, turning the cubes occasionally.

2 On 8 or 9 skewers, thread alternate pieces of lamb with broken up, small pieces of onion from the marinade, whole mushrooms pierced through the stalk and slices of courgette.

3 Baste the kebabs well with the marinade and then cook them over a barbecue or under a medium-high grill for 15 to 20 minutes, turning and basting them often.

Lamb curry with plain rice, cucumber and yogurt salad, chopped green pepper and dhal

Calories About 345 a serving; 265 a serving for the variation.

- Suitable for diabetics
- No fibre
- Very low salt (if milk allowance permits)
- Gluten-free

Trim the lamb first unless you are using a lean cut. Stewing lamb is often leaner than more expensive shoulder of lamb or prime chops. To make a complete balanced meal – and an occasion – out of curry, serve it with the traditional side dishes, such as dhal (page 115), chopped cucumber in yogurt (use the tjatziki recipe, page 59), mango chutney, diced green or red peppers, green beans or onions and chappatis, or plain brown rice.

LAMB CURRY

This authentic curry has a deep, mellow flavour, so it won't take off the roof of your mouth. *Serves 4.*

700g (1½lb) lean lamb, cubed, or 900g (2lb) stewing chops, boned and cubed
6 cardamom pods, 1 bay leaf, 6 black peppercorns, 5ml (1 tsp) cinnamon (all ground)
2 large onions, finely chopped
2 cloves of garlic, chopped
15ml (1 tbsp) fresh ginger root, finely grated
10ml (2 tsp) ground coriander
10ml (2 tsp) ground cumin
large pinch of chili powder
2ml (½ tsp) turmeric
200ml (7fl oz) stock
45 to 60ml (3 to 4 tbsp) plain low-fat yogurt (optional)
spring onion, chopped, fresh coriander leaves or parsley, to garnish

INDIAN MENU

Lamb curry **345 cals**
Dhal **110 cals**
Plain brown rice **160 cals**
Mango chutney **40 cals**
Tjatziki **45 cals**
Banana slices with lemon juice
40 cals
Finely chopped onions **20 cals**
Finely chopped red peppers
20 cals

Total calories per person **780**

---

1 Place a layer of lamb pieces in a large, thick-based saucepan and heat gently to melt out any fat. Then turn the heat up high and brown the lamb pieces on all sides. Transfer the browned lamb to a dish. Brown the rest of the lamb in batches before transferring it to the dish.
2 Put the ground cardamom, bay leaf, pepper and cinnamon and the chopped onion in the pan and cook very gently for a few minutes.
3 Add the garlic, ginger and remaining spices and cook for a few minutes more.
4 Put the lamb back in the pan, add the stock, bring it to the boil and simmer very gently, covered, for about 1½ hours, until the meat is very tender.
5 Check occasionally that the curry is not becoming too dry, although there should be less liquid than in a conventional stew.
6 Just before serving, stir in the yogurt, if using, and garnish with the spring onion, fresh coriander leaves or parsley. Do not allow the curry to boil again after adding the yogurt.

VARIATION

Use the same weight of *chicken* cut in pieces instead of the lamb. Brown the chicken in *10 to 15ml (2 to 3 tsp) oil or butter* in step 1, as the chicken won't contain enough fat to melt out.

If you want a stronger taste, add more garlic, a little *curry paste* or some extra ground coriander and cumin.

QUICK SHERRIED KIDNEYS

A 15-minute dinner that tastes as good as meals that take hours to make. *Serves 3 to 4.*

15ml (1 tbsp) oil
8 large or 12 small lambs' kidneys, cut in 5mm (¼in) slices across
5ml (1 tsp) dried rosemary, powdered
large pinch of black pepper
225g (8oz) mushrooms, sliced or small whole
15ml (1 tbsp) plain wholemeal flour
45ml (3 tbsp) dry sherry or wine
60ml (4 tbsp) plain low-fat yogurt or smetana with 2ml (½ tsp) cornflour, or well-flavoured stock
pinch of sea salt
parsley or spring onions, chopped, to garnish

Calories About 160 to 205 a serving.

• Suitable for diabetics
• Medium fibre
• Very low salt (omitting salt)
• Milk-free (using stock)
• Gluten-free (replacing flour with cornflour)

As well as providing plenty of protein and B vitamins, kidneys are as high in iron as some kinds of liver, and have less than 3 per cent fat. They are also rich in zinc.

1 Heat the oil in a thick-based pan, and gently cook together the kidneys, rosemary, pepper and mushrooms, covered, for 6 to 8 minutes, until the kidney centres are barely pink.
2 Transfer the mixture to a warmed serving dish and place it in a warm oven.
3 Mix the flour with the pan juices and cook over the lowest heat, stirring, for 1 minute.
4 Remove the pan from the heat, add the sherry and the yogurt or smetana mixed with cornflour, or the stock. Return the pan to a gentle heat, and stir so that the mixture thickens smoothly. Simmer for 3 minutes.
5 Return the kidney and mushroom mixture to the pan. Season with salt. Stir everything together over a gentle heat for a few more minutes.

6 Serve, garnished with chopped parsley or spring onions, with rice, in pitta bread, in pancakes, on chappatis or with vegetables or a generous mixed salad.

LIVER AND ONIONS

Onions are liver's natural partners, provided you choose mild Spanish onions and use plenty of them. Have you tried liver and onion sandwiches? *Serves 4.*

15ml (1 tbsp) oil
450g (1lb) mild Spanish onions, fairly thinly sliced
450g (1lb) lamb's liver, finely sliced
15ml (1 tbsp) fresh sage, chopped, or 10ml (2 tsp) dried sage, powdered
1ml (¼ tsp) black pepper
pinch of sea salt
15ml (1 tbsp) wine vinegar or lemon juice
45ml (3 tbsp) parsley, chopped

1 Heat half of the oil and 45ml (3 tbsp) water in a large pan with a lid, stir in the onions, cover and cook over the lowest possible heat for 10 minutes.
2 Transfer the onions to a warmed serving dish. Add the rest of the oil and 30ml (2 tbsp) water to the pan with the liver slices. Cook, covered, for 4 minutes, turning once.
3 Return the onions to the pan with the sage, pepper and salt and cook, stirring, for 2 to 3 minutes. Then add the wine vinegar or lemon juice, stir in the parsley and serve.

DEVILLED LIVER

Grilled liver can be horribly hard and tasteless, but devilled grilled liver is delicious. If you cut the meat in very thin slices, it will be moistly tender after the minimum amount of cooking. *Serves 4.*

450g (1lb) lamb's liver, very thinly sliced
generous 45ml (3 tbsp) plain wholemeal flour
50g (2oz) wholemeal breadcrumbs
1ml (¼ tsp) black pepper
pinch of sea salt
25g (1oz) soft margarine or butter, softened
large pinch of cayenne pepper
15ml (1 tbsp) Worcestershire sauce
5ml (1 tsp) mustard powder
about 30ml (2 tbsp) lemon juice
mild French mustard, to serve

1 Heat the grill to medium and lightly grease the grill rack.
2 Dip the slices of liver in the flour.
3 Mix together all the ingredients except the liver and the French mustard. Spread the mixture over both sides of the floured liver slices.
4 Put each slice on the grill and cook for about 3 minutes each side.

Calories About 265 a serving.

- Suitable for diabetics
- Medium fibre
- Very low fat
- Very low salt (omitting salt)
- Milk-free
- Gluten-free

Liver is rich in iron and zinc as well as containing vitamin E and all the B vitamins.

Calories About 300 a serving.

- Suitable for diabetics
- Low fibre
- Very low salt (using unsalted fat and breadcrumbs and omitting salt
- Milk-free (using dairy-free margarine)
- Gluten-free (using gluten-free breadcrumbs)

Liver is an excellent source of iron. This method of cooking adds very little fat but some fibre, and is simple and good enough to encourage you to eat liver more often. Apart from iron, liver is also rich in zinc, vitamin E and all the B vitamins, and it even has a useful amount of vitamin C.

Devilled liver, served with spinach

5 Serve with moist vegetables, such as mushrooms in soured cream (page 142) or Greek spinach (page 137), and plenty of French mustard.

STUFFINGS, SAUCES & ACCOMPANIMENTS

Although chestnut stuffing is intended primarily for turkey, the plum sauce and Peking doilies, normally accompanying the crispy duck (page 201) could easily be used with chicken or cold meat. Apple sauce, again traditionally served with duck, is also good with many cold meats.

CHESTNUT STUFFING

A very old recipe, dating from Eliza Acton's *Modern Cookery* published in 1845, this is far better flavoured than most modern versions and would make a good side dish for many other meals. *Serves 6.*

Calories About 500 for the whole recipe.

• Suitable for diabetics
• High fibre
• Very low fat (reducing fat to three-quarters of given quantity or omitting altogether)
• Very low salt (using unsalted breadcrumbs and stock)
• Milk-free (using dairy-free margarine)
• Gluten-free (using gluten-free breadcrumbs)

I've reduced the fat in the original recipe by omitting some of the fat and 2 egg yolks. Chestnuts are far lower in calories than other nuts (48 per 25g or 1oz) and have only 2 per cent protein, but are quite high in fibre and vitamins E, B_6 and some other B-group vitamins.

100g (4oz) dried chestnuts
about 200ml (7fl oz) well-flavoured stock, made with onion
2ml (½ tsp) grated nutmeg
25g (1oz) soft margarine or butter
1ml (¼ tsp) ground white pepper
pinch of cayenne (chili)
5ml (1 tsp) lemon rind, finely grated
50g (2oz) wholemeal breadcrumbs
lemon juice, to taste

1 Soak the chestnuts in hot water for a few hours or overnight. Drain them, place them in a saucepan and barely cover with the stock, including onion from the stock.
2 Bring to the boil and simmer, covered, for about 45 minutes or until tender. Drain, reserving the liquid.
3 Put the chestnuts and onion through a food processor or vegetable mill or the fine blade of a mincer, then add all the other ingredients, with lemon juice to taste.
4 Add enough of the cooking stock to make the mixture moist but not too wet.
5 Check the seasoning, and heat the stuffing through in a lightly greased covered dish for 30 to 40 minutes alongside the poultry in the oven.

VARIATION

You can also add the *minced cooked giblets* from the poultry when you process the chestnuts in step 3.

PLUM SAUCE

This recipe makes at least twice as much as you'll need for one duck. You could freeze the remainder or serve it instead of chutney with cold meat. Painted on poultry before roasting, it gives a tasty, crisp surface.

Calories About 208 for the whole recipe.

• Suitable for diabetics in small amounts (say 15ml – 1 tbsp)
• Medium fibre
• Very low fat
• Very low salt
• Milk-free
• Gluten-free (if mustard does not include flour)

A useful replacement for bought chutney, which is often half sugar.

350g (12oz) red plums, washed
10ml (2 tsp) black treacle or molasses
10ml (2 tsp) honey
10ml (2 tsp) wine vinegar
2ml (½ tsp) mild mustard
pinch of white pepper
scant 5ml (1 tsp) tomato purée, to taste

1 Put the plums in a small saucepan with about 150ml (¼ pint) water. Bring to the boil, cover and simmer for about 10 minutes, until the plums are tender.
2 Remove the plums from the liquid and stone them, retaining the stones and the liquid.
3 Purée the plums with the remaining ingredients, adding the tomato purée very cautiously at the end, as too much can overwhelm the sauce.
4 Add the kernels from the plum stones and enough of the cooking liquid to make a thick, rather solid sauce. If the sauce is too thin, simmer, uncovered, for 5 to 15 minutes, until it has thickened.
5 Taste the sauce and add a little more of any of the flavourings if desired, remembering that the result should be fruity, not piquant.

APPLE SAUCE

Delicious hot or cold, this sauce can be used to moisten any kind of cold meat, and can even be served as a dessert in its own right. *Serves 4.*

| **450g (1lb) eating apples, peeled and cored** |
| **about 15ml (1 tbsp) honey, to taste** |
| **mixed spice, to taste** |
| **squeeze of lemon juice (optional)** |

1 Chop the apples into a thick-based saucepan. Add enough water to half-cover.
2 Bring to the boil, cover and simmer over the lowest heat for about 10 minutes, until the apples are very tender.
3 Purée the apples with just enough of the cooking water for a thick consistency.
4 Flavour to taste with the honey and spice. You may also wish to add a squeeze of lemon juice, depending on the flavour of the apples chosen. Serve hot or cold.

VARIATION

Cranberry sauce Made in the same way as apple sauce, using even less water. The cranberries take about 15 to 20 minutes to burst, almost puréeing themselves. You can either put them through a food processor to give a smooth texture, or keep the shape of the berries. Cranberry sauce probably needs a little more honey.

PEKING DOILIES

These paper-thin pancakes are delicious spread with plum sauce and wrapped around crispy duck. They will stay soft and pliable if they are kept warm until needed. *Makes 16.*

| **175g (6oz) strong plain wholemeal flour, sieved and the bran set aside** |
| **pinch of sea salt** |
| **150ml (¼ pint) boiling water** |
| **30ml (2 tbsp) sesame or peanut oil, for brushing** |

1 Place the flour and salt in a bowl and pour in the boiling water.
2 Mix to a soft dough, then knead the dough on a floured surface for 8 to 10 minutes, until very smooth. Cover and leave for 20 minutes.
3 Cut the dough into 16 pieces (most easily done by halving each piece again and again).
4 Shape each small piece into a ball, then roll each ball out into a 5cm (2in) circle.
5 Brush the top of one disc of dough very thoroughly with oil, especially round the edges, then sprinkle over a little of the retained bran.
6 Place a second disc on top of the first and roll both out together to about 15cm (6in) diameter.
7 Heat an ungreased cast-iron pan or griddle well. Over moderate heat, cook the pair of pancakes on 1 side for about 1 minute, until puffy. Repeat on the other side.
8 Carefully peel the pair apart. Keep them warm on a plate over simmering water while you roll and cook the other pancakes.

DESSERTS

Cheesecake can be good for you. That's the good news for pudding-lovers. This section shows how to keep the 'sinful' taste in favourites such as cheesecake, apple tart and trifle, while preparing them in a way that makes them as high in food value as any other part of your meal.

The only people who won't be pleased are those who regard dessert simply as a vehicle for cream. Born lucky enough never to like it, I've always found myself struggling through dessert recipes to find ones that don't tuck in large amounts of cream somewhere. Here are the results of my search. And if you must have cream, there's nothing to stop you adding it. Before you pour, let me say that there's nothing wrong with a little cream here and there in meals that are generally low in fat – that is to say, low in hard cheese, oil, butter, margarine, shortcrust pastry, chocolate and assorted other hidden fats. If this is where you want to have your cream, enjoy it. Soured cream and smetana are both useful, if you like their flavour, in lowering the fat content while keeping the creaminess of foods. Soured cream is roughly 18 per cent fat, compared with about 21 per cent in single cream and 48 per cent in double cream. Smetana is a cross between soured cream and yogurt. Creamed smetana has about 10 per cent fat; regular only 5 per cent.

I haven't included fresh fruit salad. I hope you'll keep that and fresh fruit in mind – they're the healthiest desserts of all.

CHEESE-BASED DESSERTS

If you want to have a pudding instead of a meal – pick one of these, and you'll be getting a good slice of protein. The difference between these and bought ones: the food value isn't smothered in sugar and fat.

CHEESECAKE TARTLETS

Calories About 116 a tartlet.

• Suitable for diabetics, reducing honey to 10ml (2 tsp)
• Medium fibre
• No salt (using unsalted fat in pastry and unsalted soft cheese)

Miriam's cheesecake, topped with slices of kiwi fruit and halved, seeded grapes

For anyone who likes cheesecake. *Makes 12*.

1 mix of almond-carob pastry (page 260)
225g (8oz) smooth low-fat soft cheese
25g (1oz) currants
2 egg whites
few drops of natural vanilla essence
45ml (3 tbsp) skimmed milk
15 to 20ml (3 to 4 tsp) clear honey

An example of how a sweet dish can still be good value, thanks to the minimal amounts of both sugar and fat (the recipe uses low-fat cheese and the whites only of the eggs).

Calories About 190 to 235 a serving, with a further 30 to 35 a serving if adding a fruit topping.

• Suitable for diabetics
• Low fibre
• Very low fat (using all quark and omitting egg yolks, and using grapenuts for the base)
• Very low salt (using unsalted quark)
• Milk-free (using soya cheese)
• Gluten-free (replacing flour with brown rice flour and using gluten-free biscuits, page 255, for the base)

Cheesecake can be good for you! This one provides protein from cheese, eggs, yogurt and biscuits or wheat germ, with very little fat or sweetening, so you can enjoy it without feeling bad about it – provided that it follows (or replaces) a fairly light meal.

1 Heat the oven to 190°C (375°F), gas mark 5.
2 Roll out the pastry and cut circles to fit 12 small, lightly greased bun tins. Line the tins with the pastry circles. Chill while you prepare the filling.
3 Beat the remaining ingredients together thoroughly, adding honey last, to taste.
4 Pour the mixture into the pastry-lined tins, filling each about three-quarters full.
5 Bake the tartlets for 20 minutes. If you serve them straight from the oven, they are like miniature cheesecake soufflés. They quickly drop, but are tasty cold, or rewarmed.

MIRIAM'S CHEESECAKE

Inspired by something called 'yogurt pie', to which I became very attached while staying in Adelaide, Australia, this is as good to eat as any richer cheesecake. When the cheesecake has cooled, you can cover it with neat circles of fresh fruit, such as *raspberries* or *sliced kiwi fruit*. *Serves 4 to 5.*

2 eggs, separated
100g (4oz) curd cheese
100g (4oz) quark
15ml (1 tbsp) plain wholemeal flour
few drops of natural vanilla essence
15ml (1 tbsp) clear honey
50g (2oz) sultanas, raisins or chopped dried apricots, all well washed
150ml (¼ pint) thick plain low-fat yogurt
5ml (1 tsp) orange zest, finely grated (optional)
50g (2oz) crushed biscuits such as hazelnut biscuits (page 253) or wheat germ, or a half-and-half mixture

1 Heat the oven to 180°C (350°F), gas mark 4.
2 Beat the egg whites until stiff. (If you beat the whites first, you won't have to wash your egg beater before the next step; if you leave the whites till after the yolks, you will have to wash all egg yolk off the beater first.)
3 Beat the egg yolks with the soft cheeses, flour, vanilla and honey.
4 Stir in the dried fruit by hand (a beater will chew it up too much – although if you don't mind the effect on the colour, beating it in will make the cheesecake sweeter).
5 Stir in the yogurt. Add the orange zest, if using.
6 Cover the base of a small loaf-shaped ceramic serving dish with the crushed biscuits and/or wheat germ. There is no need to grease the dish unless you want to turn the cheesecake out to serve it. In this case, use a greased loose-base or spring-form baking tin.
7 Fold in the egg whites very gently. Pour the mixture evenly over the base. Bake for 25 to 30 minutes, or until the cheesecake feels firm near the edge: the centre sets as it cools. This kind of cheesecake naturally browns slightly on top and will probably crack a little on cooling. If you want to avoid browning and cracking, cover the cheesecake with kitchen foil half-way through cooking.
8 Turn the oven off and leave the cheesecake inside with the door ajar for about 1 hour, so that it cools with minimum disturbance.

PASHKA

A light version of the traditional Russian Easter cake. *Serves 5 to 6.*

Calories About 205 to 245 a serving.

- Suitable for diabetics
- Medium fibre
- Very low salt (using unsalted quark and unsalted butter)
- Milk-free (using soya cheese and yogurt)
- Gluten-free

A dessert food value similar to that of a main course. All it lacks is vitamin C. So if you team it with salad or fresh fruit, you can eat it instead of a light meal, or serve it as a dessert after a vegetable or salad meal.

450g (1lb) smooth low-fat soft cheese or medium-fat curd cheese
50g (2oz) walnut, almond or hazelnut pieces, chopped
25g (1oz) soft margarine or softened butter
10ml (2 tsp) orange zest, finely grated
25g (1oz) dried apricots, finely chopped or minced
50g (2oz) raisins or sultanas, well washed
50g (2oz) currants, well washed
1ml (¼ tsp) natural vanilla essence
a few tbsp thick plain low-fat yogurt or smetana (if using dry cheese)
about 15ml (1 tsp) honey, to taste
a few nuts (hazelnuts, walnuts or almonds, split and lightly toasted), to decorate

1 In a large bowl, mix thoroughly, by hand, all the ingredients except the yogurt or smetana, and the nuts reserved for decoration.
2 Add honey, to taste.
3 Line a large sieve or a new flowerpot with a piece of very clean, coarse-textured cloth. Arrange the nut pieces for the decoration in the base.
4 Tip in the cheese mixture, fold the ends of the cloth over the top and leave to drain over a basin in a cold place for at least 8 hours.
5 To serve, free the cloth edges from the base, invert the sieve or flowerpot over a serving plate, and remove the cloth carefully.

Pashka – a nutritious, cheese-based dessert

QUICK CHEESECAKE SUNDAES

Not set like a cheesecake, but with similar flavours – and made in minutes. If the cheese you use turns out to be too watery for your liking, you can add body by letting the sundaes stand: the dried fruit will soak up some of the liquid. *Serves 4.*

450g (1lb) low-fat soft cheese
225g (8oz) any soft or stone fruit, such as peaches or apricots, roughly chopped
22ml (1½ tbsp) honey
25g (1oz) raisins or sultanas, well washed
few drops of natural vanilla essence
25g (1oz) sunflower seeds, toasted, or nuts, chopped

1 Mix the cheese with the fruit, honey, raisins or sultanas and vanilla.
2 Divide the mixture among 4 sundae dishes or glasses and sprinkle the sundaes with the sunflower seeds or nuts. If possible, allow them to stand to let the dried fruit swell and the flavours blend.

VARIATIONS

Add a base of *2 or 3 crushed biscuits*, such as *hazelnut biscuits* (page 253); if you like, use *15ml (1 tbsp) wheat germ* to replace some of the biscuits. Place the base in the bottom of the dishes or glasses. For extra flavour, you can add *5 to 10ml (1 to 2 tsp) of your favourite liqueur.* If you find this thins the mixture too much, add *biscuit crumbs* or *wheat germ* to the cheese mixture, instead of placing them in the bottom of the dishes.
For coffee-flavoured cheesecake, omit the fruit and flavour the soft cheese with *10ml (2 tsp) freeze-dried decaffeinated instant coffee*, dissolved in *15ml (1 tbsp) water, orange juice or liqueur.* If you want the flavour of the liqueur without the alcohol, heat it slightly and set a match to it. Let it burn out, then add the coffee granules.

FRUIT DESSERTS

Light, fresh and yet satisfying, these make an excellent ending to any meal, but particularly after a substantial main course.

BAKED APPLES

Although I've given a set temperature, this adaptable pudding will cook at almost any temperature, according to whatever else is in the oven. Just adjust the cooking time. You can test whether an apple has reached the degree of firmness or softness you prefer by pushing a skewer into the middle. Bake a few extra for eating cold. *Serves 4.*

4 eating apples or not-too-sour cooking apples
50g (2oz) raisins, sultanas, dates or currants, washed and minced or chopped, with 5ml (1 tsp) mixed spice or cinnamon; or 50g (2oz) mincemeat (page 264)
2ml (½ tsp) lemon zest, finely grated
20ml (4 tsp) honey, maple syrup or treacle (optional)

Calories About 185 a serving. For coffee-flavoured version, about 170 a serving. Add an extra 15 a serving if using liqueur.

• Suitable for diabetics
• High fibre (using berry fruit), otherwise medium fibre
• Very low fat (omitting nuts)
• Very low salt (using unsalted quark)
• Milk-free (using soya cheese)
• Gluten-free

A pudding that's as good as a main course for food value, so eat it without guilt after (or instead of) a light meal.

Calories About 120 each. Add an extra 35 each if using chopped nuts.

• Suitable for diabetics (halving quantity of sweetener or omitting altogether)
• High fibre
• Very low fat (using mincemeat, page 264, or dried fruit)
• Very low salt
• Milk-free
• Gluten-free

Apples provide a good source of potassium and of fibre – especially in the skin. The skin also contains more of the vitamin C. Apples are not especially high in vitamin C, but the amount varies considerably according to the variety of apple. Bramleys and Sturmer pippins are among the highest in vitamin C; Golden Delicious and Granny Smiths among the lowest.

It's hard to think of a more natural dessert. Filling but low in calories, this goes well with a high protein but not very bulky main course, such as a soufflé, kebabs or a cold terrine.

1 Heat the oven to 200°C (400°F), gas mark 6.
2 Core the apples, but don't peel them. Put the cored apples in a shallow ovenproof dish and stuff the centres with the dried fruit mixed with spice or cinnamon, or the mincemeat, plus the lemon zest.
3 If the apples are sour, dribble honey, maple syrup or treacle on top.
4 Cover just the base of the dish with water.
5 Score around the centre of each apple through the skin, to prevent it from bursting.
6 Bake for 30 to 45 minutes, depending on the size of the apples, basting occasionally with the liquid from the dish.

VARIATIONS

Add *25g (1oz) chopped nuts* to the dried fruit filling.

STUFFED PEARS

An elegant but easy dinner party pudding, which you can make in advance. Designed to be eaten cold, it is just as good hot. *Serves 6.*

Stuffed pears – delicious hot or cold

Calories About 140 a serving.

• Suitable for diabetics (halving quantity of honey or omitting it altogether)
• High fibre
• Very low fat
• Very low salt
• Milk-free
• Gluten-free

A light pudding to finish off a substantial meal.

Calories About 195 a serving. If using honey, add an extra 10 a serving. If using almonds, add an extra 35 a serving.

• Suitable for diabetics
• High fibre
• Very low salt (using unsalted fat)
• Gluten-free (replacing flour with millet or brown rice flour)

Dried apricots and peaches are ideal partners for less sweet fruits, passing on sweetness without darkening colour as well as adding their own fibre and iron.

| **6 firm pears, such as Conference** |
| **50g (2oz) sultanas** |
| **50g (2oz) walnuts, coarsely chopped** |
| **2ml (½ tsp) cinnamon** |
| **125ml (4fl oz) water** |
| **30ml (2 tbsp) honey** |
| **150ml (¼ pint) dry red wine** |
| **thin strip of lemon zest** |
| **pieces of cinnamon bark** |
| **3 cloves** |

1 Heat the oven to 180°C (350°F), gas mark 4.
2 Peel each pear carefully, cut out a plug of flesh with the stalk from the top, then remove the core with an apple corer. Place the pears upright in an ovenproof dish.
3 Stuff the centres of the pears with the sultanas, walnuts and cinnamon, and replace the plugs.
4 Bring the water, honey and wine to the boil together. Add the lemon zest, cinnamon bark and cloves, and simmer for 2 minutes.
5 Pour the syrup over the pears, cover and bake for about 1 hour.
6 If at the end of this time there is too much syrup, drain it off and boil it in a saucepan on top of the stove to reduce it. Pour it over the pears again. Serve them hot at once, or chill them and serve them cold.

GOOSEBERRY CRUMBLE

This recipe is a model which you can follow for any fruit crumble, using dried apricots, peaches, dates or sultanas to sweeten a fresh fruit. Crumble topping can be made up in batches and kept in a closed container in the refrigerator, ready for a quick and easy dessert. *Serves 4.*

| **50g (2oz) dried apricots, washed and soaked** |
| **350g (12oz) gooseberries, washed and trimmed** |
| **about 75ml (3fl oz) water** |
| **about 10ml (2 tsp) honey (optional)** |
| ***Topping*** |
| **75g (3oz) plain wholemeal flour** |
| **15ml (1 tbsp) skimmed milk powder** |
| **25g (1oz) soft margarine or butter** |
| **22ml (1½ tbsp) fruit sugar or date sugar*** |

*If you can't find fruit sugar or date sugar, use the least refined sugar you can find.

1 Bring the apricots, just covered with water, to the boil and simmer them for about 30 minutes, until tender.
2 Heat the oven to 200°C (400°F), gas mark 6.
3 Mix the gooseberries and the whole or chopped apricots (chopped apricots make a sweeter crumble) in an ovenproof dish and add the water. If the fruit needs further sweetening, drizzle honey over it.
4 To make the topping, stir the flour and milk powder together, rub in the fat and stir in the fruit or date sugar.
5 Sprinkle the topping over the fruit and bake for about 30 minutes. Serve hot or cold.

VARIATIONS

If you are making a crumble using a fresh fruit that is particularly sweet already, such as raspberries or ripe blackberries, you can omit the dried fruit, and, if you like, combine the sweet fruit with a less sweet one, such as *plums* or *apples.* For an almond flavour, add *25g (1oz) ground or flaked almonds* and *2 to 3 drops of almond essence* to the topping mix after you have stirred in the sugar.

GLAZED FRUIT TART

This tart looks beautiful, especially if you arrange apple slices in neatly overlapping rows. A double or triple-size version makes a fine party piece. *Serves 4 to 5.*

½ mix of yeast pastry (recipe page 259)
225g (8oz) eating apples, or other fruit
10ml (2 tsp) fruit sugar or honey (optional)
15ml (1 tbsp) sultanas or currants (optional)
2ml (½ tsp) cinnamon (if using apples or pears)

Glaze

5ml (1 tsp) arrowroot
150ml (¼ pint) apple or other fruit juice, but not citrus juice
about 5ml (1 tsp) honey, to taste

1 Heat the oven to 190°C (375°F), gas mark 5.
2 Roll out the pastry to fit a 20cm (8in) flan tin with a removable base, or oven-to-table ceramic flan dish.
3 If you are using soft fruit that needs no cooking, line the flan case with greaseproof paper or kitchen foil, weight it with a handful of dried beans or pasta and bake for 15 minutes.
4 Remove the weighting and paper or foil and cook for another 2 to 3 minutes.
5 Arrange the soft fruit in the case, add fruit sugar or honey if using less sweet fruit, and glaze the tart (see step 7).
6 If you are using fruit that needs cooking, arrange it decoratively in the raw pastry shell. Neither apples nor pears need to be peeled, but slice apples very thinly as otherwise they won't cook through. Sprinkle the fruit with the fruit sugar or honey and the dried fruit and cinnamon if you are using them. Cover the shell and the fruit with foil and bake for 10 minutes. Reduce the heat to 180°C (350°F), gas mark 4, and bake for about another 10 minutes.
7 Mix the arrowroot with a little of the fruit juice to make a smooth paste.
8 Boil the remaining juice, add the arrowroot mixture and simmer for 5 minutes, stirring often. Remove it from the heat, sweeten it to taste with honey, cool it a little, then spoon it over the flan.

VARIATIONS

This flan is equally good with *wholemeal shortcrust pastry* (page 257) or *hot-water pastry* (page 258). If it is made with hot-water pastry, it is very buttery in flavour.
To make a deeper, fruitier tart, place *fruit purée* in the flan case before the fruit topping. *Confectioner's custard* (page 37) can also be used in this way, but only for soft fruit flans. Pour the custard into the flan case as soon as it is baked.

Calories About 130 to 160 a serving. Add a few extra a serving if using fruit sugar or honey.

• Suitable for diabetics (omitting sweetener)
• High fibre
• Very low fat
• Very low salt (using unsalted fat and omitting salt from pastry)
• Milk-free (using soya milk for pastry and dairy-free fat)

A dessert with a good fibre content, and, thanks to the low-fat pastry, a 'lean' dessert.

For a different glaze, warm some *no-added-sugar jam*, of a flavour to suit the fruit in the tart, with a little water. Brush it over the fruit.

REAL ORANGE JELLY

Far nicer than the gooey, synthetic-tasting blocks and powders, and just as easy. Use this recipe as a model for any fruit jelly: for some ideas for juices that you can use as a basis, see pages 40–41. *Serves 3.*

20ml (4 tsp) gelatine
45ml (3 tbsp) hot water
22ml (1½ tbsp) honey
450ml (¾ pint) orange juice, unsweetened

1 Dissolve the gelatine in the hot water with the honey, stirring until it is completely clear.
2 Add the gelatine mixture to the juice and stir it in well.
3 Chill to set.

VARIATION

Pieces of *fresh fruit* can be added to the jelly as it is almost setting, so that they stay dispersed. Do not use raw pineapple or raw papaya – their enzymes will prevent the jelly from setting at all.

Calories About 95 a serving.

- Suitable for diabetics (omitting honey)
- No fibre
- Very low fat
- Very low salt
- Milk-free
- Gluten-free

A light dessert, rich in vitamin C – a good match with many meals.

Real orange jelly, with segments of grapefruit and slices of clementine

APRICOT FLAN

A treat for anyone with a very sweet tooth, who likes gooey puddings.
Serves 4.

1 nut shell (page 262)
100g (4oz) dried apricots, washed
1 mix of confectioner's custard (page 37), cooled
5ml (1 tsp) arrowroot (optional)

1 Bring the apricots to the boil in water just to cover. Put the lid on the pan and simmer for about 25 minutes, until they are very tender. Or, if you prefer, once the apricots have come to the boil, warm a wide-mouthed vacuum flask with some of the water, return the water to the pan until it boils again, then tip apricots and liquid into the flask. Seal the flask and leave for about 30 minutes.
2 Purée half of the tender apricots with the minimum of liquid needed to make a soft purée. Stir the purée into the custard. Pour the mixture into the flan case.
3 Drain the remaining apricots of liquid and arrange them on top of the purée and custard mixture. Retain the liquid from the apricots for sweetening cereals or thicken it to make an apricot glaze for the flan.
4 To make a glaze, measure out 150ml (¼ pint) apricot-cooking liquid. If you haven't got this amount of cooking liquid, don't worry, you can top it up with *unsweetened orange or apple juice*. However, keep any juice separate for the moment and bring the apricot liquid only to the boil. Mix the arrowroot to a smooth paste with a few drops of cold water, and add it to the apricot liquid. Stir until the mixture comes back to the boil, then simmer, uncovered, for 5 minutes. Remove from the heat and add the cold juice. Wait until the syrup is thickening as it cools before spooning it over the flan.

RHUBARB FOOL

Almost any kind of fruit can be 'fooled' in this way. Exceptions are citrus fruits, pineapple and papaya – none of these benefit from cooking, and the enzymes in raw pineapple and papaya will eat into yogurt. Sweeten sour fruits with dried apricots, as here, or the same weight of dates, raisins or other dried fruit. It is best to use apricots for pale fruits, however, as the darker dried fruits will darken pale fruits if they are blended with them. *Serves 4.*

50g (2oz) dried apricots, washed and preferably soaked
450g (1lb) rhubarb, cut in 2.5cm (1in) lengths
7ml (1½ tsp) soft margarine or butter
10ml (2 tsp) honey
200ml (7fl oz) thick cold custard (use the recipe on page 231, with 15ml [1 tbsp] cornflour and only 200ml [7fl oz] milk)
150ml (¼ pint) thick plain low-fat yogurt
mint leaves or slices of fruit (optional), to garnish

1 Place the apricots in a saucepan with water barely to cover. Simmer, with the lid on, until tender – about 30 minutes.
2 Heat the oven to 180°C (350°F), gas mark 4.

Calories About 340 a serving.

- High fibre
- Very low salt (omitting salt from pastry)
- Milk-free (using soya milk)
- Gluten-free

Dried apricots are one of the most useful ingredients in the low-sugar kitchen. They sweeten, add colour and provide good food value (particularly iron and fibre) all at once.

Calories About 195 a serving.

- Suitable for diabetics (omitting honey)
- Medium fibre
- Very low salt (using milk from allowance and unsalted fat)
- Milk-free (using soya milk for yogurt and custard)
- Gluten-free

EAST EUROPEAN MENU

Poor man's caviare and
crudités **85 cals**

— • —

Lamb kebabs **260 cals**
Red cabbage **75 cals**
Kasha **95 cals**
Mixed salad **100 cals**

— • —

Kissel **90 cals**

Total calories per person **705**

*Kissel fruit dessert, made here with raspberries,
redcurrants, blackcurrants, blackberries and
cherries*

3 Transfer the apricots with 5 to 10ml (1 to 2 tsp) of their cooking liquid
to an ovenproof dish with a lid. Add the rhubarb, dot the fruit with the fat
and put the lid on the dish. Bake for about 20 to 30 minutes, until the
rhubarb is tender.
4 Mash or liquidize the fruit, add the honey and cool.
5 Whisk together the custard and yogurt, and stir in the cooled fruit.
Pour the fool into individual glasses and chill. If you like, garnish with
mint leaves or slices of fruit.

VARIATIONS

With some fruit, you will only need 350g (12oz) to serve 4; rhubarb
happens to cook down considerably.
If you are using very soft fruit, such as *strawberries* or *kiwi fruit*, omit the
cooking and just mash well before mixing with the custard and yogurt.

KISSEL

A deliciously simple way of bringing out the best in fruit, kissel has more
body than stewed fruit, without the solidity of a jelly. *Serves 4.*

Calories About 76 a serving.

• Suitable for diabetics (halving quantity of honey)
• Very low fat
• High fibre
• Very low salt
• Milk-free
• Gluten-free

If you use rhubarb or not-very-sweet gooseberries, try to mix them with a very sweet fruit (sweet apricots for instance) or add a few sprigs of sweet cicely to the pan, so that less additional sweetener is needed. Soft fruits, especially those such as currants and raspberries that contain a lot of pectin, are very high in fibre.

Calories About 150 a serving.

• Suitable for diabetics
• High fibre
• Very low fat
• Very low salt

Nice to know you don't have to keep away from traditional treats to stay fit. Team this one with a salad main course, or you won't have room for it.

BRITISH MENU

Watercress broth **95 cals**
Wholemeal melba toast
70 cals
— • —
Hare with mustard and dill
270 cals
Potatoes in their skins **150 cals**
Winter greens **30 cals**
Pease pudding **110 cals**
— • —
Trifle **150 cals**

Total calories per person **875**

450g (1lb) mixed fruit (traditionally including redcurrants or blackcurrants, with your choice of gooseberries, rhubarb, apricots, raspberries, blackberries, cherries or plums)

30ml (2 tbsp) arrowroot

150ml (¼ pint) water

45ml (3 tbsp) or less honey, depending on sweetness preferred

1 If you are using rhubarb, cut it into 2.5cm (1in) lengths. If using plums or apricots, chop them roughly and remove the stones. If you like, crack the stones and reserve the kernels to add to the mixture.
2 In a saucepan, mix the arrowroot to a smooth paste with a little of the water.
3 Whisk in the remaining water and add the fruit (except raspberries) and half of the honey. Set the saucepan on a medium heat and bring the mixture to the boil, stirring.
4 Simmer for 5 minutes to soften the fruit. If you are using raspberries, add them to the pan only 30 seconds before the end of cooking.
5 Remove the mixture from the heat, let it cool enough to taste and add the remaining honey if wanted (remember that the sweetness of honey is more pronounced in cold food). If preferred, remove the cherry stones at this stage.
6 Pour the kissel into a serving dish and leave it for several hours, until it is cold and lightly set.

TRIFLE

Trifle sounds complicated to make, but if you already have some cake (stale cake is fine), it's easy. The amount of juice needed will vary with how dry the cake is. *Serves 6.*

½ sponge cake (such as honey cake, page 243)

100g (4oz) apricot purée

60ml (4 tbsp) sweet sherry, Madeira or Marsala

30 to 45ml (2 to 3 tbsp) apple juice, unsweetened

225g (8oz) fruit; good combinations include:
either **100g (4oz) blackcurrants or blackberries and 100g (4oz) apple, chopped**
or **125g (5oz) stewed dried apricots (cooked weight) and 75g (3oz) kiwi fruit (1 large), chopped**
or **175g (6oz) plums, roughly chopped and 50g (2oz) raspberries**
or **125g (5oz) gooseberries and 75g (3oz) stewed dried apricots (cooked weight)**

15ml (1 tbsp) arrowroot

75ml (3fl oz) water

10 to 15ml (2 to 3 tsp) honey, to taste

Custard
generous 15ml (1 tbsp) skimmed milk powder

300ml (½ pint) skimmed milk

2 eggs

10ml (2 tsp) honey

few drops of natural vanilla essence

25g (1oz) ground almonds

1 Cut the sponge in thin pieces and sandwich them together with the apricot purée.
2 Arrange the sponge pieces to make a layer at the bottom of a straight-sided glass dish.
3 Pour over the sherry mixed with the apple juice, then spread any remaining apricot purée on top.
4 Place the fruit in a saucepan, excluding any kiwi fruit, raspberries or strawberries being used (they don't need cooking).
5 Mix the arrowroot to a smooth paste with the water and add the paste to the pan with the honey. Bring the mixture to the boil, stirring, and simmer for about 5 minutes, until the fruit is softening.
6 Add kiwi fruit, raspberries or strawberries if you are using them. Allow the fruit mixture to cool slightly, then pour it over the sponge layer.
7 In the top of a double boiler, or in a saucepan over simmering water in a larger pan, whisk the milk powder into the milk. Whisk in the eggs, honey and vanilla.
8 Whisk steadily for a few minutes until the custard thickens. Do not let it come to the boil.
9 Add half of the ground almonds.
10 Remove the mixture from the heat. Let it cool slightly before pouring it over the trifle.
11 Toast the remaining ground almonds for a moment on a baking tray under the grill, to brown very slightly, then sprinkle them over the trifle as a garnish. Serve when cold.

APPLE STRUDEL

You may think apple strudel looks too tricky to make at home, especially with wholemeal flour, but it's really quite simple – and very popular. *Serves 4 to 5.*

½ **mix of strudel dough (page 261)**
350g (12oz) eating apples (Cox's are ideal)
juice of 1 lemon
50g (2oz) currants or sultanas
15ml (1 tbsp) wheat germ
25g (1oz) chopped or flaked almonds
10ml (2 tsp) honey
10ml (2 tsp) ground cinnamon
10ml (2 tsp) soft margarine or butter, melted

1 Heat the oven to 220°C (425°F), gas mark 7. Grease a baking sheet.
2 Roll out the strudel dough to papery thinness.
3 Slice the unpeeled apples very thinly and in small pieces into a bowl. Pour over the lemon juice and stir in the currants or sultanas, wheat germ, almonds, honey and 5ml (1 tsp) cinnamon.
4 Spread the apple mixture evenly over the pastry.
5 Brush with half of the melted margarine or butter.
6 Roll up the pastry and transfer it to the baking sheet. Brush it with the remaining melted margarine or butter and sprinkle with the remaining cinnamon. Bake for 10 minutes, then reduce the heat to 190°C (375°F), gas mark 5, and bake for about 20 minutes more.

Calories About 210 to 270 a serving.

• Suitable for diabetics
• High fibre
• Very low fat (omitting egg yolk in pastry and halving quantity of fat for brushing)
• Very low salt
• Milk-free (using dairy-free margarine for brushing)

FRUIT PIZZA

Why only savoury pizzas? Make sure the topping for these fruit ones is fairly moist, but not runny. (See also the recipe for pizza squares on page 53). *Serves 4 to 5.*

1 mix of scone dough pastry (page 260)
450g (1lb) eating apples
about 10ml (2 tsp) clear honey
15ml (1 tbsp) currants
5ml (1 tsp) ground cinnamon

1 Heat the oven to 230°C (450°F), gas mark 8. Grease an 18cm (7in) flan tin.
2 Roughly chop half of the apples and stew them for about 6 minutes in the minimum of water needed to keep them from sticking (a few tablespoonsful).
3 Drain off the water and mash the apples with enough of the cooking water to make a thick purée. Taste and add 5ml (1 tsp) honey, or more if needed.
4 Make up the scone dough and roll it out to fit the flan tin.
5 Spread the purée over the scone dough. Top with symmetrical rings of very thin apple slices cut from the remaining apples. Sprinkle with currants, cinnamon and, if you like, more honey. Cover with kitchen foil.
6 Bake for 10 minutes covered with the foil (which helps the apple slices to cook), then for 10 minutes uncovered.

VARIATION

Use *puréed dried apricots* instead of apple purée, and top with *no-added-sugar apricot jam* and *flaked almonds*.

ICES

Sorbets and light ices are great to make in batches, ready in the freezer for when you want them. Don't forget to turn the freezer back to normal temperature once they are frozen.

COFFEE ALMOND ICE

You don't have to like yogurt to like this: the result doesn't taste like yogurt at all. *Serves 3.*

65ml (4 tbsp + 1 tsp) very strong decaffeinated black coffee
40g (1½oz) fruit sugar
10ml (2 tsp) gelatine
few drops of natural vanilla essence
2 drops of almond essence
300ml (½ pint) plain low-fat yogurt or a mixture of ⅔ yogurt, ⅓ quark
15ml (1 tbsp) almond flakes

1 Turn the freezer to its coldest setting.
2 Heat the coffee and dissolve the fruit sugar and gelatine in it.

Calories About 210 to 260 a serving. Add an extra 100 to 120 calories a serving for the variation.

• Suitable for diabetics
• High fibre
• Very low salt
• Milk-free (using soya milk in pastry)

Calories About 150 a serving.

• No fibre
• Very low fat
• Very low salt (using milk allowance for yogurt)
• Gluten-free

This is an example of a dessert which provides a significant amount of protein from the yogurt and the nuts, so can be matched up with a salad or snack meal.

3 Allow the mixture to cool to tepid. Add the vanilla and the almond extract and whisk in the yogurt, or yogurt and quark mixture, until you have a smooth blend. Stir in half of the almond flakes.
4 Transfer the ice mixture to a plastic container and put it in the freezer. It is impossible to be precise about the time it will take to freeze, as this will partly depend on factors such as the temperature of the freezer and the depth of the container. But allow for about 3 hours.
5 One hour before you want to serve the ice, transfer it from the freezer to the refrigerator, to soften slightly. Serve in scoops with the remaining almond flakes, lightly toasted, sprinkled on top.

VARIATION

If you want a smoother ice, remove the mixture from the freezer after 2 hours and beat it vigorously to break down the ice crystals. Return it to the freezer for at least another hour.

DUTCH APPLE ICE

I first met the idea of apple and cinnamon sorbet at Langan's Brasserie in London – and promptly started experimenting to copy it as it tasted so good. *Serves 4.*

450g (1lb) eating apples
150ml (¼ pint) water
2 cloves
5ml (1 tsp) gelatine
juice of about ½ lemon, to taste
about 5ml (1 tsp) ground cinnamon, to taste
15 to 30ml (1 to 2 tbsp) honey, to taste
25g (1oz) sultanas or raisins, well washed
150ml (¼ pint) plain low-fat yogurt
fresh fruit slices or extra cinnamon, to garnish

1 Turn the freezer to its coldest setting.
2 Peel, core and chop the apples and cook them gently in the water with the cloves until they are tender. Remove the cloves.
3 Purée the apples, then add the gelatine and lemon juice, cinnamon and honey to taste. Stir in the dried fruit. Make sure the gelatine is completely dissolved.
4 Allow the mixture to cool to tepid, then stir in the yogurt.
5 Pour the mixture into a plastic container and put it in the freezer.
6 After 2 hours, remove the mixture from the freezer and beat it to break down the ice crystals. Return it to the freezer for at least another hour.
7 Transfer the ice to the refrigerator about 60 minutes before serving. Serve scoops of ice with a garnish of fresh fruit slices or some extra cinnamon.

CHRISTINE'S BANANA ICE

When I was trying out recipes entered for the 'Best sunflower seed recipe' contest, I loved this, for both flavour and ease. So I asked Christine Sparling's permission to use it. *Serves 3.*

Calories About 105 a serving.

• Suitable for diabetics (halving quantity of honey or omitting it altogether)
• Medium fibre
• Very low fat
• Very low salt (using milk from allowance)
• Gluten-free

A very light dessert to finish off a substantial meal.

Calories About 210 a serving.

Dutch apple ice served with slices of unpeeled apple

- Suitable for diabetics (omitting honey)
- Medium fibre
- Very low salt
- Milk-free (using soya yogurt)
- Gluten-free (replacing wheat germ with millet flakes)

This ice tastes solid, but nutritionally it is not too heavy, although sunflower seeds add oil (rich in polyunsaturates and vitamin E), as well as some fibre and protein. Bananas are particularly rich in potassium and fairly rich in vitamin A in its carotene form. Like most ices, this goes well with a chewier main course. The meal should also provide some vitamin C in the form of salad or vegetables.

50g (2oz) sunflower seeds
275g (10oz) bananas (peeled weight)
15ml (1 tbsp) honey
15ml (1 tbsp) wheat germ
150ml (¼ pint) plain low-fat yogurt
about 5ml (1 tsp) lemon juice
a few extra sunflower seeds, to garnish

1 Turn the freezer to its coldest setting.
2 Toast the sunflower seeds, including those for the garnish, for 2 to 3 minutes in an ungreased thick-based frying pan set over a low heat. Set aside the seeds for the garnish and grind the rest to a flour in a coffee grinder or a food processor.
3 Mash the bananas and mix them with the ground sunflower seeds and all the other ingredients, adding a little lemon juice to taste.
4 When the blend is smooth, transfer it to a plastic container and put it in the freezer. Freeze for at least 3 hours.
5 About 30 to 40 minutes before serving, move the ice to the refrigerator. Serve in scoops garnished with the extra sunflower seeds.

PANCAKES

The pudding when you don't have time or ideas: you can make delicious pancake fillings from small amounts of any kinds of fruit, nuts or soft cheese.

BASIC THIN PANCAKES (CRÊPES)

Pancakes made with wholemeal flour can be just as thin as those made with white flour, and they are less stodgy. One of the quickest and most economical desserts. *Makes 12 to 14 paper-thin, 15cm (6in) diameter pancakes, to serve 3 to 4.*

100g (4oz) plain wholemeal flour
1 large egg
300ml (½ pint) skimmed milk
pinch of sea salt
10ml (2 tsp) oil, preferably corn oil
5ml (1 tsp) butter and 5ml (1 tsp) oil, for cooking

1 Place the flour, egg, milk, salt and 10ml (2 tsp) oil in a blender or food processor and whizz until smooth.
2 Traditionally, you should now let the batter stand for about half an hour or so in a refrigerator, but this is not strictly necessary.
3 Pour the batter – it should be fairly thin, like the thinnest cream – into a jug. If it looks thick, add about 15ml (1 tbsp) extra milk or water.
4 Heat a fairly small thick-based pan, preferably cast-iron, brushing it first with oil, then with butter, leaving the merest film in the pan.
5 Holding the handle of the pan with one hand so that you can swirl the batter around, pour in just enough batter to cover the base. Any excess should immediately be poured back into the jug.
6 Cook each pancake over a medium heat for about 1 minute on each side, turning it when the edges begin to curl. Tip each one on to a rack when it is done. Do not stack them until they are cool, or they may stick together.
7 Because of the oil in the batter, the pan will not need greasing again after each pancake, but, if necessary, brush it very lightly with oil or butter occasionally. Stir the batter from time to time, as the mixture will tend to separate. If the pancakes get thicker, dilute the batter with a very small amount of water.
8 Serve your pancakes with lemon juice and honey; or try one of the fillings listed below.

VARIATIONS

The following all make good fillings for dessert crêpes: *any soft or stewed fruit; kissel* (page 220); *no-added-sugar jam; confectioner's custard* (page 37) mixed with *10ml (2 tsp) liqueur, 25g (1oz) raisins* and, if you like, *2ml (½ tsp) cinnamon or mixed spice.*
Pancakes can be kept warm on a plate sitting on a saucepan of simmering water while you fill them. Fill and fold them in one of the following ways.
Cake Place each pancake as it is made on a heated serving dish, spread it with some of the filling, then place the next pancake on top. To serve, cut the pile in wedges like a cake.

Calories About 55 each (if making 12) plus calories for chosen filling.

• Suitable for diabetics
• High fibre
• Very low fat (omitting egg yolk and oil from batter)
• Very low salt (omitting salt, egg white and using unsalted butter)
• Milk-free (using soya milk)

With protein from flour, egg and milk and fibre from the flour, pancakes make a good contribution to the protein and fibre in a meal, and they add very little fat.

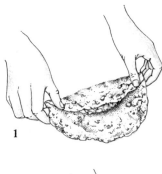

1

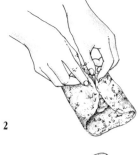

2

3

Making pancake parcels
1 Place the filling in the centre of the pancake and fold one side over the stuffing, as shown.
2 Fold in the sides.
3 Then fold over the whole pancake to make a parcel.

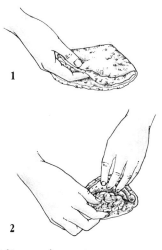

1

2

Making pancake cornets
Fold the pancake in half, and then in half again. Open up the uppermost fold and fill with stuffing.

Calories About 130 a crêpe.

High fibre
Very low fat (omitting butter and egg yolks from crêpes)
Very low salt (omitting egg white from pancakes)
Milk-free (using soya milk)

Calories About 330 each, with filling.

Suitable for diabetics
Medium fibre
Very low fat (omitting egg yolk from pancakes and using very low fat cheese and the minimum of oil for reheating)
Very low salt (omitting egg white from pancakes and salt, and using unsalted soft cheese)

Parcels Place the filling in the centre of the crêpe, then fold as shown.
Cornets Fold each pancake in 4 to make a wedge shape, and fill as shown. Serve with the filled fold uppermost.
Cylinders Roll each pancake up with a spoonful of filling inside, and place them side by side, very close to each other so they don't unwrap or look flat, on a heated serving dish.

CRÊPES SUZETTE

Makes 8, to serve 2 to 3

8 crêpes

Sauce

15ml (1 tbsp) butter

zest, finely grated, and juice of 1 large orange and ½ lemon

15ml (1 tbsp) clear honey

15 to 30ml (1 to 2 tbsp) orange liqueur, such as Grand Marnier or Curaçao

15ml (1 tbsp) brandy

1 Heat the ingredients for the sauce gently in a wide frying pan.
2 Prepare 4 pancakes at a time. Dip each quickly on each side in the mixture in the pan and fold it in 4 to make a wedge shape. Place the pancakes, points to centre, around the pan. Heat gently until the pancakes are hot, then transfer them to a warmed dish and keep them warm while you prepare the next 4 pancakes.
3 Warm the brandy.
4 When you have dipped and folded the second batch of pancakes, put the first 4 back in the pan, on top of the others. Heat quickly over a fairly high heat, then pour on the warmed brandy and set it alight – tipping the pan away from you! Serve the crêpes with orange sauce poured over.

BLINTZES

Makes 12, to serve 4 to 5

1 mix of basic thin pancake batter

Filling

350g (12oz) cottage cheese, sieved, curd cheese, ricotta or similar

30ml (2 tbsp) smetana or soured cream

50g (2oz) currants or sultanas

few drops of natural vanilla essence

pinch of salt

10ml (2 tsp) clear honey

1 Make the pancakes following the basic method, but cooking them on 1 side only. Tip each one out of the pan cooked side up.
2 Mash the filling ingredients together.
3 When the pancakes are cool, fill each one using the parcel method (opposite).
4 Brush a wide frying pan very lightly with oil or margarine. Heat the pan, then brown the pancake parcels for a few minutes on each side. Serve the blintzes with more smetana or soured cream to pour over.

PUDDINGS

No suet, no solid lump at the bottom of the tum. These are lighter and quicker than the conventional milk and steamed brigade.

GREEK LEMON CINNAMON PUDDING

A cold pudding that turns up, laden with cinnamon, on Greek islands. Good for pudding-lovers with limited time: it takes less than 10 minutes to make. *Serves 4 to 5.*

600ml (1 pint) skimmed milk
10ml (2 tsp) honey
75g (3oz) wholewheat semolina
15ml (1 tbsp) soft margarine or butter
grated zest of 1 lemon
small piece of cinnamon bark or 5ml (1 tsp) ground cinnamon
2 eggs, beaten
juice of 1 lemon
lemon zest, either in a curl or finely grated, or ground cinnamon, to garnish

1 Whisk the milk, honey, semolina, fat, grated lemon zest and cinnamon together in a pan over a gentle heat until the mixture thickens, then simmer it, uncovered, for 5 minutes. Stir often to prevent it from sticking.
2 Whisking steadily, pour the mixture over the eggs. Remove the cinnamon bark if you are using it.
3 Reheat the mixture in a double boiler or a saucepan on top of a larger one containing simmering water. Stir as the eggs thicken.
4 Remove the mixture from the heat, add the lemon juice and check the seasoning, adding a little more honey, lemon, or cinnamon if wished. Chill the pudding and serve it cold, garnished with lemon zest or cinnamon.

MILLET EGG PUDDING

Traditional milk puddings can be delicious, but take a very, very long time to cook. This one's foolproof and takes 45 minutes from start to finish. It's an attractive creamy colour. *Serves 4 to 5.*

900ml (1½ pints) skimmed milk
50g (2oz) millet flakes
2 eggs, beaten
2 strips of lemon zest
15ml (1 tbsp) honey
few drops of natural vanilla essence
ground cinnamon, to garnish

Calories About 160 to 200 a serving.

- Suitable for diabetics
- Medium fibre
- Very low fat (omitting fat and egg yolks)
- Very low salt (using unsalted fat and milk from allowance, and omitting egg whites)
- Milk-free (using soya milk)
- Gluten-free (replacing semolina with ground brown rice)

A pudding with the food value of a main course, supplying protein from the milk, semolina and eggs and some fibre from the semolina. Balance it with a course rich in vitamin C – salad, for example.

Calories About 125 to 155 a serving.

- Suitable for diabetics
- Medium fibre
- Very low fat (omitting egg yolks)
- Very low salt (using milk from allowance)
- Milk-free (using soya milk)
- Gluten-free

The milk, millet and eggs make this another main course pudding, to add protein without too much fat to a salad- or vegetable-based meal.

1 Heat the oven to 180°C (350°F), gas mark 4. Grease an ovenproof dish.
2 Simmer the milk and millet together gently for about 8 minutes, until the mixture is beginning to thicken.
3 Stir in the eggs, lemon rind, honey and vanilla, pour the mix into the ovenproof dish and bake it for 25 minutes, or until it is fairly firm.
4 Sprinkle the cinnamon on top.

VARIATION

You can use the same recipe with other flakes: *rolled oats* and *barley flakes* are especially good.
If you make lemon barley water (page 269), you can use the drained off barley and lemon zest to make this pudding. Follow exactly the same method as if you were using raw flakes, but use only about half the quantity of milk.

MRS BEETON'S FIGGY CHRISTMAS PUDDING

Mrs Beeton's figgy Christmas pudding – lighter than the traditional puddings – and served here with fresh figs

A little more crumbly than other Christmas puddings, but tasty and less heavy on the digestion – especially after a Christmas dinner. There's no flour in it. *Makes 2 medium.*

Calories About 2500 a pudding.

- Suitable for diabetics
- High fibre
- Very low salt (using unsalted breadcrumbs and fat, and omitting egg whites and salt)
- Milk-free (using dairy-free fat)
- Gluten-free (using gluten-free breadcrumbs)

This style of pudding is fruitier and less fatty, and so easier to digest, than the conventional Christmas pudding.

100g (4oz) dried figs
100g (4oz) dried dates
2 eating apples, about 225g (8oz)
225g (8oz) almonds
100g (4oz) brazil nuts
225g (8oz) fresh wholemeal breadcrumbs
generous 5ml (1 tsp) mixed spice
pinch of sea salt
2ml (½ tsp) ground nutmeg
100g (4oz) soft margarine or butter
about 10ml (2 tsp) honey
juice of 2 lemons
grated zest of 1 lemon
3 eggs, beaten
225g (8oz) raisins, 100g (4oz) currants, 100g (4oz) sultanas (all well washed and chopped)
100g (4oz) orange, scrubbed and coarsely minced, including zest
15ml (1 tbsp) brandy (optional)

1 Chop finely or mince on a medium blade the figs, dates, apples, almonds and brazil nuts.
2 Put the breadcrumbs, mixed spice, sea salt and nutmeg in a large bowl.
3 Rub in the fat, then add the honey, the lemon juice and zest, the eggs, all the fruit and nuts, and the brandy.
4 Transfer the mixture to 2 well-greased pudding bowls. Tie a buttered cloth or kitchen foil over the top and boil or steam the puddings for 3 hours.
5 Steam for a further 2 hours before serving.

POURING CUSTARDS

A genuine egg custard, and one for people who prefer 'custard powder custard', but without the sugar or colouring.

EGG CUSTARD

300ml (½ pint) skimmed milk
generous 15ml (1 tbsp) skimmed milk powder
2 eggs
10ml (2 tsp) honey
few drops of natural vanilla essence

Calories About 370 for 300ml (½ pint)

- Suitable for diabetics (in small amounts only)
- No fibre
- Very low salt (excluding egg whites and if you have enough milk allowance)
- Milk-free (using soya milk)
- Gluten-free

1 Put water to boil in a large saucepan or in the base of a double boiler.
2 Whisk all the ingredients together in a smaller pan or the top of the boiler.
3 Place the pan containing the custard mixture over the simmering water and whisk it for several minutes, until it thickens. Do not let the mixture boil or stick. If the custard becomes lumpy, sieve it. Blending it in an electric blender would make it too thin.

EGG AND CORNFLOUR CUSTARD

300ml (½ pint) skimmed milk

generous 15ml (1 tbsp) skimmed milk powder

generous 15ml (1 tbsp) cornflour

5 to 10ml (1 to 2 tsp) honey, to taste

1 large egg yolk

few drops of natural vanilla essence

1 Use a little of the milk to mix the skimmed milk powder and the cornflour to a smooth paste in the jug from which the custard will be served.
2 Stirring all the time (skimmed milk burns easily), heat the remaining milk to scalding point.
3 Stirring to mix smoothly, pour the heated milk on to the cornflour paste.
4 Return the mixture to the saucepan and heat it gently, stirring until it thickens.
5 Simmer the custard for 1 minute, then remove it from the heat and stir in the honey, egg yolk and vanilla. Stand for 2 to 3 minutes before serving.

Calories About 340 (using 10ml, 2 tsp, honey) for 300ml (½ pint)

• Suitable for diabetics (in small amounts only)
• No fibre
• Very low fat (omitting egg and using all cornflour – generous 15ml, 1 heaped tbsp, to make a sweet white sauce)
• Very low salt (if milk allowance permits)
• Milk free (using soya milk)
• Gluten-free

BREADS, CAKES & BISCUITS

Soda bread and the Grant loaf don't need vitamin C, while bagels get more rising time anyway. The dough used for making bagels can also be used to make loaves of any shape when you want extremely light bread, although it will also tend to stale quicker.

W hy bother to bake at home when there is such a variety of loaves and cakes on sale, and you're busy? Three reasons have kept me making my own bread through years of high-pressure office work. Firstly, I like eating bread, and home-made bread tastes so good you can enjoy it without having to smother it with spreads. You can eat a lot without getting fat: you get full first. On the way, you get the benefit of bread's protein, B vitamins, minerals and fibre – provided you use wholemeal flour.

Secondly, you know what you are eating. Bought bread, even wholemeal, can contain a dozen assorted additives, not to mention the mineral oil that may have been used to grease the tins. Wholemeal flour is not allowed to carry any additives at all.

Thirdly, baking bread is satisfying, relaxing and fun. I enjoy the magic of bread rising, and when you are used to making it, you don't need a recipe book or measuring cup. It becomes part of your tradition. Kneading is less of a chore, more of a relaxation. Ah, but what about the time? I never give bread more than one rising or proving. This cuts the total time taken to about 1½ hours, with only 10 to 15 minutes spent mixing or preparing. The key to one-rise bread is adding a tablet of vitamin C to the mixture. Vitamin C is ascorbic acid, one of several acids which can be used to accelerate the development of gluten, the protein in dough which develops its stretchy strands when mixed with water. The stronger those strands are, the more the bread can rise when stretched up by the gas produced by yeast. Kneading and proving encourages the gluten to develop its elasticity. Using vitamin C you can achieve the same stretchiness after one rising that you'd normally get after two.

The amount of vitamin C to add is not critical. Around 50mg per 1.5kg (3lb) of flour is enough. Because of the high temperature of baking, most of the vitamin C will be lost by the time the bread is cooked.

Whatever some recipes may say, you don't need 'strong' flour to make good bread. 'Strong' is the adjective applied to wheat and flour which are from a plant variety rich in gluten protein, so the elastic strands have the strength to hold in the gas and stretch the bread high. 'Soft' or 'weak' flour strands tend to give way under the pressure. Stronger flour does produce higher-rising bread. But the bread also tends to be drier and have less flavour. So the best bread-making flours mix 'strong' and 'weak' flours. When you can make bread that looks professional you may prefer bread with a heavier texture, using more 'soft' flour.

A selection of breads, cakes and biscuits. From the top: walnut gateau, bread rolls, oatcakes and hazelnut biscuits

Cakes and biscuits

Would you like to enjoy eating cakes and biscuits without even the faintest feeling that you shouldn't? That's what this section makes possible. It collects together recipes and ingredients for making home-baked cakes and biscuits which are delicious, yet as good for you as any other kind of food.

Some people hold the 'guided missile' theory on cakes. They have the feeling that the calories in cakes are 'different' and that instead of being used in energy, they have a built-in tendency to head straight for your hips and stay there! It's true that, when cakes are high in fat and sugar, you've much less chance of using up the concentration of calories, so more will be stored. This section picks out the cakes that are lowest in fat and in sugar, while still tasting good.

Surprisingly, this doesn't mean they are the kinds of cakes we think of as 'light'. Sponge cakes are light in texture, but it's impossible to make them without a large amount of sugar, and most contain a high proportion of fat as well. Yet some cakes that are heavier in texture, such as fruit loaf, can be made with no added fat and little or no added sugar. Because the cake is solid-tasting, it's still satisfying. Yeast-raised cakes and pastries are particularly independent of large amounts of fat or sugar.

These cakes may not contain many fewer calories, since what they leave out in fat and sugar, they add in dried fruit and flour. But the calories are more useful ones, carrying fibre, vitamins and minerals with more protein. So while eating a lot of cakes or biscuits will still put weight on you, smaller amounts can be worked into your meals or used as snacks.

All the recipes are made with wholemeal flour, and when the flour is sifted you will find that bran is left in the sieve. You can either return the bran to the sifted flour, thus keeping all the fibre, or you can set the bran aside and use it for some other purpose, such as adding to bread dough, muesli, thick soups or casseroles, or for sprinkling on breakfast cereals. If you do not use the bran, the cake will be lighter, though you may have to add some extra sifted flour to make up the weight. The disadvantage is that the fibre is removed from the recipe. You can compromise by adding half of the bran from sieving back into the mixture, keeping the rest to add to something else. And it is a good idea to make a habit of coating greased cake tins with bran, and to sprinkle some on cakes or biscuits before baking. Remember that many cakes benefit from keeping in the bran: it helps to keep gingerbreads and fruit cakes moist in texture.

You'll find several recipes that use puréed dried fruit for sweetening, thanks to the blender. Dried fruit contains fibre. small amounts of assorted minerals, including iron, and significant amounts of B vitamins, and has a good deal more filling power. Dried apricots are outstandingly high in vitamin A in carotene form, and dried peaches also provide a useful amount.

The other quality these recipes have is reliability. None requires mysterious ancestral skills, and all work well without elaborate creaming. My 11-year-old niece could make the lot.

In case you are wondering whether dried fruit has any health advantages over sugar, remind yourself that it not only provides sugar in smaller amounts, diluted with water, but it's a form of sugar that tends to be sweeter, so less is needed to make a cake sweet. While crystal sugar contains no vitamins, minerals or fibre to make it pay its way.

This chapter does not use glacé cherries or candied peel, because of their additives, especially cherry colouring, and high sugar content.

BREADS & YEAST BAKING

If you haven't made bread before, I suggest that you start with the basic wholemeal bread recipe. Once you are used to it, you'll find you can be adventurous with bread recipes, and produce delicious variations. When you want even less work, use the Grant loaf. And when you are really in a hurry, make soda bread. They all freeze well, for up to 3 months.

The step in breadmaking that worries some people is getting dried yeast nice and frothy. Water temperature is the key: it should be around 43°C (110°) or just above tepid. You can achieve this easily by mixing one-third boiling liquid with two-thirds cold. Or you can avoid the whole problem by using micronized yeast, which is added dry to the flour. However, micronized yeast weighs more than large-particle dried yeast, because the granules are smaller and so less air is trapped in the spoon. For every 15ml (3 tsp) granular dried yeast you would need about 10ml (2 tsp) micronized. So, generally, scale down the amount of micronized yeast using this guide, or use the measured sachets, as sold. After that, you can be as rough as you like with dough – it likes it!

WHOLEMEAL BREAD

Makes 1 large loaf, or 2 small loaves plus several rolls, or about 22 rolls.

25g (1oz) fresh yeast or 15ml (1 tbsp) dried
600ml (1 pint) tepid water, made by mixing ⅓ boiling water with ⅔ cold
5 ml (1 tsp) honey (if using fresh or dried yeast)
700g (1½lb) plain wholemeal flour
1 25 to 50mg vitamin C tablet, crushed
15ml (1 tbsp) fat, any kind
scant 5ml (1 tsp) sea salt

Toppings
Sesame seeds, poppy seeds, cracked wheat, bran or rolled oats, caraway seeds, fennel seeds, linseed, grated cheese

Calories About 2344 in total; about 1170 a loaf, if making two small loaves; about 105 a roll, if making 22.

• Suitable for diabetics
• High fibre
• Very low fat (fat can be omitted although bread will stale a little quicker)
• Very low salt (omitting salt and using unsalted fat)
• Milk-free (using oil)
• For gluten-free bread recipe, see page 286

1 Place fresh or large-particle dried yeast in a cup, half fill the cup with some of the lukewarm water, and whisk in the honey thoroughly. With fresh yeast, go straight on to step 2. With dried yeast, leave the cup in a warm place for about 10 minutes until the mixture is frothy. With micronized yeast, omit this step and add the dry yeast straight to the flour.
2 Mix together the yeast or yeast mixture, the flour, the crushed vitamin C tablet, all the remaining water, the fat and the sea salt. Knead with a dough hook for about 3 minutes or by hand for 8 to 10 minutes until the dough is smooth and elastic.
3 Cover it with an upturned mixing bowl, a cloth or polythene while you prepare baking tins or sheets by warming, then lightly greasing them.
4 Shape the dough into loaves and/or rolls and place them in tins or on sheets. Cover again and leave to rise: about 45 to 55 minutes for a large loaf, 35 to 40 minutes for small loaves, 20 minutes for rolls. This will take longer if the room or the dough is cold.
5 Ten minutes before you expect the dough to be ready for baking, heat the oven to its maximum temperature. Brush the bread with beaten egg for a shiny finish, and sprinkle with any of the toppings listed below. If you like, make deep cuts in the dough for decoration.

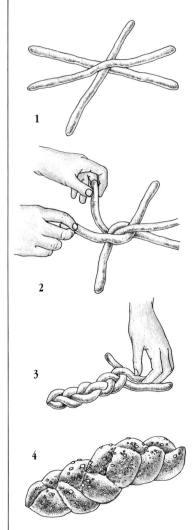

Making a French plait

1 Roll three ropes of dough and cross them over in the centre to form a star shape, as shown.
2 From the centre, start to plait the ropes towards each end.
3 Tuck the ends of the plait under to secure.
4 The finished baked loaf.

Calories About 1740 a loaf.

- Suitable for diabetics
- High fibre
- Very low fat (fat can be omitted)
- Milk-free (using soya milk and oil)

The B vitamins in flour are reduced when baking soda is used, but this recipe compensates with extra B vitamins (and protein) from the milk.

6 Bake the bread for 10 minutes at maximum temperature, then reduce the heat to 200°C (400°F), gas mark 6, for a further 5 to 10 minutes for rolls, depending on their size, and a further 20 to 25 minutes for small loaves, and 35 to 45 minutes for a large loaf.
7 Test that the loaves or rolls are done by listening to one, which should no longer 'sing', or by tipping them out of the tins and tapping their base, which should sound fairly hollow. If you want a crusty base and sides, return the loaf to the oven on a baking sheet for 4 to 5 minutes.
8 Cool the bread on a rack. If you intend to freeze a loaf, leave it until cold, then slice it before freezing.

Shapes
Tin Loaves Roll the dough into a rectangle, fold the ends loosely over the centre to make a roll to fit the tin, place in the tin with the join underneath.
Cottage Roll 2 balls of dough, one half the size of the other; place the small ball on top of the large one and push a floured finger or the floured handle of a wooden spoon deep through both.
French Roll the dough into a long cylinder and slash diagonally with a sharp knife before letting the bread rise.
Coburg Shape the dough into a large round, place on a baking sheet and cut a deep cross over the top.
Plait Roll three ropes of dough; make a 'star' crossing in the centre, then plait from the centre to each end, bringing the outermost rope to the centre. Do not plait tightly, or the bread will not be able to rise fully.
Pitta Roll out balls of dough thinly to make ovals, about ½cm (¼in) thick; bake for 15 minutes, then cover with cloth to keep the bread soft and to trap steam inside to make a pocket.
Rolls Use about 50g (2oz) dough for each large roll, adapting loaf shapes where appropriate.

Adventurous breads
Once you are used to making bread, you can experiment by replacing about a quarter of the wheat flour with *rye, barley, buckwheat* or *a mixed grain flour*. You can make rough-textured breads by mixing in a handful of one or more of these ingredients: *sprouted wheat, oatmeal, wheat germ, wheat bran, oat bran, malted wheat grains, grated cheese, grated nuts, flaked grains, cornmeal* or *toasted sesame seeds*. Or you can add *a few teaspoons of fennel seeds, caraway* or *poppy seeds* or *linseeds*. If the dough becomes stiff, add a little more warm water.

IRISH SODA BREAD

The quickest loaf – with less than a minute's work to get it into the oven.
Makes 1 large loaf.

450g (1lb) plain wholemeal flour
5ml (1 tsp) bicarbonate of soda
10ml (2 tsp) cream of tartar*
2ml (½ tsp) sea salt
15ml (1 tbsp) oil or soft margarine
150ml (¼ pint) milk, soured if possible
about 150ml (¼ pint) water
sesame seeds or rolled oats, to garnish

Irish soda bread, delicious and quickly made, served here with cottage cheese and spring onions

1 Heat the oven to 200°C (400°F), gas mark 6. Grease a baking sheet.
2 Sieve the flour, bicarbonate of soda, cream of tartar and salt. Return any bran left in the sieve to the bowl unless you want paler bread, in which case put it aside.
3 Rub or fork in the oil or fat.
4 Add all the milk and enough water to make a *very* soft dough: you may need a little more water, depending on the absorbency of the flour.
5 Draw the mixture together into a ball and knead briefly in the bowl to smooth out cracks. If you kept bran aside from the sifted flour, roll the dough in the bran, keeping any leftover bran for another use.
6 Transfer the dough to the greased baking sheet. Flour your palm and flatten the ball into a circle about 23cm (9in) across.
7 Cut out a deep cross through the top, brush the surface with milk and sprinkle with a spoonful of sesame seeds or rolled oats.
8 Bake for 35 minutes, until the bottom of the loaf is browned. Cool the loaf on a rack. If you like a soft crust, cover the bread with a cloth while it cools.

*If you use 300ml (½ pint) of soured milk instead of a mixture of water and milk, you can omit the cream of tartar.

GRANT LOAF

Calories About 2190 in total; about 1095 a loaf.

- Suitable for diabetics
- High fibre
- Very low fat (fat can be omitted)
- Very low salt (omitting salt and using oil as fat)
- Milk-free (using dairy-free fat or oil)

The recipe that Doris Grant invented makes wholemeal bread appealing to a lot of people who would never find the time for kneading. The total preparation time is only about 14 minutes. The loaf is moister and less fluffy than ordinary bread because of the extra water, but it cuts well, is slow to stale and makes excellent toast. *Makes 2 small loaves.*

400ml (14fl oz) cold water
200ml (about 7fl oz) boiling water
25g (1oz) fresh yeast, or 15ml (1 tbsp) dried yeast
5ml (1 tsp) honey
700g (1½lb) plain wholemeal flour, preferably partly strong
5ml (1 tsp) sea salt
15ml (1 tbsp) oil or soft margarine (optional, but it helps to keep the loaf fresh)

1 Mix the cold and the boiling water in a warmed jug.
2 Mix fresh or large-particle yeast in a cup with the honey and about half a cup of the water, and whisk with a fork. With fresh yeast, go on to step 3. With dried yeast, leave the cup in a warm place for about 10 minutes until the mixture is frothy. If you use micronized yeast, omit this step: add the yeast to the flour and the honey to the water.

Bagels, served with low-fat soft cheese and smoked salmon

3 Mix the flour and salt in a large bowl, and the yeast or yeast mixture and the water, then the fat, if using.
4 Stir vigorously with a wooden spoon for about 80 strokes. The consistency should be much thicker than a thick pancake batter, but just too wet to knead. Add a little more flour if the mixture is too wet, and a little more warm water if it is too dry.
5 Warm and grease well 2 small loaf tins or cake tins. Divide the mixture between the tins, cover the tins with polythene and leave them to stand in a warm place.
6 Thirty minutes later, set the oven to 200°C (400°F), gas mark 6.
7 Let the oven heat until the bread has risen to the lip of the tins. Bake for 35 to 40 minutes, until the bread doesn't 'whistle' when you put your ear close. If in doubt, tip the loaf out of the tin and see if the base looks well cooked. Cool on a rack.

BAGELS

Make them big for the traditional Jewish fillings: lox (smoked salmon), soft cheese, onions and chopped liver. Make them small for children and for breakfast. They're not just like any bread; they're very light in texture. *Makes about 24 small bagels or about 16 larger ones.*

15ml (1 tbsp) fresh yeast or 10ml (2 tsp) dried yeast
5ml (1 tsp) honey
200ml (7fl oz) lukewarm water
500g (18oz) plain wholemeal flour, preferably strong
1ml (¼ tsp) sea salt
2 eggs, lightly beaten
15ml (1 tbsp) oil

1 Mix fresh or large-particle dried yeast with half of the honey and half of the water in a warm cup. Whisk with a fork. With fresh yeast, go on to step 2. With dried yeast, leave the cup in a warm place for about 10 minutes until the mixture is frothy. If you use micronized yeast, omit this step: add the yeast direct to the flour and add all the honey to the water.
2 Mix half of the flour with the yeast or yeast mixture; add the rest of the honey and the remaining water, and stir vigorously with a wooden spoon or a dough hook for 2 minutes. Cover the bowl with a cloth or with polythene and leave for about 20 minutes until the dough has risen.
3 Add the rest of the flour, the salt, the eggs and the oil. Work the mixture to form a soft dough, transfer to a floured surface and knead for about 8 minutes.
4 If you have time, place the dough in a lightly oiled bowl, cover with oiled polythene and chill in the refrigerator for 12 to 24 hours. Otherwise, go straight on to step 5.
5 Divide the dough into 4 pieces, and shape each piece into a long 'rope' about 1cm (½in) thick. Cut the ropes into 18cm (7in) lengths and wind each length around your hand to make a ring. Pinch the ends together and put the ring on a floured board. Make the rest of the dough into rings in the same way. For larger bagels, make the 'rope' of dough thicker.
6 When all the bagels are shaped, cover them with a cloth or sheet of polythene and leave to rise for about 30 minutes, or until the bagels are slightly puffy.

Calories About 80 each (if making 24); about 120 each (if making 16).

- Suitable for diabetics
- High fibre
- Very low fat (omitting egg yolks and halving quantity of oil)
- Very low salt (omitting salt and egg white)
- Milk-free

7 Meanwhile, boil water in the widest saucepan you have.

8 Ten minutes before the bagels are due to be ready, heat the oven to its highest temperature. Grease 2 baking sheets.

9 Carefully drop a few bagels at a time into the simmering water, cook for a few minutes until they rise to the surface, turn them over with a slotted spoon and cook about 1 minute longer.

10 Transfer the bagels, as they are ready, to a baking sheet. Place them in the oven for a minute to dry water off the tops, then turn them over and bake for 15 minutes until browned. For larger bagels, reduce the oven temperature to 220°C (425°F), gas mark 7, so that they do not get too brown. If, after 15 minutes, they are not a good golden colour, increase the baking time by a few minutes. Cool on a rack.

Toppings

Bagels can be given an extra sheen by reserving some of the beaten egg, and using it to brush them before baking.

The beaten egg can be used to fix on any of the traditional bagel toppings: sesame seeds, poppy seeds, caraway seeds, or finely chopped onion softened in a little oil over a low heat for 10 minutes.

VARIATIONS

This is a rich dough; for a more solid bagel use one less egg.

You can use the same dough, without the poaching stage, to make a light-textured 'chollah', a large plaited loaf. Follow the recipe to the end of step 4, then divide dough in 3, shape each piece into a 'rope' about 4cm (1½in) thick, and plait loosely. Leave to rise, brush with egg, sprinkle with poppy seeds and bake for about 30 minutes at 200°C (400°F), gas mark 6.

DANISH PASTRIES

Probably the longest recipe in this book – but nice to know you can make these when you feel like it. They freeze well. *Makes about 16.*

15ml (1 tbsp) fresh yeast or 10ml (2 tsp) dried yeast
5ml (1 tsp) honey (if using fresh or dried yeast)
150ml (¼ pint) lukewarm water + 30ml (2 tbsp) extra water
250g (9oz) plain wholemeal flour, preferably strong
10ml (2 tsp) honey
pinch of sea salt
100g (4oz) hard vegetable fat or butter, chilled
Fillings
100g (4oz) dried apricots, well washed and preferably soaked for a few hours
a few drops of almond essence
25g (1oz) currants, well washed
50g (2oz) ground nuts, preferably almonds
10ml (2 tsp) ground cinnamon
75g (3oz) fairly dry curd cheese mixed with 5ml (1 tsp) honey and a few drops of natural vanilla essence
1 egg, beaten, to glaze
25g (1oz) flaked almonds, to garnish

Calories About 154 each.

- Suitable for diabetics (occasionally)
- High fibre
- Very low salt (using unsalted fat and soft cheese, and omitting salt)
- Milk-free (using fruit fillings only and dairy-free fat)

Although these are only slightly lower in fat than bought pastries, the fat is of a more useful type, and these pastries are also lower in sugar, higher in fibre, and free from any colourings or additives.

Danish pastries: shown here, cartwheels and apricot squares

1 Mix fresh yeast or large-particle dried yeast with 5ml (1 tsp) honey and half of the water and whisk with a fork. With fresh yeast, go on to step 2. If you use dried yeast, leave the mixture in a warm place for about 10 minutes until frothy. If you use micronized yeast, add it straight to the flour (step 2), without wetting it first.

2 Combine the yeast or yeast mixture with the flour, 10ml (2 tsp) honey, sea salt, and the remaining water and mix together to make a kneadable dough. Knead on a floured surface for 8 to 10 minutes until the dough is smooth and elastic.

3 Roll out the dough into a rectangle about 5mm (¼in) thick, with the narrow end facing you.

4 Cut the vegetable fat or butter into 1cm (½in) cubes. Dot half of the cubes evenly over the centre third of the dough. Fold the top or bottom third of the dough over the cubes. Dot the rest of the cubes over the top of the folded section, then fold the other end of the dough over the top. Press the edges of the parcel of dough lightly to seal, transfer the dough to a greased plate or baking sheet, cover with greased polythene and place in a refrigerator for 30 minutes or longer.

5 Place the chilled dough on a lightly floured surface, with the narrow end facing you. Roll out to a 5mm (¼in) thick rectangle again, and fold as before (but without adding the fat). Turn the narrow side of the folded dough towards you, and roll out and fold for a third time.

6 Chill again for at least 30 minutes.

7 Meanwhile, simmer the apricots in water to cover until they are tender (about 30 minutes). Remove 8 apricots or apricot halves for decorating the pastries and purée the remaining apricots with just enough of the cooking liquid to make a spread without the mixture becoming watery. Stir in the almond essence.

8 Cut the chilled dough in half. Roll one half into a rectangle not less than 5mm (¼in) thick, and about 23cm (9in) long.

9 Brush the rolled-out dough with some of the apricot purée, sprinkle with the currants, the ground nuts and half of the cinnamon.

10 Roll up loosely from the shorter side into a sausage shape. Cut across in slices about 2cm (¾in) thick: it should make 7 or 8 slices. Transfer the slices one by one to a greased baking sheet, pushing each one lightly into a circle shape. When the batch is completed, cover the sheet loosely with polythene and leave for about 1 hour at room temperature but not in too warm a place or the fat will leak.

11 Meanwhile roll out the other piece of dough into a rectangle about 20cm (8in) wide and 40cm (16in) long. Using scissors, cut the dough into 8 squares.

12 Brush the squares with some of the apricot purée. Place a large teaspoonful of the curd cheese mixture in the centre of each square, top with one of the reserved apricots, then fold in the corners of the pastry to half cover the apricot.

13 Transfer the squares to a greased baking sheet, cover with polythene and leave to stand at room temperature.

14 When all the pastries are puffy – the time will depend on the temperature of the room and the dough – set the oven to 200°C (400°F), gas mark 6.

15 When the oven is hot, brush the pastries with beaten egg and sprinkle with the remaining cinnamon.

16 Bake the pastries for 10 minutes, then brush with the rest of the apricot purée and sprinkle with almond flakes. Bake for a further 5 to 10 minutes, then cool on a rack.

VARIATIONS

You can also make a 'cock's comb' shape by cutting slices about 4cm (1½in) wide from the filled sausage shape of dough, rolling the slices flat, then cutting 4 deep slits into the wide side of each piece.

HAMANTASCHEN

Traditional Jewish three-sided pastries baked in February or March to celebrate an ancient victory over a tyrant called Haman – but a handy recipe all the year round when you want a pastry that's a little different. *Makes about 20.*

1 mix yeast pastry, (page 259)
a little clear honey, warmed, to glaze
Filling
75g (3oz) poppy seeds
75ml (3fl oz) water
22ml (1½ tbsp) soft margarine or butter
15ml (1 tbsp) honey
40g (1½oz) raisins or sultanas
25g (1oz) walnuts, chopped
2ml (½ tsp) finely grated lemon zest (optional)

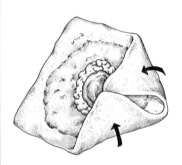

Apricot cheese pastries
Brush each square of dough with apricot purée, and top with a spoonful of curd cheese and an apricot. Then fold in the four corners to half-cover the apricot – the corners will pull away during baking.

Calories About 85 each (if making 20); if using prunes, about 70 each (if making 20).

• Suitable for diabetics (occasionally)
• High fibre
• Very low salt (omitting salt and egg whites from pastry and using unsalted fat throughout)

Poppyseed is similar to sesame seed in food value – high in oil, but providing fibre, vitamins and some protein.

This recipe is traditional, showing that 'leaner' cookery with lower fat pastry is not at odds with traditional tastes.

Folding hamantaschen
Bring up two sides of the pastry over the filling and then the third side up to meet them, pinching the edges together to seal.

Calories About 1215 in total.

• High fibre
• Milk-free (using soya milk and dairy-free fat)

Sponge cakes are popular but it's impossible to make a low-sugar version as the sugar levels are important to the texture. This recipe offers a good alternative that most people would identify as a sponge cake, yet has only half as much sweetening and a quarter of the fat, and contains more fibre.

1 Roll out the pastry 5mm (¼in) thick, and cut out circles about 8cm (3in) in diameter.
2 Place the circles on a lightly greased baking sheet.
3 Set the oven to 190°C (375°F), gas mark 5.
4 Grind the poppy seeds in a coffee mill or food processor.
5 Add the ground seeds to all the other ingredients in a saucepan, stir while bringing slowly to the boil and simmer, uncovered, for about 5 minutes, until the mixture thickens.
6 Allow the mixture to cool and check the flavouring: if you like, add a little finely grated lemon zest to taste.
7 Place a good spoonful of filling in the centre of each circle, then pull the pastry up at 3 points, drawing the edges together to make a triangular patty. Pinch the edges together.
8 Brush the tops with a little warmed honey and bake the pastries for about 25 minutes, until golden brown. Cool on a rack.

VARIATION

Replace the poppy seeds with *75g (3oz) prunes*, simmered in very little water until tender, then minced or finely chopped.

CAKES

The cake recipes in this section dispense with all forms of crystal sugar, using honey or dried fruit as sweeteners. Dried fruit helps to give fruit cakes and gingerbread plenty of deep flavour.

HONEY CAKE

The nearest recipe in this book to a sponge cake. This method requires no skill or prolonged creaming or beating. *Makes an 18cm (7in) diameter cake.*

40g (1½oz) butter or soft margarine
60ml (4 tbsp) honey
150ml (¼ pint) skimmed milk
few drops of natural vanilla essence
200g (7oz) plain wholemeal flour
10ml (2 tsp) baking powder
2 egg whites

1 Heat the oven to 200°C (400°F), gas mark 6.
2 Gently heat the fat and honey in a saucepan until melted.
3 Remove the pan from the heat, add the milk and vanilla essence.
4 Sieve the flour and baking powder, reserving any bran left in the sieve.
5 Grease an 18cm (7in) diameter tin and dust with the bran (keep any leftover bran for another recipe).
6 Combine the wet and dry blends.
7 Beat the egg whites until stiff, then gently fold them into the mixture.
8 Spoon the mixture into the tin and bake for 20 to 25 minutes. Turn the cake out of the tin and cool it on a rack.
9 Split the cake and fill with any of the fillings suggested on pages 35–6.

FRUIT LOAF

This belongs to that traditional group of 'cut and come again' cakes to have handy in an airtight tin. *Makes 1 medium-sized loaf.*

225g (8oz) raisins, sultanas or currants, mixed together and well washed
45ml (3 tbsp) clear honey
75ml (3fl oz) fruit juice, unsweetened
160g (5½oz) plain wholemeal flour
15ml (1 tbsp) baking powder
2ml (½ tsp) mixed spice
1ml (¼ tsp) ground nutmeg
1 large egg, beaten

1 Heat the oven to 160°C (325°F), gas mark 3. Grease a small loaf tin thoroughly.
2 Mix together the dried fruit, honey and fruit juice and leave to stand.
3 Sieve the flour, baking powder, mixed spice and nutmeg, returning any bran left in the sieve to the bowl.
4 Add the beaten egg to the fruit mixture, then stir in the flour mixture.
5 Tip the mixture into the tin and bake for 40 to 50 minutes, until the top of the loaf is springy to the touch.

Calories About 1370 in total.

• Suitable for diabetics (halving quantity of honey, or omitting it altogether)
• High fibre
• Very low fat
• Milk-free

No added fat apart from the egg, very little sweetening and lots of fruit make this a good standby for hungry moments, without lots of 'empty' calories.

Carrot cake – a moist and nutritious addition to the tea table

CARROT CAKE

Every recipe book should have one. Carrots can add sweetness and moistness to many kinds of fruit cake, and when you eat less sugar, you notice how sweet they are.

Calories About 2120 in total.

- High fibre
- Very low salt (using low-salt baking powder)
- Milk-free

Carrots are famous for their vitamin A, in the form of carotene, but did you know that they also offer useful amounts of B vitamins, vitamin E and the ability to convince slimmers that they are full?

3 eggs
60ml (4 tbsp) oil
225g (8oz) carrots, grated
45ml (3 tbsp) honey
225g (8oz) plain wholemeal flour
5ml (1 tsp) baking powder
5ml (1 tsp) bicarbonate of soda
generous 5ml (1 tsp) ground cinnamon
100g (4oz) raisins or sultanas, well washed
50g (2oz) walnuts or toasted almonds, chopped
few drops of natural vanilla essence

1 Heat the oven to 180°C (350°F), gas mark 4. Grease and flour a large loaf or cake tin.
2 Beat the eggs, add the oil, grated carrot and honey and beat well.
3 In another bowl, sift together the flour, baking powder, bicarbonate of soda and cinnamon.
4 Add the raisins, chopped nuts and vanilla essence to the flour.
5 Pour the egg mixture into the flour mixture and mix the two together. Pour the mixture into the tin.
6 Bake for about 1 hour, or until the cake is risen and firm. Cool on a rack.

VARIATION

For a lighter cake, add the lightly beaten egg yolks to the mixture at step 4 before folding in the egg whites at step 5.

GINGERBREAD

Rich flavour, good texture – and very easy to make well. *Makes an 18cm (7in) diameter, deep cake.*

Calories About 2210 in total.

- High fibre
- Very low salt (using unsalted fat and low-salt baking powder instead of soda, and omitting egg white)
- Milk-free (using dairy-free fat)

Not especially low in fat, but very much lower in sugar and higher in fibre than conventional versions – though just as luscious.

100g (4oz) sultanas, well washed
50g (2oz) dried apricots, well washed and soaked for 1 to 2 hours, then drained
150ml (¼ pint) water
5ml (1 tsp) vinegar
100g (4oz) soft margarine or butter
30ml (2 tbsp) honey
30ml (2 tbsp) molasses
1 egg, beaten
250g (9oz) plain wholemeal flour
5ml (1 tsp) bicarbonate of soda
15ml (1 tbsp) ground ginger
5ml (1 tsp) ground cinnamon

1 Simmer the sultanas and apricots in the water for 15 minutes, cool slightly, then liquidize.
2 Heat the oven to 150°C (300°F), gas mark 2. Grease an 18 to 20cm (7 to 8in) round or square cake tin.
3 Combine the vinegar, fat, honey and molasses and mix into the purée.
4 Add the beaten egg to the mixture.
5 Sieve the flour, bicarbonate of soda, ginger and cinnamon.
6 Add the wet mixture to the dry ingredients, beat the mixture quickly but thoroughly and if necessary add a little hot water to obtain a consistency that will drop from the end of a spoon.
7 Pour the mixture into the tin and bake for about 1¼ to 1½ hours, or until a skewer pushed into the centre of the cake comes out dry. Cool on a rack.

RICH FRUIT CAKE

With expensive cakes for special occasions, it's tempting to stick to the family's traditional recipe. But this one is worth the effort of tackling something new: it works well and isn't difficult. It also lasts well – you can store the cake in an airtight tin for a few weeks or in the freezer for up to 3 months. *Makes an 18cm (7in) diameter cake.*

Calories About 3540 in total.

- Suitable for diabetics
- High fibre
- Very low salt (using unsalted fat and low-salt baking powder and omitting egg whites)
- Milk-free (using dairy-free fat)

50g (2oz) dried apricots, washed and soaked
100g (4oz) block of dates, chopped and all stones removed
150ml (¼ pint) water
75g (3oz) soft margarine or butter, or a mixture of the two
3 eggs, beaten
225g (8oz) plain wholemeal flour
10ml (2 tsp) baking powder
7ml (1½ tsp) mixed spice
25g (1oz) ground almonds or ground toasted hazelnuts
625g (1lb 6oz) mixed currants, raisins and sultanas, washed
zest of ½ an orange, finely grated
15ml (1 tbsp) brandy or whisky
few drops of almond essence

1 Heat the oven to 160°C (325°F), gas mark 3. Grease an 18cm (7in) diameter cake tin and line with baking parchment or greaseproof paper; if you use greaseproof paper, grease the inside as well.
2 Cook the apricots and dates together in the water, simmering for about 15 minutes. Cool a little, then put the fruit and the cooking liquid into a blender or processor and liquidize until smooth.
3 Add the margarine or butter and whizz again.
4 Transfer the mixture to a large bowl, then beat in the eggs a little at a time.
5 Sieve together the flour, baking powder and spice, returning any bran left behind in the sieve to the mixture. Stir in the wet mixture, then the almonds or hazelnuts, the mixed fruit, orange zest, brandy or whisky, and the almond essence. The mixture should be soft enough to drop from a spoon, but too thick to pour.
6 Spoon the mixture into the tin, smooth the top with the back of a wet spoon and make a slight depression in the centre to prevent the cake forming a peak.

Rich fruit cake with an almond paste topping

7 Bake for 30 minutes, then reduce the heat to 150°C (300°F), gas mark 2, and bake for another hour, covering the top loosely with foil to prevent browning.

8 Test with a skewer to see if the cake is cooked through: the skewer should come out dry and not sticky. Leave the cake in the tin a few minutes before turning it out on to a rack to cool.

Calories About 775 in total.

• High fibre
• Milk-free
• Gluten-free

About 61g fat since almonds are relatively high in fat.

ALMOND PASTE

This takes no time to make – and tastes much better than bought varieties. Brush the cake thinly with warmed apricot jam or honey before coating it with almond paste. *Makes 1 layer for an 18 cm (7in) diameter cake.*

1 egg white
45ml (3 tbsp) clear honey, warmed
10ml (2 tsp) lemon juice
few drops of almond essence
few drops of orange flower water (optional)
100g (4oz) ground almonds
5 to 10ml (1 to 2 tsp) soya flour

1 Beat the egg white to a very soft peak.
2 Still beating, drizzle in the honey, followed by the lemon juice, almond essence and orange flower water, if used.
3 Stir in the ground almonds and enough soya flour to make a kneadable paste. Roll out the paste between sheets of polythene or greaseproof paper. Use straight away, brushing cake thinly with warmed apricot jam or honey before applying the paste.

VARIATIONS

This mixture not only makes a cake topping, but can also be used for petits fours.
Apricot petits fours Wash good-quality dried apricot halves and stuff each one with a tiny ball of almond paste. Top with a little soft cheese mashed with honey and, if you like, garnish with unsweetened dried coconut.
Nut petits fours Shape tiny balls of paste and squash each one between 2 walnut or almond halves.
Prune petits fours Stuff prunes in the same way as suggested for apricots.

WALNUT GATEAU

This kind of mixture is often used to make fruit loaves, but here it makes a moist and easy-to-handle basis for a gateau that requires much less beating than a traditional recipe, and is more foolproof. *Makes a 18cm (7in) diameter cake.*

170g (6oz) stoned, dried dates
170ml (6fl oz) skimmed milk
50g (2oz) soft margarine or butter
30ml (2 tbsp) corn or sunflower oil
2 eggs
170g (6oz) plain wholemeal flour
2ml (½ tsp) bicarbonate of soda
5ml (1 tsp) cream of tartar
50g (2oz) chopped walnuts
50g (2oz) oat flakes
15ml (1 tbsp) lemon or orange juice
Filling
350g (12oz) low-fat soft cheese
45ml (3 tbsp) finely chopped walnuts
15ml (1 tbsp) honey
generous 5ml (1 tsp) decaffeinated instant coffee
10ml (2 tsp) coffee or orange liqueur
walnuts, halved, to decorate

1 Heat oven to 180°C (350°F), gas mark 4.
2 Bring the dates to the boil in a saucepan with the milk, then remove from the heat. Allow to cool. Grease 2 18cm (7in) sandwich tins.
3 Transfer dates and milk to liquidizer, add the eggs, and fats, and blend until smooth.
4 Sieve together the flour and raising agents, retaining the bran in the

Calories About 2500 in total; about 250 per slice (if the cake is cut into 10 slices), without filling. Add 30 per slice for coffee and walnut filling, 50 per slice for plum filling and 55 per slice for peach filling.

• Suitable for diabetics
• High fibre
• Very low salt (using low-salt baking powder, unsalted fat and milk from allowance, unsalted soft cheese or fruit for filling and omitting egg whites)
• Milk-free (using soya milk and fruit filling, such as kissel, page 220)

Protein is supplied by the cheese, eggs, milk, nuts and flour, making this recipe an excellent dessert to follow a main-meal salad, for example.

sieve. Stir in the nuts and oat flakes. Combine the wet and dry mixtures, mixing well. Add the juice.

5 Transfer the mixture to the tins, smooth the surface and make a slight dip in the centre. Sprinkle the reserved bran on top of the mixture, and bake for about 30 minutes, until the cakes are just firm, but springy in the centre. Turn out and cool on a rack.

6 To make the filling, mix the ingredients by hand, adding a little *milk* or *yogurt* if necessary to make a good spreading consistency.

7 When the cakes have cooled, split into two and sandwich layers with filling, topping with filling. Decorate with walnut halves, if wished.

VARIATIONS

An alternative filling can be made by mixing the cheese with *225g (8oz) red plums, stewed and puréed*, sweetened with a little honey, or with *100g (4oz) stewed and puréed dried peaches* (no sweetener is needed).

GRETL'S TEACAKE

Very sweet – like Gretl. *Makes 1 large loaf.*

450g (1lb) mixed dried fruit, well washed
300ml (½ pint) Indian tea, hot or cold, or 1 large mug
60ml (4 tbsp) honey
1 egg, beaten
225g (8oz) plain wholemeal flour, or 2 mugs
15ml (1 tbsp) baking powder

1 Soak the dried fruit in the tea and honey overnight.
2 Heat the oven to 160°C (325°F), gas mark 3. Grease a large loaf tin.
3 Stir in the egg, flour and baking powder. Add a little more liquid if needed to make a soft, dropping consistency.
4 Transfer the mixture to the greased loaf tin, bake for about 1¼ to 1½ hours, until the centre is firm and the edges are shrinking slightly from the tin.

SCONES

Great food when you are in a hurry – ready in about 12 minutes. Don't keep them for cosy winter teas – use them for lunch-boxes, picnics and breakfast as well. *Makes 8 large scones, 8cm (3in) across.*

225g (8oz) plain wholemeal flour
pinch of salt
20ml (4 tsp) baking powder or 2ml (½ tsp) bicarbonate of soda and 5ml (1 tsp) cream of tartar
40g (1½oz) soft margarine or butter
about 150ml (¼ pint) skimmed milk

1 Heat the oven to its highest temperature.
2 Sieve together the flour with the salt and baking powder (or bicarbonate of soda and cream of tartar). Retain any bran left in the sieve for rolling out the scones.
3 Rub the fat into the dry ingredients.
4 Add most of the milk, until the consistency is very soft but not wet.
5 Transfer the dough to a surface dusted with bran and pat or roll out

Calories About 2135 in total.

- High fibre
- Very low fat
- Very low salt (using low-salt baking powder)
- Milk-free

Ideal for very low fat teas. For ideas on spreads see pages 35–6.

It provides two kinds of fibre – cereal and fruit.

Calories About 135 a scone. For fruit scones, add an extra 10 per scone. If using honey, add about 5 per scone. For cheese scones, add about 25 per scone. The calories for spice, buttermilk and herb scones are the same as for plain scones.

- Suitable for diabetics
- High fibre
- Very low fat (halving quantity of fat or omitting it altogether)
- Very low salt (using low-salt baking powder and unsalted fat and omitting salt)
- Milk-free (using soya milk and dairy-free fat)

The same basic recipe as all scones, but using wholemeal flour for extra fibre. Scones are naturally low in fat compared to almost any other kind of bun or cake.

TEA PARTY MENU

*Cucumber sandwiches with dairy spread and wholemeal bread **205 cals each***
*Egg sandwiches with mashed hard-boiled eggs and cottage cheese **240 cals each***
*Fruit scones **160 cals each***
*Glazed fruit tart **150 cals***
*Cherries or grapes **50 cals***
Favourite tea

Calories About 70 each, before filling. Add an extra 24 each for coffee filling, an extra 45 each if using double cream as well and 40 calories for the rum and almond version.

• Suitable for diabetics (occasionally), using fruit filling
• High fibre
• Very low salt (using unsalted fat, omitting 1 egg white and using unsalted quark in filling)

Not a low-fat recipe – this has the same level of fat as other choux doughs (page 257). The difference is the high level of fibre, although the éclairs are still very light.

until about 2cm (¾in) thick. Handle the dough as little and as quickly as possible.
6 Shape the dough with biscuit cutters or a knife, transfer the shapes to an ungreased baking sheet, brush them with milk and bake for about 10 minutes.
7 The scones are done when, if you squeeze their sides, they feel dry and firm, not wet or mushy.

VARIATIONS

Buttermilk scones Instead of the skimmed milk, use the same volume of buttermilk or soured milk and omit the cream of tartar, adding only bicarbonate of soda. Scones made this way are particularly light and tangy. Any of the variations below can be used.
Fruit scones Add 75g (3oz) well-washed sultanas, raisins or currants, or a mixture of all three, after rubbing in the fat, and mix 15ml (1 tbsp) honey into the milk. Alternatively, liquidize half of the fruit in the milk, and leave out the honey.
Spice scones Sieve 2ml (½ tsp) of mixed spice, cinnamon, nutmeg or ginger with the flour, and add 15ml (1 tbsp) honey to the milk. Spices can also be added to fruit scones.
Cheese scones Add a good pinch of celery seeds or celery salt, mustard powder and paprika to the flour instead of sea salt and add 50g (2oz) mature Cheddar cheese, finely grated, to the mixture after rubbing in the fat.
Herb scones Add 5ml (1 tsp) mixed dried herbs to the flour, or about 15ml (1 tbsp) of freshly chopped herbs. The same amount can also be added to cheese or buttermilk scones.
Honey and lemon scones Add 10ml (2 tsp) finely grated lemon zest to the flour, and 15ml (1 tbsp) honey to the milk. You can also replace 15ml (1 tbsp) milk with the same amount of lemon juice.
Orange scones Make in the same way as honey and lemon scones, replacing the lemon with orange and adding a sprinkling of ground coriander to the flour.

COFFEE ÉCLAIRS

An item with mystique – yet easy to make and reasonably healthy too. This is a classic choux pastry – richer than the one given on page 257. *Makes 12.*

75g (3oz) plain wholemeal flour
50g (2oz) butter or high PUFA margarine
150ml (¼ pint) water
2 standard eggs
honey, to glaze

1 Sieve the flour on to a plate or a sheet of paper, tipping any bran left in the sieve back into the flour.
2 Heat the oven to 220°C (425°F), gas mark 7.
3 In a medium-sized saucepan, bring the butter or margarine and the water to the boil. Remove from the heat immediately.
4 Quickly tip all the flour into the pan. Beat well with a wooden spoon until the mixture forms a smooth ball that leaves the sides of the pan clean.
5 Allow the mixture to cool slightly, while you thoroughly grease a

baking sheet or an éclair tin.

6 Beat the eggs lightly together, then add them to the mixture in the pan, a little at a time, beating steadily after each addition to prevent lumps from forming. When all the egg has been added the paste should be smooth and glossy.

7 Pipe out the mixture in 3 to 10cm (1½ to 4in) lengths, using a piping bag with a 1 to 1.5cm (½ to ¾in) nozzle. If you don't have a piping bag, you can use a polythene bag cut across at one corner.

8 Bake for 30 minutes, remove the tin from the oven, and quickly slit each éclair along its long side so that steam can escape. Return the éclairs to the oven for 3 to 4 minutes. Lift them on to a rack to cool.

9 Fill the éclairs when they are completely cold – they are too crisp to fill when warm. Glaze them with a little warmed honey.

Fillings

Coffee Dissolve a scant 5ml (1 tsp) decaffeinated instant coffee in 2ml (½ tsp) vanilla essence and a little yogurt; blend with 100g (4oz) fromage blanc or low-fat cheese. Flavour with honey to taste: you will probably need about 30ml (2 tbsp).

Cream For a creamier filling, mix 50g (2oz) whipped double cream with half the above mixture.

Rum and almond Use the first filling, replacing the coffee with a few drops of almond essence if you prefer, and add 25g (1oz) chopped toasted almonds and 15ml (1 tbsp) rum.

Coffee éclairs – glazed with honey and filled with coffee-flavoured low-fat soft cheese

CAROB BUNS

Carob offers hope for the chocolate addict! It doesn't taste like chocolate, but offers a dark brown sweetness with a hint of the same appeal, but without chocolate's high fat, high sugar, caffeine and migraine potential. *Makes 12.*

25g (1oz) carob powder
125g (5oz) plain wholemeal flour
1ml (¼ tsp) bicarbonate of soda
2ml (½ tsp) cream of tartar
pinch of sea salt
7ml (1½ tsp) mixed spice (optional)
50g (2oz) soft margarine
45ml (3 tbsp) honey
1 egg, beaten
few drops of natural vanilla essence
50ml (2fl oz) water
15ml (1 tbsp) lemon juice

1 Heat the oven to 200°C (400°F), gas mark 6.
2 Sieve the carob powder, flour, bicarbonate of soda, cream of tartar, salt and mixed spice (if used), reserving any bran left in the sieve.
3 Cream the margarine and honey together until fluffy.
4 Beat in the egg thoroughly.
5 Add half of the sifted dry ingredients to the mixture, stir in the vanilla, water and lemon juice, add the rest of the dry ingredients and mix well.
6 Grease well a 12-hole bun tin or set out 12 paper cases; sprinkle the surfaces with the reserved bran.
7 Fill each container about three-quarters full with the batter.
8 Bake the buns for 15 to 20 minutes. Cool them on a rack.

VARIATION

Add *50g (2oz) washed sultanas* to the mixture after step 5.

BISCUITS

If biscuits have a high food value, as these do, there's a lot to be said for using them to top up a lunch-box or light meal – especially if the alternative is sweets.

OATCAKES

Traditional, crisp, unsweetened oatcakes to go with soups, cheese, dips and sweet spreads. *Makes about 28.*

225g (8oz) medium oatmeal
large pinch of sea salt
large pinch of bicarbonate of soda
40g (1½oz) butter or chicken fat
about 100ml (4fl oz) boiling water

Calories About 95 each (if making 12). Add an extra 11 per bun for the variation.

- Suitable for diabetics
- High fibre
- Very low salt (omitting salt and egg white and using low-salt baking powder and unsalted fat)
- Milk-free (using dairy-free fat)

Buns no one would suspect of being 'good for you'.

CHILDREN'S TEA PARTY MENU

Carob buns **95 cals each**
Real orange jelly **70 cals**
Bagels with soft cheese and apple slices **150 cals each**
Bananas **80 cals each**
Carrot cake **200 cals**
Fruit juice mixed with mineral water **30 cals**

Calories About 45 each (if making 28).

- Suitable for diabetics (halving quantity of honey)
- High fibre
- Very low fat
- Very low salt (omitting salt and using unsalted fat)
- Milk-free (using dairy-free fat)

The fibre in oatmeal seems to be particularly beneficial in tackling high blood fat and high blood sugar levels – so choosing these biscuits seems both a sensible and an enjoyable mouthful of protection. If you like, you can exchange 50g (2oz) of the oatmeal for oat bran.

1 Heat the oven to 180°C (350°F), gas mark 4. Grease a baking sheet.
2 Mix the oatmeal, salt and bicarbonate of soda in a heat-proof bowl.
3 Melt the fat in half of the water, then pour the boiling water mixture into the oatmeal.
4 Add just enough extra boiling water to make a fairly soft dough.
5 Roll out the dough until about 3mm (just over ⅛in) thick. Cut the dough into 7cm (2½in) rounds and bake for about 20 to 25 minutes until the biscuits are dry in the centre. The oatcakes can also be cooked on a griddle.

CHEESE CRACKERS

Very easy, crisp and tasty biscuits which you could serve with drinks, with cheese or with dips. *Makes 30, 5cm (2½in) diameter, biscuits.*

225g (8oz) plain wholemeal flour
10ml (2 tsp) baking powder
pinch of sea salt
5ml (1 tsp) garlic powder (optional)
2ml (½ tsp) chili powder or ground cumin
50g (2oz) Parmesan or mature Cheddar cheese, grated
15ml (1 tbsp) soya sauce
45ml (3 tbsp) oil
water, to mix
paprika, to garnish

Calories About 40 each (if making 30)

• Suitable for diabetics
• High fibre

It's impossible to make a crisp biscuit without a significant amount of fat, but this recipe works well with a minimum of fat from oil and cheese, and the result also provides fibre. Extra bran can be added if wished.

1 Heat the oven to 220°C (425°F), gas mark 8.
2 Mix together the first six ingredients, then add the soya sauce, oil and enough water to make a stiff dough.
3 Roll out the dough until 5mm (¼in) thick, brush the surface lightly with oil and sprinkle with paprika.
4 Cut the dough into shapes, place them on a greased baking sheet and bake for 10 minutes.

VARIATION

Add *2ml (½ tsp) ground cumin*, or *cumin seeds* to the dry ingredients, and sprinkle a little *finely grated cheese* on the biscuits before baking.

HAZELNUT BISCUITS

Crisp, nutty and delicately flavoured. *Makes 20.*

125g (5oz) plain wholemeal flour
50g (2oz) medium oatmeal
5ml (1 tsp) cream of tartar
2ml (½ tsp) bicarbonate of soda
50g (2oz) soft margarine
40g (1½oz) hazelnuts, toasted then grated
30ml (2 tbsp) clear honey
water, to bind
25g (1oz) whole hazelnuts or 20 almond flakes, to decorate

Calories About 70 each.

• Suitable for diabetics (halving quantity of honey)
• High fibre
• Very low salt (using low-salt baking powder and unsalted fat)
• Milk-free

Not especially low in fat, but the recipe contains a more useful form of it, as some of it comes from hazelnuts which also have B vitamins, fibre, protein, iron and zinc, and a particularly high level of vitamin E.

1 Heat the oven to 200°C (400°F), gas mark 6. Grease a baking sheet.
2 Stir together thoroughly the flour, oatmeal, cream of tartar and bicarbonate of soda.
3 Fork in the margarine, then the grated nuts, the honey and enough water to bind the mixture.
4 Place tablespoons of the mixture on the baking sheet.
5 Use a fork to flatten each mound and make lines on the top.
6 Brush the base of the whole hazelnuts or almond flakes with a tiny dab of honey or jam and press one into the top of each biscuit (without this, the nuts tend to fall off).
7 Bake the biscuits for 15 to 20 minutes, until a pale gold colour. Cool on a rack.

GINGERBREAD MEN

Calories About 60 each (if making 20).

Gingerbread men (and women) – decorated with currants and slivers of nut

This recipe makes the kind of gingerbread that won't bake very hard, but if you like gingerbread men chewy, leave the biscuits to cool and then bake them again for 15 minutes. A good snack for tea, or for a picnic or a lunchbox. *Makes about 20 small biscuits.*

- High fibre
- Very low fat
- Very low salt (using low-salt baking powder and omitting salt)
- Milk-free

CHILDREN'S PARTY MENU

Pizza squares 115 cals each
Carrot sticks 20 cals
Tofuburgers in buns with tomato sauce and lettuce 275 cals
Chicken liver pâté open sandwiches 200 cals each
Gingerbread men 80 cals each
Bananas 80 cals each
Real orange jelly 70 cals
Fruit juice ice lollies 20 cals each
Carob buns 95 cals each

Calories About 105 each (if making 15).

- Suitable for diabetics
- High fibre
- Very low salt
- Milk-free
- Gluten-free (replacing the rolled oats with millet flakes and the wheat germ with rice bran)

Oats, wheat germ, sunflower seeds and soya flour all contain particularly high food value, providing essential oils, vitamin E, fibre, protein, B vitamins and other useful nutrients. Here's a way of enjoying them.

25ml (1fl oz) oil
15ml (1 tbsp) honey
45ml (3 tbsp) molasses or black treacle
125ml (4fl oz) water
2ml (½ tsp) bicarbonate of soda
pinch of sea salt
good pinch of ground cloves
1ml (¼ tsp) ground cinnamon
15ml (1 tbsp) ground ginger
about 250g (9oz) plain wholemeal flour
currants and almond flakes, to decorate

1 Beat together all the ingredients except the flour in a mixing bowl.
2 Stir in the flour gradually until the dough forms a ball that leaves the sides of bowl.
3 Cover the bowl and place it in the refrigerator for at least 3 hours and up to 24 hours.
4 When the dough is well chilled heat the oven to 180°C (350°F), gas mark 4. Grease a baking sheet.
5 Roll out the dough on a floured surface until it is about 5mm (¼in) thick.
6 Cut out gingerbread men or other shapes.
7 Transfer the shapes to the greased baking sheet and decorate them with currants and almond flakes to make eyes, mouths, buttons and any other fancy touches. Press fruit in firmly so that it stays in place.
8 Bake the biscuits for 10 to 15 minutes. Cool them on a rack.

MISS STRINGER'S HANDFUL COOKIES

A recipe borrowed with permission from Kathleen Stringer of Huddersfield, who won a prize with it in the 'Best sunflower seed recipe' contest. It must also qualify as one of the easiest recipes ever, producing the dark brown flavour of carob which appeals to chocolate addicts. *Makes about 15 – depending on how big your hand is!*

4 handfuls rolled oats
2 handfuls buckwheat flour
2 handfuls sunflower seeds, toasted
1 handful wheat germ
1 handful unsweetened dried coconut
1 handful carob powder, sieved to remove lumps
2 handfuls raisins, chopped
15ml (1 tbsp) soya flour
30ml (2 tbsp) oil
water, to mix

1 Heat the oven to 190°C (375°F), gas mark 5.
2 Mix all the ingredients together, adding the oil last, with enough water to make a soft dough.
3 Divide the dough into about 15 little heaps on a greased baking tray and bake for 25 to 30 minutes.

PASTRY & OTHER CRUSTS

Pastry is one of the treats of life, with most people's favourite foods including an apple pie like mother used to make, éclairs that squish with creamy filling, or a meaty pie from a delicatessen or wine bar.

Here are some ways of making pastry more of a balanced food but at the same time no less of a treat. For ordinary pastry is distinctly low in nutrients, while extraordinarily high in calories. That's because the flour with which it is made is of the most refined kind, and consequently low not only in fibre, but also in vitamins and minerals. Meanwhile, the most modest shortcrust pastry is roughly one-third fat, while flaky and puff pastry can soar to almost half fat – so about three-quarters of the calories come from fat.

Even if you are not concerned about what such a concentration of calories – some 150 per 25g (1oz) you eat – may do to your waistline, that's just too much fat for general health or good digestion.

The fats used in commercial pastry are usually of the hardest type, least useful to the body. In the recipes that follow I've used the softest fats that will suit the pastries. Butter comes in, though. First, thanks to its water content, it is actually less fatty than lard or dripping (82 per cent fat to lard's 99 per cent). Second, it carries with it more nutrients – particularly vitamin A, vitamin D and vitamin E. Third, the flavour of butter is so beloved of many that it's worth mixing it with another fat to get the best of both worlds. Fourth, for some pastries, notably hot-water pastry, it's necessary to have a fat with a high melting point, and butter provides a much more attractive choice than lard or suet. Choose unsalted or slightly salted butter, as salted versions can carry a surprisingly large amount of added sodium.

This chapter begins with shortcrust pastry made with wholemeal flour, for those who'd like to get better food value out of their pastry, but want to keep shortcrust in their repertoire. Then comes wholemeal choux pastry – for éclairs with more fibre. I go on to give a whole range of lower-fat pastries and other crusts, with examples of how to use them successfully.

PASTRY

In spite of using wholemeal flour, the result is no heavier. Most of these pastries also require less skill than either shortcrust or flaky. I haven't invented any of them – they are all established, just under-used.

WHOLEMEAL SHORTCRUST PASTRY

Calories About 734 in total.

- High fibre
- Very low salt (using unsalted fat)
- Milk-free (using dairy-free margarine)

Even wholemeal shortcrust pastry still has a high level of fat and I have not found it possible to reduce this without spoiling the result.

A mixture of soft margarine and butter produces a good compromise for those who love the flavour of butter. Most of the shortcrust pastry that can be bought ready-made contains neither. It is nearly all made with cheaper and more saturated fats such as lard, hardened margarine or hardened vegetable fats.

Wholemeal pastry is tastier, nuttier and, once you get used to it, far more appetizing, with either savoury or sweet fillings than shortcrust made with white flour. If you roll out the pastry and line your dish in the way suggested here, you will avoid the problem of pastry crumbling when you transfer it to the dish to be lined. *Makes a 20cm (8in) flan case.*

100g (4oz) plain wholemeal flour
50g (2oz) soft margarine, butter or a mixture
a little very cold water

1 Sieve the flour into a bowl. For nutty pastry, return the bran to the flour. For finer pastry, keep the bran in the sieve and use it to dust the surface on which you roll the pastry out. This way the bran stays on the pastry but does not affect the texture.
2 Fork or rub in the margarine or rub in the butter, until the mixture resembles fine breadcrumbs.
3 Add water very cautiously until the mixture will stay together.
4 Roll the pastry out on a sheet of polythene or kitchen foil dusted with flour or bran.
5 If you are using the pastry to line a dish, upturn the dish on top of the pastry and turn the whole thing over so that the pastry is over the dish. Line the dish loosely with the pastry. Peel off the backing sheet carefully.
6 Continue with your recipe, remembering to time the baking since you can't judge when this pastry is done by its browning: it's brown already.

VARIATIONS

Lighter pastry In some areas you can buy a finely ground wholemeal flour that makes pastry which is smoother and easier to roll out.
Nuttier pastry Add 30ml (2 tbsp) coarse wheat bran to each 100g (4oz) flour. This produces a pastry with a higher fibre content, and a taste you'll either love or loathe!
Oat bran pastry Add 30ml (2 tbsp) oat bran to each 100g (4oz) flour. Oat bran provides the other kind of fibre, the smooth type associated with lowering blood fat and sugar levels, and you will find that it is barely perceptible in the finished pastry.
Shorter pastry Add 2ml (½ tsp) baking powder to 100g (4oz) flour. This slightly reduces the vitamin B_1 content of the result.

CHOUX PASTRY

Calories About 925 in total.

- High fibre
- Milk-free (using dairy-free fat)

One of the easiest pastries to make well, and very light when made with wholemeal flour. This recipe makes a more solid version than those containing more fat (see coffee éclairs, page 250). It's the pastry used for éclairs and profiteroles, and is suitable for use with either savoury or sweet fillings. *Makes 12 éclairs or 1 choux ring.*

Not particularly low in fat, but even though it's made with wholemeal flour, it's surprisingly light. The eggs add a substantial amount of protein.

150ml (¼ pint) water
50g (2oz) soft margarine or butter
100g (4oz) plain wholemeal flour
3 eggs, lightly beaten

1 Put the water and the fat into a saucepan and set it on a medium heat. When the fat has completely melted, increase the heat and bring the water to the boil.
2 Tip in all the flour at once, and stir vigorously until you have a thick paste that forms a ball in the middle of the saucepan.
3 Cool the paste slightly, then, using a wooden spoon or an electric beater, beat in the egg a little at a time. Each time egg is added the mixture will separate, but it will smooth out again when the egg is blended in. Always make sure the mixture is smooth before you add any more. When all the egg is incorporated the paste will be ready to use.
4 Pipe out the required shapes using a piping bag with a 2cm (¾in) nozzle. Or transfer the paste to a polythene bag, cut a small snip from one corner of the bag and pipe the mixture through that.
5 Bake in an oven pre-heated to 220°C (425°F), gas mark 7, for 20 to 30 minutes, using the shorter time for small shapes like éclairs and profiteroles, longer for large rings.

HOT-WATER PASTRY

The ideal pastry for people who think they can't make pastry. Foolproof, easy to handle and cook, it's the sort of pastry used for raised meat pies but is equally suitable for use with sweet fillings. It's now rarely made at home. Rediscover it. *Makes 1 very large pie or 2 medium-sized pies.*

Calories About 2745 in total.

• High fibre
• Very low salt (using unsalted fat, omitting salt and egg white)
• Milk-free (using vegetable fat)

Lower in fat than shortcrust pastry. Some recipes use only 125g (5oz) fat per 450g (1lb) flour. I find this produces too hard a pastry, and prefer to balance the higher fat count by using low-fat pie fillings.

450g (1lb) plain wholemeal flour
175g (6oz) butter or solid vegetable fat
about 125ml (4fl oz) water
pinch of sea salt
1 egg, beaten, for glaze
150ml (¼ pint) stock (optional)
5ml (1 tsp) gelatine (optional)

1 Place the flour in a bowl.
2 Bring the fat, water and salt to the boil. Tip the mixture into the flour all at once, and, using a wooden spoon, mix to a soft dough.
3 Knead the dough until it is smooth – about a minute. Flours vary in their absorbency, and you may need another few spoonfuls of very hot water to make a soft but workable dough. Keep the dough warm to use.
4 Cut off a quarter of the dough and set it aside, keeping it warm.
5 Pat or roll out the remaining dough to line a large cake tin or 2 loaf tins. Use tins with detachable bases or line them with foil or baking parchment before greasing them.
6 Fill as required.
7 Roll out the reserved dough to make a lid. Cut a hole in the centre with a small biscuit cutter or scissors.
8 Damp the edges of the pastry and press the lid into place, sealing the edges by pinching. Knock up the edges to give a decorative frill. Use the pastry trimmings to make decorative leaves, or other shapes to suit your filling (for example, fish or birds). Brush the pastry lid with the egg.

9 Bake the pie for 20 minutes in an oven pre-heated to 200°C (400°F), gas mark 6, then reduce the heat to 180°C (350°F), gas mark 4, for the remainder of the baking time, which will depend on the size of the pie and the type of filling.

10 When the pie is done, remove it from the oven and extract it from the tin. Brush it twice with egg, to give it a shiny glaze, and return it to the oven for 5 to 10 minutes.

11 Pies made with hot-water pastry may be served hot or cold. If your pie is to be eaten cold and you want it to contain well-flavoured jelly, heat the stock and sprinkle on the gelatine. Dissolve the gelatine completely, then allow the stock to cool a little. When the pie has half cooled, pour the warm stock through the hole in the pastry lid. If you find that the pastry leaks when you add the stock, wait until the pie is cold to fill it; warm jellied stock gently to dissolve it before pouring it into the pie.

YEAST PASTRY

This kind of pastry needs no deft handling, and produces an excellent light result if rolled really thin to allow for thickening as it rises. If you use strong wholemeal flour you will be able to roll it thin without its breaking. Yeast pastry is suitable for use with savoury or sweet fillings. *Makes 2 20cm (8in) flan cases or 12 open tartlets plus 1 20cm (8in) flan case.*

10ml (2 tsp) fresh yeast or 5ml (1 tsp) dried yeast
175g (6oz) plain wholemeal flour, preferably strong
75ml (3fl oz) skimmed milk, heated to lukewarm
5ml (1 tsp) honey
25g (1oz) soft margarine or butter, softened
1 egg
pinch of sea salt

1 If you are using micronized yeast, add the yeast to the flour. Whisk the skimmed milk and the honey together. If using fresh yeast or large-particle dried yeast, whisk the yeast with the milk and honey. With fresh yeast, go on to the next step immediately. With dried yeast, leave the mixture in a warm place until it froths – this takes about 10 minutes.

2 Add half of the flour to the milk mixture, stir well and cover. Let the mixture stand for about 40 minutes.

3 Add the remaining flour with the fat, the egg except for a small amount reserved for glazing, and the salt. Turn the mixture, which will be fairly soft, on to a floured working surface. Knead it for about 8 to 10 minutes to a soft but smooth dough, adding just enough flour to avoid stickiness and dipping your kneading hand into warm water if the dough gets too dry.

4 Cover the dough and leave it to relax while you prepare your filling.

5 You can use the pastry after about 10 minutes. Do not knead it again, but roll it out very thinly (remember, it will thicken as it rises). Because it is stretchy and strong, yeast pastry is particularly useful for wrapping. It can also be used for lining a dish or topping a filling.

6 Brush the filled pastry with the reserved egg and bake it for about 25 minutes in an oven pre-heated to 200°C (400°F), gas mark 6.

Calories About 870 in total.

- Suitable for diabetics
- High fibre
- Very low fat
- Very low salt (using unsalted fat, egg yolk only and omitting salt)
- Milk-free (using soya milk)

Only a third of the fat content of shortcrust pastry, plus an egg. But the eggs provide protein and many vitamins, as well as fat. Because of its low fat content, this pastry is, along with scone dough and strudel pastry, the best food value of the pastry varieties for regular use, so make it in larger batches, and freeze some, as it freezes well.

Calories About 835 in total.

• Suitable for diabetics
• High fibre
• Very low salt (using low-salt baking power, unsalted fat and omitting salt)
• Milk-free (using soya milk)

Very different from shortcrust pastry, but quite as tasty and far lower in fat. Using baking powder slightly reduces the vitamin B1 value of the flour, but as this pastry also includes milk, you gain a small amount of B vitamins from that.

SCONE DOUGH PASTRY

Scone dough pastry can be used with either savoury or sweet toppings. Roll the dough out fairly thinly – it will rise and thicken as it cooks. Because baking powder starts working as soon as it meets moisture, scone pastry should be baked as soon as possible after mixing. So have the topping ready before you start. It is one of the quickest to make – little rubbing in is needed and it is quick to cook. *Makes a 30 × 18cm (12 × 7in) pizza, or 1 20cm (8in) flan case plus a few tartlets, or 12 tartlets with lids.*

175g (6oz) plain wholemeal flour
7ml (1½ tsp) baking powder
pinch of sea salt
40g (1½oz) soft margarine
about 60 to 75ml (4 to 5 tbsp) skimmed milk

1 Prepare your topping first, as this pastry is best when baked quickly after mixing.
2 Heat the oven to 230°C (450°F), gas mark 8. Grease a baking sheet or flan tin.
3 Sieve the flour with the baking powder and salt. Return the bran to the flour.
4 Fork or rub in the margarine.
5 Add enough milk to make a very soft dough.
6 Roll out thinly – scone dough rises during baking – on a sheet of polythene or kitchen foil. If you are using a baking sheet or tin, upturn it on top of the dough and turn them over together so that the dough is on top. Peel off the backing sheet.
7 Bake according to the recipe, but usually for 15 to 20 minutes.

ALMOND-CAROB PASTRY

Calories About 945 in total.

• High fibre
• Very low salt (using unsalted fat)
• Milk-free (using dairy-free spread)

Carob doesn't really taste like chocolate, but can help some people to beat their craving for chocolate. The powder is very sweet, free from the caffeine content of cocoa, and low in fat. It does not contain the substance known as tyramine, contained in chocolate and some other foods, which seems to trigger migraine in people with that tendency.

A little less fatty than regular pastry, this is a good pastry to use for sweet dishes. The carob, with its dark brown colour and flavour, disguises the wholemeal. Time the baking of this pastry carefully, as its colour won't guide you. *Makes about 15 open tartlets or 1 20cm (8in) flan case.*

generous 10ml (2 tsp) carob powder
125g (5oz) plain wholemeal flour
10ml (2 tsp) cinnamon
50g (2oz) soft margarine
30ml (2 tbsp) flaked almonds
few drops of almond essence
60ml (4 tbsp) cold water
enough egg yolk to bind

1 Sieve together the carob, flour and cinnamon. Return the bran to the mixture.
2 Rub or fork in the margarine.
3 Add the flaked almonds, almond essence, cold water and just enough egg yolk to make a firm but uncracking dough.
4 Roll the pastry out.
5 If you are baking the pastry as an empty flan case to be filled later,

place greaseproof paper or kitchen foil in the pastry shell and weight it with dried beans or pasta. Bake the pastry case in an oven pre-heated to 200°C (400°F), gas mark 6, for 15 to 20 minutes, until the centre is cooked.

VARIATIONS

This mixture makes biscuits which are very crisp, although barely sweet. You may like to add *more almonds* and *a little more almond essence*. Roll the pastry out and cut it into shapes. Bake in an oven pre-heated to 200°C (400°F), gas mark 6 for 15 to 20 minutes.

STRUDEL DOUGH PASTRY

This is a very adaptable pastry, capable of turning savoury or sweet bits and pieces into a rather elegant dish. You really do need strong flour for strudel dough, however. Only strong flour lets you stretch the dough out until it's almost translucent. When it is, it cooks up delightfully crisp-topped and thin-layered, so it enhances rather than dominates the filling. Once you've got the hang of stretching the dough thinly, strudel is a very easy pastry to make. *Makes 2 strudels, serving 4 people each.*

225g (8oz) strong plain wholemeal flour
30ml (2 tbsp) olive oil
1 small egg, beaten
about 150ml (¼ pint) warm water
pinch of sea salt
10ml (2 tsp) soft margarine or butter, melted, for brushing

1 Sieve the flour into a bowl, adding back the bran from the sieve.
2 Make a well in the centre and pour in the oil, the beaten egg and about half of the water. Add the salt.
3 Mix with a fork, gradually adding just enough water to make a soft but not sticky dough.
4 Turn the dough out on a floured board and knead it for 5 minutes, until it is springy and smooth. Cover it with a cloth or a polythene bag and leave it for 30 minutes.
5 Place the dough on a clean floured cloth. Do not knead again, but roll and stretch it very, very thinly, in a square shape, until you can almost see through it.
6 Spread the dough generously with savoury or sweet filling. Brush with half of the melted margarine or butter. Lift the end of the cloth nearest to you and use it to push the edge of the dough over the filling. Carefully pull the cloth, with the dough so that the dough gradually rolls itself round the filling.
7 Tip the roll on to a greased baking sheet and brush it with the rest of the melted fat. Bake for 10 minutes in an oven pre-heated to 220°C (425°F), gas mark 7. Then reduce the heat to 190°C (375°F), gas mark 5, and bake for about 20 minutes more.

Calories About 1075 in total.

- Suitable for diabetics
- High fibre
- Very low fat (omitting egg yolk)
- Very low salt (omitting salt and using unsalted fat and egg yolk only)
- Milk-free (using dairy-free margarine for brushing)

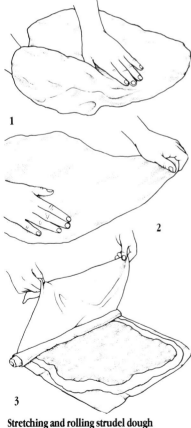

1

2

3

Stretching and rolling strudel dough
Strudel dough must be very thin. It can be stretched using either of the methods shown in (**1**) and (**2**) above. By stretching the dough on a cloth, you can then pull the cloth up to help roll the dough over the filling. (**3**).

OTHER CRUSTS

Pastry isn't the only way to make a dish go further – and look more attractive – by adding a case or topping. Here are two easy crusts which add food value without too much fat.

NUT SHELL

Too crumbly for something you want to cut in slices, but a tasty base for fruit and cheesecake desserts, and also for savoury fillings, with a nutty bonus. *Makes a base for an 18cm (7in) diameter flan.*

40g (1½oz) wholemeal breadcrumbs
25g (1oz) rolled oats
50g (2oz) plain wholemeal flour
40g (1½oz) hazelnuts, toasted then grated
35ml (2 tbsp plus 1 tsp) oil
pinch of sea salt
few drops of almond essence

1 Heat the oven to 190°C (375°F), gas mark 5. Grease an 18cm (7in) diameter flan tin.
2 Mix all of the ingredients.
3 Pat and press the mixture on to the flan tin.
4 Bake the nut shell empty for 15 to 20 minutes, until it is crisp.

Calories About 780 in total.

• Suitable for diabetics
• High fibre
• Very low salt (omitting salt and using unsalted bread for crumbs)
• Milk-free

Much lower in fat than those bases made from digestive biscuits glued together with loads of butter. Compared to shortcrust's ratio of 1 part of fat to every 2 of flour, this contains only 1 part of fat (counting the hazelnut oil) to more than 3 of the non-fat ingredients.

MILLET-CHEESE TOPPING

A protein-rich, relatively low-fat topping to use instead of pastry for savoury pies. *Makes a topping for 1 medium-sized pie.*

1 onion, sliced
5ml (1 tsp) oil
100g (4oz) millet
450ml (¾ pint) stock or water with 5ml (1 tsp) vegetable concentrate
50g (2oz) mature Cheddar cheese, grated
good pinch of nutmeg
pinch of white pepper
soya sauce (optional), to taste
10ml (2 tsp) sesame seeds

1 Cook the onion in the oil in a covered pan for 10 to 15 minutes.
2 Add the millet and stock and simmer for 20 minutes until the grain has a stiff, mushy consistency.
3 Remove the millet mixture from the heat and stir in three-quarters of the cheese, with the nutmeg and pepper.
4 Check the seasoning and add a little soya sauce if wanted.
5 Pile the topping on top of your pie filling, sprinkle with the remaining cheese and the sesame seeds and bake the pie for 30 minutes in an oven pre-heated to 190°C (375°F), gas mark 5.

Calories About 615 in total.

• Suitable for diabetics
• High fibre
• Gluten-free

Turns a vegetable filling into a main meal, since millet is one of the most useful grains for protein, and more protein is supplied by the cheese.

PRESERVES

The mark of a proud cook was once the rows of bright jars of jams and pickles in the larder; now, you may feel much the same about a well-stocked freezer, or freezer compartment in your refrigerator. The freezer has removed dependence on sugar and salt for their ability to preserve. For nutritional reasons, that's an excellent change. Freezing food is also easier and less time-consuming than making jars of preserves.

On the other hand, there are some traditional flavours that it would be a pity to lose, and here are recipes for some of them. By combining traditional ingredients with the use of the freezer, you can avoid using sugar without sacrificing the convenience of preserves. (See page 307 for more ideas on making the most of a freezer or the freezing compartment of your refrigerator.)

'Freezer jam' is my name for a method of making fruit spreads without as much sugar as is normally needed for preserving. Unfortunately, it's almost impossible to make at home the no-added-sugar jam you see in shops, because it uses special pectin – quite different from the pectin you can buy.

Next time you have a basket of blackcurrants, for instance, freeze them in 450g (1lb) bags. Then, when you want jam, take out a bagful, and stew the currants gently in the minimum of water, with a few sprigs of sweet cicely, if you can get some, to reduce the tartness. Add honey or fruit sugar to taste, then purée or mash the currants to make a much fruitier spread than you'll find in any jam jar. It will keep for 5 to 6 days in the refrigerator, so make only a week's supply at a time. You can use the same technique to make marmalade, mincing Seville and sweet oranges.

HONEY LEMON CURD

Calories About 515 per jar.

- Almost no fibre
- Milk-free (using dairy-free margarine instead of low-fat spread)
- Gluten-free

Lower in fat and sugar than bought types, with a better, more lemony flavour.

Easy to make and very sweet – especially the orange version – but tasty. It is useful for sweetening desserts, ices, and fruit, or for filling cakes. It will keep for about 3 months, unopened. Refrigerate once opened.
Makes 1 jar (275g [10oz] curd).

45 to 60ml (3 to 4 tbsp) of any favourite honey
3 egg yolks
2 egg whites
juice and zest of 2 lemons
40g (1½oz) low-fat spread

1 Sterilize jar in boiling water and dry it well in a very low oven.
2 Combine all the ingredients in a saucepan over a larger pan of simmering water or in the top of a double boiler.
3 Stir the mixture over a low heat until it thickens to the point when it will coat the back of a spoon. This takes no longer than 15 minutes.
4 Transfer to the warmed jar. Seal when cold.

VARIATION

Substitute *50ml (2fl oz) orange juice* and the *zest from a small orange* for half the lemon juice and zest.

MINCEMEAT

An all-fruit version. The absence of suet and sugar doesn't spoil the taste but does mean that the mincemeat won't keep for longer than a few weeks unless frozen. The mixture will mature as the fruit plumps up and the flavours mingle. If you want to make a lot of mincemeat for the year ahead, allow the mixture to sit in the refrigerator for several days before transferring it to freezer storage. *Makes 2 350g (12oz) jars.*

100g (4oz) each of sultanas, raisins and currants, well washed
25g (1oz) dried apricots, well washed
225g (8oz) eating apples (2 medium), peeled
25g (1oz) almonds
5 to 10ml (1 to 2 tsp) cinnamon
10ml (2 tsp) mixed spice
honey to taste, try 10ml (2 tsp)
juice of 1 orange
zest of 1 lemon, finely grated
30ml (2 tbsp) brandy, if liked (it helps mincemeat to keep)

1 Sterilize the jars in boiling water and dry them well in a very low oven.
2 Mince finely the sultanas, raisins, apricots, and half of the currants. Stir in the remaining currants, whole.
3 Mince the apples and almonds finely and stir them into the mixture.
4 Stir all the remaining ingredients into the minced mixture, adjusting the spices and honey to taste. (If you are not using brandy, you may want to add a little more orange juice to the mixture.)
5 Pot the mixture into the jars, seal them firmly and keep them in the refrigerator.

APRICOT SPREAD

A multi-purpose spread, for filling cakes, spreading on scones, mixing with custard or yogurt for an instant dessert, or for sweetening muesli or stewed fruit. It will keep for about 10 days, covered, in a refrigerator, or can be frozen. *Makes 1 350g (12oz) jar.*

140g (5oz) dried apricots

1 Wash the apricots well by rinsing them in boiling water, then put them in a saucepan and just cover with water.
2 Bring to the boil, cover and cook gently for about 30 minutes until very tender. This can be done conveniently by transferring apricots and water, after 1 to 2 minutes' cooking time, to a warmed, wide-mouthed vacuum flask (in which there's no risk of the fruit drying out). Leave in the flask for about 1 hour or until the apricots are tender.
3 Reserving most of the cooking water, liquidize the apricots or put them through a food mill to purée them. If preferred, leave in some chunks for a rougher texture. Add just enough of the cooking water to make a thick but soft spread.

Calories About 1055 per jar. Add about another 70 for the brandy.

• Suitable for diabetics (using as little honey as possible)
• High fibre
• Very low fat
• Milk-free
• Gluten-free

If mincemeat kept in the refrigerator ferments, you can still use it – it will just taste more alcoholic. But if mould develops, throw the mincemeat away; mould can be dangerous.

Once you've got a low-fat, low-sugar, high-fibre mincemeat, don't save it for Christmas. It can be used to stuff baked apples or to add sweetness, instead of sugar, to recipes.

Calories About 230 per jar.

• Suitable for diabetics
• High fibre
• Very low fat
• Very low salt
• Milk-free
• Gluten-free

Apart from their useful sweetness and tangy flavour, dried apricots are very rich in vitamin A (in carotene form) and contribute a range of B vitamins, potassium (very high) and fibre (very high).

4 Pot the spread in a clean, warmed jar and store in a refrigerator.

VARIATION

The spread can also be sterilized to keep longer by bottling it, then placing the jars on a trivet in a large saucepan, and submerging them up to the neck in cold water. (Leave the screw lids loosely fastened so that steam can escape during cooking.) Bring the water in the saucepan to the boil, and boil the jars for 5 to 10 minutes.

Tighten the tops on the jars and then leave to cool. The next day, test the seals. If they are not tight, use the contents of the jar as if they were fresh – within a week to 10 days.

PICCALILLI

This is a useful pickle to have in store to spice up sandwiches, cold meat or grain dishes. *Makes 2 large jars, about 1.5kg (3lb) total.*

Calories About 435 per jar.

- Suitable for diabetics
- Medium fibre
- Very low fat
- Very low salt (omitting salt)
- Milk-free
- Gluten-free (replacing wheat flour with cornflour or maize flour)

900g (2lb) mixture (untrimmed weight) of any of the following vegetables: carrots, cauliflower, courgettes, cucumber, French beans, green tomatoes, marrow and pickling onions, cut into dice about 12mm (¼in) in diameter
sea salt
15ml (1 tbsp) mustard powder
30ml (2 tbsp) turmeric powder
15ml (1 tbsp) plain wholemeal flour
600ml (1 pint) white or red wine vinegar
15g (½oz) fresh ginger root, grated finely
a few peppercorns
10ml (2 tsp) celery seeds

1 Put the diced vegetables on a non-corrosive dish and lightly sprinkle them with salt. Let them stand overnight, then rinse the salt off thoroughly and drain them well. (This step can be omitted, but it does help to keep the vegetables crisper.)
2 In a large saucepan, mix the mustard, turmeric and flour to a smooth paste with a little of the vinegar, then add remaining vinegar, ginger, peppercorns and celery seeds.
3 Heat the mixture and simmer it, covered, for 10 minutes. Add the vegetables, simmer for 5 minutes more, then pour the mixture into clean, warmed jars. Seal when cold and store for about 1 month before using. It can be kept in the refrigerator for up to 3 months.

PICKLED ONIONS

An enjoyable ritual for a cold autumn evening, as onions are best pickled, and cheapest, just after harvest. Using red wine vinegar gives a nice colour. *Makes about 9 standard-sized jars.*

Calories About 56 per jar.

- Suitable for diabetics
- Medium fibre
- Very low fat
- Very low salt (omitting salt)
- Milk-free
- Gluten-free

If you omit the brining step to reduce the salt, the onions do lose some crispness.

2kg (4lb) small pickling onions or shallots
100g (4oz) sea or rock salt
1 litre (2 pints) malt, wine or distilled vinegar
scant 5ml (1 tsp) each cloves, allspice berries, mace, 8cm (3in) cinnamon stick, a few peppercorns, whole, *or* 25g (1oz) pickling spice

1 Make a brine by adding the salt to 1 litre (2 pints) water and boiling it. Allow it to cool.
2 Put the onions or shallots in a bowl, cover them with boiling water for 1 minute to loosen the skins, then remove the onions or shallots, peel them and return them to a large bowl.
3 Pour the brine over the onions or shallots and leave for 24 hours.
4 Boil the vinegar with the remaining ingredients for 1 minute, cover and leave until cold.
5 Rinse the salt off the onions or shallots thoroughly, drain them well, and then pack them into clean jars, allowing 1cm (½in) clear space at the top.
6 Pour the cold spiced vinegar over, seal and leave for 1 month before using, to allow flavour to develop. It can be kept in the refrigerator for up to 3 months.

MANGO CHUTNEY

A priority for the store cupboard, because bought chutney is seldom as good, and mango chutney is so versatile, suiting meat, cheese, rice and curries, fish and chicken. *Makes 2 standard-sized jars.*

900g (2lb) mangoes
10ml (2 tsp) sea salt
450ml (¾ pint) wine vinegar
75ml (5 tbsp) honey
25g (1oz) root ginger
2 cloves of garlic (optional), crushed
5ml (1 tsp) allspice
50g (2oz) raisins

1 Cut mangoes into 2.5cm (1in) cubes.
2 Mix them with salt, leave for 3 hours and drain.
3 Add all remaining ingredients, transfer to a saucepan and simmer very gently, uncovered, for about 1 hour.
4 Transfer to clean, warmed jars and seal well. It can be kept in a refrigerator for up to 3 months, or can be frozen.

Calories About 580 per jar.

- Suitable for diabetics (in small amounts)
- Medium fibre
- Very low fat
- Very low salt (omitting salt)
- Milk-free
- Gluten-free

Very much lower in sugar than bought chutney.

DIETS FOR SPECIAL NEEDS

HEALTHY DRINKS

Today, coffee and tea are considered almost essential lubricants of social life. However, neither was in use in the West before the seventeenth century. It might be useful to remember that, if you feel that it's impossible to live normally without these drinks or even to use less of them.

For the more difficult you find it to cut down, the more benefit you will probably derive from doing so. If you drink more than one or two cups of strong tea or coffee a day, you are taking enough of their stimulant ingredients, caffeine and tannin, to experience an effect from them. While, in small amounts, caffeine and tannin certainly 'pick you up' (and that's the reason these drinks continue to reign supreme), larger quantities are likely to make you feel nervy, affect your digestion and sleep, and lead eventually to your feeling only half-alive without them. Exaggeration? Try stopping for a week and see how dependent you've been, if you regularly drink cup after cup of either drink during the day.

What can you drink instead?

Decaffeinated coffee
Decaffeinated coffee doesn't solve all the problems of coffee's effects on the digestion, but it reduces them markedly. There has been some concern that residues of the solvent used to extract the caffeine may be left in the beans and may affect health, but water-processed decaffeinated coffee is now available as beans, freshly ground, or in the form of instant coffee. Few people can distinguish good decaffeinated coffee from ordinary coffee.

Coffee substitutes
You can buy dandelion 'coffee' and a variety of other substitutes, usually made from grains. Dandelions and chicory are positively helpful to digestion. Otherwise, it's a matter of finding which drink you like instead.

Herb teas
Making tea weaker, or using a lower-tannin variety, available from health food stores, obviously reduces its stimulant effect. Herb teas provide another alternative. Except for matté tea, most herb teas contain little or no caffeine or tannin.

The tea plant is, of course, a herb itself, so there's nothing outlandish about switching to tea made from another plant. In many European countries herb teas, or tisanes, are used routinely. They are made in much the same way as conventional tea, using dried or fresh herbs or teabags. Allow two teabags or 10ml (2 tsp) of dried herbs (20ml [4 tsp]

fresh herbs) to 600ml (1 pint) of very hot water – the water doesn't have to be absolutely boiling, as it does with ordinary tea. Pour the water on to the herbs and leave to infuse for a few minutes, then strain. Or you can use a tea infuser, a perforated metal container which enables you to trap the leaves. Place the infuser containing the leaves in a cup or pot of hot water, and when the tea has infused sufficiently lift out the infuser. These infusers were originally devised for making ordinary tea. But they suit herb teas, where the bits of leaf are often larger, even better. Herb teabags are easy to carry around, so that wherever you are, you need only hot water to make a hot drink.

If you don't like the first herb tea you try, don't despair. Buy only a small amount and try another – there are dozens to choose from. Of the teas made from single herbs, the most commonly found are the following: chamomile: which herbalists use as a relaxant; fennel: used as a digestive – a traditional wind-queller; hibiscus (*Malva*): a refreshing pink brew, often mixed with other herbs; limeflower (lindenflower): a tea with a slight sweetness, and a low caffeine content; peppermint: probably the most popular after-meal drink; rosehip: a pleasant pink tea – rosehips are rich in vitamin C, but when they are served in tea form the quantity used is too small to yield a lot of the vitamin; verbena or vervain: used as a relaxant, for insomnia and for coughs. There are also dozens of mixtures of these and other herbs.

The flavour of herb teas, like that of ordinary tea, deteriorates with long storage, especially if the teas are exposed to air, heat or light, so buy them in small packs and keep them in airtight tins.

Other hot drinks
The following hot drinks are also well worth trying: lemon juice with hot water and a little honey: tomato juice, heated, with or without a dash of Worcestershire sauce; vegetable concentrate with hot water, making a vegetable consommé; yeast extract with hot water.

Cold drinks
Get away from the sugar, additives (and, in cola drinks, caffeine) of soft drinks. Even those described as fruit drinks, squashes or crushes may contain only a very small percentage of fruit. Fruit nectars contain a much higher proportion of juice, and you may be prepared to tolerate their small amount of added sugar for the sake of the wide variety of flavours they offer. Proportions of juice and sugar are usually declared on the label.

Cold drinks which provide a healthier alternative, especially for children, who tend to drink more of them, include the following: herb teas, chilled: especially varieties designed for serving cold, usually the 'pink' ones containing rosehip or hibiscus; juices (page 40); juice cocktails (pages 41, 269 and 290); juice spritzers: juice mixed half and half with sparkling mineral or soda water; lemon barley water, home-made (right); skimmed milk, chilled, flavoured with decaffeinated coffee; water: but don't drink softened water, as it's too high in sodium from the softening process; yogurt or buttermilk fruit shakes (page 42).

Alcohol

Although alcohol is never good for your health, small amounts are unlikely to hurt you, particularly if you stick mainly to wine or beer. But what is a small amount? The alcohol tolerance of individuals varies widely, with women generally having much less leeway than men before they damage their livers. However, up to fifteen drinks a week, preferably spread out over several days, but having a few alcohol-free days each week, is considered acceptable by most studies. A drink is counted as 300ml (½ pint) of beer, a glass of wine, a small glass of fortified wine such as sherry, or a measure of spirits.

Pregnant women, evidence clearly shows, can harm their babies by drinking. The best course is to stop all alcohol, but one drink a day is the maximum allowable.

A range of de-alcoholized wines and beers is available. Other people drown a small measure of alcohol with a large glass of soda water, mineral water or other mixer. If you want to drink something else, what are the options? Any of the drinks already listed under Cold Drinks; non-alcoholic cocktails: some of these are well established – most are based on fruit juices and syrups, but the syrup can be replaced by honey; bitters are essential to give a cocktail atmosphere.

Caffeine content of drinks

Over 250mg of caffeine is recognized medically as a stimulant. Just 2 or 3 cups of ground coffee will supply well over this amount.

Ground coffee contains 100 to 150mg caffeine per average cup, depending on the strength of the brew, and size of cup.

Instant coffee contains 60 to 90mg per cup, depending on strength.

Tea contains 50 to 80mg per cup, depending on strength.

Cola drinks contain 40 to 60mg per average glass, depending on the brand.

LEMON BARLEY WATER

A refreshing drink that will keep in a screw-topped bottle in the refrigerator for several days. *Makes 600ml (1 pint).*

30ml (2 tbsp) barley
600ml (1 pint) water
zest and juice of 1 lemon
honey, to taste

1 Wash the barley in a sieve, bring to the boil in the water.
2 Put the thinly peeled zest and the juice of the lemon in a china or pottery jug.
3 Pour the barley and boiling water over it, stir well and leave until cool.
4 Taste, and add honey cautiously to flavour.
5 Strain to use.

PUSSYFOOT

One of the best known 'mocktails'. There are many variations on the theme of citrus juice and egg yolk. The egg keeps the mixture frothy. *Makes 2 generous cocktail glasses.*

1 egg yolk
2 ice cubes
juice of ½ lemon
scant 150ml (¼ pint) orange juice, unsweetened
juice of ½ lime, made up with water to same amount as lemon juice
2ml (½ tsp) clear honey
2ml (½ tsp) angostura bitters, or to taste

1 Place all the ingredients in a blender and whizz until very frothy.
2 Pour into glasses. Garnish each glass with pieces of fruit, on the rim of the glass or on a cocktail stick.

VESPER

Means 'evening' – a good aperitif before dinner, especially. It is nice with 'cloudy' (unfiltered) apple juice. *Makes 1 long drink.*

½ wine glass of good-quality apple juice
juice of ½ lemon
2ml (½ tsp) angostura bitters
sparkling mineral water to top up (about same amount as apple juice)

1 Mix the apple juice, lemon juice and bitters.
2 Add mineral water to taste.
3 Pour over ice cubes in a whisky glass.

HELPING YOUR HEART

The rise of heart disease in Western communities is levelling off, but the incidence is still very high. Research emphasizes three worrying points. First, more young people are developing heart disease and dying from heart attacks. Many people don't mind the far-off prospect of a quick death from a fatal heart attack at a good old age. But most of us know men under 40 who've suddenly succumbed. Even if heart disease doesn't bring a fatal attack, it can reduce sufferers to invalids with the pain of angina, poor circulation and breathlessness.

Secondly, more women are succumbing to heart attacks in their pre-menopause years, when in the past such women seemed to have some mysterious protection. This rise has been blamed on social changes, ranging from an increase in the number of women who smoke to a new kind of stress suffered by women in high-pressure jobs.

Thirdly, it's clear that the build-up of fatty deposits in arteries, possibly leading to a fatal blockage with the heart failing through the loss of oxygen-carrying blood supply, starts very young, in childhood.

In spite of controversy about what causes heart disease, experts generally agree that there are five factors which will influence your risk level. Because of the invasion of younger age groups by the disease, prevention needs to be tackled by developing a healthier lifestyle at a very young age. Four of the factors can be built into such a lifestyle; they are: no smoking; eating in the style of those populations that don't suffer high levels of heart disease; exercising regularly; and deliberately learning methods of coping with stress. The fifth factor accepted as influencing heart disease risk is not in your hands: it's the inherited health status you're born with. But by improving your own health habits, you may be able to pass on lower risks to your children.

Other factors, such as the balance of minerals in water, may play a part in heart disease, but these remain controversial. No one really knows, either, why the level of heart disease has stopped rising in some Western populations, or has actually fallen. It may be the result of the undoubted efforts of huge numbers of people to change their health habits, or it may be some factor we don't yet understand.

Smoking This is the single most harmful habit you can have. As well as increasing your risk of heart disease, it can make you more likely to suffer a stroke. One in eight heavy smokers gets lung cancer, but smoking is linked with an estimated one in three of all cancers, because it can also encourage other types of cancer.

Exercise This can play more than one role in reducing the risk of a heart attack. As well as training your heart to use oxygen more economically, it helps weight control, reducing the burden of work on the heart, and is valuable in reducing stress. It can do this both directly, by relaxing tense muscles through their use and by stimulating the production of natural mood-raising chemicals in the body, and indirectly, by improving physical confidence and self-image, and providing an outlet for pent-up emotions.

Stress Although it is sometimes claimed that stress has no effect on heart health, few people would deny that an individual's reaction to stressful situations can affect general health, which includes the heart. It's important to recognize that while stress can be the result of inescapable outside circumstances, a great deal of tension is either self-created by unrealistic schedules or commitments, or is the result of the way we react. The serenity of some individuals in circumstances that make others frantic illustrates that such reactions are partly or even mainly under our control.

New methods of reacting, and of avoiding self-created stress, can be learned. Techniques now widely available include meditation, yoga, exercise, relaxation classes and deep breathing, plus counselling on ways of reorganizing your life so that you don't create avoidable stress. Many people have their own ways of avoiding the build-up of stress: by playing music, for instance, having a massage, walking the dog or scrubbing the floor.

Diet This is another important factor in any strategy against heart disease. Ideally, it should be started so early that it becomes natural, rather than a sacrifice or effort. For many years, people have had the idea that if they just ate less cholesterol (one of the fats found in considerable quantities in the plaques which block the arteries of heart patients) they would be safe. Now, the panacea for many people is to add bran to food.

Unfortunately, the answer is not so simple. While the 'butter versus margarine' battle goes on, everyone agrees that the safest way to tackle the role that fat plays in heart disease is to eat less of all fats: animal and vegetable, hard and soft. Of the fats that are still eaten – and some fat is vital to good health – between a third and a half should come from vegetable sources, such as oils (preferably unrefined), nuts, seeds such as sunflower or pumpkin, wheat germ and whole grains.

Eating less fat automatically reduces cholesterol intake. It also brings the fat level in Western diets down closer to that of countries where heart disease is rare. Eating less fat has been shown to lead to reductions in the levels of fat and cholesterol in the blood, both of which are indicators of the risk of heart disease.

What about eggs? Many diets for heart disease limit eggs to three a week, because of their high cholesterol level. Although it has not been con-clusively shown that eating more eggs does push up blood cholesterol levels – and remember that the body makes cholesterol itself for various jobs – it's sensible to eat no more than about 3 to 4 eggs a week until more is known on this point.

If you already have a high blood level of fat or of cholesterol, it's wise to cut down more sharply on all fats, and also on eggs. The easiest way of doing this is to use only egg whites, which contain almost no fat or cholesterol, and omit the yolks.

Shellfish is a puzzle, because it is low in fat yet high in cholesterol. As a result, diets for heart patients often suggest restricting its use to no more than once a week.

Reducing fatty food can also help heart problems by reducing the total number of calories eaten. Although plumpness is not thought to increase the risk of heart disease very much, obesity not only increases the work of the heart but also discourages the exercise which can help the heart.

Because a low-fat approach has been followed throughout this book, most people interested in avoiding heart disease can use the recipes without further fat reduction. When a recipe suggests a choice of fats, it's sensible to use softer fats, such as margarines high in polyunsaturates (see page 10) or to use oil more often than butter, since you are likely to get some of the more saturated, harder fats (associated with populations with a high rate of heart disease) from the meat and dairy foods you eat. But just substituting polyunsaturated fats for saturated fats is a less effective way of reducing blood levels than is eating less of all fats, though keeping more of the soft ones.

The second aspect of eating to help heart disease is to choose more fibre-rich foods. Although there is much about fibre still to be learned, it seems clear that it can affect the way the body deals with fat. Studies suggest that cereal fibre, such as wheat bran, increases the amount of fat that the body excretes. The physical form of the fibre seems to matter, too. Eating whole apples, for instance, where the fibre is in large particles, may produce a slightly different digestive pattern from that produced by eating stewed, puréed apples, which in turn will be differ-ent from the pattern that results from drinking the same amount of apples turned into juice. Although research on this subject has a long way to go, it seems sensible to take a good deal of food in its chewier, natural shape.

The kind of fibre that occurs in foods like beans and lentils, and also in oats, has been reported to be more effective than wheat fibre in bringing down the level of fat and cholesterol in the blood stream. The work on oat bran by Dr James Anderson at the University of Kentucky suggests oat bran can usefully reduce blood fat levels if about 50g (2oz) a day is taken. He believes that this is the result of a special mechanism, where the oat bran 'switches off' the body's own cholesterol-making system. Dr Anderson has also shown that oat bran can be used to bring down raised blood pressure directly, rather than by reducing the patients' weight. (In this experiment he used only lean volunteers.)

Oat bran is now available in shops. It can be added to many foods, from bread and cereals to soups and stews. It is less flaky than wheat bran, and more like oatmeal. When mixed with water, oat bran forms a sticky, soft gel rather like porridge.

Recipes throughout this book are generally high in fibre, because they use unrefined grains. But with heart health in mind, it's sensible to include beans, peas, lentils and oats – either as oatmeal or oat bran – in your meals often. That way, you'll get both kinds of fibre.

Sugar excess hasn't been convincingly shown to encourage heart disease directly. However, it can worsen matters indirectly in two ways. First, by encouraging obesity, which puts extra work on the heart. Secondly, by taking up calories that should be spent on the foods rich in the vitamins, minerals and fibre which would provide the heart with a better nutritional context.

Anyone who suffers from high blood pressure will benefit from cutting down more determinedly on salt (see pages 278–80).

Other eating habits that are proven aids to heart health include the following:
1 Eating generous amounts of garlic. Garlic has been shown to help the body correct its blood fat balance after absorbing high levels of cholesterol.
2 Avoiding heavy drinking, which can push up both blood fats and blood pressure. Blood pressure is a measure of how hard your heart has to pump to push blood round the body. Raised blood pressure is one of the clear indications that you have a higher risk of a heart attack or a stroke. The amount of alcohol that can be consumed without damage to health varies from individual to individual but anyone who has a tendency to raised blood pressure or heart disease is well advised to keep their alcohol consumption low (see page 269).

3 Avoiding large amounts of caffeine and related stimulants – from coffee, strong tea, cola drinks and chocolate – which may push up blood pressure. People who drink five or more cups of coffee a day, one survey shows, are more likely to develop heart disease: this might be a direct result of the high coffee consumption, or the coffee drinking in itself might be an indication of general stress.

4 Finally, it is a wise precaution to ensure that your system has access to all the vitamins and minerals it may need by eating the least refined foods you can, without throwing away your appetite on empty calories in the form of sugary or overcooked foods. However, available evidence suggests that changing only the food side of your lifestyle is unlikely to make much impact on your risk of heart disease. It is essential to pay attention to the exercise, relaxation and smoking aspects too.

Eating to help your heart

As a preventive measure:

1 Follow the menu planning outlined on pages 14–20.

2 Where recipes give alternative fats, choose the softest fat.

3 Except for occasional use, avoid dishes such as hot-water crust pastry where butter must be used.

4 Make a point of eating beans and lentils frequently, say three or four times a week. The dishes you choose can include lentil soups, bean salads, bean sprouts, humus and bean casseroles. As well as providing a particularly useful kind of fibre, these foods are low-fat sources of protein.

5 To add fibre to what is already a fairly high-fibre style of eating, use oat or soya bran, adding up to 30ml (2 tsp) a day to cereals, porridge, soups or stews. Choose oat dishes, such as muesli, porridge, oatcakes, mock duck or tofu burgers, often.

6 Favour the use of garlic. No, there isn't any way of stopping the smell after eating it. If you don't like it,

consider taking capsules of garlic oil, which definitely smell much less. Odourless garlic capsules are now available from health food stores. Onions have a milder but still useful effect.

7 Explore alternatives to caffeine-rich drinks: for ideas, see page 268.

8 Limit eggs to 4 a week, unless you use only the whites, which can be eaten freely.

9 Don't eat shellfish more than once a week.

10 If you are overweight, follow the suggestions on pages 296–300.

As a control measure:

1 Follow the low-fat diet plans on pages 276–8.

2 Cook without adding salt, using the ideas given on pages 278–80.

3 Follow the Pritikin Program, a method of treatment devised by Dr Nathan Pritikin at his clinic in California, where visitors come for a month at a time to follow a very restrictive diet. Fat is reduced to a very, very low level, salt and sugar are cut out, and fibre and unrefined foods increased. Alcohol, caffeine and tobacco are barred. Coupled with a carefully monitored programme of exercise and relaxation, this regime results in many sufferers achieving normal blood pressure (without taking drugs) by the time they leave and it has produced startling improvements in patients who have suffered severely from angina pain or from circulation problems, and who have been heavily dependent on drugs. The regime may seem intolerably restrictive, but people whose life is already very restricted and threatened by the symptoms of severe heart disease may find changing their lifestyle a small price to pay for feeling better. *The Pritikin Program for Diet and Exercise* by Nathan Pritikin and Patrick McGrady (New York, 1980) gives detailed eating plans, recipes and back-up advice, and is the most useful book for those seeking natural treatment for existing heart and blood pressure problems.

HIGH-FIBRE EATING

The easiest way of adding fibre to food might seem to be keeping a packet of wheat bran handy, and adding a little to all kinds of moist dishes. This isn't necessarily a good way to organize a high-fibre diet – and certainly not the tastiest.

Fibre is a family word, covering a number of substances found in the cell walls of plants. And although a great deal about the various types still has to be studied, it's clear that they behave in different ways inside us. This means that it's advisable to plan a high-fibre diet around a variety of different kinds of fibre.

Using the recipes in this book will raise most people's fibre intake without further attention. However, if you have been advised to follow a particularly high-fibre diet, here are some points that are worth bearing in mind.

Fibre intake

There's no known 'ideal daily intake' for fibre. People today eat very much less cereal fibre than they did 150 years ago, but obtain more fibre from fruit and vegetables. The result is an average intake estimated at around 20g per day – although people such as hospital patients, on institutional diets, have

been shown in some instances to have as little as 14g per day. The most generally used target is 30g of fibre per day. You can see from the chart below how this might be made up. Eating a little more than this won't hurt you. However, as with most things in life, more is not necessarily better.

Increase fibre intake slowly. Even if you are following a high-fibre diet as treatment for an illness, taking too much extra fibre at once is likely to make you feel bloated and uncomfortable, as it is by nature bulky and many forms will absorb fluid inside you. Rather, increase your fibre intake bit by bit over several months so that your system will get used to it. Remember that there are many other sources apart from wheat bran (see page 275), so try different sources if one makes you uncomfortable or you dislike the taste.

Cereal fibre

If an intestinal problem has resulted in your need for a higher fibre diet, cereal fibre will probably be the most useful source. It has the greatest ability to absorb fluid, and increase the bulk of waste material travelling down the intestine. This is particularly important in diverticular disease, where pieces of

TWO SAMPLE HIGH-FIBRE DIETS VERSUS LOW-FIBRE DIET

High-fibre diet (1)		High-fibre diet (2)		Low-fibre refined diet	
BREAKFAST					
Original muesli	4	2 slices wholemeal toast	6.4	2 slices white toast	1.9
Orange	2	Spread and honey	–	Spread and honey	–
		Apple	2	Bacon	–
LUNCH					
Wholemeal sandwich, 1 round	6.4	Baked beans on 1 slice wholemeal toast	16.2	Sausage, egg and mash (100g [3½oz] potato)	0.9
Salad, mixed: average 200g (7oz)	7	Salad, mixed (100g [3½oz])	3.5	Custard tart, 100g (3½oz)	1.1
		Banana	3.4	Peas, 75g (3oz)	4.0
MAIN MEAL					
Lentil soup	7	Wholemeal pasta with sauce (fibre for pasta alone)	5.7	Lamb chops	–
Slice of wholemeal bread	3.2	Green vegetables or salad: average 100g (3½oz)	3.4	White rice, 55g (2oz) uncooked weight	1.3
Grilled fish	–	Kissel *or* soft fruit (average depending on soft fruit chosen)	7.5	Lettuce salad, average with tomato	1.5
Spinach, 100g (3½oz)	6.3			Apple crumble with custard (e.g. 140g [5oz] crumble)	3.5
Baked apple, with 15g (½oz) dried fruit stuffing	2.8				
Yogurt or custard on apple	–				
Total fibre (g)	38.7		48.1		14.1

waste material, which through lack of fibre are small and hard, cause problems to the rings of muscle along the intestine that use a 'ripple' effect to push material down the tube. When waste material is small, the muscle rings have to strain to 'get a grip', and great pressure can build up. The result can be a 'blowout' or pocket forming in the wall of the intestine between rings. Such pockets are more the rule than the exception in elderly Westerners. They may cause no problems, but if waste becomes trapped in one, painful infection can set in.

Cereal fibre has been shown to result in a shortening of the transit time of food from 'in' to 'out'. This, together with its bulking effect, make it effective in solving constipation. The condition known as 'spastic' or 'irritable' colon is also often treated with cereal fibre for its bulking effect.

Bran by the spoonful is not the best way of taking cereal fibre: as our chart shows, other foods may give you more just because they taste better, so your portion will be bigger. Secondly, uncooked bran contains a natural substance called phytic acid. This can combine with minerals in food, making compounds that the body cannot absorb. By this mechanism, the body may lose a little zinc, calcium and iron. If you eat your bran in its natural form, wholemeal bread, brown rice or other unrefined cereals, this loss is less important: first, because in proving bread a substantial proportion of phytic acid is broken down; secondly, all these cereals are richer in such nutrients than their white refined equivalents, so you have more available and can afford to lose some of it. In the same way, if you eat bran in the unrefined foods where it occurs naturally, you are also getting more of the other nutrients, most of which are lost from refined white bread with bran; for instance, useful minerals like chromium or B vitamins.

For most people, wholemeal bread, unrefined breakfast cereals and crispbread will be the main sources of cereal fibre. However, don't forget brown rice, wholewheat pasta, wholemeal flour in baking and other 'whole grains' like barley. ('Pot' or 'Scotch' barley is the unrefined type, equivalent to brown rice; 'pearl' is more refined.)

Don't automatically reach for a packet of bran cereal – the attraction of its high-fibre content may be outweighed by a high sugar or salt content: read the label. Ideal cereals are unsugared muesli, Shredded Wheat, Puffed Wheat, frumenty (page 45) and porridge made with rolled wheat flakes.

If someone has been taking laxatives for a long time, their digestive system may need a considerable quantity of extra fibre to stimulate it into acting by itself without the irritant effect of the laxative. This is the best use for wheat bran, adding up to 30ml (2 tbsp) per day to food, until laxatives can be dispensed with. The amount of bran should then be gradually reduced, as the natural stimulus is re-established.

Don't forget that lack of fibre is not the only cause of constipation. Lack of fluid can also play a part. Poor circulation can also be a cause – with the answer lying in exercise and a generally much improved diet.

Finally, cereal fibre should not be the only fibre used, as general health probably benefits best from a mixture.

Oat and bean fibre
For diabetes, heart problems, high fat or cholesterol levels in the blood and high blood pressure, it seems as though the *'gummy' fibres* may be the most useful.

Oat fibre and bean fibre in particular have been associated with reducing the level of fat in the blood, which is useful for circulatory disorders including heart disease, where a high blood fat level is an alarm signal.

Diabetics may also benefit because these fibres slow down the progress of food from stomach to digestive tract. This produces a slower release of sugar into the blood stream, a help in keeping blood sugar levels steady.

A reduction in high blood pressure by using a low-fat diet with oat fibre has also been achieved in a test group. As a result of such research, both oat bran and soya bean fibre are now sold as products in their own right. Oat bran differs completely in character from wheat bran. It is not fibrous, but consists of small particles which form a sticky porridge-like consistency when mixed with water. It can be added to cooking without producing wheat bran's 'bitty' texture – and used in all kinds of moist foods as well as baking.

As with wheat bran, eating the whole of the oat has a nutritional advantage, both because oat bran also contains phytic acid, which can reduce mineral absorption, and because that loss is less important if you are also eating the mineral-rich grain.

Soya 'bran' is different in character again, with a distinct taste which not everyone enjoys, so start cautiously. It is said by the supplier to be 70 per cent fibre, with only 25 calories per 25g (1oz). It is best added to savoury dishes like casseroles and flan fillings, for instance.

Although you can up these types of fibre by eating more oats or beans, if you have been advised to use a high-fibre diet, the brans will provide more fibre than you could get in even large normal helpings of the whole food: 50g (2oz) of oat bran a day, for example, was used in the successful blood fat-lowering trials. To get that from oats, you would need to use about 225g (8oz) of raw oats.

Fruit and vegetable fibre

Fruit and vegetable fibre varies considerably between plants. Peas and beans, for instance, naturally share the type of fibre in the dried pulses – and make an often-ignored source. Sweetcorn is high in fibre too. Other notable sources are the soft fruits, particularly those high in pectin, such as blackberries, black and red currants, loganberries and raspberries.

Dried fruit is high in fibre simply because it has been concentrated by removal of water. However, not all the laxative effect of figs, for instance, can probably be ascribed to their high-fibre content: they also contain ingredients with a laxative effect.

All these items are far higher in fibre than the food on which too many people rely for their fibre supplies: salad. Nor are potatoes as high in fibre as people suppose. Their contribution is only important for those people who eat a lot of them. To get the same amount of fibre as would be provided by 100g (4oz) garden peas, for instance, you'd need to eat either 260g (9oz) of baked potatoes (skins are no richer in fibre than the insides) or almost 350g (12oz) of lettuce.

An effect particularly associated with pectin is the elimination of some harmful materials, such as heavy metals like lead, from the body. Pectin has also reduced blood cholesterol level in tests, and slowed

HELPING YOURSELF TO FIBRE: THE RICHEST SOURCES

Food	Typical helping	Dietary fibre (g)
CEREAL FIBRE		
Wholemeal bread	70g (2½oz) 2 medium slices	6.4
Wholewheat pasta	56g (2oz) uncooked weight	5.7
Shredded Wheat	40g (1½oz) 2 biscuits	5
Granary bread	70g (2½oz) 2 medium slices	4.8
Puffed Wheat	25g (1oz) large cereal bowlful	3.9
Brown bread (not wholemeal)	70g (2½oz) 2 medium slices	3.6
Wheat bran, plain	7g (¼oz) added to a dish	3
Rice bran	40g (1½oz) more like flour than bran	3
Ryvita	25g (1oz) 3 crispbreads	3
Hovis bread	70g (2½oz) 2 medium slices	2.5
Wholemeal flour	25g (1oz) half of pancake recipe, for example	2.4
Brown rice	56g (2oz) raw weight for main dish portion	2.4
Barley, pot	25g (1oz) raw weight for side dish portion	1.6
FRUIT AND VEGETABLES		
Blackcurrants	100g (3½oz)	8.7
Redcurrants	100g (3½oz)	8.2
Raspberries	100g (3½oz)	7.4
Figs, dried	40g (1½oz)	7.4
Blackberries	100g (3½oz)	6.3
Spinach	100g (3½oz) cooked weight	6.3
Loganberries	100g (3½oz)	6.2
Apricots, dried	25g (1oz)	6
Dates, dried	56g (2oz)	4.8
Sweetcorn kernels	100g (3½oz)	4.7
Brussels sprouts	100g (3½oz) cooked weight	4.2
Potatoes	225g (8oz)	4
Prunes	25g (1oz)	4
Almonds	25g (1oz), shelled	3.6

Food	Typical helping	Dietary fibre (g)
FRUIT AND VEGETABLES (*continued*)		
Peaches, dried	25g (1oz)	3.6
Coconut, dried	15g (½oz)	3.5
Banana	100g (3½oz) peeled weight	3.4
Green beans	100g (3½oz)	3
Leeks	100g (3½oz)	3
Fresh figs	100g (3½oz), about 2	2.5
Brazil nuts	25g (1oz), shelled	2.3
Plums	100g (3½oz), 2 large	2.3
Apple	100g (3½oz) weight eaten	2
Orange	100g (3½oz) peeled weight	2
Raisins	25g (1oz)	1.7
Sultanas	25g (1oz)	1.7
Currants, dried	25g (1oz)	1.6
PULSES AND OATS		
Red kidney beans	56g (2oz) raw weight	13.8
Baked beans in tomato sauce	180g (6oz) not allowing for any toast	13
Butter beans	56g (2oz) uncooked weight	12
Chick peas	56g (2oz) uncooked weight	8.4
Split peas	56g (2oz) uncooked weight	6.6
Lentils	56g (2oz) uncooked weight	6.5
Processed peas	75g (3oz)	5.9
Garden peas	100g (3½oz)	5.2
Broad beans	100g (3½oz)	4.2
Muesli	1 serving	4
Soya flour	25g (1oz) – used in cooking	3
Oat bran	20g (¾oz) – used in porridge or baking	2.7
Oatmeal	30g (generous 1oz) for porridge	2.1
Oatcakes	3 small	1.6

the progress of food from stomach to digestive tract.

Fruit and vegetable fibre is particularly helpful when aiming to lose weight, because its bulk helps slimmers feel full even though produce is generally low in calories. Nuts are also rich in fibre, but a less important source because their high oil and calorie content means you will eat less of them.

Another main attraction of fibre from produce is that these foods carry a rich supply of assorted vitamins and minerals too.

LOW-FAT DIET

No one should ever aim for a fat-free diet. We need far smaller amounts of fat than most of us eat, but we all need a certain quantity, since fats perform assorted vital functions in the body.

However, while a no-fat diet is dangerous, a diet with even less fat than the low level provided by recipes throughout this book may be prescribed in some situations. These include gall bladder disease and gallstones, certain kinds of jaundice and other illnesses related to injury to the liver, lack of fat-digesting enzymes, and other cases where fat cannot be tolerated.

In addition, diets very low in fat, when coupled with mild exercise, relaxation lessons and careful supervision, have been reported to produce encouraging improvements for sufferers from high blood pressure, angina and other circulatory problems.

The Pritikin Program (see page 272), which involves such a low-fat diet, has brought about startling improvements after only one month in patients who have been severely restricted by angina pain or circulation problems. A large proportion of those who visit the Pritikin clinic become able to dispense with medicines. (The clinic has also had great success in treating sufferers from maturity-onset diabetes.)

Because reducing fat removes large amounts of calories from meals, following a diet very low in fat usually leads to weight loss. Nutrient and fibre intake goes up, because any food eaten instead of fat (except for sugar) will contribute more.

Anyone following a diet for more than a few weeks that is extremely low in fat should consult his or her medical practitioner about how to ensure that he or she doesn't suffer any shortage of the essential fatty acids, especially linoleic acid, only available in fats we eat. While vitamins A and D, both carried in fats such as dairy foods, oily fish and butter or margarine, can be supplied from other sources (carrots and other yellow and green vegetables for vitamin A in carotene form; sunlight on skin for vitamin D), some kind of linoleic acid supplement may be advisable. For instance, this could take the form of capsules of safflower oil, the oil containing about 75 per cent of this acid. The estimated daily requirement of linoleic acid is 2 to 5g. Some of this will be supplied by wholegrain cereals, but several oil capsules a day would make up the amount.

Low-fat meals

Recipes throughout this book have been designed to use the minimum of fat compatible with a successful result, so the opportunities for reducing still further the fat level of any particular recipe are limited. Although you can get used to eating very little fat, cutting it down drastically affects food flavour.

Foods to be avoided

The following foods are high in fat, and dishes containing them should be avoided.

Avocado pears	Mackerel
Biscuits, bought	Mayonnaise
Butter and margarine	Milk, full-fat
Cakes, bought	Nuts, except chestnuts
Cheese, hard	Oil-based salad dressings
Chocolate (30 per cent fat)	Olives
Coffee creamer	Pork (except lean ham)
Cream	Salad cream
Cream cheese	Shortcrust, flaky, choux and
Delicatessen meats and	puff pastry – use only
sausages	strudel type (page 261)
Duck and goose	White sauce made by the
Egg yolks	usual method of blending
Fatty meat or fatty fish	fat and flour; substitute
Fried foods	low-fat wholemeal sauce
Herrings	(page 27)
Lamb, except leanest cuts	

VERY LOW-FAT SALAD DRESSING

Makes 150ml (¼ pint).

150ml (¼ pint) thick plain low-fat yogurt or soft cheese

pinch of French mustard

pinch of black pepper

Flavourings
Choose between: chives and other fresh herbs, chopped; 5 to 10ml (1 to 2 tsp) tomato purée; spring onions, chopped; lemon juice, to taste; paprika; mango chutney (page 266); garlic, crushed

For a thick sauce, mix all the ingredients by hand. Use a food processor only if you want a fairly liquid texture.

HIDDEN FATS IN FOOD

An average Westerner eats between 100g (3½oz) and 125g (4¼oz) fat daily. Here are some of the foods you may not think of as fatty: aim to eat at least 25 to 30g (around 1oz) less fat a day than you do now.

Food	Typical helping	Fat (g)	Alternative food	Typical helping	Fat (g)
Avocado pear	100g (3½oz), typical half, no dressing	22*	**Globe artichoke**	1 whole, no dressing	negligible
Cheese, Cheddar	Matchbox-size piece, 25g (1oz)	8.3	**Cheese, cottage**	25g (1oz), 15ml (1 tbsp)	1
Chocolate	4 squares, 25g (1oz)	7.4	**Banana**	Large, 140g (5oz) peeled weight	0.4
Doughnut	70g (2½oz)	11	**Currant bun**	70g (2½oz)	5.3
French salad dressing	30ml (2 tbsp)	18	**Oil and lemon dressing**	30ml (2 tbsp) from recipe on page 150	
Lean steak	175g (6oz) rump	13	**Rabbit casserole**	175g (6oz)	7
Milk	225ml (8fl oz) glass	8.5	**Skimmed fresh milk**	225ml (8fl oz) glass	0.2
Peanut butter	25g (1oz), generous 30ml (2 tbsp)	13	**Apricot spread**	25g (1oz)	negligible
Pork sausages, grilled	2 × 50g – total 100g (3½oz)	24.6	**Shepherd's pie**	200g (7oz)	12
Salami	Small helping, 25g (1oz)	11.3	**Lean ham**	25g (1oz)	1.3
Scotch egg	100g (3½oz)	21	**Baked potato with cottage cheese**	225g (8oz) potato with 50g (2oz) cheese	2.2
Sponge cake, light	100g (3½oz) slice	26**	**Honey cake**	100g (3½oz) slice	7.3
Steak and kidney pie	140g (5oz) individual size	29.7	**Sandwich, chicken salad**	1 round; 7g (¼oz) butter or margarine and 50g (2oz) chicken	7.7
Wholemeal quiche lorraine	140g (5oz) medium slice	39.3	**Wholemeal pizza**	140g (5oz) piece	16.1

Varies from 11 to 39 per cent depending on season

** *Unless it's fatless variety, but this is rarely sold ready made as it stales quickly.*

Low-fat foods in restaurants

The person on a low-fat diet has some irksome restrictions when eating out, since some dishes, while low in fat when made following my recipes, can be very oily. So in restaurants it's safest to stick to very plain foods.

FIRST COURSES	
Artichoke	
Asparagus	With a squeeze of lemon, no butter
Consommé	
Corn on the cob	Without butter
Grapefruit	
Melon	
Mixed salad	Without dressing

MAIN COURSES	
Baked beans on toast	With grilled tomatoes, if you like
Baked jacket potatoes	With cottage cheese and/or chives or onions
Chicken	Grilled, roast or casseroled; discard skin and ask for sauces to be omitted
Ham	If very lean
Lamb's kidneys	Grilled, and not more often than once every ten days, because of high cholesterol content
Peas, beans, sweetcorn	A useful source of protein in a restaurant meal, provided you ask for them to be served unbuttered

MAIN COURSES (*continued*)	
Pizza	Without cheese, olives, anchovies or salami; try mushroom, pepper and tomato topping
Rabbit	Roast or casseroled; ask for sauce to be omitted
Rice	Plain boiled or steamed
Salad	Without dressing, or ask for cottage cheese or lemon to moisten
Shellfish	Only in Japanese restaurants, where they don't add fat, and not more often than once every ten days
Turkey	Roast or casseroled; the leanest meat
Vegetables	All kinds, lightly cooked
White fish	Grilled or poached, without sauces

DESSERTS	
Baked apple	
Fresh fruit	
Fresh fruit salad	Without cream
Jelly	
Stewed fruit	

FINE-LINE PASTRY

There's no pretending that this is as tasty as pastries with some fat, but if it's eaten hot it's quite acceptable. *Sufficient for a 20cm (8in) diameter flan tin.*

100g (4oz) plain wholemeal flour
generous 30ml (2 tbsp) skimmed milk powder
7ml (1½ tsp) baking powder
pinch of sea salt
cold water, to mix

1 Heat the oven to 200°C (400°F), gas mark 6. Lightly grease a flan tin.
2 Mix all the dry ingredients thoroughly.
3 Add enough cold water to make a soft dough.
4 Transfer to the flan tin and fill (see suggestion right). Bake for about 25 minutes.

Filling

This mixture makes a low-fat but still delicious filling for a savoury flan. *Sufficient for a 20cm (8in) diameter flan.*

175g (6oz) vegetables, chopped, such as celery, mushrooms (lightly browned in a barely oiled pan for 5 minutes), watercress, spring onions, etc.
30ml (2 tbsp) plain wholemeal flour
100g (4oz) cottage cheese
generous 15ml (1 tbsp) skimmed milk powder
150ml (¼ pint) water or stock
1 egg white
5 to 10ml (1 to 2 tsp) soya sauce, to taste

Mix all the ingredients and pour the mixture into the flan case before baking.

LOW-SALT DIET

Although everyone aware of the effect of food on health is now concerned with reducing the amount of excess salt eaten, and the recipes in this book minimize salt, for some people a more drastic reduction is necessary. It is not sufficient for them to reduce the amount of salt (of which sodium forms 40 per cent) added to food, they must also avoid it completely, together with foods which have already had salt added to them, either in processing or in cooking, and cut down on foods naturally high in sodium. For most people, this is a major effort. Most of us find food without *any* salt bland and uninteresting. While some people don't like their food salted much, they probably don't eat an excess of salt anyway. However, the amount of salt we eat is to a large extent a matter of habit, and most of us can adapt our taste buds within a few weeks to want much *less* salt. Instead, the no-salt cook can flavour foods with some of the following seasonings: garlic and onions, herbs, such as parsley, fennel, dill, rosemary, thyme and other aromatics; lemon juice is one of the best salt substitutes in salad dressings, soups, dips and other savouries. Add to taste. Natural yogurt has a tang from the lactic acid, which can add flavour to many savouries. Low-salt yeast extract and powder add taste.

Salt substitutes

Two types of salt substitute are available. One type mixes ordinary salt half and half with potassium-based salts, so you should be able roughly to halve the amount of sodium eaten. The second type is made entirely from non-sodium compounds. Although the second kind is obviously far lower in sodium, I do not find it very helpful. It does not taste like salt, and, if used in significant quantities, leaves a bitter after-taste. If you are allowed some sodium, the first type is more useful.

Medical advice should be sought on both types if you have a heart or kidney condition that may be affected by the amount of potassium they contain.

Salt-free ingredients

Ordinary *baking powder* contains sodium, as does *bicarbonate of soda*. To replace them, buy salt-free baking powder at health food stores, or ask a chemist to make one up.

Bread with no salt is one of the foods to make the low-salt dieter wince. To overcome the lack of flavour, you can mix the bread dough with yogurt or buttermilk instead of water – both have a tang – and add in flavours such as toasted crushed sesame seeds, toasted grated sunflower seeds, grated carrot or caraway seeds.

Unsalted *butter* is readily available, but there are few brands of unsalted *margarine*, apart from Vitaquell. You can make a high-in-polyunsaturates spread using unsalted butter and sunflower or safflower seed oil, following the recipe for sunshine spread on page 34. For a lower-fat spread, follow the dairy spread recipe (page 34), using unsalted butter or margarine and home-made soft cheese.

Avoiding salt-based additives

Many food additives are based on sodium, and, while the amount is too small to upset a reduced-sodium diet, people who need to follow a diet very low in salt should avoid them.

Food additives based on sodium

E201	sodium sorbate	E339(b)	disodium hydro-gen orthophos-phate
E211	sodium benzoate		
E221	sodium sulphite		
E222	sodium hydrogen sulphite	E339(c)	trisodium ortho-phosphate
E223	sodium metabisulphite	E401	sodium alginate
E237	sodium formate	E450(a)	disodium dihyd-rogen diphos-phate tetrasodium diphosphate
E250	sodium nitrite		
E251	sodium nitrate		
E262	sodium hydrogen diacetate		
E281	sodium prop-ionate	E450(b)	pentasodium triphosphate
E301	sodium-L-ascor-bate	E450(c)	sodium polyphos-phates
E325	sodium lactate	E466	carboxymethylcel-lulose, sodium salt
E331	sodium dihydro-gen citrate di-sodium citrate tri-sodium citrate		
		E470	sodium* salts of fatty acids
E335	sodium tartrate	E481	sodium stearoyl-2-lactylate
E339(a)	sodium dihydro-gen orthophos-phate		

* Not all these products are based on sodium.

Sodium quantities in common foods

Common salt or sodium chloride is around 40 per cent sodium. This means that each 400mg of sodium in a food represents roughly 1g of salt.

The World Health Organization suggests that in one in five Westerners a high salt intake may be a cause of high blood pressure, a sign of considerably higher risk of heart attack or stroke. UK consumption is estimated at 12g per day. A target of 5 to 6g of salt a day for the general population, and around 3g a day for the person on a very low sodium diet is suggested. This translates into a maximum of 2 to 2.4g of sodium a day, or 1.2g for the low-sodium dieter.

In this context, *high-sodium foods* are those which contain anything between 400mg and 750mg in a typical day's eating. The serving size is important. Tomato juice, for instance, contains sodium quantities of around 230mg per 100ml, far lower than bacon, at around 1000 to 1500mg per 100g. But you might easily drink a large 225ml (8fl oz) glass of tomato juice, contributing around 500mg sodium.

Medium-sodium foods are those which supply between 100mg and 400mg sodium per typical daily

AVERAGE SODIUM CONTENT OF SOME COMMON FOODS

High-sodium foods

Bacon and any smoked or cured meat
Baking powder and bicarbonate of soda
Beef extract
Bread, unless home-made with less or no salt
Breakfast cereals (almost all except muesli, oats, unprocessed flaked cereals)
Butter, unless unsalted
Cakes made with baking powder, such as scones
Cheese, except home-made soft cheeses, which are medium-sodium, and a few shop cheeses labelled low-sodium
Convenience foods (most)
Crisps
Fish convenience foods, such as fish fingers
Kippers and cured fish
Low-fat spreads
Margarine, unless low-salt
Olives
Pastry, unless made at home with unsalted fat
Salad dressings, bought
Salted nuts

Sausages, beefburgers, pasties and other made-up meat dishes
Savoury crackers and biscuits
Self-raising flour
Shellfish, especially oysters
Soups, tinned and dried
Soya and tamari sauce
Stock cubes
Take-away meals (most)
Tinned savouries (most)
Tinned tomato juice and vegetable cocktail juices
Tinned vegetables (not tomatoes)
Yeast extract

Medium-sodium foods

Beer
Beetroot
Bought pickles and chutney
Carrots
Celery
Chocolate bars
Cocoa powder and drinking chocolate
Coconut milk
Custard powder
Dried fruit, unless cooked in water

Egg whites
Fresh fish and fresh roe
Fresh meat and game apart from rabbit, hare and turkey
Glucose, liquid
Golden syrup
Horlicks and Ovaltine
Lemon curd, with eggs
Milk – goat's milk is 20 per cent lower in sodium
Mincemeat, bought
Peanut butter
Seaweed vegetables
Spinach
Stout, brown ale, strong ale
Tomato purée, salted
Turnips
Watercress
Wine, sweet
Yogurt

Low-sodium foods

Barley
Beans, dried**
Cream
Egg yolks
Fresh fruit, except olives
Fresh vegetables, except those in medium-sodium list

Hare
Honey
Lentils**
Mustard, dry
Nuts, unsalted
Oatmeal*, rolled oats and porridge without salt
Pasta
Potatoes
Puffed Wheat
Rabbit
Rice
Rye
Shredded Wheat
Soya flour
Sugar
Vegetable oils
Wheat and plain wheat flour
Wheat germ

* Between low and medium, but in most cases would be cooked, so sodium content would be diluted with water.
** May seem fairly high in sodium on charts, but these are usually values for dried pulses; when cooked, sodium content per 100g (4oz) falls by almost two-thirds.

portion. They can be used sparingly or occasionally by the low-salt dieter.

Low-sodium foods contain so little sodium that it need not be counted carefully. Eaten in generous helpings, these foods are still unlikely to add up to a high-sodium total.

Following a low-salt diet

Those under medical care for a condition requiring a low-salt intake should establish how strictly they are advised to control sodium. A daily milk allowance, for instance, may be advised. On the other hand, those with high blood pressure that is being controlled by drugs can do themselves no harm by cutting down on salt. The average person needs only about a tenth of what he normally consumes.

Many recipes from this book are naturally low in sodium, while others can be adapted to reduce sodium content. The main ways of doing this are:

1 Omit added salt, using flavouring with lemon juice and herbs instead.
2 Use special no-sodium baking powder.
3 Eat foods naturally higher in sodium, such as celery, less often.
4 Buy unsalted versions of margarine, butter, crispbreads and other foods.
5 Make your own low-salt bread, using the recipe on page 235, but reducing salt or omitting it altogether, and using whatever you can spare from your milk allowance in the form of yogurt for part of the mixing liquid.
6 Choose recipes which avoid foods that are naturally high in salt.
7 Limit the amount of meat and fish eaten, in favour of lower-sodium sources of protein, such as rice and other grains, pulses and nuts.
8 If the amount of milk you are allowed is restricted, you may want to use a low-sodium substitute.

ARE YOU ALLERGIC?

Many health problems can be caused by allergy – that is, by an individual's adverse reaction to a substance (or several substances) harmless to other people. Skin complaints, digestive problems, depressed and restless moods, excessive sweating, swollen ankles, irritable bowels, asthma attacks, headaches and itching are among the symptoms that are now recognized as possible signs of allergic reaction. And this is by no means an exhaustive list.

How do you know if any health problem you may have is caused by an over-sensitive reaction to something around you? There are, of course, many possible causes for physical illnesses which have nothing to do with allergy. If you are wondering whether you or a member of your family is suffering impaired health because of an allergy, ask yourself the following questions.
1 Is there allergy in the family? Roughly half of those with allergic reactions have a parent who has the same tendency, although the substances to which they are allergic may differ.
2 Is the health problem new? Although it's possible to have an allergy for many years without realizing it, a new symptom suggests that something around you may be upsetting your system.
3 Have you consulted your medical practitioner and excluded physical illnesses known to cause similar symptoms?
4 Has the health problem got a pattern? It's useful to keep a record of fluctuation of symptoms. This may provide clues to their cause. Symptoms that come and go are suggestive of a reaction to something that occurs from time to time, not every day. If the

answer to all these questions is 'yes', it's likely that allergy could be playing a part.

Environment

Remember that allergy isn't necessarily connected with food. And you don't have to swallow anything: it's enough to sniff or touch it. Common allergens include many items in the world around us, among them washing powder, cigarette smoke, nickel in earrings and hair slides, cosmetics, certain fabrics, paint fumes, animal hair, flowers and parrots. Only if you can't spot a non-food cause should you begin to suspect food.

If you have a new health problem that you think might be linked with allergy, the first counter-step is to make a systematic list of what you did last week, to recall every substance with which you've been in contact. A new piece of jewellery, a new aftershave or even a new brand of salad cream is the kind of suspect to look for – because it's new.

It's easy to pin down the cause of a food allergy when you eat the substance only occasionally. Many people are allergic to strawberries, for instance, or to lobster. It's much harder when the villain is something that is eaten often. This can be the cause of a long-standing allergy, or it can be something to which you mysteriously become allergic after years of using it.

The first suspects are the foods most often found to cause allergies: interestingly, several of these are the foods most of us encounter first in our lives. These are cow's milk, eggs, oranges and wheat. Also in the top ten are: cheese – which is, of course, cow's milk in another form – coffee, tea and chocolate. These substances share another link: they are all among the foods that commonly trigger migraine. Cheese, chocolate, citrus fruit, fermented foods, red wine, pickled herrings and some other rarer foods contain proteins which can dilate blood vessels in the head, setting off migraine in vulnerable people. A link between allergic reactions and migraine was suggested by a study in *The Lancet* (Oct. 15, 1983), where 82 out of 88 children who suffered recurrent migraine were found to be allergic to one or more of a wide range of foods and responded to dietary treatment. But milk, eggs, chocolate, orange, wheat and cheese were the most common culprits. Half of the children stopped suffering migraines when they stopped drinking cow's milk.

There is some suspicion that feeding infants with solid foods, especially wheat, and with cow's milk in the first weeks of life can encourage the develop-ment of adverse reactions, because the child's system is not sufficiently mature to cope with the foods. The revived popularity of breastfeeding, together with more emphasis on delaying the introduction of cow's milk, wheat or eggs until a baby is three- and, preferably, four- to five-months old, may lead to a fall in allergic reactions to these foods.

An important point to note is that the word 'allergy' is often used loosely to cover reactions to foods that don't fall within the strict medical mean-ing of the word. There may be foods to which you aren't medically speaking allergic, but which your system doesn't tolerate well.

Testing

Avoidance is the key to both diagnosis and relief of allergy and severe intolerance. Working out whether you have an adverse reaction to food is a simple but tedious process. It means avoiding even the slightest trace of a single food you suspect, for about ten to fourteen days. The rest of your meals should be more or less as usual. If that particular food is the culprit, the health problem should get better in that time. In that case, you can then confirm your suspicions by taking a very small amount of the food, and watching for a relapse. If your condition doesn't change, either while you are avoiding that food or when you start eating it again, you can restore the food to your meals and for the next ten to fourteen days avoid the next most likely suspect food.

A disadvantage of this method is that your reac-tions may be influenced by your expectations. You know what you are avoiding and then taking again. If you have a hunch that a certain food makes you feel ill, it probably will. Allergy clinics try to ensure that you don't know what food is being tested by giving you an unrecognizable extract, which is put under the tongue, or mixing a small amount of the food with another food that masks it. If you can arrange for someone to 'fool' you like this at home, it may make your reactions more reliable.

Because of the newness of allergy testing it's an uncertain science, and home detection can be just as good. If you do decide to seek professional help, be wary, as testing services are not always reliable. Some offer diagnoses from a spot of blood or piece of hair sent to them, some start out believing that everyone should avoid certain foods, such as milk or wheat. You could end up being advised to stick to a very restrictive diet, for no good reason. Choose a well-established medical clinic if possible, and ask to be put in touch with some successfully treated patients who can pass on their views.

Treatment

If you find you are allergic to, or severely intolerant of, one food, the simplest and most successful treatment is to avoid it completely. This is naturally easier if it is a food you don't eat often. But all the main allergens are foods that are everyday for most of us. Indeed, it may be over-use of them that has led the body to rebel, although whether this is so has not been established.

Multiple allergy

If you find that you have become increasingly intolerant of many foods, it's time to stop trying to avoid them, and to look instead at why you have become over-sensitive to natural substances. Build-ing up your general health may be the best way of getting your system to be more tolerant again. Consider the following factors.
1 Stress seems to play a part in allergy. Making a deliberate effort to rearrange your lifestyle to be less stressful may be necessary. Exercise can help relieve stress, and keep your physical system working as it should.
2 Smoking can make not only you, but also those in close contact with you, more liable to allergy.
3 Improving your general style of eating by moving towards natural foods with a higher nutritional value may restore your system's reactions to normal. (Try following the menu plans on pages 14–20.)
4 Making sure that supplies of vitamins and minerals are at the levels which give your body the best raw materials for health is part of building up your resistance to any disturbance of normal reactions. Include in your diet plenty of dark green leafy vegetables for carotene and vitamin C, and low-fat proteins such as fish, poultry, low-fat yogurt and wheat germ for B vitamins. In addition, this may be one time when taking multi-vitamin/mineral sup-plements can be useful, especially if your nutritional

status has become run down. Unusual stress, a poor eating pattern or the consumption of substantial amounts of alcohol may all affect levels of vitamins B and C. Choose a vitamin brand offering at least 100mg of vitamin C and a wide selection of the B group vitamins in each day's recommended dosage. Then follow the suggested course – don't think that because two tablets or capsules are recommended, four must be better.

YEAST FRUIT CAKE

Use fruit and spice generously to turn a bread into a cake with very little fat and no added crystal sugar or eggs. *Makes a large cake, weighing about 900g (2lb).* Total calories: 2120.

75g (3oz) dried apricots
20ml (4 tsp) fresh yeast or 10ml (2 tsp) dried yeast
about 225ml (8fl oz) lukewarm water
275g (10oz) plain wholemeal flour
30ml (2 tbsp) concentrated apple juice or clear honey
generous 10ml (2 tsp) mixed spice
generous 5ml (1 tsp) ground cinnamon
2ml (½ tsp) nutmeg, grated
75g (3oz) raisins
75g (3oz) sultanas
75g (3oz) nuts, chopped
75g (3oz) apple, peeled and chopped
25g (1oz) soft margarine

1 Bring the apricots to the boil in water to cover, simmer for 2 minutes, then throw the water away. Chop the apricots fairly finely.
2 Mix fresh yeast or large-particle dried yeast with about a third of the lukewarm water in a cup, and whisk in 5ml (1 tsp) of the flour with a fork. If you are using fresh yeast, move on to the next step. If using dried yeast, leave the yeast mixture in a warm place for about 10 minutes, until it is frothy. If using micronized yeast, omit this step and step 4, and add the yeast to the other ingredients in step 3.
3 Mix all the other ingredients in a bowl, with the chopped apricots.
4 Pour over the yeast mixture and stir vigorously for about 2 minutes.
5 Grease a large, warmed cake tin thoroughly. Add a little more warm water if necessary to give the mixture a dropping consistency.
6 Pour the mixture into the tin, cover it with polythene and leave it in a warmish place for about 1 to 1½ hours, until it is bubbly and risen.
7 Heat the oven to 220°C (425°F), gas mark 7.

8 Bake the cake for about 40 minutes, until it is firm. To avoid over-browning, cover it with foil half-way through the baking time.
9 When the cake is just shrinking from the sides of the tin, and no longer 'singing' when you put your ear to it, it should be ready. Remove it from the tin and cool it on a rack.

Avoiding possible allergens
Baking Yeast baking doesn't require eggs for rising.
Binding can be done with breadcrumbs or soya flour instead of egg. See tofu quiche (page 121) for how tofu can be used as a binding agent in flan fillings.
Cakes such as the yeast fruit cake, left, for instance, don't need eggs.
Coffee, tea and chocolate drinks, see ideas for Drinks, pages 268–9.
Eggs Many recipes without eggs have been included in this book. However, eggs crop up in all kinds of recipes, and even a small amount will upset anyone who cannot tolerate them.

MILK-FREE DIETS

Eczema (especially in childhood), catarrh, sinus blockages and sometimes migraine and diarrhoea are the symptoms most often associated with intolerance of cow's milk.

Avoiding cow's milk also means no cheese, cream, butter or margarine containing whey, or milk ingredients in other foods. However, people who are intolerant of cow's milk sometimes find that they can eat cow's milk yogurt without ill-effects.

It is much easier to follow a diet free of cow's milk if you have a convenient source of good-quality goat's milk, to which fewer people are allergic. The only problems are that it is almost impossible to obtain low-fat goat's milk, as it is rarely skimmed; and that, unlike cows, goats have not been bred to give milk all year round. The first difficulty is often solved by the dip in other fat intake when you stop eating cream, cheese and butter. Otherwise, aim to eat a little less fat in other foods. The second problem can be overcome by freezing goat's milk for the winter. Soya milk can also be used as a substitute for cow's milk, though again it is higher in fat than skimmed cow's milk. Both soya and goat's milk are sold in powder form. Formulae for babies and infants who prove intolerant of cow's milk must be worked out with a medical practitioner, as for very young infants you can't just substitute goat's milk for cow's, but some specialized products are available.

Kosher margarine is always free from whey. In Europe, Vitaquell margarine is also free from milk substances, and is excellent nutritionally, with over 40 per cent polyunsaturated fatty acids (PUFAS), a low-sodium content and no artificial additives or hardening. Granose also produce a margarine with no milk ingredients, and about 20 per cent PUFA.

Chinese, Japanese, Malaysian and Arab styles of cooking all use little or no milk, and offer all kinds of ideas for interesting food without it. Westerners have been taught to see milk as an essential food, but it isn't. All the vitamins and minerals milk certainly provides can be obtained from other foods. You may be particularly concerned about the loss of calcium, and it is true that it is difficult without any dairy foods to reach the high level of calcium provided by typical Western diets. However, many people have more calcium from food than they need. Goat's milk has almost as much calcium as cow's, and the following are other good sources:
Almonds and Barcelona nuts □ Dark green leafy vegetables, such as watercress, parsley, etc. □ Fish where you eat the bones, such as sardines, whitebait, canned salmon or pilchards □ Sesame seeds, ground – although most of this calcium may be poorly absorbed □ Shellfish, especially shrimps, cockles, oysters, lobster and whelks □ Soya

Calcium supplements free from cow's milk are readily available.

Cooking points
1 Use goat's milk or soya milk where milk is essential for a recipe, and for making yogurt and soft cheese. For thickening, use goat's milk or soya milk powder, or boil goat's milk for about 25 minutes to reduce the water content.
2 Stock can often be used instead of milk in sauces and soups. Use a whey-free margarine throughout. Low-fat spreads usually contain whey.
3 Soak muesli in fruit juice overnight instead of adding milk.
4 Fruit juice or purée can often be substituted for milk in fruit cakes.
5 Read the labels of bought products carefully: milk crops up in unexpected places.

GLUTEN-FREE DIETS

A surprising number of people follow gluten-free diets, but what is gluten? It is defined by *Webster's Dictionary* as 'A tenacious elastic protein substance, especially of wheat, that gives cohesiveness to dough'. Gluten is mainly found in wheat, but it is present to a lesser extent in barley and rye too, and a substance similar to gluten exists in oats.

When gluten meets water and is kneaded into dough, it develops elàstic strands, and the more gluten in the grain, the stronger the strands. This property is essential to the kind of high-rising bread we're used to: when yeast gives off gas, it forces the bread dough to expand, producing bubbles to hold the gas. Flour with plenty of gluten can stretch a long way without breaking so producing high-rising bread. This kind of flour is called 'strong' or 'hard', while low-gluten flour is called 'weak' or 'soft'.

Coeliac is the term used for people who are allergic to gluten. When they eat it, their mechanism for absorbing nutrients through the lining of the intestine is fouled up. As a result, they literally become malnourished, especially of the nutrients carried in fat, such as vitamins A, D and E. They can easily fail to grow well, tending to be smaller in height and very thin. They may be anaemic through lack of iron, and suffer digestive problems ranging from cramp to abdominal swelling or diarrhoea. Mouth ulcers are another possible symptom. For example, a questionnaire of 10,000 people showed that about one in five who suffered from recurrent mouth ulcers had undiagnosed coeliac disease. Others who suffer in this way may be allergic to wheat, without having a full coeliac condition. In the past, coeliacs have also shown a higher than average rate of a particular form of bowel cancer. It is not known whether this is related to the amount of gluten eaten before diagnosis, or, often by accident, after. The fact that avoidance of wheat or the substitution of very refined wheat starch can lead to a diet very low in fibre can't help health either.

Until the 1950s little was known about this illness, and many people grew to adulthood struggling constantly against ill health. Now, most cases are diagnosed in childhood, when a baby weaned on to wheat- or barley-based cereals fails to thrive. Some of these cases may be associated with a too-early introduction to gluten-bearing cereals, and there's been a definite move away from feeding a baby anything containing gluten for several months after birth, in case its system is too young to cope and reacts badly.

Some people still fail to be diagnosed until they are adult while others develop a coeliac condition after they are grown up.

The treatment for coeliac disease is simple but not easy to stick to: gluten must be avoided for the lifetime of the sufferer. Even small traces in a convenience food, for instance, can produce a relapse in the state of the intestine. The Coeliac Society helps coeliacs identify all the foods with 'hidden gluten', ranging from wheat-based alcoholic drinks to soya sauce and many, but not all, brands of baking powder.

EXAMPLES OF GLUTEN-FREE MEALS

Main meals

Liver pâté with crudités OR with
gluten-free bread*
—•—
Biryani*
Mixed salad
—•—
Real orange jelly with fruit OR
fresh fruit OR
slices of fresh orange marinated in
liqueur or with coconut

Lorna's butterbean tarragon
soup*
—•—
Fish terrine
Jacket potatoes*
Creamy herb sauce
Green salad
—•—
Fresh fruit OR
baked apple

* provides cereal or bean fibre

Mushrooms à la grecque
—•—
Kedgeree*
Watercress salad
—•—
Baked pears

Chawanmushi
—•—
Kidney bean and chick pea salad*
Green salad
Jacket potatoes OR
new potatoes
Creamy herb sauce
—•—
Kissel

Humus* and crudités
—•—
Winter pie*
Green vegetables in season
—•—
Coffee almond ice

For special meals

Corn on the cob with dairy
spread*
—•—
Lamb curry
Boiled rice*
Dhal*
Tjatziki
Mango chutney
Side dishes of chopped peppers
and onions
—•—
Dutch apple ice

Carrot and caraway soup
Gluten-free bread*
—•—
Lamb kebabs
Pease pudding*
Boiled rice*
Vegetables in season OR
mixed salad
—•—
Fruit fool OR
pashka

EXAMPLES OF GLUTEN-FREE FOODS

Breakfasts

Browned mushrooms, with
rice, grilled tomatoes or
slices of cold baked potato,
grilled hot
Buckwheat, cooked, eaten
cold with skimmed milk
and a little salt
Dried fruit compôte
Egg dishes, with gluten-free
toast
Fruit and fruit drinks
Gluten-free bread or toast,
with spreads as usual
Haddock, poached in milk

Kedgeree
Kippers
Muesli, made with the same
grains as porridge
Plain low-fat yogurt, with
fresh fruit
Popcorn (home-made fol-
lowing instructions on the
packet), eaten as a breakfast cereal, with skimmed
milk
Porridge, made from rolled
millet flakes, buckwheat
flakes or rice bran

Main Meals

Beans and lentils
Fish
Meat
Rice dishes
Salads (avoid commercial
salad dressings if labels
show any flour, rusk,
starch, etc.)
Vegetable dishes

*Thicken sauces with millet
flakes, buckwheat or rice
flour or vegetable purées*

Desserts

Crumbles (use millet flakes
and ground rice for
topping)
Custard, using cornflour or
millet or buckwheat flour
(buckwheat makes a
darker-coloured, stronger-
flavoured custard)
Fresh fruit and fruit salads
Fruit juice jellies
Rice and millet flake
puddings
Sorbets and ices

The coeliac faces a definite restriction on eating out, but need not be too disheartened. He or she still has a wide repertoire of natural foods to choose from, and may end up considerably healthier than others who fail to avoid junk food.

Because of the loss of fibre when you eliminate wheat, oats, barley and rye from your meals, coeliacs need to make a point of replacing it with roughage from other sources. For most people the easiest way

of doing this is to use gluten-free bread and biscuits made from unrefined gluten-free cereals, such as brown rice. Meals should also be planned to include other kinds of fibre, such as beans, peas or lentils and brown rice and other grains. Although fruit and vegetables will not supply an adequate replacement for the different kind of fibre that cereals provide, eating plenty of fruit and vegetables is obviously an excellent habit. The lavish supply of vitamins and minerals so provided may be particularly useful to a coeliac who has had to struggle to absorb enough nutrients, and may not have optimum body levels.

Some coeliacs have particular difficulty in digesting fat. The low-fat style of recipe throughout this book should keep fat intake down to a level where this is no problem. Otherwise, coeliacs avoiding gluten cereals can accidentally eat high amounts of meat and dairy food, all high in fat.

Gluten-free diets are also used to treat a rare skin condition called *dermatitis herpetiformis*. More controversially, many people with multiple sclerosis shun gluten, following in the steps of those who report a remission of symptoms on doing so.

There are also a number of other people for whom wheat disrupts physical or mental health, although they are not coeliacs. Such cases are well described in *Not All in the Mind* by Dr Richard Mackarness (London, 1976).

Gluten-free foods

Rice, millet, maize and buckwheat replace wheat, barley, rye and, for most gluten-free eaters, oats (although a few can tolerate oats).

Looking to Eastern-style food shows how varied a gluten-free diet can be. But even Chinese and Indian foods often incorporate small amounts of wheat flour, so you need to be careful to avoid soya sauce, for instance, replacing it with Japanese tamari.

The conventional flour for gluten-free diets is wheat flour with the gluten removed. I can't recommend this at all. First, it produces very tasteless results, because it is so refined. Secondly, refining has removed much of its food value, including fibre. Thirdly, traces of gluten may well remain. I think it's far healthier to use flours from other foods, and these are more and more available. Rice flour, maize flour and buckwheat flour can all be used to thicken foods, or in pancake recipes. Use buckwheat flour cautiously at first, both because some coeliacs find it does upset their digestions and because some people don't like the taste, although they may find they do quite like it when it is mixed half and half with rice flour. It is preferable to use flour made from brown rice rather than ground white rice, and brown rice flour is now fairly readily available. You can also make flour at home in a coffee grinder from ingredients such as raw buckwheat, split peas or walnuts. Brown rice will ruin most coffee grinders. It's too hard.

The most difficult food to replace is bread, but a recipe for gluten-free bread is given on page 286. This recipe comes from *The First Clinical Ecology Cookbook* by Rita Greer (Larkhall Laboratories, London, 1979). Rita's brown bread will also provide you with gluten-free breadcrumbs and so, poten-

tially, with dishes such as bread pudding, summer pudding and charlottes. Rita Greer is the foremost writer on gluten-free cookery, having used a special diet with great success to help to treat her husband's multiple sclerosis. In particular, she tackles that most difficult area of gluten-free cookery – baking breads and cakes – with excellent results. Rather than using the conventional wheat flour with gluten removed, Rita uses unrefined flours from foods which never contain gluten, as recommended above. So her dishes have more food value, especially fibre, which the gluten-free eater may go short of.

For biscuits, try the gluten-free version of Miss Stringer's handful cookies (page 255).

For baking powder, use brands that are gluten-free: check the label, or buy gluten-free types from health food stores.

Replace soya sauce with tamari, and check food labels for gluten cereal derivatives.

GLUTEN-FREE FRUIT LOAF

Makes 1 small loaf.

15g (½oz) almonds
15g (½oz) yellow split peas
15g (½oz) walnut pieces
15ml (1 tbsp) soya flour
generous 5ml (1 tsp) micronized yeast
2ml (½ tsp) bicarbonate of soda
5ml (1 tsp) mixed spice
125g (5oz) buckwheat flour
50g (2oz) eating apple, cored weight
50g (2oz) carrot, roughly sliced
75g (3oz) sultanas or raisins
25g (1oz) soft margarine or butter
15ml (1 tbsp) honey
150ml (¼ pint) skimmed milk or apple juice or a mixture

1 Place the almonds, the split peas and half of the walnuts in a coffee grinder and reduce them to a flour-like consistency.
2 Sieve the ground nuts and peas with the soya flour, yeast, soda, spice and buckwheat flour into a mixing bowl, adding back any bran from the sieve.
3 In a blender, liquidize the apple, the carrot, about half of the dried fruit and the fat with the honey and the milk or apple juice.
4 Heat the mixture to just above lukewarm.
5 Heat the oven to 180°C (350°F), gas mark 4. Grease a small loaf tin and flour it with buckwheat flour.
6 Add the liquid mixture to the flour mixture and beat thoroughly to a very wet consistency.

7 Chop the remaining walnuts and stir them in, with the rest of the dried fruit.
8 Pour in the mixture and bake for about 30 minutes, or until the loaf is slightly leaving the sides of the tin. Remove the cake from the tin and allow it to cool on a rack.

RITA'S BROWN BREAD

Closer-textured than ordinary bread, but easy to handle, versatile and good when toasted as well. You'll notice that some of the measurement equivalents given in the list of ingredients are slightly different from those in the rest of the book. This is because exact quantities are more important in this kind of baking. *Makes 1 medium loaf.*

110g (4oz) brown rice flour
generous 10ml (2 tsp) dried yeast granules
250ml (9fl oz) lukewarm water
25g (1oz) soya flour
125g (5oz) potato flour
20g (¾oz) yellow split-pea flour
scant 10ml (2 tsp) pectin powder
15g (½oz) ground almonds
5ml (1 tsp) fructose (fruit sugar)
scant 1ml (¼ tsp) sea salt
15ml (3 tsp) oil
generous 5ml (1 tsp) carob powder

1 Heat the oven to 180°C (350°F), gas mark 4. Grease a medium-sized loaf tin, and flour it with a little of the brown rice flour.
2 Whisk the yeast thoroughly into the water. Leave in a warm place for about 10 minutes.
3 Put all other ingredients in a bowl and mix well.
4 Add the yeast mixture and beat. This makes a very liquid mixture, but don't worry.
5 Pour the mixture into the tin. Bake for 1 hour. Remove the loaf from the tin and cool it on a rack, covered with a clean cloth.

VARIATION

Rita Greer doesn't use buckwheat, but I like to replace half or all of the rice flour with *buckwheat flour*. Making this by pulverizing buckwheat in a coffee grinder has an advantage over bought flour which may have traces of gluten from being ground in a mill used for wheat.

Ideas for packed meals

Baked apple	Liver pâté
Bean sauce on jacket potato*	Plain low-fat yogurt with
Fresh fruit	fresh fruit
Fresh fruit salad	Popcorn*
Fruit bars*	Rice salad*
Fruit jelly	Sandwiches made with
Gluten-free biscuits	gluten-free bread*
Green salad	Taramasalata
Kissel*	
Lentil soup*	** Dishes that provide a substantial amount of fibre.*

HOW TO AVOID MIGRAINE

Food is far from being the only cause of migraine. But there is evidence (as shown by a report in *The Lancet* on 5 July 1980) that as many as two out of three migraine sufferers have at least one food allergy. The food to which the sufferer is allergic acts not as sole cause but as a trigger for the attacks.

Read the section on allergy for information on how to identify whether you have an allergy (pages 280–86).

The most common trigger foods for *migraineurs*, as chronic sufferers are described, are those which contain a substance known as tyramine. This is a natural protein, but one which can dilate blood vessels. It is the abnormal contraction, then dilation, of blood vessels in the head that causes the painful pressure of migraine.

Tyramine occurs in mature cheese, red wine (particularly Chianti), pickled herrings, citrus fruits, broad bean pods and a few other less common foods. Chocolate and cocoa contain another amine

which can trigger migraine. Many migraine sufferers react to only one or two foods from the likely list. And they may find they react to some other kind of food more. The form of the food can matter too. It's possible, for instance, to find that instant coffee triggers a migraine, while ground coffee does not.

If you cut out a suspect food to see whether your migraines lessen, you probably need to exclude it for at least six weeks – considerably longer than when testing other food allergies. This is because few people get migraines more than about once a fortnight, and you need to cut out the food for two or three times the period you would normally expect between migraines. Knowing that you are watching out for the effect of the exclusion on migraine might hold off your migraine once or twice, but the influence of wishful thinking wears off if you give it time, producing a more realistic test. So allergy testing – and perhaps having to avoid particular foods permanently – can be well worthwhile.

Another way that food affects some migraine sufferers is through the timing of meals. They find they are more vulnerable to attacks when the blood sugar level is low, and bouts will tend to occur after any unduly long gap between meals (and sometimes also after strenuous exercise). If migraine occurs mainly in the early morning or is there on waking, a before-bed snack to shorten the gap between the evening meal and breakfast can prevent attacks. Something which is digested slowly, such as yogurt, cereal with milk or a slice or two of toast, is preferable to a sugary snack.

Liverish?

What's the difference between a migraine and a headache? Experts don't all agree, but in general, to qualify as a migraine, the attack must include either visual disturbance or a bilious attack (many people get both).

But there's also such a thing as a bilious headache – the kind that occurs the morning after a night of heavy eating and drinking. The solution to this latter sort of headache is obvious: restraint. But it may also indicate that your liver would like you to eat less fatty food (which the recipes in this book can help with) and also that it may be generally under strain. Apart from reducing your intake of alcohol and fat, you should also cut down on coffee, eat more fresh fruit and vegetables, which make life easier for your digestive system, generally eat less, and take more exercise. Stopping smoking will help too.

Some foods can positively help the liver. These include dandelion leaves in salads, dandelion coffee, chicory drinks and a variety of herb teas specifically sold for liverishness. Most of these teas include a laxative, and many headaches are certainly connected with constipation. Again, if you follow the style of menu suggested throughout this book your diet should provide enough fibre for you to avoid that problem.

Plan of campaign

1 Check for allergies.
2 Reduce the amount of liver-straining fatty foods, alcohol and coffee in your diet.
3 If migraines occur after long periods without eating or after heavy exercise, adopt a 'little and

often' style of eating, avoiding sugary foods since they may encourage your blood sugar level to drop again too quickly.
4 Avoid constipation by eating plenty of foods that are high in fibre, especially fibre from grains.

Other factors

Migraine is a very individual problem, but tackling food alone is rarely the complete answer. The following common contributory factors should also be considered.
1 Mental or emotional tension can lead to physical tension, and as the immediate cause of migraine is tightening of blood vessels in the head – followed by over-expansion – this may trigger a migraine. Tension can also produce contracted, tight neck muscles, which can restrict blood flow and set off a headache that turns into a migraine. Biofeedback, yoga, meditation and relaxation exercises may all help. So can osteopaths and chiropractors, who can both encourage the muscles into relaxation by manipulation, and help you identify physical causes for tension in your back and neck, such as habitual sitting positions, poor-fitting driving seats, spinal displacements lower down the back for which your upper spine is compensating, and more. Massage should not be under-rated as a method of relieving physical and emotional tension.
2 Some migraines seem to come with 'heavy' weather, fumes or high winds. Migraines of this type may be alleviated by the use of an ionizer, which changes the positive electrical charges produced in the air during such conditions to the negative charges or ions associated with fresh mountain air.
3 Giving up smoking can often reduce migraines sharply.
4 Migraine attacks may start or intensify when women take oral contraceptives. If so, the link should be recognized, and alternative methods of contraception explored.

Recently, a herb called feverfew (*Chrysanthemum parthenium*) has been used successfully by many migraine sufferers. It is taken daily in capsule form or in the form of one or two fresh leaves. Because the leaves contain camphor, which can blister the mouth, sandwich them between two pieces of bread.

EATING UNDER PAR

Feeling ill, or under unusual stress, changes our eating patterns and often our likes and dislikes too. Here are some of the situations you may meet, and how best to cater for them.

UNDER STRESS

Stress often precedes or accompanies illness, and although we think of it as a mental problem, it produces physical changes, such as sleeping more or less, digestive disturbances, panic sweats, tense and painful muscles in the neck, the back or the tops of the arms, and more. Individuals vary widely in their reactions, but appetite is usually one of the first things to change.

You can divide stressed people roughly into two groups: those who lose their appetites and those who reach for the chocolate biscuits!

Both the people who lose their appetites and those who tend to binge are vulnerable to a particular threat to nutritional balance: under stress, many of us use more alcohol, tobacco or coffee. Alcohol uses up extra B vitamins, and also diverts the digestive system from coping with food, so what we eat may not be so well absorbed. Tobacco, apart from its many proven serious ill-effects, is claimed to use up extra vitamin C at the rate of at least 25mg per cigarette. Although this has not been officially accepted, it is sensible for those who smoke to make sure they get extra vitamin C. Coffee (and strong tea) are powerful stimulants. Taking a lot of either can make people nervous, jumpy and more stressed.

Loss of appetite
Loss of appetite is in some ways a natural reaction, and in the short term it is not worrying. It relieves the body of the work of digestion and waste elimination – considerable drains on its energy – leaving its resources free to concentrate on the stressful problem. Taken to an extreme situation, when a frightening situation occurs, the body gets ready to run faster or fight harder than it would normally be able to, and the digestive system shuts down. In this situation, there's no point in forcing food down, making life more uncomfortable.

Problems start if the stressful situation lasts a long time, or keeps recurring. Then the body is constantly working itself up to face an emergency, and the appetite and general normal working of the body remain disturbed. Over anything more than a few days, such a stress will result in the body going short of those nutrients which it barely stores, that is, most of the B group of vitamins and vitamin C. There's

evidence that people use more of these vitamins when they're under stress, too.

Sheer lack of energy may also become a problem, because the calories aren't being provided. Although most people have enough fat to break down into energy to last weeks, in response to this 'starvation situation', the body is likely to slow down its energy use, so weight loss may be mainly water at first, and there may be a feeling that the body is 'going slow'. On the other hand, the stressful situation may produce a kind of 'high' which gives a sense of never being tired, and even of euphoria. This is likely to end in a dramatic fall of mood and energy once the crisis is over.

Solving the problem
There's no reason why an individual should stick to his normal diet when every instinct goes against it. But to counter the loss of vitamins, people under stress should resist the temptation to ignore what they eat, just grabbing a snack here and there. Instead, when appetite is small, the food chosen should be far higher in concentrated food value than usual. Drinks that are high in food value are even more useful, as most people go on drinking even when they don't feel like eating.

The natural answer to this situation is juices. Fruit and vegetable juices concentrate most of the vitamin and mineral value of the produce in a small volume – see how many oranges you need to squeeze for a single glass of juice. They provide a good supply of vitamin C and vitamin A (though the body is less likely to lack vitamin A, since it can be stored). If you juice leafy greens you will also be getting the B vitamin folic acid, calcium, iron and assorted other nutrients. Orange juice is particularly useful for vitamin B_1, but this vitamin is fragile, so the juice needs to be freshly squeezed. In the vegetable field, watercress juice, parsley juice and potato juice (raw) are the best sources of vitamin B_1. Wheat germ will add a good slug of B vitamins to any juice. And yogurt is an excellent source of B vitamins, and particularly easy to digest. Both will also provide protein, and the yogurt, calcium. When you can't face food, the anti-stress cocktail (page 290), combining orange juice, wheat germ and yogurt, provides an excellent meal replacement.

The other way of getting a lot of nourishment into a liquid form is in a vegetable soup, such as watercress broth (page 73); include the whole of the egg and not just the white. More watercress can be added, and, if liked, some celery. Add the celery during the liquidizing stage.

Although vitamin supplements cannot replace a healthy style of eating, they can supply a level of the nutrients that the person who has lost his appetite would otherwise miss. A general multi-vitamin/mineral supplement is advisable, since many nutrients work in combination; to get higher levels of the B and C vitamins, products which combine these are available. You can't 'eat your way out of stress' with food or vitamin pills, but you can avoid some side-effects while you sort out your problems.

The urge to binge

Malnutrition might not seem a problem for the other group of stressed people: those who react by stuffing themselves with sweet, gooey foods, and, particularly, with chocolate.

The presence in chocolate of certain chemicals which mimic the natural mood-raising chemicals in the brain is currently being investigated. The way in which carbohydrate may lead to raised levels of soothing brain chemicals is also being researched.

But speculation about why anger, distress, fear or loss of confidence sets off the urge to eat is of little immediate help to the person under stress. He still has to resist the temptation to eat everything in sight. Instead, he should see himself as needing special VIP treatment, to include eating only food of the highest quality. This doesn't mean champagne and caviare, but the food with the most nutritional value.

For this type of person, raw food, in the form of salads, is ideal. Because of the urge to eat, this person is likely to want to eat a lot, to feel full, and to eat foods which take a good deal of chewing. Salads, which should include not only fruit and vegetables but chopped nuts, wheat germ and yogurt dressings (all of which will add protein), provide all this, are easy to prepare and to digest, and won't add unwanted weight gain to the worries of the eater under stress (provided they don't eat more than 25 to 50g [1 to 2oz] of nuts).

An effort should be made to plan meals in advance, so that lunch-boxes of salad can divert attention from the cake or sweet shop when away from home. Apples, raisins or other fruit can be carried with you to ward off the urge.

The alternative for the person who doesn't like salads – either because he dislikes chewing or because he just hates the taste – is to cook vegetables lightly, and eat them straight, puréed or diluted with well-flavoured stock and turned into vegetable soup.

COOKING FOR AN INVALID

It's natural for those who are ill to lose their appetites for a while – and the advice given above for those who lose their appetites under stress applies here too. Juices and soups are often the most acceptable foods, and are best served 'little and often'. Don't feel that you always have to get a sick person to eat solid food to 'keep his strength up'. It may just divert the system's energies from recovery, and the food value may not be well absorbed. Patients are often very thirsty, and it is worth planning a variety of drinks which include some food value rather than using soft drinks which are only nutrient-empty sugar, water and additives – plus caffeine in the case of cola drinks. Apart from juice, hot lemon drinks with a little honey, cold lemon barley water (page 269), yogurt or buttermilk (yogurt can be thinned with fruit juice) mixed with fruit or honey to sweeten, and yogurt mixed with tomato juice are easy to make, and all provide something useful. Make small amounts at first, in case they aren't liked.

When appetite is recovered, a 'soft' diet may be advised. This can include a far wider variety of foods, if you use a blender. But keep on using a high proportion of vegetable and fruit juices, as freshly made as possible, as few other foods carry their concentration of vitamins and minerals.

Suggestions for soft meals

Custard Made with eggs, sweet type or as in consommé cubes, cooked for a shorter time so the custard will be softer, or served in soup

Eggs Soft poached

Fruit Stewed and puréed

Meat and fish Minced after cooking, using recipes such as fish pie or liver and onions, thinned with a little stock or milk if wanted

Muesli Made fairly liquid with extra milk or fruit juice

Plain low-fat yogurt With puréed fruit

Porridge Which many people like when they're sick even if they dislike it normally

Quick cheesecake With the fruit minced and the texture thinned with milk

Sorbets and ices

Soups Put through a blender if the patient can't chew. Particularly useful: chawanmushi (in this case mince the meat before adding it to the soup); Scotch broth; lentil soup; butterbean soup.

Vegetable purées Especially potato purée mixed with smaller amounts of other mashed vegetables and enough milk or stock to thin it down.

The food value of many dishes can be boosted by stirring in 10ml (2 tsp) per portion of either wheat germ or brewer's yeast. The latter must be added cautiously, as, although it is very rich in food value, it can't be called delicious. Both foods provide B vitamins, a high proportion of protein, and minerals.

Cooking for a post-operative patient

Operations can increase the patient's need for vitamin C, protein and zinc, all necessary to the healing and regrowth process.

Concentrated protein drinks, yogurt and milk drinks and the extra protein of wheat germ and milk powder all come into use here. The vitamin C is best obtained from vegetable and fruit juices (see pages 40–41). Zinc is richest in shellfish and other seafood, nuts and liver. You can also buy zinc supplements, the most easily absorbed being the chelated form. Brazil nuts, the richest in zinc, can be blended into yogurt and juice cocktails (liquidize the nuts in the juice before adding the yogurt). Liver can be bought in dried form, but many people find it more agreeable to eat liver pâté. Chicken liver and lamb's liver are highest in iron, but a little lower in zinc than calf's and pig's liver.

Presentation

Making food look appetizing is even more important when the appetite is half-hearted. Small helpings, nicely arranged with all the clichéd but still effective trimmings of flowers, napkins and pretty plates,

make a lot of difference to how much someone feels like eating. This is true even if you are preparing food for yourself: make it a ritual, and you are more likely to eat well than if you simply stand by the refrigerator door.

ANTI-STRESS COCKTAIL

Made in seconds, ideally with fresh-pressed juice. *Makes 1 large glass.*

75ml (3fl oz) orange juice, unsweetened
15ml (1 tbsp) wheat germ
75ml (3fl oz) plain low-fat yogurt

1 Mix the orange juice and the wheat germ in a blender.
2 Add the yogurt and whizz briefly.

VARIATIONS

Add some soft fruit, such as *raspberries*, *strawberries* or *stoned apricots* to the mixture.

You can replace the orange juice with a half-and-half mixture of *carrot* and *apple juice*.

THE NEW DIABETIC DIET

A revolution has taken place in the diet recommended to diabetics. For many years, they have been told to limit the amount of carbohydrate eaten, as well as to exclude sugar from meals. This resulted in a diet which relied heavily on meat, fish, dairy foods and eggs. While we think of these as 'protein foods', most of them, apart from the leanest meat and poultry, white fish and low-fat milk and cheese, are also high in fat. Because of the tight limit on carbohydrate, meals based on these types of food provided little fibre.

It's argued that this style of eating may have been one cause of the very high rate of heart disease among diabetics, along with other complications. While those who have no close contact with a sufferer may think that a special diet, with or without insulin, is all that a diabetic needs to live a normal life, those who get closer to the day-to-day reality of a diabetic's routine quickly become aware how easily control of the disease can be upset, for instance, by a meal's being delayed for an hour; and how serious health problems can result from poor control over a period of time.

A few years ago, diabetes research teams came forward with a new style of diabetic diet that produced more stable health from day to day, and which, they believe, will also reduce the long-term threats to health that often accompany diabetes.

Instead of restricting carbohydrate, the new diet recommends that at least half of the diabetic's calories come from it – but almost all from carbohydrate eaten in an unrefined form, that is from wholemeal bread, pulses, all kinds of unrefined cereals, vegetables and fruit. Sugar is still barred, but instead of limiting carbohydrate units rigorously, the new diet shows the diabetic who is counting carbohydrate how to choose the right type, and ensure that he or she is eating enough of it. The second major change is that diabetics are urged to follow a regime that is very low in fat. *The Diabetic's Diet Book* by Dr Jim Mann and the Oxford Dietetic Group (London, 1982) gives a clear and simple account of how to use the high-carbohydrate diet. The new regime can be summed up as 'more fibre, much less fat'. Although all kinds of fibre are useful, the 'gummy' type found in pulses and oats seems to be particularly effective in improving blood sugar stability. Work by Dr James Anderson and his team at the University of Kentucky has established that oat bran is more effective in this respect than wheat bran. But any kind of bran is best eaten in the high-fibre foods where it naturally occurs.

The new diet suggested for diabetics is remarkably similar to the general one suggested throughout this book, with these special points.
1 Diabetics need to avoid sugar, by itself or in food,

far more strictly than the rest of us. Although many diabetics can cope with very small amounts of sugar, they should avoid using it at home. Fruit is their main source of sweetness.

2 Most diabetics who develop the condition after the age of 40 are overweight, and can control their condition without drugs if they can get down to their ideal weight. So weight control is crucial. Diabetics who take insulin can't 'crash diet' – it's even worse for their health than for other people's. Weight has to be lost more slowly, by reducing calorie intake per day to about two-thirds of the quantity that it is usually.

One way in which you can work out approximately what your calorie consumption needs to be in order to lose weight is to keep a record of everything eaten or drunk during three days of normal eating. Then add up the total calories, divide the total by three and reduce the figure by at least 200 to 500 calories a day. To lose weight, diabetics should continue on the same pattern of eating, but take smaller helpings.

Diabetics *must* always consult their doctor or dietitian before dieting, especially if they're taking insulin, as the amount needed for good control may go down when less food is eaten.

3 Regular meals are essential for good control of the kind of diabetes where insulin has to be taken. This is one of the most difficult restrictions for the diabetic. Not only must he eat regularly, but the amount eaten at each meal should stay roughly the same from day to day. To do this successfully, a diabetic needs to work out early on a pattern of eating that is practical for his lifestyle, and suits his tastes, and think ahead so the timetable of eating can be followed – he may need to take packed meals, or work out where to break a journey for a meal, for instance.

A new eating plan
Diabetics should never change their eating patterns without consulting their dietitian, but here is a sample of how a healthy seven-day pattern of meals might look. The menu plan is not intended to be

SAMPLE SEVEN-DAY MENU PLAN

The diet plan on this and subsequent pages includes snacks and drinks from the list below. The recipes suggested in the diet plan are those given in the recipe section of the book.

Drinks
400ml skimmed milk daily, 132 calories and 20g carbohydrate
  plus *unlimited*
coffee, preferably decaffeinated
tea and herb tea
tomato juice
mineral water
bouillon and yeast extract drinks

Biscuits
providing about 100 calories and 10g carbohydrate
1½ hazelnut biscuits
1 bran biscuit
2 cheese crackers
2 oatcakes
4 crispbreads, eg Ryvita (eat with yeast extract and salad)

Fruit portions
120g orange (peeled weight)
200g melon
100g apple
150g apricots, fresh
150g blackberries, raw
100g cherries or pineapple
100g figs, fresh
65g grapes
100g peach or nectarine (stoned weight)

	Calories	Carbo-hydrate
MONDAY		
Breakfast 40g carbohydrate		
muesli using only 50g apple	221	37g
hazelnuts, 15g	54	–
fresh fruit, 100g (eg ½ grapefruit)	22	5g
Break 10g carbohydrate		
biscuits from list	100	10g
Lunch 80g carbohydrate		
lentil soup	190	32g
wholemeal roll, 50g	108	21g
large mixed salad, vegetables only, 225g	55 approx.	4g
Caesar dressing, 15ml	95	–
rhubarb fool, omitting honey	145	22g
Break 10g carbohydrate		
fruit from list	40	10g
Evening meal 150g carbohydrate		
fish cakes, using all white fish **and**	240	30g
brown rice, 35g (raw weight) **or**	126	31g
biryani, using half amount of honey	332	61g
tjatziki	45	6g
runner beans, 65g	17	3g
2 crispbreads, 15g	60	10g
cottage cheese, 100g	96	1g
Snack 10g carbohydrate		
biscuits from list	100	10g
Total calories and carbohydrates (including daily milk allowance)	1846 or 1812	252g

Continued overleaf

followed precisely, but should be used as a model for balanced meal planning, depending on the diabetic's carbohydrate allowance. This plan supplies about 2000 calories and 250g carbohydrate a day, with about 50 per cent of the calories provided in the form of carbohydrate, mainly from various types of unrefined food (1g carbohydrate provides 3.75 calories).

This menu plan can only be used with recipes from this book, as dishes with the same names made following other recipes may include far more fat or sugar, or may be in larger or smaller portions. Except where portion size is noted on the plan, portions given in the chart can generally be taken to be average-sized.

All measurements are in metric, as rough approximations between metric and imperial are too imprecise for diabetics, and for diabetics who are not overweight, grams of carbohydrate are the main item to be counted. In a number of countries people work in carbohydrate units instead, counting 10g as 1 unit.

The meals build in beans, lentils and oats for plenty of 'gummy' fibre. Because the menus are low in fat, which takes up little space for its calories, the foods that make up the calorie total are bulkier. For the many diabetics who are overweight, this form of diet should make it easier to take smaller portions and so help weight loss.

Each day includes at least two helpings of fresh fruit, and enough vegetables to provide a good level of vitamin C. Dark green leafy vegetables, such as watercress, Savoy cabbage, spring greens or broccoli, should be chosen wherever possible, as they combine a high vitamin C content with plenty of carotene for vitamin A, folic acid, vitamin K and minerals.

Some diabetics need regular snacks between meals to keep their level of blood sugar steady. The recipe for bran biscuits (page 295) is designed to provide approximately 100 calories and 10g carbohydrate per biscuit, to make a regular snack item so that the diabetic can always have the right kind of nibble handy.

TUESDAY	Calories	Carbo-hydrate
Breakfast 40g carbohydrate		
wholemeal toast or bread 60g (2 large thin slices)	130	25g
low-fat spread, 20g or soft margarine or butter, 10g	73	–
apricot spread, 50g	44	10g
fresh fruit, 100g (eg honeydew melon)	21	5g
Break 10g carbohydrate		
biscuits from list	100	10g
Lunch 80g carbohydrate		
spring rice salad, with chick peas and brown rice (50g each, raw weight)	480	73g
oil and lemon dressing, 15ml	30	–
cottage cheese, 100g	96	1g
apricots or blackberries, 100g	29	6g
Break 10g carbohydrate		
fruit from list	40	10g
Evening meal 150g carbohydrate		
lamb kebabs	260	5g
brown rice, 50g (raw weight) **or**	180	45g
butterbean bobottie **and**	290	49g
1 hardboiled egg	80	–
watercress salad	20	–
red cabbage	95	17g
oil and lemon dressing 10ml	30	–
quick cheescake, choosing sweet fruit and omitting honey	190	12g
Snack 10g carbohydrate		
biscuits from list	100	10g
Total calories and carbohydrates (including daily milk allowance)	1970 or 2020	250g or 249g

WEDNESDAY	Calories	Carbo-hydrate
Breakfast 40g carbohydrate		
'whole' cereal, 40g (eg Shredded Wheat – 2 biscuits	120	27g
skimmed milk, extra 100ml	33	5g
Edam cheese, 35g	105	–
fresh fruit, 100g (eg 1 peach)	32	8g
Break 10g carbohydrate		
biscuits from list	100	10g
Lunch 80g carbohydrate		
tofu burgers	190	19g
wholemeal rolls or bread, 90g (2 rolls or 3 slices)	195	38g
mixed vegetable salad	40	2g
yogurt, 30ml, mixed with herbs to dress salad	30	2g
banana, 100g (peeled weight)	80	19g
Break 10g carbohydrate		
fruit from list	40	10g
Evening meal 80g carbohydrate		
liver and onions **or**	273	8g
vegetable soufflé	225	7g
peas, fresh or frozen (not tinned) 100g	52	7g
buckwheat or barley, 50g raw weight	190	44g
stuffed pears, omitting honey or using only half amount	138	20g
Snack 10g carbohydrate		
biscuits from list	100	10g
Total calories and carbohydrates (including daily milk allowance)	1850 or 1802	249 or 248g

Foods of value in improving diabetic control

Beans and lentils These include peas and broad beans

Liver and brewer's yeast Rich in something known as 'glucose tolerance factor', of which the mineral chromium is an ingredient.

Oats Any recipes made with oats.

Rice More effective than potatoes in keeping blood sugar levels steady.

Salads and vegetables All kinds are suitable for diabetics. An increased consumption of vegetables has been shown to improve diabetic control. This may be a direct result of the high fibre and mineral content of vegetables, or it may be because they tend to be eaten instead of fattier, sweeter foods, or it could possibly be a combination of the two.

Wholegrains These are also rich in chromium, in contrast to refined versions. For example, an estimated 40 per cent of the chromium in wheat is lost in the refining process.

Sweeteners

Many diabetics buy or are given 'diabetic' jams, chocolate, fruit squashes and biscuits. Unfortunately, these are not of much benefit except for an occasional treat. They are often sweetened with sorbitol or other sugar substitutes, because these are absorbed more slowly than ordinary sugar (sucrose), and so are less likely to upset the blood sugar balance. That's their only advantage over sugar. They contain just as many calories (and for the person who becomes diabetic later in life, reducing calories is usually the key to control). They are just as empty of useful nutrients as sugar, too. What's more, if you eat more than about 25 to 30g (about 1oz) a day – a modest amount compared to the average person's sugar intake – you may well react with a deterioration of blood sugar control, and/or stomach cramps and diarrhoea.

Saccharin, acesulfame and aspartame contain no, or negligible, calories, and so may be more useful for diabetics. For most diabetics, the implications of a diet which poorly controls their condition out-

THURSDAY	Calories	Carbo-hydrate
Breakfast 40g carbohydrate		
wholemeal toast or bread, 75g (2½ slices)	162	31g
low-fat spread, 15g or soft margarine or butter, 7g	55	–
browned mushrooms, 100g plus 5ml oil	55	–
fresh fruit, 100g (eg ½ peach)	37	9g
Break 10g carbohydrate		
biscuits from list	100	10g
Lunch 80g carbohydrate		
sardine salad sandwiches made with wholemeal bread, 140g (4 slices)	303	59g
sardines, 75g	220	–
salad, 75g	20	–
low-fat spread, 15g	55	–
large banana, 110g (peeled weight)	87	21g
Break 10g carbohydrate		
fruit from list	40	10g
Evening meal 150g carbohydrate		
tarragon chicken, 225 joint (raw weight)	260	8g
baked potato, 100g **or**	85	20g
courgette bake	325	29g
spinach, 100g	30	1g
sweetcorn kernels, 100g	76	16g
fruit with ice, 120g	50	13g
Dutch apple ice, omitting honey or using only half amount	95	21g
Snack 10g carbohydrate		
biscuits from list	100	10g
Total calories and carbohydrates (including daily milk allowance)	1965 or 1945	249g or 250g

FRIDAY	Calories	Carbo-hydrate
Breakfast 40g carbohydrate		
porridge	140	24g
Edam cheese, 32g (modest slice)	100	–
small banana, 80g (peeled weight)	63	15g
Break 10g carbohydrate		
biscuits from list	100	10g
Lunch 80g carbohydrate		
minestrone soup, omitting pasta	156	19g
wholemeal pitta bread or wholemeal rolls, 75g (¾ pitta or 2 small rolls)	162	31g
humus	190	15g
raw vegetable 'dippers'	30	2g
dried apricots, 30g	61	13g
Break 10g carbohydrate		
fruit from list	40	10g
Evening meal 80g carbohydrate		
mushroom and spinach lasagne	260	35g
green salad	30	1g
Caesar dressing, 7ml	48	–
garlic wholemeal bread, 45g plus low-fat spread, 20g, or soft margarine or butter 10g	174	19g
Christine's banana ice	210	26g
Snack 10g carbohydrate		
biscuits from list	100	10g
Total calories and carbohydrates (including daily milk allowance)	1993	250g

Continued overleaf

weigh in seriousness the doubts about the safety of saccharin. Aspartame, which has only recently become accepted for general sale, has not been accused of ill-effects, except for people suffering from intolerance of a particular natural protein, called phenylalanine. Some aspartame products also include lactose, so they aren't suitable for those allergic to milk; make sure you check the label before using them.

Fruit sugar (fructose), the kind of sugar extracted from fruit, has the same amount of calories, and the same lack of nutrients, as sucrose. However, it can be used by most bodies without insulin and it is less liable to upset most diabetics' blood sugar balance than sucrose. It is also sweeter than sucrose, so less is needed. Very small amounts are allowed in many diabetics' meal plans – it would be wise though to consult your doctor first.

The obvious problem about the regular use of sweeteners by diabetics is that it does nothing to discourage a sweet tooth. And when food does need sweetening, all of us, but diabetics especially, are better off using fruit – fresh, dried or puréed – or sweet spices.

Alcohol

Alcohol need not be a problem for diabetics, although many tend to react much more strongly to it than non-diabetics do. They need to limit it to small amounts, and must never drink on an empty stomach. Dr James Anderson suggests no more than 60ml (2fl oz) a day, to be taken with food. A tough tot to swallow.

Some other authorities, while not recommending alcohol for diabetics, suggest that a glass of dry wine or 300ml (½ pint) of beer or lager or a single measure of spirits can be tolerated occasionally.

Various sweet and fortified drinks, such as port and liqueurs, can upset the diabetic more, and are best avoided. So-called diabetic beer is not recommended, because it contains more alcohol and calories than ordinary beer, and is more liable to upset the diabetic's sugar balance.

	Calories	Carbo-hydrate
SATURDAY		
Breakfast 40g carbohydrate		
Scotch pancakes	160	25g
low-fat spread, 15g or soft margarine or butter, 7g	55	–
apricot spread, 50g	44	10g
fresh fruit, 100g (eg a small orange)	26	6g
Break 10g carbohydrate		
biscuits from list	100	10g
Lunch 80g carbohydrate		
monster salad, including brown rice and red kidney beans (50g each, raw weight) raisins 15g, mixed vegetables, 200g, oil and lemon dressing, 30ml, or use only 25g beans and have a 100g apple with or after salad instead of the other 25g beans	500 approx.	80g
Break 10g carbohydrate		
fruit from list	40	10g
Evening meal 150g carbohydrate		
fish pie **or**	300	35g
lentil and cheese savoury	370	35g
carrots, 100g, plus a dot of soft margarine	80	5g
spinach or greens, 100g	30	2g
glazed fruit tart	180	32g
plain low-fat yogurt, 100ml	52	6g
Snack 10g carbohydrate		
biscuits from list	100	10g
Total calories and carbohydrates (including daily milk allowance)	1800 or 1870	251g

	Calories	Carbo-hydrate
MONDAY		
Breakfast 40g carbohydrate		
kedgeree	210	22g
fresh fruit, 100g (eg 1 nectarine)	50	13g
plain low-fat yogurt, 45ml	40	5g
Break 10g carbohydrate		
biscuits from list	100	10g
Lunch 80g carbohydrate		
roast chicken, meat only, 100g	148	–
baked potato, including skin, 180g **or**	153	36g
aubergine roast	157	12g
baked potato, including skin, 100g	102	24g
apple strudel	312	38g
plain low-fat yogurt, 100ml	52	6g
Break 10g carbohydrate		
fruit from list	40	10g
Evening meal 150g carbohydrate		
tortillas	147	23g
bean sauce	220	35g
mixed salad, large	40	2g
Caesar dressing, 15ml	95	–
real orange jelly **omitting** honey	80	16g
and hazelnut biscuit to eat with jelly	70	7g
Snack 10g carbohydrate		
biscuits from list	100	10g
Total calories and carbohydrates (including daily milk allowance)	1947 or 1990	253g

BRAN BISCUITS

A useful snack item. Oat bran is particularly beneficial to diabetics. *Makes 15.*

100g plain wholemeal flour
100g wholewheat semolina
40g coarse wheat bran or oat bran or a half-and-half mixture
a pinch of sea salt
80g soft margarine
1 egg
skimmed milk, to mix

1 Heat the oven to 180°C (350°F), gas mark 4. Grease
a baking sheet lightly.
2 Mix the wholemeal flour, semolina, bran and salt
and rub in the margarine.

3 Stir in the egg and just enough milk to form a stiff
dough.
4 Roll out the dough to about 5mm (¼in) thick, and
use a cutter approximately 8cm (3in) across (such as
a large glass) to cut it into 15 rounds. Alternatively, if
you prefer, cut the dough into square shapes with a
pastry wheel.
5 Transfer the dough shapes to the baking sheet,
prick 3 sets of holes in each one with a fork and bake
for 15 to 20 minutes.

VARIATION

For biscuits with a nuttier texture, use *100g rolled
oats* instead of the semolina. In this case, you will
need slightly more milk to make a dough that will
stick together.

You can also vary the flavour by adding *spice*, such
as *cinnamon*, or *celery seeds*.

WEIGHT

Being unhappy about your weight is understandable
if you are obese or very thin. However, many people
who are neither are still dissatisfied, often because
they are too influenced by the 'standard body'
glorified by photographers in fashion and cosmetic
advertisements. 'If only I were a different weight, life
would be great' is a common misconception among
such people, and one which can get in the way of
enjoying life.

It's important to accept that while self-confidence
can certainly be improved by keeping your weight to
a level where you feel comfortable, getting over-
anxious about the perfect shape can lead to unhappy
obsession with food and figure. Never try to model
yourself on a body build radically different from
your own. You'll know without weighing yourself
when your shape is getting out of hand.

GAINING WEIGHT

Naturally thin people rarely succeed in gaining
weight by simply eating more. They seem to have the
most efficient mechanisms for burning off extra
calories, rather than storing them, and if they *do* gain
a pound or two, it may be in the form of a 'tummy',
and not where they necessarily want it. For such
people the best solution may be to just enjoy being
thin, as do famous 'skinnies', like Mick Jagger and
most top fashion models. However, some people
may be thin for reasons other than their calorie-
burning efficiency.

In a small proportion of cases, being very thin
means that food is not being absorbed effectively

from the digestive tract. This may be because of an
intestinal problem: for example, coeliacs, who are
allergic to gluten, suffer damage to the intestinal wall
whenever it comes into contact with this cereal
protein, and may therefore often remain thin until
the condition is diagnosed and gluten excluded
from their meals (see pages 283–6).

In other cases, thin people who eat refined,
processed foods most of the time may find that their
body seems to use food more effectively if they
switch to eating natural foods. (There may be other
reasons for poor absorption, in which case a medical
check-up may be required.)

In some cases, being underweight may simply be
due to tension. Highly strung, tense people may find
that they burn up calories more slowly, and therefore gain weight, if they deliberately learn how to
relax and unwind. Ways of doing this range from
meditation, yoga and relaxation exercises to a
deeper re-thinking of basic attitudes to life.

Anorexia
Sometimes being thin can be due to *anorexia
nervosa* (meaning 'nervous loss of appetite') – a
condition in which people literally starve themselves
to death. Although anorexia has only recently 'come
out of the closet' into public debate and research, it
certainly isn't new. The factors that set it off,
however, are still uncertain, despite some characteristics common to many sufferers, namely: nine
out of ten are women; most cases start during the
teenage years; it's far more common among middle
and upper income and education groups; sufferers
may have a 'fatty' in the family whom they fear

becoming like; there may be a fear of close relationships; the sufferer may like the feeling of being in control that limiting food successfully gives her.

Symptoms of anorexia – and this is almost the only way to spot the problem, since sufferers go to great lengths to conceal and deny their thinness – go beyond emaciation and include: cessation of periods (women generally stop menstruating if under 38kg [6 to 6½ stone], give or take 3 to 4kg [6½ to 8½lb]); growth of downy hair on the body and face; refusal to eat with others, although the anorexic often enjoys preparing food for other people; loss of enamel from teeth if the sufferer is starving herself by vomiting after eating (the digestive acids eat away enamel) – a symptom of *bulimia* (see opposite); unrealistic insistence that she is fat; excess energy, often shown in intense sporting activity; hatred and fear of overweight; fear of eating carbohydrates; hiding food and pretending to have eaten it.

This condition needs expert treatment. One of the main problems lies in persuading the sufferer that something is wrong, and that treatment is needed. The threat to health comes not just from starvation, but possible heart damage if the sufferer is taking laxatives or vomiting. Underlying the sufferer's apparent energy is depression, and this can lead to a higher-than-average chance of suicide.

In many cases, the condition is in some way connected to relationships within the family, and the sufferer may need to go away from home to have a good chance of recovery.

Treatment usually consists of psychological work to help sufferers overcome their desperate fear of food, and especially of carbohydrates, of losing control if they eat more, and concentrates on the emotional background of the home situation, combining these tactics with by-hook-or-by-crook persuasion (for example, if you eat this, you can get out of bed) to eat.

However, about half (at best) of sufferers do not fully recover, and can relapse in future times of stress, remaining abnormally thin.

Thinness may be due to some other undiagnosed health problem. Basically, any large weight loss needs investigating. Anyone who suddenly loses anything over about 7kg (15lb) without changing their diet or environment should go for a medical check-up.

The exceptions to this rule are people who've just undergone some unusual form of stress, which can affect the body's ability to absorb food as well as appetite and eating tastes.

Exercise
Many 'six-stone-weaklings' have built up their bodies through exercise, without changing what they eat deliberately. However, as they gain muscle and bulk, they probably do feel hungrier. Although women don't usually want to put on noticeable muscles, exercise routines with light weights are probably the most effective method for slim people to improve their shape.

Losing Weight

By definition, fat is stored energy, and people have too much of it because *they take in more energy*, measured as calories or joules, than they use up. But that isn't the whole story.

Among the high proportion of Western people who are too heavy, there are the following groups:

Slow-burners
Many overweight people are 'slow-burners': in other words, they eat no more or less than their thinner colleagues, but their systems burn energy more slowly so that they remain heavy. This tendency runs in families, but can also suddenly 'arrive' during adult life, for reasons that aren't understood. While many people take in calories that aren't used by the body but gain no weight (or very little) because the excess tends to be 'burnt off', 'slow-burners' store it all as fat.

It isn't impossible for such people to lose weight, but to do so they have to limit their food intake much more severely than most people – a striking case of life not being fair! Metabolic rate – the rate at which the body functions and burns fuel for those functions – can be boosted at least temporarily by exercise, so forget all those warnings that exercise will use up barely any extra calories and make you hungrier. If you get hot from exercise, you will probably find your appetite reduced, not increased, and the rise in metabolic rate may increase the calorie-burning tempo for hours afterwards.

So although exercise is advisable for *all* overweight people it's particularly important for the 'slow-burners'.

Finally, although 'slow-burners' need to limit food intake tightly, they should not attempt starvation diets, since these may only cause the body to slow down even more to conserve the energy.

Health problems
A small number of those who gain weight on little food do so because of a more general health problem.

Although glandular problems are rare, they do occur. A slow-running system can be the result of an underactive thyroid. The thyroid is the gland in the neck which produces thyroxine, a substance which is necessary for the metabolism to work normally. If not enough thyroxine is secreted, the body slows down as does the rate at which calories are used.

Thyroxine is 64 per cent iodine, and lack of iodine is one, though not the only, cause of shortage. To avoid thyroid problems, which occur mainly in areas where the soil is naturally low in iodine, it's wise for everyone routinely to use iodized salt – added or sea salt; and sea food, either in the form of sea vegetables like kelp or Japanese seaweeds, or as sea fish and shellfish.

It is dangerous to self-diagnose thyroid problems. However, a possible symptom is a temperature of under 36.5°C (97.8°F) on first waking in the morning. The temperature must be measured before you move from your bed (shake down the thermometer the night before) and taken for about 10 minutes. A low temperature can mean low thyroid activity, but proper medical testing is necessary to confirm it.

Always bear in mind that it is dangerous to take extra iodine except under supervision, and that thyroxine given by a doctor can only help overweight if a deficiency exists. Otherwise, it can have dangerous side-effects.

Compulsive overeating

A large proportion of overweight people *do* overeat – for emotional reasons. Food is a common outlet used for comfort or to suppress feelings at times of stress and strain, in the way that alcohol is also sometimes used.

Women in particular seem especially vulnerable to developing an obsessional relationship with food. This may be partly due to the unrealistically thin image they aim towards for the sake of fashion – a woman who is constantly trying to eat less than her body wants, and to stay underweight, is, likely to think about food a lot. It may also be due to women having readier access to food, to it being cheaper than alcohol and less socially noticeable or re-proved.

Some people can come to see food as their enemy – a temptation that undermines their 'success' in being thin – instead of as a necessary and enjoyable fuel. Sometimes, too, a 'love–hate' relationship can develop, where food becomes a comforting friend when the eater is upset, but an enemy when she or he feels they have over-indulged – even if they haven't. Many in this situation feel a sense of panic just from feeling full. If they eat just one of the foods they regard as 'naughty', they may feel that they've spoiled their diet completely. Their rigid control has little give in it and may snap – so they turn to a binge of more forbidden foods.

We all overeat sometimes, but when it's ac-companied by these powerful emotions, it's no longer a question of being mildly greedy, but of being driven by forces that have little to do with enjoyment of food. The foods eaten on a binge are almost always sweet ones: cakes, chocolate, biscuits and pastries. When such behaviour gets a hold, it can be hard to shake off. Taken to extremes, a pattern of 'binge and starve', known medically as *bulimia*, can set in. To get rid of the discomfort of being stuffed with vast amounts of food, and to fend off over-weight, the binger may take large amounts of laxatives or make himself or herself sick after eating. Both can injure health, causing serious loss of potassium, which, in extreme cases, can result in heart problems. Vomiting will eventually result in loss of tooth enamel from contact with stomach acids. These stratagems may keep weight fairly normal, so the situation goes unnoticed for years.

How do people reach this low ebb? Studies of people with obsessional relationships with food suggest that their difficulty in forming close relationships with other people may have something to do with it. There certainly seems to be some correlation between the appetite for food and the appetite for love: think how many people lose weight and appetite when they fall in love, and think of how you can use food to comfort you when lonely or bored.

From a practical point of view, no one with even a slight emotional use of food is going to find it easy, or possible, to eat less – or to eat in a balanced way – unless they become aware of why they eat too much for their energy needs. They may follow diet after diet, losing weight but then regaining it with equal speed. What such people need, in fact, is not 'the right diet', but a close, if often painful, look at what's going on in their head – by, say, joining a self-help group of others with similar problems – or finding a counsellor or psychotherapist who can help them find a way round their food cravings. Other self-awareness training methods that may help include yoga and meditation. Self-help may not completely solve the problem, although it may help by making the person aware of what's going on in their mind. It can also often be a great relief – and surprise – for people to realize how many others share their food obsessions.

All these steps can raise the individual's self-image and make them less willing to abuse their body with binges of unhealthy food.

Habit overeating

Habit overeating is one way that overweight is passed on in families. If you grow up in an atmosphere where meals are large, snacks frequent and the choice of menus rich, you are likely to adopt some of these habits yourself.

Although a normal-burning metabolic rate will

enable many people to 'burn off' such excess calories in the short term, the pounds may go on steadily in the longer term. For example, eating just one extra plain digestive biscuit a day (about 70 calories) provides a surplus 25,550 calories a year, which, at the rate of about 3500 calories in 450g (1lb) fat, would lead to an overall annual weight gain of 3kg or 7lb. Even if your body burnt up half of this, by the end of six years you would be almost 10kg (22lb) heavier.

Solving the problem

Given that most of us vary what we eat considerably from day to day, it's a tribute to the body's weight-maintaining ability that so many of us stay around the same weight year in, year out.

In contrast to the abstemious 'slow-burner' who still has a perpetual weight problem unless they eat very carefully, the person who started out their adult life slim but has gradually put on a pound or two a year until it's become a problem has an easier job – the mechanism for burning excess calories may have faltered under the repeated strain, but the overeating that's mainly a habit is easiest to correct.

Behavioural therapists, who work with both compulsive eaters and slow-burners, can teach overweight people to avoid some of the common habits of the overweight. These include eating very quickly, or eating while doing something else. In both cases, the food slips down barely noticed and, in the end, the taste buds ask for more. People can learn to eat slowly and savour what they eat so that the experience is more satisfying.

Similarly, smaller helpings can become a habit, as can getting up after meals before thinking about second helpings. Natural dislike of food waste can be changed from an excuse for finishing off leftovers to a reason for serving less in the first place.

The habit of eating because it's a certain time of day, or because you want to be polite, or because you pass a particular café or shop – all common among overweight people – can be overcome relatively easily once you know that you are doing it. Family pressure to eat more is more difficult to resist, since big changes in someone's weight can alter the 'balance of power' within marriages or the routine of family life (going out more; fewer 'ritual' family meals, for instance). Slimming clubs can enable the overweight person to share 'confessions' and tips for re-arranging eating habits.

Exercise For all the groups, as indeed for anyone interested in eating for health, exercise is the essential other side of the balance. Although exercise rarely uses up more extra calories than you'd get in a modest sandwich, it can help people keep their

weight down by all the following methods:
1 Making people more aware of their bodies, improving motivation to control food, and increasing awareness of hunger or its absence.
2 Increasing body heat – speeding up the calorie-burning rate for several hours, and for most people, discouraging overeating.
3 Toning muscles – good muscle tone can do as much to improve body shape as losing weight.
4 Enhancing self-image and self-confidence, so 'comfort eating' is less appealing.
5 Providing an emotional outlet and activity other than of food, so 'tension eating' isn't inviting, and people are less likely to eat because of boredom.

In terms of energy use, a 30-minute brisk walk every day of the year would, at an average use of 3.5 calories per minute, use up an extra 38,325 calories a year – equivalent to roughly 5kg (11lb) of weight lost. This is one reason why a daily exercise session is more valuable in using calories than a weekly burst: the calories add up, plus your metabolism gets a more frequent boost.

Plan of campaign If you fall into any of the groups discussed above, you should regulate your lifestyle accordingly:
Slow-burners Don't eat fewer than 800 calories a day, and make sure each one 'pays its way' with high vitamin and mineral content. Take a multi-vitamin/mineral to ensure against going short of nutrients accidentally.

Exercise more, especially with daily sessions of a form of activity that makes you hot.
If you suspect you suffer from an underactive thyroid Check your morning temperature, family history and the likelihood of iodine deficiency in your area. Then consult your doctor (do this also if you gain weight while on medication).
Compulsive eating Recognize that this is common, in varying degrees, and needs to be tackled not with diet but by bringing your underlying emotions into the open.
'Habit' overeating If you've gained weight slowly from a slim youth, you should be able to lose it fairly easily by re-training your eating habits – then following a lower-calorie diet.

How to eat fewer calories and stay healthy The successful diet is the one you have only to follow once – because it has gone hand-in-hand with re-training eating habits which means you don't regain the weight you have lost. It should also provide a good nutritional balance, so that you won't get run down, putting your health at risk and often destroying your willpower to eat less.

1000-CALORIE-A-DAY DIET

Here's an example of a low-calorie diet which provides a good range of nutrients; once weight has been lost, portions can be increased until a level is found at which weight is maintained.

This form of diet will produce a weight loss of about 1kg (2lb 2oz) per week in most women, although this may be much greater during the first two weeks. This may seem too slow, but the heavier you are, the more you will tend to lose at first; and eating less than this can be counter-productive, since you may not be eating enough to get all the food value you require, and your system may well slow down in response to a very low food intake, so that you burn calories more slowly. Exercise can speed up weight loss in many cases, as well as distracting your attention from eating.

Allowances
A daily allowance of 150 calories is allowed, for:
300ml (½ pint) skimmed milk
Drinks Decaffeinated, dandelion or grain coffee; herb or other tea; mineral, soda and tap water (but not tonic); bouillon and yeast extract drinks; lemon juice and water.
Vegetables for nibbling Cabbage, carrots, cauliflower, celery, chicory, Chinese leaves, courgettes, fennel, green beans, mushrooms, parsley, peppers, spinach, spring onions, swedes, tomatoes, turnip, watercress.

A 150ml (¼ pint) glass of dry wine contains roughly 95 calories, and can be added to the pattern when wanted. Do not use wine instead of another food. Remember that wine will tend to relax your resolve to stick to your diet.

Points to watch
This pattern can be used as a model using any dishes of suitable calorie content in the book. However, you should:
1 Keep the milk allowance to provide calcium, unless you replace it with yogurt or low-fat cheese dishes. Goat's milk or soya milk can be used.
2 Keep the high-fibre breakfasts, preferably alternating.
3 Keep the salad-a-day meal, because it provides un-processed vitamins and minerals with fibre.
4 Use fish and liver regularly unless vegetarian. Vegetarians can base their evening meal on any of the book's bean or grain recipes with a comparable calorie value.

	Approximate calories	
BREAKFAST		
25g (1oz) unrefined cereal (soak muesli overnight in water or milk from allowance) or rolled oats (for porridge). No sugar	100	
Milk from allowance		
Fresh fruit (not banana)	50	
		150
OR		
½ grapefruit	20	
50g (2oz), 2 small slices wholemeal bread	125	
7g (¼oz) butter/margarine or 15g (½oz) low-fat spread	55	
		200
OR		
125g (5oz) plain low-fat yogurt	75	
125g (5oz) fresh fruit, any type, or 1 small banana	60	
15g (½oz) wheat germ	45	
10ml (2 tsp) wheat bran, if liked	neg.	
		180
LIGHT MEAL		
Base 1 meal a day on salad, using a wide variety of leafy and root vegetables, sliced, shredded or in chunks	40	
Dressing: 10ml (2 tsp) oil with 45ml (3 tbsp) plain low-fat yogurt, flavoured with mustard, herbs, lemon juice or vinegar	100	
50g (2oz) bread or 4 crispbreads or wholewheat pasta or brown rice or beans, all cooked from 35g (1¼oz) raw weight	120	
	50	
1 piece fresh fruit (not banana**)		
		310
MAIN MEAL		
Melon or grapefruit or consommé or tjatziki or globe artichoke	40	
125 to 175g (5 to 6oz) grilled or baked white or shell fish or 100 to 125g (4 to 5oz) grilled or roast turkey, rabbit, chicken or game or liver*	150	
Vegetables from list		
100g (4oz) baked potato or brown rice or pasta 25g (1oz) raw weight	100	
1 piece fresh fruit (not banana**)	50	
		340
Total depending on breakfast chosen	950–1000	

Once a week use liver for iron and oily fish for vitamins A and D, unless vegetarian. (Vegetarians should use margarine rather than butter for higher A and D, and vitamin-fortified skimmed milk.)
**Keep to eat between meals, if preferred.*

1500-calorie-a-day diet
Most men can lose weight while eating 1500 calories a day. Add to the above pattern:
50g (2oz) more bread – 123 calories
7g (¼oz) more butter/margarine or 15g (½oz) more low-fat spread – 55 calories
Slightly larger portions of all other meals

A well-balanced diet can form the basis of a lifelong style of eating on which you can maintain roughly the right weight. Almost everyone goes up and down by a kilo or so, and being *exactly* the same weight all the time should not become an obsession.

It's also important not to aim for a body shape that is totally removed from your own. If you are a natural mesomorph – fairly strong-boned, wide-shouldered, muscular – find your admired models among other mesomorphs such as Rodin sculptures or, say, Ingrid Bergman. Don't hanker to be a fine-boned sylph such as David Bowie or petite like Lulu, or you'll never be happy with your shape, no matter how thin you get.

All kinds of body shape can be beautiful, as has been proved by the great artists. In fact, a good way of liking your body more is to visit an art gallery. Among the men and women painted, you're bound to find a physical type like yours – whether you are a Modigliani, Titian, Renoir, Burne-Jones or Egon Schiele type – which you recognize as beautiful. Judge yourself by these standards, and not by the narrow criteria of this year's fashionplate.

Having decided what you are realistically aiming for, keep a diary for at least four days (including a weekend) of what you eat now – don't try to change what you eat, or eat less. The diary will give you a basic guide to your usual eating patterns, which you can use to decide where you can most easily cut down. Since fat and sugar provide about 60 per cent of all our calories, and are both the most concentrated-calorie foods and the least nutrient-rich, any well-balanced diet will reduce intake of these first. (A similar ruling applies to alcohol – for many people, another major source of 'empty calories'.)

This book already does this, and you can use the menu planning section and recipes without change to build up a low-calorie regime, confident that calories are not being 'thrown away' on foods that provide no nutritional value other than energy. A slimming diet should simply consist of smaller helpings of the same foods that provide a healthy diet: low or no sugar, low fat, high fibre, low salt, plenty of fruit and vegetables. A diet rich in fibre is also more filling.

Alcohol and sugar can be omitted completely if you like, but never try to adopt a no-fat, rather than a low-fat, diet. Forget the older diets which barred carbohydrates (apart from salads), in favour of large amounts of meat, fish, dairy foods and eggs. They provided too much fat, too little fibre and a style of eating that was both too expensive and too unnatural to be adopted permanently. The eater lost weight, but often re-gained it, since this sort of pattern did not re-train everyday eating habits.

Calories from carbohydrate are no more fattening than those from protein – and both types of foods have almost the same calorie content per gram as shown below.

1g carbohydrate = 3.75 calories; 1g protein = 4 calories; 1g alcohol = 7 calories; 1g fat = 9 calories.

Maintenance diet
The end of a successful diet should not produce a rush for cream cakes. Although there is no harm in a celebratory cake or bar of chocolate, anyone slimming should aim to re-shape their food tastes as well as their figure, so that their idea of a treat becomes a banana or an extra sandwich – foods which won't swamp the calorie count, and which provide a good range of nutrients for their calories. This change in tastes does happen, and it's heartening, if a little disappointing, to find you don't enjoy sweet or rich foods as much as you used to.

Other methods of losing weight are as follows:

Crash diets May produce quick weight loss, but most of it will be fluid which will be regained immediately. Can leave you grumpy and jumpy. Don't re-train your appetite or tastes.

Slimming clubs Offer useful moral support and tips for dieters, but ensure that the diet they suggest is a modern one, i.e. provides fibre by allowing some wholemeal bread, cereals and beans.

Slimming drugs and injections Drugs that speed up metabolism can speed up weight loss, but are dangerous; you can get addicted to them. You may also develop a tolerance for them so that they don't work any more. And you can't go on taking them permanently – so unless you change your eating habits too, you are likely to regain the weight.

Special 'diet' foods Can only be lower in calories by adding some non-calorific element, such as water (turning margarine into low-fat spread) or air (in airy, 'slimming' bread). No particular food can promote slimming except by helping you lower your total calorie intake. Some people find controlled-portion products useful in replacing will-power.

EATING FOR SPORT

'Steak' used to be the key word for athletes in training. Nowadays, although many still eat it, expert opinion recognizes that most athletes' need for protein is no greater than that of an active adult man. Instead, the good sports diet is based on larger portions of the same balance of foods as in an ordinary well-organized style of eating; in other words, low in fat, sugar and salt, and high in fibre, fruit and vegetables.

Salt

Because athletes usually sweat more than other people, it might be thought that they need to add extra salt to their food. In fact, the amount of salt normally consumed – even with the style of lower-salt cooking described in this book – is still several times more than the body actually needs. Extra salt may strain the kidneys which have to dispose of it, hinder the excretion of surplus fluid from the body, and make the athlete drink more and then sweat more as a result.

Supplements

Many athletes swear by vitamin and mineral supplements as aids to peak performance. So far, there's no scientific backing for this, although it is generally accepted that stress from great effort can lead to greater usage of the B group vitamins and vitamin C. Favourite items among athletes are the natural cell-protectors, vitamins C and E and substances alleged to improve the oxygen-carrying capacity of the blood stream, notably octocosanol, extracted from wheat germ, and selenium (a mineral which works in combination with vitamin E).

Preparing for events

Contestants in endurance events have for several years been attracted to the so-called 'carbohydrate-loading diet' as a means of preparing themselves for competitions.

It is almost impossible to assess the effectiveness of the carbohydrate-loading diet, as there's no way of measuring how well the same person could have performed that day without it. However, some athletes (who can be notoriously superstitious about what makes them do well) believe it really helps them: it could all be in the mind, but who can say? Others claim that the carbohydrate-starved part of the week upsets them so much that the end result is not helpful. In the present state of knowledge, it's impossible to say who is right.

A long-distance runner racing on a Saturday, for instance, will start his or her preparation on the previous Monday, Tuesday and Wednesday by avoiding all carbohydrate foods. This is not only difficult to do, but may leave him or her feeling light-headed and weak. The idea behind it is to starve the muscles of glycogen, the fuel store for energy.

On Thursday and Friday, he or she will then tuck away large meals of carbohydrate-rich foods. The theory is that the glycogen-drained muscles will 'suck up' the absolute maximum stores, thus putting the runner in peak form for the race. On the actual day of the competition, light meals based on easily digested carbohydrates like fruit are chosen for early events; meals like pasta for later ones. The idea of steak dinners on the day of the event has long been rejected, for this form of meal will not be sufficiently digested to reach the body for several hours – probably after the event has finished. In the meantime, the digestive process could slow the contestant down a little and make him or her feel uncomfortable.

Long-distance events

Contestants in marathons and other endurance events benefit by being unusually light in weight, and the desire to stay thin may be their overriding consideration in planning what they eat. This can sometimes come into conflict with their need for a good supply of nutrients unless they choose their low-calorie meals carefully. Although many take vitamin supplements, these cannot fully replace nutritious food, which simply provides a wider range of nutrients – as well as carbohydrates, protein, fats and fibre – than any pill, however well-designed.

Heavy training can also interfere with good nutrition, since no one wants to go running on a full stomach, and the athlete may feel too tired to be hungry afterwards.

Because of the need for concentrated nourishment, juices are particularly useful when the appetite is not very good.

Sugar

If you were to ask a random sample of people whether athletes need sugar, almost all would say 'yes'. And yet although we need glucose sugar for energy, the body can manufacture it from many foods without our ever touching crystal sugar. Although the latter is a quickly absorbed form of energy, it isn't necessary for athletic performance. On the other hand, endurance event athletes who take sugary drinks may get away with doing so much more than the 'Saturday athlete' who imagines that a game of football justifies a few chocolate bars. This is because the endurance athlete will be regularly using up more than the average number of calories and so will probably get his vitamins and minerals even if he 'throws away' a small proportion of calories on a food which doesn't supply many nutrients. The Saturday athlete on the other hand is less likely to use up so many calories as to have any to spare for 'no food value' items.

Individuality

Athletes are good examples of how each human being is a unique combination of talents and characteristics: the top league may share certain charac-teristics of build to suit their particular event, and yet still also differ enormously in both physique and personality.

This difference also shows when it comes to designing diets for athletes. Apart from the obvious benefit of eating the food which provides good supplies of vitamins, minerals and other nutrients, it's not possible to design a perfect diet for athletes; they vary too much in what food makes them feel on top form. Using the general menu-making plans in this book will provide a sensible base to adapt to individual tastes. In general, when extra food is wanted, it should be provided by carbohydrate-based dishes.

EATING OUT

The same principles used in the choice of recipes and cooking methods throughout this book will help you make the healthiest selection from any menu you are faced with, whether it's at a late-night take-away, or on an elegant evening out.

Here are some of the choices: many of the recommended dishes may not be prepared as healthily as you would prepare them at home, but they are the best of what's on offer.

Drinks

Choose juices rather than squashes, crushes, colas or other combinations of water, flavourings and sugar. Tomato juice, mineral water, and spritzers of fruit juice half-and-half with sparkling mineral water are all widely available in cafés.

More restaurants now serve decaffeinated coffee and, less often, tisanes or herb teas (see page 268 for ideas on these). You can also ask a restaurant to make up a herb tea bag which you've brought with you.

As for alcohol, follow the suggestions on page 269. Watch carefully how much wine is poured and always drink mineral water as well as any alcoholic drink, or dilute dry white wine with it to make a spritzer.

TAKE-AWAY FOOD

Baked potatoes	With cottage cheese, salad, baked bean, chili bean, chicken curry or other relatively lean fillings; ask for butter to be left off
Barbecued chicken	Remember this is often available in fish and chip shops
Cakes and buns	If you must have buns, choose yeast-raised cakes and buns – they have a lower percentage of fat and sugar than anything made with pastry or sponge. Pick currant buns or hot cross buns rather than Danish pastries or fried doughnuts, which have a high fat level. Look out for the growing number of wholemeal scones available. A banana sandwich made with wholemeal bread is a still better 'sweet'
Corn on the cob	Without butter
Desserts	Add a chopped apple or peeled mandarin orange to plain yogurt, rather than buying the sugary versions made with preserved fruit
Doner kebab	With pitta bread and salad
Fish and chips	Peel off the batter, or tuck in wholeheartedly and make other meals leaner to balance
Hamburger	With salad only, preferably omitting bun
Ice cream	Choose sorbets, which contain sugar but less fat than ice cream
Pizza	Short on fibre, but healthier than high-fat quiche
Sandwiches	Made with wholemeal bread when possible, with leaner fillings such as chicken, salad, yeast extract, bananas, cottage cheese, mashed fish, etc., more often than peanut butter or hard cheese. Avoid mayonnaise (choose plain boiled egg, not egg mayonnaise), cream cheese, corned beef (usually very fatty) and salami (average 45 per cent fat)

CHOOSING HEALTHIER FOOD IN RESTAURANTS

FIRST COURSES	
Artichoke	Ask for dressing to be served separately, so you can limit how much you add, or ask for a squeeze of lemon instead
Asparagus	Ask for dressing to be served separately, or for lemon instead
Caviare	Usually served with wholemeal bread
Crab salad	Ask for dressing to be served separately, or for lemon instead
Crudités	Get used to being sparing with a mayonnaise dip, or ask for some cottage cheese or smooth pâté to dip the vegetables
Fish terrine	Will probably contain cream, but portions tend to be small
Grapefruit	If you don't like added colourings, don't eat the cherries. Ask them not to sugar it
Humus	Ask them not to pour on extra oil
Melon	Ask them not to add sugar
Moules marinière	
Oysters	Ideal: ask for the brown bread to be only sparingly buttered
Pâté	Ask for wholemeal toast and hope it's a fairly lean pâté; team with a low-fat main course
Prawn cocktail	Ask for dressing to be served separately, or for lemon instead
Prawn tikka	
Sashimi	Japanese raw fish – some people may not like it, but it's very healthy
Side salad	Green or mixed, makes an excellent, fresh-tasting first course almost any restaurant can produce easily. Ask for dressing to be served separately
Smoked salmon	Usually served with wholemeal bread
Soups	Choose the less creamy types, such as minestrone, Scotch broth or gazpacho
Tjatziki	
Vegetable terrine	

MAIN COURSES	
Beef	Choose roast beef or grilled steaks, asking for the standard butter pat to be omitted. Casseroled beef can be low or high in fat, depending on the recipe and cut used
Café food	Apart from sandwiches, consider baked beans on toast (preferably wholemeal) with tomatoes; poached or boiled eggs; shepherd's pie and other potato-based dishes in preference to pies, flans or pasties; meat-and-two-veg in preference to a fry-up with chips
Chicken and turkey	Grilled, casseroled, roast (hot or cold), but dodge 'Maryland' or other methods involving frying. If you are on a strict low-fat diet, remove the skin. Ask for sauces either to be added half-measure or served separately, so you can enjoy the taste but use less

MAIN COURSES (*continued*)	
Chinese food	Almost all healthy, except for deep-fried dishes such as spring rolls, sweet and sour meat in batter, and white rice. Lean choices are vegetable and almond, chicken or prawn chop sueys, stir-fried dishes and 'hot-pot' style recipes
Duck and goose	Go for roast only with both meats, except in Chinese restaurants, where the cooking methods remove a large proportion of the fat
Fish	Any kind, but not fried. Many restaurants will grill instead of fry, and omit the decorative butter pat on top, if asked. Ask for rich sauces to be either halved or served separately so you can limit the amount you add
Game	A good choice casseroled or roasted, but avoid rich sauces
Indian food	Vegetable, chicken and prawn or fish curries are by nature the leanest curries. Biryani dishes are a sensible choice at a good-quality restaurant, where the rice has not been re-fried – although they won't be as nutritious as the same dishes made at home with brown rice. Dhal, chappatis (which are often made with wholemeal flour) or nan, with raita (cucumber with yogurt) and lassi (a yogurt drink) make up a balanced meal, with or without a curry. Tandoori is one of the healthiest of all cooking styles
Lamb	Choose roast or grilled lamb, or traditional dishes such as Lancashire hot-pot, Irish stew or moussaka, where the lamb is mixed with generous amounts of vegetables. Liver and kidney dishes are often the leanest
Pork	Difficult to find low-fat pork dishes, but roast would be leanest
Veal	A lean meat, but usually fried or smothered in a high-fat sauce. A grilled veal chop is a good choice

DESSERTS	
Fruit	Fresh pineapple, melon slices, strawberries (ask for sugar not to be added), fresh fruit salad, oranges sliced in liqueur (but not caramelized oranges) or fresh fruits of any kind make the best desserts. Although some sugar may have been added to fruit salad or other prepared fruit, it's usually a small amount compared to what's in other desserts, and not significant unless you are diabetic, or eat desserts daily
Ice cream	Pick sorbets whenever available: they have less fat, though still some sugar
Pancakes	Choose plain pancakes with lemon or pancakes with a fruit filling, and ask not to have sugar sprinkled on top. Again, not as healthy as you could make with wholemeal flour at home, but the best of what's available

KITCHEN EQUIPMENT

'The average kitchen in a well-to-do household contains too many things, and the young housewife is apt to forget that what is a suitable *batterie de cuisine* in a home where cook and kitchenmaid are kept is absurd in a lesser household, where even if the cook knew the use of some of the articles, she certainly would not have time to keep them clean.

When choosing the culinary outfit let your maxim be: "Everything in this kitchen will have to be cleaned".' These words from the *Daily Mail Cookery Book* of 1919 are even more relevant today. People with lots of clever gadgets don't turn out reliably better food than those without them. They may save time during cooking and then spend more time on extra clearing up. They may find themselves doing by hand a job for which they have just the machine, because the thought of taking out, assembling, dismantling, washing up and putting away the machine is too daunting.

The equipment that you really find worthwhile will vary from household to household, according to the size of your family, what you like to cook and your personal temperament. A friend of mine, for instance, prefers to grind coffee beans by hand, both as a pleasant diversion between courses and because he thinks electric grinders bruise the beans and detract from their flavour. And many people, however attractive the new products on the market may be, inherit most of their kitchen ideas together with the equipment to carry them out.

Here are some of the items which particularly suit the style of cookery in this book. They are chosen because they save time or effort, or because they retain food values better than other equipment does, or because they give a 'plus' to cooking. Some of them are items you may not have thought of, whose charms I'd like to bring to your attention. You don't need them all, and you won't want them all.

POTS & PANS

Saucepans made of stainless steel are one of the best investments a cook can make: they won't react chemically with any food or affect the value or taste of food in any way; and provided that you do invest and buy the best you can find, they will retain their high standard of looks and performance for many years. Always look for a heavy pan, with a layer of copper or aluminium sandwiched between the layers of steel on the base. The base itself should be finely ground so that it is completely flat. The layer of another metal is needed to improve the heat-conducting properties of the pan, because stainless steel is a poor conductor of heat. A flat base helps the heat spread evenly, so that hot spots which encourage food to stick or burn don't form, and the pan doesn't warp over the years.

Copper pans should be avoided unless they are lined with stainless steel or aluminium. Because it is so sensitive to temperature, copper is the chef's traditional choice, but unlined copper reacts chemically with a wide variety of substances, and it destroys vitamin C in food. Tin-lined copper is not really satisfactory either, as tin is of dubious value to the body, and some is bound to be eaten since it is a soft metal.

Aluminium pans are popular because they are economical and they carry heat well. But some people dislike the fact that aluminium can combine with substances in food, so you eat some of it. In theory it should pass through the body harmlessly, but there have been claims that it can cause ill-effects, such as memory damage or allergy. Aluminium certainly reacts with acid fruit, and most people would be unhappy about leaving a batch of cooked rhubarb or plums in an aluminium pan for any length of time.

Glass – Pyrex or Corningware, for example – is like stainless steel, a material with which you can feel very safe, as it doesn't affect any food. Glass kettles are common in the US, and like glass pans they have a strong visual appeal. They look so clean, and you can see just what's cooking. You can take Corningware pans straight out of the freezer and heat them on the stove or in a microwave oven. They are good-looking enough to serve from, too. However, neither these nor Pyrex pans resist sticking as well as heavy stainless steel or cast-iron pans.

Cast-iron and enamelled pans conduct heat well. Their disadvantages are that iron may cause some cut fruit to blacken, that enamel can chip – allowing food to touch unstable metals underneath – and that both are very heavy to handle. However, they do have good looks and perform well.

My own choice is a set of stainless steel Cuisinox saucepans, in which I can happily make porridge or scramble eggs knowing that there won't be a nasty burnt mess to wash off. My set of three pans has the added attraction of detachable handles, so they stack for compact storage and take up little room if used to store leftovers in the refrigerator. The set I use also offers items I don't have, among them a big casserole pan which holds a stainless steel steamer big enough for a whole chicken or a fish. The lid of the casserole doubles as a large sauté pan.

When it comes to **frying pans**, I strongly prefer cast iron. Cast-iron pans are heavy to handle, but think of what you gain. They conduct heat evenly, so they're very good for cooking pancakes, for instance, and they rarely stick, so you can use less grease when cooking, and need to stir less often. Unlike non-stick pans, they don't have to be washed with enormous care, for fear of hurting the coating; nor do you have to ponder how much of the coating you may be eating. Most models are made complete with cast-iron handles, so you can put the whole pan under the grill or in the oven to brown food, without worrying about melting plastic. And I think these pans look attractive enough to use for serving a paella or an omelette. They're also cheap.

Use a pastry or a paint brush to brush pans or baking tins with oil, and you'll find you use far less fat than if you pour oil from a bottle. Many recipes which specify that onions should be softened in quite a large quantity of butter work just as well if the onions are cooked in a heavy pan just smeared with oil from your brush, and this is one of the best ways to lighten your cookery and your calories. Keep your brush in a jar or pot of your favourite oil.

NUTRITION-SAVERS

A gravy jug with a spout that starts right at the bottom means that you can pour out the juice while the fat stays in the layer at the top. You'll find transparent models for the kitchen, so you can see when you're getting too much fat, or elegant table jugs, which usually have a spout at either end, one set low to pour off juice, the other starting higher up, to pour off fat.

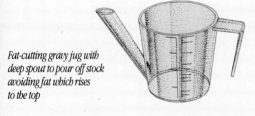

Fat-cutting gravy jug with deep spout to pour off stock avoiding fat which rises to the top

Use a **metal rack** to hold your roasting meats clear of the oven pan, and you'll find the results much less greasy. The bottom of the meat will also crisp much better.

A **stainless steel pressure cooker** is useful if you often cook in a hurry or have a large family. So much is generally accepted. What is less well known is that this method can also produce the same health bonus as a **steamer**. In neither case does food touch the water that draws out vitamins and minerals; pressure cooking can be even better than steaming,

because the food is heated for a shorter time. But you must use a **timer**, as otherwise vegetables easily turn from nutritious crunch to mush.

A **timer** is also almost essential for baking, in my view. It's so easy to forget how long food's been cooking, and if you use wholemeal flour you can't judge by colour, as dishes are already a little brown before you start. If you time vegetables too, results are more consistent.

Scrub vegetables with a **stiff brush**, and you can often save vitamins as well as time spent peeling. If you need to peel, use a good quality **peeler**, and you'll remove only the thinnest layer of skin, avoiding waste and vitamin loss.

STORAGE EQUIPMENT

Next time you buy a **refrigerator**, think of your health – and think big. The refrigerator is the best place to keep your vegetables and salads, if you want them to retain their condition and food value longer. As soon as produce is harvested, heat, light and exposure to oxygen begin to affect its freshness. This shows in wilting, loss of colour and condition. What you can't see is that vitamins – notably vitamins C, A and B_1 – are also suffering. Storing fresh vegetables in the refrigerator helps to retain their goodness.

In your refrigerator, it's useful to keep a **stock jug**, into which you automatically strain the liquid when you've cooked the vegetables. If you don't have a special container for such stock, you'll be tempted to throw it out. Keep it and use it to make your soups or sauces, and you'll gain back most vitamins and all minerals that have leached from the food to the water. Choose a jug with measures marked on the side, so that you'll know just how much you are pouring out without needing to pour it into a separate measuring jug first. Keep a lid on the jug, and use up the contents every three or four days.

CUTTING WORK

Dislike of chopping food is one reason why many people are prepared to pay so much extra for ready-prepared soups, vegetables or salads.

One of the most useful kitchen aids is an **electric blender or liquidizer**. It's not just elbow grease that's saved when you purée a soup in seconds instead of laboriously rubbing it through a sieve. It's also food value. When you can whizz produce to a smooth consistency electrically, it doesn't have to be nearly as soft – so overcooked – as when you sieve it, so you keep more vitamins. Again, sieving keeps the fibre back, but electric blending leaves the fibre in, chopping it so finely that it's unobtrusive.

Of the many devices designed to speed up the chopping process, few beat the sharp **knife**. Good knives are worth paying for. You get faster, and safer, results since many cuts occur when a blunt knife slips on the surface of food. A sharp one cuts safely through to the board beneath. I like stainless steel knives, as they don't have to be washed and dried as carefully as carbon steel. They stay shiny and sharp effortlessly. My own favourites are Victorinox knives, because the small handles fit my hand, and they seem to make onion slicing so easy. Moreover, stainless steel knives won't discolour fruit or vegetables.

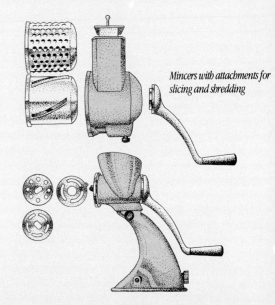

Mincers with attachments for slicing and shredding

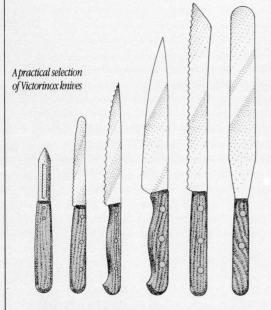

A practical selection of Victorinox knives

For making quick salads, I like to have a stainless steel, **four-sided grater**, which offers a stable shape and a variety of cutting surfaces. The same jobs can be done faster – with not too much extra washing – with a **vegetable mill** which has a variety of grating and shredding discs. If you handle a lot of food, and don't already have a good blender, you might prefer to buy a food processor.

If you chop large quantities of nuts a food processor will do it very nicely, but if you are using small amounts, a **Moulinex Junior** will chop them, and an **electric coffee grinder** will turn them to flour-like consistency or fine particles, depending on how long you whizz them. The coffee grinder will also make excellent breadcrumbs (as will the food processor). If you like decaffeinated coffee, but suspect your friends don't, grind decaffeinated coffee beans, and they'll never know the difference from the flavour.

Breadcrumbs can also be made using the fine blade of a **mincer**. Only worth buying if they have metal screws (I find the plastic type frustratingly feeble), mincers open the way to quicker marmalade, mincemeat, chopped dried fruit, and meat or fish pâtés – in fact, any mixture too dry for a blender. A food processor will do this job too. If you buy a mincer, look for the type with two tops, one for mincing, one for slicing or shredding. If you use it to mince or make pâté, you can also reduce fat content, since bought varieties are frequently very greasy.

This list shows how useful a **food processor** can be, but are they really worth having? Your decision will depend partly on the size of your kitchen. If you don't have a surface on which to keep one of these reasonably bulky machines, you may find getting the processor out such a chore that you'll leave it languishing in the cupboard. If you already have a blender, mincer and electric mixer, you may feel a food processor is unnecessary – or you may welcome a machine that will do all these jobs, as well as that of a grater. When choosing a food processor, think what extras you might want later. If you beat many egg whites, choose one which a demonstrator can convince you does this job well. Most food processors don't. If you like juice, pick a model where this attachment is available.

People who cook for lots of mouths may be better off with a machine like the **Kenwood Chef**. It's bulkier than a food processor, but has a larger capacity, particularly when it comes to kneading dough, mixing pastry or beating cakes. It also has a much wider range of optional extras: a good pasta-maker, a juicer, a flour mill, a sausage-maker and more. If you don't cook much, you may resent this large object on your work surface. If you cook a lot, you may see it as your best pal.

Finally, when it comes to cutting, don't forget good **scissors**. They'll speed up all sorts of jobs, from trimming pastry edges to chopping fresh herbs finely.

Things you might not have thought of
If you have a **tea infuser** or 'ball' you can make a cup or pot of any tea or herb tea as neatly using leaves as with a tea bag. Infusers are also handy when you want to put cloves or bay leaves in a casserole – and fish them out easily afterwards. Choose a stainless steel one.

A **sprouter** gives you access to your own fresh bean sprouts, as well as lentil, alfalfa, mustard and cress, wheat or chick pea sprouts, to add interest and high food value to meals. Especially in winter, when salad ingredients are less varied and more expensive, you'll find them welcome and fun to grow.

Sprouter with two of its customary three tiers, for growing beansprouts all year round

Woks have hit the fashion, and they do fry with least fat. But if you don't have gas to cook with, forget it: on electricity, the heat changes are too slow and the bottom tends to wobble even with a trivet. For many people, a large cast-iron frying pan does just as well, and it takes less storage space. If you buy a wok choose one with a lid, which widens the range of recipes you can make with it.

Fancy moulds and cutters seem a whim, but do the useful job of making food look prettier. This is particularly important if you are introducing people to less familiar dishes: it makes them look more professional and well-tried, even if they're new to your household. Children will eat all kinds of food if it's cut into bunnies whose heads they can nibble!

A selection of fancy cutters

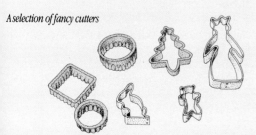

Oven-to-table dishes halve your washing up. Need we say more? Corningware and cast-iron dishes that can be used on the hob as well as in the oven are even more useful.

Wide-mouthed vacuum flasks are a versatile investment. You can use them to make yogurt (page 24) or soft cheese (page 25), to cook dried fruit (page 43) or porridge (page 44) overnight, or to take hot meals on picnics or to work. Make sure your flask has a metal, not foam, lining. It will retain heat for longer, and so be more effective for transporting hot food, for instance.

Electric juicers seem expensive, but freshly extracted juices are far superior to bought juices in flavour and food value. You can also make a much wider variety of juices than you can buy, and your home-made vegetable juices won't have added salt as most bought ones do. Remember too that all bought juices, unless just squeezed, have been pasteurized or otherwise heated to make them keep. Choose between the following types.
1 A juicer attachment with a food processor or table mixer: this is very little more expensive than a really good separate juicer, and if you already have a processor, is the best choice.
2 A 'continuous' electric juicer, which throws the pulp of the fruit or vegetable out into one container while juice flows into another. This type is useful if you make a lot of juice. Look for a sturdy machine with a powerful motor.
3 A less expensive electric juicer, where the pulp stays in the centrifugal juicing chamber. You have to clear this out after each batch of fruit or vegetables, but this isn't difficult – although it's inconvenient if you are processing large amounts.
4 The electric version of a hand citrus press – which is fine if you only want citrus juice. These machines are very economical and easier to store.

FREEZERS

Freezing is by far the best method of preserving food. It's safer, easier and retains flavour and goodness far better than any of the traditional methods of drying, canning and pickling.

It's not perfect: contrary to what many people think, food doesn't remain in the same condition for ever in the freezer. Over the weeks and months, losses of vitamins as well as of flavour and texture take place. So you need to use up your frozen food regularly and keep an eye on how long you store it.

That said, freezing can certainly ease the way to a healthier style of eating. It enables you to store foods that aren't available near you, so you can buy items such as goat's milk, fresh vegetables, soft fruit, favourite breads or unusual fish in bulk when you come across them, or make a trip to fetch them.

You can save a good deal of money by freezing vegetables when they're in season (but don't freeze salad vegetables – they would lose all their crispness). It's a good idea to freeze chopped herbs in ice cube trays. Chop the herbs into the trays and cover with water. Take the cubes from the trays when they are frozen, store them in bags in the freezer and remove individual cubes as needed to add to your cooking.

If you come into a wealth of home-grown or cheap soft fruit, you're much better off freezing it than preserving it (your jam will have to be frozen anyway if it's not at least half sugar, see page 263). With a supply of fruit in the freezer you can have fruit out of season for desserts, spreads and cake toppings and fillings.

You need never run out of top-quality bread if you freeze some you've bought or baked; cut it into slices first so that you can toast a slice as you want it, instead of having to wait for a whole loaf to thaw. Cakes and pastries freeze well too, and uncooked doughs can also be frozen.

Fish, provided that it is very fresh, freezes well. It seems to keep its character after freezing better than meat or vegetables. Moreover, only thick pieces, say over 2cm (¾in) need to be thawed before cooking. Shellfish, however, is better when thawed slowly for several hours in a refrigerator.

Freezer guidelines
Running costs per cubic metre are less for a larger freezer. Costs are also reduced if the freezer is kept full, and in a cool place so it does not have to fight the outside heat.

Freezing fresh food There are three important rules to obey:
1 Freeze it fast, as the more quickly food is frozen the better it retains its texture. If you are freezing a large amount of food at once, activate the fast-freeze mechanism, or set the freezer to its maximum temperature the day before you plan to freeze (don't forget to switch back to the normal temperature once the food has been in the freezer for twenty-four hours). It is not necessary to adjust the temperature if you are just adding a small quantity to the freezer, but in either case put the food to be frozen in the coldest part of the freezer – usually at the bottom, or next to the walls.
2 Pack foods in portions of the size you are likely to use at any one time. Or freeze small items separately, then bag them together, so that you can take out individual pieces as needed. Otherwise, you'll find yourself thawing a larger pack than you need and

wasting the extra. Use secure packaging – flimsy wraps are a false economy, as if they tear in the freezer the food will be spoilt. Make all packs as airtight as possible (but when you freeze liquids leave a little space to allow for expansion as they freeze), and use airtight fastenings: wire twists or string for bags, tape for polythene wrapping or boxes.
3 Label food clearly, including details of portion size and date and an 'eat by' date. If you are very methodical, keep a freezer book with a record of what you put in, crossing items out as you use them. Otherwise, always try to put food in at one side and take it out at the other, so that you follow a system of stock rotation, moving food along as you put new items in.

Blanching vegetables This is not as essential as it's said to be, provided that you freeze them quickly and don't plan to keep them for more than two months. Although blanching retards the enzyme action that causes loss of colour, flavour and food value, it inevitably affects the character of the food and removes a proportion of its water-soluble B and C vitamins, especially as the boiling stage is usually followed by cooling by rinsing with water, in which more nutrients can dissolve. In general, it's best not to cut vegetables into small pieces before freezing, as this increases the surface area, so more vitamins will be lost.

Freezing cooked dishes Freezing some of the dishes which take a considerable time to cook turns them into convenience foods, provided that you remember to transfer your planned evening dish from freezer to refrigerator in the morning (or have a microwave oven).

Aim to use *meat, fish, vegetable and fruit produce* within four months, to limit the slow but inevitable deterioration in quality. However, most fruit will keep, if necessary, for up to twelve months.

Aim to use *bread, cakes, pastries and uncooked doughs* within three or four months.

Thawing Vegetables and most fish can be cooked from frozen without thawing. With most other foods, slow and thorough thawing is essential if texture and flavour are to be retained. With meat, it's also important to avoid food-poisoning organisms, which may fail to be cooked out of meat and poultry if the centre of the meat is still too cold to get hot enough to kill bacteria during cooking. Keep the liquid that drips from meat and fish as they thaw: it contains some dissolved minerals and vitamins.

Refreezing This is generally undesirable.

MICROWAVE OVENS

Microwave cooking arouses strong emotions, for and against. For it are those who value its convenience and speed. Against it are those who dislike the loss of the subtle flavours connected with browning and caramelization, produced by direct heat, and those who suspect that microwave ovens can leak health-damaging rays.

Manufacturers are working to improve both these points. Many ovens now incorporate a setting which turns the microwave into a conventional oven for long enough to brown food; and the risk of leakage from an oven in good condition is very small.

Given these improvements, a microwave oven is particularly appealing to the freezer owner, who can then thaw foods so quickly that emergency meals from the freezer are much more practical. It's also useful for anyone who cooks in a hurry.

In nutritional terms, microwaves can help retain vitamins in food because many items – such as vegetables – can be cooked barely touching water, in which vitamins and minerals dissolve during conventional cooking.

CONVERSIONS & MEASUREMENTS

WEIGHTS & VOLUMES

Like most cookery books, this one generally gives approximate rather than exact equivalents for metric and imperial measures, to avoid complex arithmetic. However, for some special diets and for the technical information given in the introduction to the book, where accuracy is needed, more exact equivalents are used. When following a recipe, always use either the metric or the imperial measures.

Measurements under 25g (1oz) dry weight or 75ml (3fl oz) fluid volume are normally given in spoons. Use standard measuring spoons, as ordinary spoons differ considerably in size. All measures are level unless otherwise stated.

CALORIES

The calorie counts for the recipes are, again, necessarily approximate. They are intended as a working guide for anyone who, for whatever reason, needs to count calories. The counts are based on the figures and conversion rates given in the standard British text *The Composition of Foods* (Her Majesty's Stationery Office, London). The conversion factors suggested by *The Composition of Foods* (some other figures differ slightly) are

1g fat = 37kJ (kilojoules) = 9 calories
1g protein = 17kJ = 4 calories
1g carbohydrate = 16kJ = 3.75 calories
1g alcohol = 29kJ = 7 calories
1 calorie = 4.19 kilojoules

DRY WEIGHTS (approximate equivalents)	
25g (28.35)*	1oz
40g	1½oz
50g	2oz
75g	3oz
100g (113)	4oz
125g	5oz
175g	6oz
200g	7oz
225g	8oz
250g	9oz
275g	10oz
300g	11oz
350g	12oz
375g	13oz
400g	14oz
425g	15oz
450g	16oz, 1lb
700g	24oz, 1½lb
900g	32oz, 2lb

* For your interest some exact figures are given in brackets

FLUID VOLUME MEASURES (approximate equivalents)	
1ml	¼ tsp (teaspoon)
2ml	½ tsp
5ml	1 tsp
15ml	1 tbsp (tablespoon)
75ml	3fl oz
125ml (113)	4fl oz
150ml	5fl oz, ¼ pint
175ml	6fl oz
200ml	7fl oz
225ml	8fl oz
250ml	9fl oz
300ml (285)	10fl oz, ½ pint
325ml	11fl oz
350ml	12fl oz
375ml	13fl oz
400ml	14fl oz
450ml (425)	15fl oz, ¾ pint
475ml	16fl oz
500ml	18fl oz
600ml (570)	20fl oz, 1 pint
900ml	30fl oz, 1½ pints
1000ml, 1 litre	40fl oz, 2 pints (35fl oz, 1¾ pints)

TEMPERATURE CONVERSIONS	
Gas Oven Marks	Electric Oven °C (°F)
¼	110°C (225°F)
½	130°C (250°F)
1	140°C (275°F)
2	150°C (300°F)
3	160°C (325°F)
4	180°C (350°F)
5	190°C (375°F)
6	200°C (400°F)
7	220°C (425°F)
8	230°C (450°F)
9	250°C (500°F)

Eggs
Standard size 3 (55g) eggs are used throughout, except where otherwise stated.

Vegetables
These generally need be peeled only where stated in the recipes, but this is, of course, a matter of taste.

GLOSSARY OF BASIC INGREDIENTS

Agar agar *see* Thickeners.

Arrowroot *see* Thickeners.

Bran Bran is the outer layer of any cereal grain. As well as containing almost all the fibre of the grain, it is also high in protein, and much higher in B vitamins, vitamin E, zinc, magnesium, iron and other minerals than the part of the grain used in white bread or white rice. Theoretically, *wheat bran* contains 52 calories per 25g (1oz) but because of its physical form, even fewer calories may be absorbed. It's not necessary to buy packets of bran unless you want a particularly high fibre diet, as using wholemeal flour, brown rice and wholewheat pasta, for example, will provide the fibre in situ.

Rice bran provides less dietary fibre per 25g (1oz), but is likely to be used in larger amounts, because it is more like flour in appearance, and therefore more useful in baking or for making porridge, without making food seem 'branny'. It is gluten-free, but contains phenylalanine, a natural protein to which some people have an inbuilt intolerance. It contains on average 87 calories per 25g (1oz).

Oat bran is usually sold as a combined product with oat 'germ'. The combined product is 18 per cent dietary fibre, and is like a finer-ground oatmeal, becoming very 'gummy' when mixed with liquid. It can be added to muesli, porridge, oatcake or soup recipes almost unnoticed. Oat bran has about 96 calories per 25g (1oz).

Soya bran, like oat bran, provides a type of fibre particularly linked with lowering blood fat level and cholesterol level, and improving diabetic control. It is roughly 70 per cent dietary fibre but because of its fine texture is often less noticeable than wheat bran when added to food. It is added in small amounts to bread, cake and dessert recipes, or in slightly larger amounts to savoury recipes. It can also be used to coat burgers or added to pancake batter. Soya bran has approximately 25 calories per 25g (1oz), and 14 per cent protein.

Cheese *see* Soft cheese

Dried fruit Read dried fruit labels to avoid 'Food grade white mineral oil', otherwise known as liquid paraffin, which, in large amounts, has been associated with hindering the absorption of fat-soluble vitamins. Fruit can be bought without it or dressed with vegetable oil. Sulphur dioxide gas is applied to all pale-coloured dried fruit and is vitamin B-destructive. Some sulphur can be 'boiled off' by boiling fruit for a few minutes, then throwing the water away and starting the recipe from there (but weigh fruit before you boil it). *See also* Sweeteners.

Flour There are many different types:
Wholemeal flour is often thought of as useful only for bread, but it can be used for almost any recipe; if you want a paler flour, you just sieve it and reserve the bran left in the sieve. Apart from its higher protein, vitamin, mineral and fibre content, wholemeal flour differs from refined white flour in being free from additives. It is, however, more vulnerable to rancidity unless kept cool and used up within 2 to 3 months.

Many different varieties of wheat are used for wholemeal flour. Most flour sold specially for bread mixes strong and less strong flour, the latter having a better flavour and avoiding the bread being tough in texture. Other wholemeal flours are 'all-purpose' mixtures with more 'soft' or 'weak' low gluten wheats included. Wholemeal flour can be 'stoneground' or 'roller-milled' – and choice between them depends on personal preference. High gluten 'strong' or 'hard' flours are used for recipes requiring a strong and stretchy dough, such as bread, strudel or pasta. The amount of fluid in recipes may need slight alteration, usually increasing by a tablespoonful or two when using 'strong' flour which is high in gluten protein.

Self-raising wholemeal flour is available, but this has no advantage over adding raising agents to the flour when required, which gives more flexibility in suiting the amount to the recipe.

Brown flours, sometimes called 'wheatmeal', have a minimum fibre content by law of 6g per 100g (4oz) flour, but some will contain more than others. They are no more useful in cooking when a paler flour is wanted than sieved *wholemeal flour*.

White flour is recognized as a deficient food and legislation requires some vitamins and minerals to be added. However, wholemeal flour is still generally richer in nutrients, and those restored to the white version represent only a few of those lost in refining.

Less commonly used flours:
Soya flour does not have the same thickening properties as cereal flours, and is mainly useful as a way of adding extra food value to dishes. It is extremely high in protein – around 40 per cent – as well as in B vitamins, iron, magnesium, and potassium.

Rye flour is not always 'wholemeal', although unrefined versions are available. It's mainly used for bread. *Buckwheat flour* is used mainly for pancakes, although it can be used to replace a quarter of the wheat flour in any recipe. *Rice flour* can be obtained made from unrefined brown rice. It will be more finely ground than pudding-style ground rice. *Maize flour* is used mainly for pancakes and cornbread. It can be used to replace a quarter of the wheat flour in bread. *Pea flours* are made from split peas, or chick peas, and used either in Indian cookery or in gluten-free recipes. Split-pea flour can be made in a coffee grinder.

Gelatine *see* Thickeners

Grains For fast cooking, keep wholewheat pasta, buckwheat, bulgur wheat or millet in your larder. They all cook in 12 to 20 minutes. *Brown rice* comes in short and long grain forms. The long grain is more versatile, and easier to cook perfectly. *Barley* should be bought as 'pot' or 'Scotch' unrefined grains, rather than as the less nutritious, more polished 'pearl' barley. *Buckwheat* can be bought plain or roasted, when it is called kasha. You can easily 'roast' your own, by stirring it in an ungreased thick-based pan over lowest heat for a few minutes until it starts browning slightly. The best quality buckwheat has large grains. *Whole dried maize grains* are mainly used as popcorn. *Whole wheat grains* are mainly useful for making Frumenty, page 45; for sprouting (see **Sprouting**); or for crushing and then sprinkling over bread loaves before baking.

Margarine Look for brands which state on the label that they are all-vegetable, and that they contain a high level of polyunsaturated fatty acids (PUFAS) or over 50 per cent of linoleic acid in its natural form, known as 'cis cis'. Ideally, choose an unhardened (unhydrogenated) brand with no added salt.

Mirin A kind of Japanese *sake* (rice wine). If unavailable, use dry sherry.

Miso A thick paste made from soya beans, brown rice, water and sea salt. The soya makes it rich in protein, but it is too salty to use in more than small amounts. It can be used anywhere that you might use yeast extract.

Mustard Because of their value as fairly low-sodium flavourings, mustards deserve some attention, with many varieties and tastes available. *Powdered mustard* is low-sodium and also has a considerable mineral content but too little is eaten for the latter to be useful. Check labels for additives, if any. *Made-up mustards* usually have added salt, but as small amounts are used, this can be unimportant, especially if you then omit added salt from the recipe. Check label for additives.

Nuts These keep better when bought whole, and unroasted. Fresh-grated nuts have most flavour, but exposure to air hastens rancidity and loss of taste. Many packed nuts have been vacuum-packed or oxygen-removed by nitrogen flushing to improve keeping. These keep best while unopened. Opened packets should be used up within a month or two and kept cool. Most nuts, apart from walnuts, can be made much tastier by lightly toasting in a heavy-based skillet, ungreased, over a very low heat for a few minutes until just colouring. *Hazelnuts* have 50 per cent lower fat content than most nuts and high vitamin E; *walnuts* have a high PUFA content; *almonds* have high calcium and vitamin E content; peanuts have the top protein content (25 per cent).

Oils Oil has even more calories – average 225 per 25g (scant 1oz) – than butter or margarine – average 184 per 25g (scant 1oz). But its use may still be beneficial to health because it tends to lower the level of cholesterol in the blood stream. Some oils are also particularly rich in the essential fatty acids that the body uses for assorted functions, and which tend to be low in processed foods. From a cooking point of view, the oil you choose will depend on how much you want to heat it. The oils highest in PUFAs burn easily when heated. Overheated oil structure can break down to produce substances which are an irritant and possibly harmful to the body.

For use cold, an oil with a high PUFA content is fine. The five highest are, in descending order of PUFA content, safflower, soya, sunflower and, with similar content, corn and cottonseed oil. If available, walnut and linseed oil are also in the top league.

For higher temperature use, olive oil, which is low in PUFA, but still unsaturated, is more stable. Refined corn oil is also fairly stable under heat.

However, for general use, unrefined oils – 'cold-pressed' oils – have more flavour, cost more and are more natural.

If you keep in stock a bottle of olive oil and a high-PUFA oil, both preferably cold-pressed or unrefined, you can provide for all cooking needs.

Salts *Sea salt* is a less refined form of salt, but it has virtually as much sodium as *refined table salt* which is almost entirely sodium. So while sea salt can add extra trace elements, particularly iodine, to food, it must still be cut down if you want a low-sodium style of eating. *Sesame salt* combines ground sesame seed with sea salt. This is a way of reducing sodium while adding another flavour, but if you use a lot, the high oil content of sesame seed must be taken into account.

Sea vegetables A new name for seaweeds, which are used in many countries, notably Japan, as food. They are rich sources of assorted minerals, with guaranteed iodine which is sporadic among land-grown foods. Most are salty, and if you want to reduce this, rinse seaweeds thoroughly in water before cooking.

Kombu comes in finger-shape strips, which are immersed briefly in boiling water or stock to make 'dashi', the basic Japanese stock (to which fish flakes are also normally added). The kombu is then discarded. *Nori* comprises paper-thin sheets of dried seaweed, used in Japan to wrap rice savouries to give them flavour. They are crisped before use by passing near a flame or other heat for a second or two. *Arame* are fine shreds of sea vegetable, used as a vegetable or in soups; *wakame* are thick strands of sea vegetable, used as a vegetable.

Seeds Sunflower, sesame, poppy, linseed and pumpkin seeds are all useful nutritionally, with a similar make-up to nuts, giving protein, fibre, vitamins and minerals but also a lot of oil so they need to be used sparingly.

Sunflower seeds are particularly rich in iron – about 3 times higher than peanuts, for instance, contain 24 per cent protein (more than most meat) and are the richest of nuts and seeds in vitamin E. *Sesame seeds* would be high calcium providers if the mineral were absorbed: you can help this to some extent by crushing seeds, which also releases flavour and calories. *Poppy seeds* are mainly used as garnish. *Linseed* is widely used in Europe for its mucilaginous type of fibre, which gives it a mild laxative property and is also soothing to the digestive system. *Pumpkin seeds*, which tend to be expensive, are a pleasant snack or addition to fruit cake instead of nuts, but are mainly valued for their very high

zinc content. Often taken for prostate conditions.

All these seeds make a useful extra for topping cakes, salads, cereal dishes and vegetables, giving them a nutritional 'booster' – but they should all be used in small amounts because of high oil level.

Smetana Like *soured cream* but is cultured on lower fat dairy produce. While soured cream has an average 18 per cent fat, smetana has only 5 to 10 per cent with a lower fat and a creamy version available. You can make your own smetana by following the instructions for yogurt, but using half-and-half single cream and full-fat milk (usually 3.8 per cent fat) for 11 per cent fat smetana, or skimmed milk for 9 per cent fat smetana. Instead of stirring in yogurt to start, stir in either some smetana itself or some sour cream. Incubate as usual.

Like yogurt, smetana will separate if heated to boiling point unless stabilized, when cold, by mixing with an egg white and 10ml (2 tsp) cornflour or wheat flour. If using cornflour, the mixture must be simmered for at least 1 to 2 minutes to get rid of the raw flour taste; with wheat flour, for 5 to 6 minutes.

Soft cheese Low fat-soft cheese can be obtained in several forms: **1** home-made recipe (page 25) using yogurt cheese method to make soya cheese; **2** as sieved cottage cheese, the most widely available type, unfortunately often containing preservative; **3** as 'quark', which is unsalted and ranges from very low fat to 40 per cent fat (check the label); **4** as 'medium-fat curd cheese', widely sold loose, containing 11 per cent fat, and around 40 to 45 calories per 25g (1oz); **5** as skimmed milk soft cheese which is like unsalted quark. All soft cheese should be kept well covered and refrigerated.

Soya sauce Traditionally, a soya bean extract with water, fermented over 1 to 2 years. This fermentation process is now often skipped, but you can still buy traditional *soy* or *shoyu* sauces free from flavour enhancers or caramel. Soya sauce contains wheat, so is not suitable for gluten-free diets. *Tamari* is a similar product, without wheat. Use as flavourings, omitting salt from recipe as both are very salty.

Sprouted grains and pulses Sprouts are one of the super foods nutritionally. As the shoot grows, vitamin C increases and protein, vitamin and mineral levels are not only high but unaffected by processing, storage and handling.

Beansprouts give an authentic touch to stir-fry vegetables and help to dress up plain vegetables such as sprouts or cabbage. They also make a versatile salad ingredient. Use them as well to add crunch to sandwiches with soft-textured fillings like cottage cheese or mashed fish. *Wheat and barley sprouts* can be used in salads or in baking to provide a pleasantly 'chewy' texture to the bread.

To sprout wheat and bean seeds (not barley, as it has too tough a skin): **1** rinse a cup of *whole* wheat grains or pulses under the tap in a sieve. Don't use cracked or split wheat, as it won't sprout. **2** Leave the grains or pulses in a warm place in the sieve to drain thoroughly. **3** Run them under cold water twice a day, returning them to the drying place in between. The whole process takes about 2 to 4 days for beans, and three to seven days for wheat. Once the sprouts are the same length as the grain or pulse, they are ready to use. Rinse them a final time before use. They can be kept in the refrigerator in a covered container for a few days for later use.

Special seed sprouters can be bought (page 307), making the process easier.

Sweeteners Dried fruit and honey are the main sweeteners used in this book.

In general, *dried fruit* is the best way of sweetening food, particularly if used as a purée. It provides fibre, minerals, some vitamins and fruit sugar, at about 65 calories per 25g (1oz). The most effective way to use it is in recipes which include liquid, which should be liquidized with the fruit in a blender before adding to other ingredients.

Honey has several advantages over sugar: **1** It's sweeter weight for weight, so less needs be used, especially in cold foods; **2** It contains only about 72 calories per 25g (scant 1oz), compared to 100 calories per 25g (scant 1oz) for white or brown sugar; **3** Provided there is already some glucose in your liver, your system should not break down the fructose or fruit sugar, which is the main element in honey, to glucose (also present), or produce such a rapid rise in blood sugar – nor require insulin to be turned into energy. It is therefore better for diabetics than crystal sugar.

Honey is best bought unpasteurized, ideally in the comb, from bees fed on natural products. *Clear honey* is easier to handle in cooking than *set honey* – although the latter is just as natural. All honey crystallizes naturally eventually, with no harm. However, to avoid this for as long as possible, keep honey warm. If replacing sugar in cooking with honey, use 2 measures of honey for every 3 suggested for sugar. Honey can be replaced by *real maple syrup* in sweetening. Because the latter is more liquid, you may need to reduce the liquid in a recipe very slightly. Another form of the main sugar in honey is pure *fructose*, or fruit sugar, which looks like a fine crystal, completely white sugar. It has the same number of calories per gram or ounce as sugar, and no vitamins or minerals to speak of. However, like honey, it is sweeter than sugar so less should be needed.

Brown sugar has no real advantages over white, apart from very small amounts of trace elements. One of these, chromium, may be significant because the body needs it to cope with sugar. So if you do use crystal sugar, brown is better.

Molasses, the residual syrup after sugar cane is boiled and sugar extracted, is not an 'empty calorie' food, as it contains useful amounts of minerals. At around 62 calories per 15ml (scant 1 tbsp), it's a lower-calorie way of sweetening food; although it is less sweet than sugar or honey, it adds its own distinctive flavour too. Use cautiously so as not to overpower other tastes. *Black treacle*, a more refined version, has half the mineral value.

Concentrated apple juice is a useful sweetener in small amounts but in larger amounts it is too acid. It is also convenient for making hot or cold soft drinks just by adding hot or cold water. It has similar food value to apples, in a more concentrated form in terms of calories, and with less fibre.

Date sugar is equivalent to other dried fruit used in sweetening, but more concentrated as almost all the water has been removed.

Tamari *see* **Soya sauce**.

Thickeners There are several types:
Powder gelatine is usually sold in boxes of sachets containing just over 5ml (1 tbsp) each designed to set 575ml (exactly 1 pint). The main rule for success is always to add the gelatine to the liquid, not the other way around. The liquid should be very hot but never boiling.

Leaf gelatine comes in transparent sheets. To set 575ml (exactly 1 pint) of liquid, soak 15g (½ oz) gelatine (about 4 sheets) in 10 to 15ml (2 to 3 tbsp) of cold liquid taken from the recipe. Meanwhile, heat remaining liquid, sweeten as necessary, add the soaked gelatine and stir briskly until well dissolved. The mixture should be very hot but not allowed to boil.

Vegetable gel powders are used by people who dislike the idea of gelatine, which is made from animal bones, and they also contribute some dietary fibre. To set 575ml (exactly 1 pint) of liquid, 10ml (2 tsp) vegetable gel powder are mixed to a smooth paste with a little of the cold liquid, then added to the remainder. The mixture is boiled and simmered for 2 minutes.

Agar agar, also known as kanten, is an edible seaweed/vegetable setting agent, used routinely in Japan. To set 575ml (exactly 1 pint) of liquid, whisk it with 10ml (2 tsp) agar agar and bring to the boil stirring. Simmer for 5 minutes.

Arrowroot is a fine white powder made from tropical plants. It won't gel liquids, but will thicken them without flavouring them. To thicken 575ml (exactly 1 pint) of liquid, mix 10ml (2 tsp) arrowroot to a smooth paste with a little of the cold liquid, whisk in remaining liquid until smooth, bring the mixture to the boil and simmer for 2 to 3 minutes.

Cornflour is a very refined form of maize flour, but as such small amounts are used, the lack of food value is unimportant. It is gluten-free.

Vinegar Vinegar has almost no calories, no fat and no vitamins but does have a sprinkling of minerals in small amounts. Although some people find it irritates their digestive system, for most it's a useful flavouring, particularly since it is low in sodium. It's fun experimenting with the wider range of vinegars now available, from tarragon to raspberry flavoured.

Yeast *see* page 235.

Yeast extract One of the most useful kitchen ingredients, because it makes a hot drink, a spread for bread and a flavouring that's particularly useful for non-meat meals. Yeast extract is packed with protein, B vitamins and assorted minerals including iron. However, it's usually eaten in very small amounts because it is so salty – so don't count on it for many nutrients in practice. You can buy a low-salt version.

INDEX

Trout
  Hazelnut trout in an
    overcoat *15*, 170–1
Tuna
  Salade niçoise 155
  See also Hazelnut trout in an
    overcoat
Turkey
  roasting 198–9
  See also Rabbit pie
Turkish chicken 192–3, *193*
Turnips
  cooking methods 128
  See also Carrots and
    parsnips
Tyramine 286

V

Vacuum flasks 307
Vegetable gel powders 312
Vegetable mill 306
Vegetables
  fibre content 275–6
  freezing 308
  preparation and cooking
    124, 126–9, 305
  vitamins and minerals in 12–
    13, 124, 126
  Piccalilli 265
  Scotch broth 82
  Stir-fried vegetables with
    cashew nuts *138*, 138–9
  Vegetable juices 40, 41
  Vegetable macaroni 112–13
  Vegetable sauce 28–9
  Vegetable soufflé 136
  Vegetable terrine *50*, 61–2
  Winter pie 140
Vegetable spaghetti marrow
  cooking methods 129
Venison
  roasting 184
  Venison in port 191–2
  Venison in the pink 190–1,
    191
Verbena tea 268
Vervain tea 268
Vesper 269
Vichyssoise 79
Vinegar 312
Vine leaves
  Almond-rice stuffed vine
    leaves 101–2
  Stuffed vine leaves 59–60,
    60
  See also Vegetable terrine
Vitamins 12–13, 122, 124, 148
  against allergies 281–2
Vulgar bulgur 91–2

W

Waffles, nutmeg *42*, 49
Waldorf dip *57*, 57–8
Waldorf salad 159
Walnuts 310
  Cheesecake-style filling or
    topping 35–6

Walnuts ctd
  Stuffed pears *215*, 215–16
  Walnut dressing 151
  Walnut gâteau *232*, 248–9
  Walnut petits fours 248
  See also Tarator hazelnut
    sauce
Watercress 18, 73
  cooking methods 127
  Watercress and mushroom
    soufflé 133
  Watercress and orange salad
    16, 151, *187*
  Watercress and pear salad
    157
  Watercress broth 73
Weight
  gaining 295–6
  losing 296–300
Wheat bran 274, 309
Wholemeal bread 235–6
Wholemeal shortcrust pastry
    257
Wholemeal white sauce 27
Winter pie 140
Woks 307
Won ton *67*, 67–8, *68*

YZ

Yams
  cooking methods 129
Yeast
  for bread making 235
  Yeast extract 34, 313
  Yeast fruit cake 282
  Yeast pastry 259
Yogurt 22, 24
  Blue cheese dressing 151,
    154
  Coffee almond ice 223–4
  Creamy herb sauce 32, *135*,
    196
  Home-made yogurt 24, 25
  Original muesli 43
  Tjatziki 59, *145*, *203*
  Very low-fat dressing 276
  Walnut dressing 151
  Yogurt cheese 26, *26*
  Yogurt fruit shake 42
  See also Mushrooms in
    soured cream

Zinc 122, 205, 206, 290

RECOMMENDED READING

Health and Nutrition
Buss, D. and J. Robertson, *Manual of Nutrition*, HMSO, London,
  1976
Hauser, Gayelord, *Look Younger, Live Longer*,
  Faber and Faber, London, 1951
Kenton, Leslie and Susannah, *Raw Energy*, Century, London, 1984
Mann, Jim (Dr), *The Diabetic's Diet Book*, Martin Dunitz,
  London, 1982
Mervyn, Leonard, *Minerals and Your Health*, Allen and Unwin,
  London, 1980
Paul, A. A., and D. A. Southgate, *The Composition of Foods* (bible of
  food values and analysis), HMSO, London, 1980
Pleshette, Janet, *Health On Your Plate*, Hamlyn, London, 1983
Polunin, Miriam (ed), *The Health and Fitness Handbook*, Sphere,
  London, 1983; *The Right Way to Eat*, Dent, London, 1984
Pritikin, Nathan, and Patrick McGrady, *The Pritikin Program*,
  Bantam Books, New York, 1981
Stanway, Andrew (Dr), *Taking The Rough With The Smooth*, Pan,
  London, 1982

Cookery
Elliot, Rose, *Your Very Good Health recipes for healthy eating*,
  Fontana, London, 1981
Ewald, Ellen Buchman, *Recipes for a Small Planet*, Ballantine,
  New York, 1977
Hambro, Nathalie, *Particular Delights: cooking for all the senses*,
  Norman and Hobhouse, London, 1981
Mann, Jim (Dr) and Roberta Longstaff, *The Diabetic's Cookbook*,
  Martin Dunitz, London, 1984
Martin, Peter and Joan, *Japanese Cooking*, Penguin, London, 1972

USEFUL ADDRESSES

Action against Allergy
43 The Downs, London SW20 8HG

Anorexic Aid
The Priory Centre, 11 Priory Road, High Wycombe,
Buckinghamshire

British Diabetic Association
10 Queen Anne Street, London W1M 0BD
Hon. Sec. Mrs M. Perry 95 Hanover Street Edinburgh EH2 1DJ
Hon. Sec. Mrs M. James 21 Millrace Close, Lisvane, Cardiff,
S. Glamorgan
Hon. Sec. Mrs L. Spratt, 6 Finch Way, Taughmonagh, Belfast,
N. Ireland

British Naturopathic and Osteopathic Association (who can give
you the name of your nearest nutrition therapist using nature cure)
Frazer House, 6 Netherhall Gardens, London NW3

Cancer Help Centre (for treatment and advice on nutrition to help
fight cancer)
Grove House, Cornwallis Grove, Clifton, Bristol BS8 4PG

Coeliac Society (will only deal with diagnosed coeliacs or
dermatitis herpetiformis, not with wheat allergy; it offers useful lists
of which food products are gluten-free, but its recipes use low-
fibre wheat starch flour; has seventy local self-help groups)
P.O. Box 181, London NW2 2QY

Foresight Association (for advice on pre-conceptual nutrition for
healthy babies)
Woodhurst, Hydestile, Godalming, Surrey GU8 4AY

Health Education Council
78 New Oxford Street, London WC1A 1AH

Henry Doubleday Research Association (association for organic
gardeners, who publish directory of organic growers)
Convent Lane, Bocking, Braintree, Essex

Hyperactive Children's Support Group (send SAE for information
about food reactions in children)
Hon. Sec. Sally Bunday, 59 Meadowside, Angmering, Sussex
BN16 4BW

Jewish Vegetarian Society
Bet Tava, 855 Finchley Road, London NW11 8LX

Migraine Trust
45 Great Ormond Street, London WC1N 3HD

National Childbirth Trust (also covers advice on feeding infants)
9 Queensborough Terrace, London W2 3TE

Soil Association (for information on organic food and suppliers)
Walnut Tree Manor, Haughley, nr Stowmarket, Suffolk

Vegan Society
47 Highlands Road, Leatherhead, Surrey

Vegetarian Society
53 Marloes Road, Kensington, London W8 6LA

for Eire
Health Education Bureau
34 Upper Mount Street, Dublin 2

Irish Cancer Society
5 Northumberland Road, Dublin 4

Irish Diabetic Association
Ballyneety House, St Laurence Road, Clontarf, Dublin 3

Irish Organic Growers
Life Force Foods Ltd, 4 Halston Street, Dublin 7

Vegetarian Society of Ireland
457 Collins Avenue, Whitehall, Dublin 7

ACKNOWLEDGEMENTS

The publishers would like to thank the following individuals and
organizations for their help: Gina Carminati, for styling the
photography, Jane Suthering and Caroline Ellwood for preparing
food for photography; Jacqui Hurst for helping with photography.
Emmalee Gow and Gill Edden for checking recipe and nutrition
information; Esther Eisenthal and Pippa Rubinstein for initial work
on the book; Fred Gill and Miren Lopategui for proof reading,
Elizabeth and George Galfalvi and Gillian Bussell for typing and
Vicki Robinson for the index.
    For the loan of kitchen utensils, the publishers would like to
thank David Mellor of Sloane Square, London SW1, Divertimenti of
Fulham Road, London SW3 and Ceramic International of King's
Road, London SW10.

General editor Susan Berry
Art editor Steven Wooster
Principal text editor Josephine Christian
Designer Louise Tucker
Assistant text editors Margot Levy, Miren Lopategui, Lindy
Newton

Art director Debbie MacKinnon

Illustrations Sandra Pond, Will Giles and Venner Artists

Typesetting Tradespools Ltd, Frome, Somerset
Reproduction Newsele, Milan